D0915538

South Carolina at the Brink

South Carolina at the Brink

*Robert McNair and the
Politics of Civil Rights*

Philip G. Grose

University of South Carolina Press

BOWLING GREEN STATE
UNIVERSITY LIBRARY

© 2006 University of South Carolina

Published by the University of South Carolina Press
Columbia, South Carolina 29208

www.sc.edu/uscpress

Publication of this volume made possible in part by a grant from the Caroline McKissick Dial Fund,
University Libraries, University of South Carolina

Manufactured in the United States of America

15 14 13 12 11 10 09 08 07 06   10 9 8 7 6 5 4 3 2 1

Library of Congress Cataloging-in-Publication Data

Grose, Philip G., 1938–
  South Carolina at the brink : Robert McNair and the politics of civil rights / Philip G. Grose.
      p. cm.
  Includes bibliographical references and index.
  ISBN-13: 978-1-57003-624-8 (cloth : alk. paper)
  ISBN-10: 1-57003-624-1 (cloth : alk. paper)
  1. McNair, Robert E. (Robert Evander), 1923– 2. Governors—South Carolina—Biography.
3. South Carolina—Race relations—History—20th century. 4. South Carolina—Politics and
government—1951– 5. African Americans—Civil rights—South Carolina—History—20th
century. 6. Civil rights movements—South Carolina—History—20th century. I. Title.
  F275.42.M35G78 2006
  975.7'043092—dc22

                                        2006003515

For Virginia

Contents

List of Illustrations   ix

Preface   xi

Chronology   xv

   1 The Old Order Changeth   1

   2 Growing Up in Hell Hole Swamp   22

   3 Coming of Age: War, Education, and Election   43

   4 Learning the Ropes in a Rural State   66

   5 A Circuitous Route to the Governor's Office   82

   6 Preparing for the Showdown   108

   7 A Full Term and a Mandate for Moderation   141

   8 A Blueprint for South Carolina   159

   9 The Gathering Storm at South Carolina State   176

  10 A Tragedy at Orangeburg   198

  11 The Rise of Soul Power   241

  12 South Carolina Runs Out of Time, Courts   266

      Epilogue   295

Notes   305

Bibliography   345

Index   349

Illustrations

Following page 114

Claudia Crawford McNair
Daniel Evander McNair
Robert Evander McNair, age 3
Athlete Bob McNair
Scholar Bob McNair
Lieutenant (j.g.) McNair
Representative McNair
Lieutenant Governor McNair
Russell sworn in as Senator
Campaigning in 1966
The electorate was changing
I. DeQuincey Newman
McNairs were big winners in 1966
Celebrating in style
Democrats still in control
Tourism became big business
Industry grew and diversified
The executive staff
The First Family
Creating the Capital Complex
First Lady
An LBJ insider
Off the cuff with the press
Coffee-cup diplomacy
Orangeburg under siege
Aftermath of shootings
S.C. State students protest
Hospital workers protest
SCLC leaders

Local leaders
The young governor
The outdoorsman
The battle-weary governor
A last farewell
McNair at his home place

Preface

Civil rights change came to South Carolina through various channels. Most visibly, it was the product of federal court orders and acts of the U. S. Congress, landmark events that largely grew out of such forces as emerging black political strength, grassroots public pressure, organized campaigns and demonstrations, and legislative initiatives at the state and local levels.

At no step along the way, however, did actual change—the altering of the way people carried on their day-to-day lives—come about without the application of the political process. It was politics, the practice of negotiation, cajoling, and compromise, that converted the promise and ideals of civil rights measures into the reality of civil rights change. It was politics, as well, that often determined the nature of public response to civil rights change, and established precedents and patterns that inspired either peaceful acceptance or violent reaction to those changes.

In the latter part of the 1960s in South Carolina, at the peak of the civil rights transformation in America, the state was governed by a man of vigorous political pragmatism. His name was Robert Evander McNair. While much of the South yielded to emotional and primitively violent reaction to civil rights change, he guided South Carolina along the sometimes-tortuous path of moderation and created the political atmosphere in which peaceful change could take place.

This book examines how McNair was able to nudge the power structure, for the most part a legislative oligarchy of rural political figures, not only into acceptance of change, but also into support of legislative initiatives designed to address the economic, educational, and social inequities that had resulted from the state's long tradition of racial separation. It also addresses his refusal to adopt populist strategies in dealing with the South Carolina public, and his determination to offer instead the often risky strategy of engaging the public in straight talk.

By design, the book is neither biography nor history, although it contains elements of each. It is intended instead as a journalistic view of McNair's life in the context of the events that shaped his career and formed the political agenda of his years in various roles of public leadership. The text draws heavily on accounts from a remarkable cadre of professional journalists whose informed opinions and conscientious attention to the daily events of South Carolina government and politics made them qualified analysts, as well as skilled recorders of the history of those critical times.

Much of the production of this book is owed to the University of South Carolina, particularly to the Institute for Southern Studies and its director, Walter B. Edgar. This was not only where the book had its conception, it was also the place where office space, equipment, support, and kind encouragement were generously supplied. The author is also indebted to Herbert Hartsook and the South Carolina Political Collections for access to documents, photos, and records, and for additional workspace, support, and friendship. From the University of South Carolina Press, Alex Moore, Karen Beidel, and Scott Burgess provided the professional guidance, support, and remarkable patience to see the manuscript through the many stages of development.

The book's primary source of material from McNair himself and other leaders of the day is an extraordinary oral history conducted in the early 1980s by scholars and historians led by C. Blease Graham of the University of South Carolina. Edited transcripts of these insightful interviews will provide rich materials for researchers exploring the pivotal years of the 1960s in South Carolina and will bring attention to issues far beyond the limited scope of those addressed in this text.

Other key sources came from Charleston attorney Kaye Koonce, whose paper on the Charleston Hospital Strike of 1969 was brought to the author's attention by Paul Beazley, and which provided valued information, candid interviews, and historical perspective on that event. Much of the account of USC's campus antiwar protests of 1970 came from Paul Fidler, who made available the faculty account of those events, "The Months of May." John Sproat generously provided articles he produced on the role of Senator Marion Gressette and his education committee in influencing moderation in state policy toward school desegregation. Archivist Aimee Berry gave the author full access to the extensive South Carolina State files on the "Orangeburg Massacre," and the FBI documents that make up that file. Jerry Dell and Ben Gimarc produced Southern Regional Council reports that put South Carolina's experience in regional perspective. The author gained new insight into 1966 gubernatorial candidate Joseph O. Rogers from conversations with his son, Joe Rogers Jr., and documents of his father's he made available.

The author is also indebted to many who offered valued insight, information, advice, criticism, and support all along the way, including Governor John West, Cyril Busbee, Jesse Coles, Fred Carter, Jim Konduros, Wayne Corley, Claire Fort, Bill Saunders, Cleveland Sellers, Don Fowler, Ike Williams, Carl Stokes, Ernie Ellis, Bob Ellis, and especially John Bryan for his tutoring. Special thanks also go to researchers Aaron Marrs and Adam Mack for their scholarly assistance, and to Janet Bryan, Gayle Levine, Kate Moore, and Tibby Steedly for their friendship and many acts of support.

Deep gratitude goes to Governor McNair himself, who graciously made himself available on all occasions for inquiries and follow-up interviews, and who on no occasion attempted to influence in any way the text of this manuscript.

Much credit belongs to the author's family—especially the encouragement and support received from his daughter, Patricia—and, undeniably, the book's production is attributable to the inspiration, steadfast determination and insight of the author's wife, Virginia, who found ways through the rough spots and whose contributions are far too great in scale and value to enumerate.

Chronology

JANUARY 1, 1896
New state constitution goes into effect, disenfranchising most black South Carolinians with its literacy and property-ownership requirements.

MAY 28, 1896
The U.S. Supreme Court decision *Plessy v. Ferguson* upholds segregation of public accommodations.

DECEMBER 14, 1923
Robert Evander McNair is born at Cades, South Carolina.

OCTOBER 29, 1929
Prices collapse on New York Stock Exchange, setting off decade-long economic depression.

SEPTEMBER 6, 1934
Six people are killed and fifteen are seriously wounded as special deputies open fire on strikers at Honea Path during General Textile strike.

SEPTEMBER 1, 1939
Germany invades Poland, setting off World War II in Europe.

DECEMBER 7, 1941
Japan attacks U.S. Navy base at Pearl Harbor in the Hawaiian Islands, bringing the United States into World War II.

DECEMBER 1944
Lieutenant (j.g.) Robert E. McNair participates in the invasion of Leyte and Lingayen Gulf, campaigns that led to the Japanese surrender of the Philippines.

1944
Progressive Democratic Party is established by blacks in South Carolina to organize and encourage political activity.

1944
In its *Smith v. Allwright* decision, U.S. Supreme Court rules that the Democratic Party primary cannot be limited to white-only participation.

SEPTEMBER 2, 1945
World War II ends with surrender of Japan.

JULY 12, 1947
Judge Waties Waring of Charleston, in his *Rice v. Elmore* decision, brings an end to all-white Democratic primary in South Carolina.

JUNE 1948
McNair loses his first political race for House of Representatives in Berkeley County.

NOVEMBER 11, 1949
Black parents in Clarendon County bring suit against school board, challenging segregated school system, in *Briggs v. Elliott.*

JUNE 1950
McNair is elected to House of Representatives from Allendale County.

APRIL 15, 1951
South Carolina General Assembly enacts Governor James F. Byrnes' recommended 3 percent sales tax, largely to upgrade black public schools and avoid court-ordered desegregation. McNair supports measure.

MARCH 19, 1954
Under McNair's leadership as chairman of House Labor, Commerce and Industry Committee, General Assembly adopts "right-to-work" legislation, outlawing closed-shop union organizations.

MAY 17, 1954
U.S. Supreme Court rules that the "separate but equal" doctrine is unconstitutional in its *Brown v. Board of Education* case. The S.C. case *Briggs v. Elliott* was incorporated into the *Brown* case.

JUNE 12, 1962
McNair is elected lieutenant governor in Democratic primary race against Marshall Parker of Oconee County by a margin of 58 percent to 42 percent. Black voters play a major part in the McNair victory margin.

AUGUST 21, 1962
Lunch counters in Columbia are desegregated after sit-in demonstrations, and city policies for employment are liberalized.

JANUARY 28, 1963
Harvey Gantt is admitted to Clemson College as the institution's first black student. Eight months later, the University of South Carolina is desegregated by Henri Monteith and James Solomon.

NOVEMBER 22, 1963
President John F. Kennedy is assassinated in Dallas, Texas. Vice President Lyndon Baines Johnson becomes president.

JULY 2, 1964
U.S. Civil Rights Act, outlawing discrimination in public accommodations and employment, becomes law.

NOVEMBER 3, 1964
Senator Barry Goldwater becomes the first Republican candidate for president to carry South Carolina in the twentieth century. Lyndon Johnson is elected president.

APRIL 18, 1965
U.S. Senator Olin D. Johnston dies in office.

APRIL 22, 1965
McNair becomes governor to fill out term of Donald S. Russell after Russell resigns. Subsequently, McNair appoints Russell to replace Johnston in U.S. Senate.

AUGUST 6, 1965
U.S. Voting Rights Act becomes law, protecting blacks' voting and registration rights.

DECEMBER 14, 1965
McNair calls a special session of the General Assembly to comply with a federal court order requiring the reapportionment of the S.C. Senate on a one-man, one-vote basis.

NOVEMBER 8, 1966
McNair is elected to a full four-year term as governor over Republican Joseph O. Rogers of Manning by a margin of 58 percent to 42 percent, almost the same as his margin of victory over Marshall Parker in race for lieutenant governor four years earlier. An estimated ninety thousand black votes are cast for McNair.

MARCH 2, 1967
A campus-wide student boycott is called by class presidents at South Carolina State in protest over suspension of three students and other related issues. McNair is involved in resolution of the boycott, which leads to resignation of S.C. State president Benner Turner.

MARCH 30, 1967
The Department of Parks, Recreation, and Tourism is established, pursuant to an early McNair proposal.

FEBRUARY 8, 1968
Three black students are killed and thirty-one are wounded by members of the South Carolina Highway Patrol during a demonstration on the S.C. State campus. Civil rights groups subsequently place responsibility with McNair and call for investigation. McNair relies on FBI to provide report on the shootings.

JANUARY 15, 1969
In his State of the State message, McNair unveils proposals pursuant to a wide-ranging set of recommendations known as the "Moody Report." Central to the recommendations are state-funded kindergartens and measures to address the state's high dropout rate.

MARCH 20–JUNE 28, 1969
Strike by Charleston hospital workers brings thousands of demonstrators into the streets and gains national attention from labor and civil rights groups. McNair intervenes to help resolve local issues and end the hundred-day walkout.

MARCH 3, 1970
White boycott leaders wielding ax handles, mace canisters, and billy clubs attack school buses bringing black children to newly desegregated Lamar High School, overturning two of the buses only moments after the children had been escorted inside.

MAY 11, 1970
Antiwar demonstrators take over Osborne Administration Building at the University of South Carolina during eleven days of protest. National Guard is called, along with Highway Patrol and Columbia police, to quell the disturbance. With Guardsmen and other law enforcement on campus, McNair insists that school remain open, as it does.

SEPTEMBER 1970
Massive desegregation of public schools in South Carolina begins. McNair cautions, "We have run out of time and run out of courts. We will comply with the court rulings."

OCTOBER 15–16, 1970
A. C. Flora High School in Columbia is closed after two days of racially oriented fights among students on campus. Part of the outbreak is linked to campaign workers for GOP gubernatorial candidate Albert W. Watson.

NOVEMBER 3, 1970

Democrat John C. West defeats Republican Albert W. Watson in close race for governor. Also elected are the state's first black House members since 1895—Herbert Fielding of Charleston and I. S. Leevy Johnson and James Felder of Columbia.

JANUARY 19, 1971

John C. West is sworn in as governor, vowing to end poverty in the state and pledging a color-blind administration. McNair returns to private practice of law, establishing, along with senior staff members James Konduros and Wayne Corley, the firm of McNair, Konduros and Corley in Columbia.

(Portions of the above information came from *A South Carolina Chronology, 1497–1992,* by George C. Rogers and C. James Taylor [Columbia: University of South Carolina Press, 1994].)

South Carolina at the Brink

1

The Old Order Changeth

In the wee hours of Easter Sunday morning, 1965, the political clock in South Carolina came to a brief stop. The mark in time was the unexpected death of Olin Dewitt Johnston, the durable senior U.S. senator whose career spanned almost fifty years, covering a grim half-century of economic futility and racial alienation in South Carolina. In the aftermath, intensifying social and economic tremors began to rearrange the state's political and racial underpinnings as new leaders emerged.

Viewed in the context of ensuing years, the senator's death and the events subsequent to it would prove to be a defining moment in the state's politics. A political generation whose roots could be traced to the days of deep racial division and hostility of the early twentieth century was giving way to a generation of leaders bred in the Depression, toughened by World War II, and endowed with a healthy skepticism about the political absolutes that had guided the state's past. Set in motion that day would be a chain of developments that would not only change the faces at the top of the state's political ladder, it would also shift attention from the state's ideologically murky past and bring to prominence a practitioner of the state's newly fashioned political moderation.

That practitioner was Robert Evander McNair, a small-town attorney whose quiet demeanor well suited the forces of postwar pragmatism emerging to challenge the powers of political absolutism which had dominated the state for more than half of the twentieth century. During McNair's sixty-eight months as governor, South Carolina would become a battlefield where long-subdued differences over racial, economic, and political realities would flare into open, and often explosive, conflict. South Carolina would also endure along with the rest of the states a decade that saw the nation beset by civil disorder and torn by political divisions threatening the very survival of American democracy. It would be

McNair's fate to preside over the collision of these endemic forces during his term in office and to oversee the painful transformation of the stalwart old Confederate state into a member in good standing of the economically ambitious "New South" of the latter decades of the twentieth century.

Such portentous developments, however, seemed illusively off in the distance in those spring days of 1965 in which the state's political community was caught by surprise at the loss of one of its most prominent members. Olin Johnston commanded a formidable position in South Carolina's public hierarchy, both as an officeholder of some seniority in Washington and as a political figure with few peers in winning elections and sustaining voter support.

At his death, Johnston was remembered as a champion of the downtrodden, a practitioner of the politics of resiliency, and a resolute defender of the racial status quo. He supported programs of public power, public welfare, public housing, and public education and even broke with most southerners in casting a rare Dixie pro-labor vote against the Taft-Hartley Act. But when it came to other issues of public interest, namely, those identified with civil rights, Johnston was strictly a traditionalist, joining his other southern colleagues in resisting the civil rights initiatives of every president from Franklin Roosevelt to Lyndon Johnson.[1]

As measured against his colleague Strom Thurmond, Johnston's racial views were considered for his time to be "moderate," but it was a judgment applied only in the latter years of his senatorial career. As governor, in the months preceding his 1944 election to the U.S. Senate over arch-segregationist Ellison D. "Cotton Ed" Smith, Johnston affirmed his own racial credentials by masterminding a plan designed to prevent court-ordered black-voter participation in the state's Democratic primary, the political contest that at the time was the dominant election for state and local offices. "White supremacy will be maintained in our primaries," Johnston promised South Carolinians.[2]

As race became an issue of increasing political and public urgency in the postwar years, Johnston's intransigence on civil rights cast him as something of a throwback to the state's virulently segregationist past, particularly in the eyes of a new generation of political leaders that was beginning to view racial conflict as an unsightly impediment to the state's ambitious economic plans and strategies. It was, in fact, a matter of some symbolic significance that Johnston and his predecessor, "Cotton Ed" Smith, had held the same Senate seat for fifty-seven years (Johnston for twenty-one years and Smith for thirty-six years), a span that included years in which "South Carolina [and Mississippi] put the white supremacy case most bitterly, most uncompromisingly, and most vindictively [and] used the floor of the U.S. Senate as a forum for white supremacy oratory."[3]

In a state where incumbent senators were rarely defeated, particularly after they had two or three terms under their belts, Johnston's death not only opened up the most coveted office in the state's political order, it also loosened the leadership chain sufficiently to create an opportunity for some new faces and new thinking to come forward. South Carolina, in fact, was already making something of a break with its long entrenched political past, having accomplished the peaceful court-ordered desegregation of its two major institutions of higher education—Clemson College (later University) and the University of South Carolina in 1963—and having averted, at least for the moment, major racial violence in its accommodation of civil-rights-oriented public demonstrations earlier in the decade.

Moderate Stirrings for Change

Emerging as ringleaders of the state's newly found moderation were South Carolinians who could scarcely be regarded as rebellious or iconoclastic. For the most part, they were homegrown, conservative-minded, occasionally progressive-thinking public figures who were rarely—if ever—seen in heroic charges against the political barricades of the times. They were most comfortable as infighters battling within the existing rules and structures of the state's political and governmental establishment. Their fights, however, were clearly directed toward issues that had lain dormant for generations, issues such as public education, economic diversification, and racial equity. They recognized in their own carefully modulated tones and strategies that the state's overall condition was desperate and that a lot of things had to change before it got much better.

If anything, the emergent leaders were probably more economy builders than social crusaders. They advocated aggressive industrial recruitment as a means of gaining economic diversity, and they recognized that good public schools were an essential ingredient of economic strength and stability. It was a strategy that had its detractors, particularly among traditional business and industries, heavily dependent on a low-wage workforce. Also contentious to some was the suggestion that a new economic strategy required a new political enlightenment, at least to the extent of recognizing that racial peace should be embraced as much for its usefulness in an overall economic development package as for any compelling human or societal value.

The ranks of the reformers were not limited to politicians, particularly when it came to maintaining racial peace. There were corporate leaders who believed civil disruption was bad for business. There were ruling members of the state's political oligarchy, who saw disorder as a threat to their control. There were middle-class black leaders holding fast to the gradual process of court relief as the best strategy to address their grievances. There were some notable church leaders of both races seeking to use their congregations as bridges for peaceful resolution of differences. There were even some political progressives—many of whom shared World War II experience—who staked their careers on the perception that the state was willing to accept the inevitability of significant change to its long-defended way of life.

Among the political progressives in those pivotal spring days of 1965 were two sometimes bitter rivals—Ernest F. Hollings, an up-and-coming young former governor who had helped engineer the peaceful Clemson desegregation, and the sitting governor, Donald S. Russell, a former president of the University of South Carolina whom Hollings had beaten soundly in the 1958 Democratic primary for governor. For all their political rivalry, they shared a common interest in racial peace for South Carolina, and it was during the latter days of Hollings's gubernatorial administration and the early days of Russell's term as governor in 1963 that the two competitors forged at least a temporary truce to carry out the peaceful desegregation of Clemson College.

A little over two years later—on that Easter morning in 1965 as South Carolina bade farewell to its senior senator, Olin Johnston—another important decision awaited Donald Russell. As governor of the state, he was empowered to appoint the interim successor to the suddenly vacant seat in the U.S. Senate. It was a decision charged with immediate political consequences and severe political hazards. It was also a decision that could say a lot about the state's long-term racial future.

To some, Russell seemed a political neophyte. Much of his political experience had been gained as a protege and assistant to James F. Byrnes during the latter's service as director of the nation's war-mobilization efforts in World War II, and Russell's election as governor in 1962—on his second try—represented the first, and only, elective political office he ever held.

Nonetheless, Russell took his place prominently in the politics of the 1960s as a racial moderate and a progressive, business-minded governmental leader. A wealthy attorney with southern courtliness and keen intellect, Russell had been a popular dollar-a-year president of the University of South Carolina (1952–1957) who invested personal moneys in renovations and scholarship funds at that institution. By the time of his death in 1998, the value of Russell's endowments at the university had reached $2.4 million.[4] He had also stirred segregationists' ire when he invited black South Carolinians to his lawn party at the governor's mansion following his inaugural in January 1963.

At age fifty-nine, Russell had the look of a CEO, tall and erect with a polished bearing that belied his impoverished childhood and the toughening early years of his practice as a small-town lawyer in Union, South Carolina. Russell's public career was launched when he joined the prestigious Spartanburg firm of which Byrnes was a partner, and his political niche was established in Washington, where he served under Byrnes in several key wartime and postwar positions, including as Byrnes's deputy secretary of state in 1945 under President Truman.[5]

He was also one of few men in the state's recent history who became governor without first serving an apprenticeship in the General Assembly, and for some— despite his experience in high-level federal posts—that made him something of a political outsider in his own home state. Russell was described by one State

House newsman as "an intellectual, aloof, something of a 'loner,' painfully shy and comfortable only in the company of friendly peers."[6]

Solomon Blatt, the state's legendary Speaker of the House who had tutored many a governor-to-be in the fine art of political infighting, said of Russell that "Donald was a very honorable fellow. He was clean and had one of the finest legal minds of any lawyer that ever lived in this state. And, he made a good governor. He was honest. But Donald wasn't a good mixer."[7]

There was, in fact, the feeling that Russell's real ambition was to return to Washington to rejoin the environment he had enjoyed under Byrnes. One insightful Democrat, Attorney General Daniel R. McLeod, recalled, "I don't think Governor Russell liked being Governor . . . in my opinion, he couldn't be divorced from the University. I believe Governor Russell . . . wanted to go to Washington."[8]

In those pivotal spring days of 1965, speculation grew that Russell might opt to set in motion the forces required to have himself designated to succeed Johnston on an interim basis. It seemed politically logical for a man longing for the trappings of Washington; it was also politically dangerous for a man who had won public office only once. The passing of political icons such as Johnston—particularly on something of an unexpected basis—was often accompanied by strong public emotion and even something of an extended political wake and mourning designed to accord the deceased a period of tribute and reverence uncluttered by dispute or contention. Johnston had been a South Carolina political institution for more than four decades, and his political strength came largely through his personal appeal to the thousands of textile workers who made up the core of South Carolina's industrial labor force.

The product of a tenant farm and himself a child laborer in textile mills, Johnston was described as a "skilled campaigner [who] was at his best at the crossroads, the county courthouses, and the textile mills. . . . He would appear with dust on his shoes and a suit showing signs of hard travel. Most of those who turned out to greet him would be called by name. . . . Textile workers loved him. When campaigning through a mill, the tall senator would stop at a disabled loom, quickly tie an expert weave knot in the right place, and set the machine to humming again."[9]

Conventional political wisdom would have argued for Russell to make a symbolic or sentimental choice to replace the popular Johnston and to honor the tradition of undisturbed political repose for the deceased legend. Nine years earlier, on September 6, 1954, on the occasion of the sudden death of the state's senior senator, Burnet R. Maybank, Governor Byrnes had appointed popular industrialist Charles E. Daniel to serve the remaining few months of Maybank's term before giving way to Strom Thurmond, who won in the remarkable write-in campaign over state senator Edgar Brown in November 1954.[10]

Russell thus had several options in choosing a successor to Johnston, and within two days of the senator's death, newspapers were speculating about those options and suggesting a number of candidates, ranging from the sentimental to the substantive. Among them were two members of the Johnston family—wife Gladys, a popular campaigner on the trail with her husband, and brother Bill, the affable mayor of Anderson. The family had become politically significant in its own right, and one of Olin and Gladys Johnston's three children, Elizabeth J., would later serve three terms in the United States Congress from the Fourth District, known after her marriage to Dwight F. Patterson Jr. of Laurens as Liz Patterson. Other candidates mentioned in the speculation were the seventy-six-year-old Edgar Brown, who had lost in three previous Senate bids, former Governor Byrnes, and Columbia mayor Lester Bates, who had twice been a candidate in the Democratic primary for governor, losing to Byrnes in 1950 and to George Bell Timmerman Jr. in 1954.

By April 20, 1965, two days after Olin Johnston's death, public conjecture also began to appear that Russell would claim the seat for himself. One newspaper analyst noted that Russell could gain the advantage of "some 20 months of seniority and more than a year of experience to offer the 1966 voters." By law, the interim appointment would be in effect only until the state's next general election, November 8, 1966. The analyst also warned, "such a course might prove so unpopular with the public that Russell would be committing political suicide to follow it."[11]

Russell Opts for the Senate

Political suicide or not, Russell's decision was known publicly a day later. He would claim the U.S. Senate seat for himself. Columbia newsman Charles H. Wickenberg Jr., a governmental insider who had served as executive secretary to Governor Timmerman (1955–1959) and was executive news editor of the *State* newspaper, broke the story in that newspaper's April 21 edition, citing "unimpeachable sources" that revealed, "The decision to go to the U.S. Senate was urged on the . . . governor by individual legislative, business, industrial and labor leaders." Wickenberg's account quoted a source as saying, "We need a strong Democrat in Washington now, right now, to replace Johnston. There are vital issues concerning our state such as the one-price cotton matter that involves the textile industry. We cannot wait for a senator; Russell holds the most recent mandate of South Carolina voters to state office. In November 1966, he will have to answer to them for his record in the U.S. Senate."[12]

The news account proved accurate and prophetic. Wickenberg had, in fact, been in close touch with Russell's press secretary, Fred R. Sheheen, who was a former colleague when both were South Carolina bureau chiefs for the *Charlotte Observer*. Sheheen later recalled that prior to publishing the story, Wickenberg had called to confirm its contents and had read a draft of the story to him. "I thought the story was extremely favorable to Governor Russell because it did recount these factors about the textile people demanding that they needed someone strong [in Washington] to protect the textile interests." Sheheen passed the word back to Russell about the story, and, after a conversation about its contents, he called Wickenberg and said, "I can't confirm or deny the story, but if I were Governmental Affairs Editor of the *State* newspaper, I'd run it."[13]

Later that day, the word was hurriedly spread that Russell would indeed step down as governor, touching off events that would result in his becoming U.S. senator the next day—April 22, 1965—and elevating to the office of governor a young attorney by the name of Robert Evander McNair, victorious two years earlier in his first statewide race for lieutenant governor after five two-year terms in the South Carolina House of Representatives.

McNair recalled that Russell had actually tipped his hand as early as Sunday afternoon—hours after Johnston's death—about his plans:

> Mr. Russell called [on Sunday] and said, "I think we ought to sit down and talk. Could you and Josephine [Mrs. McNair] drive up to Columbia?"
>
> We did. We made arrangements, mutually agreed, that we should not come in our car. So we borrowed an automobile and drove to Columbia.
>
> I had a good, lengthy discussion with Governor Russell that Sunday afternoon. We agreed that any discussion about Senator Johnston's replacement should be very confidential. . . . Governor Russell was not in any way going to indicate what he was going to do. He simply wanted to talk about it.[14]

The conversation, according to McNair, went along the lines that "he wanted to know how I felt about it, and I recall saying, . . . 'Mr. Russell, this is a decision that you have to make' . . . I think I did say that I thought his decision, if he chose to go, would be well-received, that people were accustomed to having strong people [in Washington], that he had a good background, that . . . most of his career had been spent in Washington, and he certainly could render this state a great service."[15]

Speaker Blatt later recalled his views on the transition:

> Bob McNair came by Barnwell with his wife and picked me up and took me to Columbia with them. [McNair recalled that the Blatts and McNairs traveled to Columbia together for the swearing-in ceremony on April 22. Representative William Rhodes and his wife, Elizabeth, were also in the party.] They talked with me about it and what the effect of it would be, and I told them, of course, the danger of it. But I said I just want to tell you one thing, "Donald wants to be a U.S. senator and Bob wants to be governor. This is the only way I know of that it's going to happen, both of you getting what you want. Now I don't know what payday is coming—what's going to happen—I don't know.

But there's going to be a lot of people mad about it. And your friends—most of them—that are really your friends are going to be happy because you have accomplished what you've wanted for yourself."[16]

McNair Becomes the "Surprise" Governor

It all happened quickly. At precisely noon on Thursday, April 22, 1965, Donald Russell resigned as governor and McNair was sworn in by South Carolina Supreme Court justice Claude A. Taylor in a House of Representatives chamber crowded by senators, house members, and guests. An hour later, McNair signed the interim appointment naming his predecessor, Russell, to fill the vacancy left by the death of Olin Johnston four days earlier.

As predicted, Russell's decision set off mixed reaction among South Carolinians. The late senator's family was reported as being "miffed" at being excluded from the decision, and Johnston's widow, Gladys, was quoted as saying, "No member of the Johnston family was consulted on my husband's successor."[17] Would-be aspirant, brother William Johnston, "acknowledged that many friends suggested" that he fill his brother's post, but he said, "I did not discuss the matter with anybody. I didn't know what the Governor [Russell] had decided until I heard it on the radio in my office Wednesday [April 21] morning."[18]

Charlotte Observer columnist Jack Claiborne reflected the following Sunday that Russell's move was a "dangerous one." "Not only did it make the Johnstons unhappy," he wrote, "it also set up Russell as a target for Hollings."[19] Hollings, who had defeated Russell in the 1958 governor's race, followed the counsel of his political advisers, who encouraged him to stay adamantly noncommittal about the self-appointment decision. Hollings praised Russell's political courage and strong beliefs but was nonetheless measuring his chances against Russell in the upcoming special election for the full Senate term nineteen months hence. He remarked pointedly, "I am certain the people of South Carolina will express their own opinions of Russell's 'self-appointment' in the Democratic primary next year."[20]

Lost, at least for the moment, in all the speculation about palace intrigue, political hurt feelings, and personal career opportunities were some larger questions about South Carolina and its immediate political and racial strategies in the post-Johnston era. The peaceful desegregation at the University of South Carolina and Clemson had gained some positive national attention for the state and for individuals like Brown, Hollings, textile industry lobbyist John Cauthen, Clemson president Robert C. Edwards, and others. But elsewhere the political rifts were widening as two-party politics and the deepening sentiments over the state's racial future became increasingly prominent. The state's political community was crowded with powerful figures of highly divergent stances, including Thurmond and his GOP allies, who scorned what they considered capitulation to court orders and who actively promoted the belief that there was still a chance for racial segregation to be retained.

Much of that lurking contention was obscured by traditions of civility and surface perceptions of political stability as the state welcomed and assessed its new governor. Bob McNair's arrival as the state's chief executive—unexpected as it was in the public life of the state—was no political fluke. It simply came a little ahead of time for a man who had set his eyes on the governor's office some years earlier and had spent much of his career preparing himself for the job.

McNair's rise through the ranks, in fact, was a rapid one. During his first term in the House, in 1951–1952, he had toed the line by supporting the 3 percent sales tax in a strategy championed by Governor Byrnes to upgrade the state's all-black schools and thereby salvage its "separate but equal" segregated school system.[21] As a protégé of Speaker Blatt, McNair was subsequently fast-tracked through leadership positions in the House, chairing two key standing committees—Labor, Commerce, and Industry and then Judiciary—before he was forty years old. He was thus able to sponsor, among other key measures, right-to-work legislation, which helped earn him popularity among the state's industrial and corporate leaders. He had been the leading candidate to replace Blatt as Speaker in 1958, but when Blatt abandoned plans to run for a position on the South Carolina Supreme Court, McNair turned his attention to a run for lieutenant governor in 1962.

In that race, he defeated popular upcountry senator Marshall Parker of Oconee County, establishing along the way his credibility as a statewide political figure and defying at least two of the state's unwritten election rules: House members are not supposed to beat senators; and candidates from little places like Allendale were not supposed to put together effective statewide organizations.

There was another distinctive aspect of McNair's victory in 1962. He gained a substantial portion of the still relatively small black vote in the state, a vote that would expand to become his margin of victory in the 1966 governor's race. At a time when direct linkages between black and white public figures were considered politically risky, McNair had the support of an aggressive young NAACP lawyer named Matthew J. Perry, who had already gained some attention as Harvey Gantt's attorney in the desegregation of Clemson and who would later become the state's first black federal judge.

A Popular Insider

Along the way, McNair had also begun to attract attention from many quarters—lobbyists, state employees, municipal officials, lawyers, corporate directors, ministers, community leaders, and others who made it their business to keep up with the inner workings of the state's governmental and political machinery.

The brief ceremony swearing in McNair as governor drew a description from Robert McHugh, the veteran governmental affairs editor of the *State* newspaper who had succeeded Wickenberg in that post: "The reservoir of affection McNair's former legislative colleagues have for him could be measured in the spontaneity of the standing ovation they gave him."[22]

Other accounts of the McNair inaugural were similarly upbeat. Charleston's Hugh Gibson, whose reservations about Russell's political skills had been expressed only days earlier, scarcely concealed his enthusiasm for McNair in his front-page coverage in the *News and Courier* on April 22. "The 41-year-old Allendale attorney unquestionably is one of the most popular figures ever to come to that office," he wrote, predicting that "South Carolina's 77th governor [will] usher in an 'era of good feeling' in both state governmental and legislative circles."[23]

Gibson, a pipe-smoking Marine veteran who was particularly known for his coverage of the S.C. Senate and who was treated by some of its members as if he were one of them, had seen McNair in action as the lieutenant governor presiding over the state's upper chamber. Gibson could be curmudgeonly on occasion, but with McNair he was uncharacteristically warm:

> Veteran legislators cannot recall a chief executive more genuinely loved in both houses of the General Assembly. . . . This popularity is by no means accidental. It stems, in part, from his own friendly and easy disposition; in part, from his 12 years in the House; in part, from his firm but friendly service as the Senate's presiding officer.
>
> And, most of all, it stems from the fact that for some eight years McNair has been working at the business of winning friends and votes to reach the prize which fell into his hands yesterday.[24]

The usually taciturn Associated Press, whose bureau chief was another Senate denizen, a colorful red-haired Georgian named Al Lanier, let down its hair long enough to describe McNair as a "square-built, cherubic-looking Allendale attorney [who] is a vote-getter without being a back-slapper. . . . He set his sights on the governorship years ago but has never let tireless campaign work interfere with a heavy legislative load that doesn't reach the public eye."[25]

> McNair's office on the Senate side of the State House is a hangout for visitors and legislative hangers-on who are drawn there by McNair's tolerant attitude toward all who want to see him. A newsman, chatting idly in McNair's office just last week, posed this question: "Bob, Governor Russell has used the education angle and former Governor Fritz Hollings made his pitch on industrial advances. What pitch are you going to use if you become governor?"
>
> "I'm going to finish what they started," McNair shot back.[26]

The quick retort found its way into McNair's brief formal remarks following his swearing-in as governor. "I pledge myself to carry out to the best of my ability those programs which have been inaugurated by my predecessors and to be alert as God gives me vision to any and all possibilities of improving the welfare of our citizens," he said.[27]

McNair's short speech was filled more with signals than it was with recommendations for action. "There was nothing specific," he said. "I did not spell out any program or anything. It was just tone-setting for the approach we wanted to take."[28] It was also a speech tailored for legislative ears, reminding them that he still considered himself, after all, one of them. "I wanted to set the tone that this was going to be a 'we' administration and . . . I was really looking for cooperation from the General Assembly and all people in government to work together to move the state forward."[29]

Blatt, Brown, and the Legislative Alliances

McNair got quick reciprocation from the General Assembly on his invitation to be part of a "we" administration. Within six days of his swearing-in, the usually feuding budget chiefs of the S.C. Senate and House of Representatives declared a truce and, in a virtually unprecedented act of harmony, presented the new governor with something of an inaugural gift, a state appropriation bill passed by both houses without the necessity of a conference committee to negotiate the differences between the two bodies' versions of the bill. "I took that as being a gesture of good will on their part," McNair said, "and I think that it started us off on a feeling of cooperation."[30]

The feeling of cooperation was, as McNair well knew, more than a political nicety or a gesture of goodwill. For a young, newly inaugurated chief executive, it meant access to a valuable source of power for South Carolina governors weakly endowed by the state constitution at the time—power granted voluntarily by legislative leaders who dominated much of the state's governmental process. Born in one of the state's original counties, rural Berkeley County, and elected from tiny Allendale, the state's newest county at the time, McNair had the advantage of growing up politically in small-county politics, and he had regularly made common cause with the small-county barons as allies and fellow travelers during his legislative career.

As a member of the House leadership and later as lieutenant governor presiding over the Senate each day, McNair could also bridge the chasm separating the oft-feuding Senate and House leaders in the state's General Assembly. Unlike his two urban predecessors as governor—Hollings of Charleston and Russell of Spartanburg—McNair was a member in good standing of the ephemeral "Barnwell Ring," a loose confederation of small-county legislators who in recent years had drawn their allegiance more from the rural nature of their causes than from their geographic proximity to Barnwell County.

In the days before one-man, one-vote rulings tied representation to population in the South Carolina legislature, counties were the election units for both houses of the General Assembly, and many of the legislative fights were between small and larger counties. The advantage in that fight often lay with politically crafty rural leaders like Brown and Blatt, whose abilities and electoral endurance had lifted them to positions of virtually unchallenged power in the Senate and House. For all their political skills, however, the two Barnwell leaders did not get along with each other, and McNair was one of the few who could bridge the often wide and deep gap between the two.

"The Blatt-Brown thing was there," McNair recalled. "You had two very powerful leaders who naturally were going to have their differences. Their differences would surface and would then get into the General Assembly and tie it up sometimes for weeks and weeks. . . . There were personal differences between them because of the nature of the people; they were different personalities and had different backgrounds. They also had differences on certain basic issues and politics, as well."[31]

Blatt, the feisty son of Jewish immigrants who had escaped the pogroms of Russia, ruled the House with strict and sometimes testy authority. Brown, witty and engaging, conveyed a gentle but assertive influence within the entrenched leadership of the Senate, where seniority determined rank and power. When McNair took office as governor in 1965, Brown was seventy-six and Blatt sixty-nine, and the two old rivals were still capable of putting up a good fight either for or against each other. In a state where personal politics counted heavily, the new governor's ability to penetrate that simmering rivalry was an early and major source of power for his administration.

McNair's friendship with Blatt went back to his first term in the House, when Blatt had been a mentor to the young Allendale representative, and McNair recalled, "We were such good friends and the fact that I had come along as a protégé of his gave me a big lift. That gave us a good relationship to start with, and we worked at it. We worked at trying to improve, at least, the communications between the two bodies."[32]

With regard to Brown, McNair said, "I think I came along at a good time to catch Senator Brown in his mellowing time. . . . The press and everyone portrayed him as a fellow with horns, [but] he was one of the most likable, lovable gentlemen you would ever know. He could be very tough—no one could question that—but also one of the easiest people to work with that you could find. He had an extremely good disposition and personality, and as most people were aware, he also had a good sense of humor."[33]

The Gathering Civil Rights Storm

For all the perception of goodwill and good wishes, McNair was taking office at a deceptively perilous time. The peaceful desegregation of Clemson and USC, cheered as signs of the state's newfound racial maturity, had actually been highly orchestrated dress rehearsals for a long-deferred main event, desegregation of the state's entire public-school system, a certain storm that lay ominously just over the horizon for the new administration.

Eleven years earlier, the U.S. Supreme Court had ruled in *Brown v. Board of Education* (1954) that the segregation of public schools by race was unconstitutional. A subsequent ruling, known as *Brown II,* provided that the states would be required to merge the systems "with all deliberate speed," and six southern and border states and the District of Columbia moved promptly to desegregate their public schools in the years immediately following *Brown.*[34] Other states chose stern resistance, pursuing a strategy later described by President Richard Nixon's civil rights chief, Leon Panetta, when he wrote, "it was in the Deep South where the collective heel was dug in."[35]

South Carolina was not among those that rushed to comply, nor was it part of the collective resistance that characterized its Deep South neighbors. The state had chosen its own course of defiance, which included a unique effort to meet the requirements of the "separate but equal" doctrine by upgrading its shabby black schools and—having done that—embarking on a high-level defense of its segregated system. The strategy, masterminded by legendary South Carolina statesman James F. Byrnes, created conditions under which many of the state's white leaders believed their segregated system would be upheld in court. While shrill voices of protest against segregation were being heard across Dixie, South Carolina remained almost smug with a confidence that seemed to obviate the need for public violence and political demagoguery, and even after the *Brown* decisions of 1954 and 1955, the state continued its series of legislative and legal schemes to delay the implementation of *Brown.* From the outset of such strategies, there was an ongoing effort to counsel and reassure South Carolinians of an orderly and lawful—though artfully undefined—outcome.

As years passed, and *Brown* withstood a bevy of legal challenges from South Carolina and elsewhere, there settled across the state a kind of political ambiguity, a fitful interlude of peace and long-delayed judgment that was hailed as a sign of the state's evolving political moderation. While some applauded the state's protracted indecision, others complained that South Carolina's slow and fitful response deprived the state of the kind of confrontational crisis that they contended provided cathartic, substantive resolution of racial differences in states like Alabama and Mississippi. There have ensued to the present day disagreements over South Carolina's relatively quiet post-*Brown* behavior. Some have contended that the state—as Hollings said—knew it was whipped and was using delaying tactics to smooth the way for peaceful acceptance of *Brown* and its consequences. Others believe that South Carolina persisted in legal and legislative resistance to school integration because it retained faith that its segregated schools would somehow be rescued from the provisions of *Brown.* Whatever the motivation, the outcome was essentially the same: official resistance and reluctant compliance.

Cyril B. Busbee, who was state superintendent of education during the contentious years of South Carolina's last legal stands in the late 1960s, recalled that the year after the *Brown* decision, the General Assembly "repealed a bunch of laws . . . and created a committee which all were clearly intended to impede and to delay the integration process as long as possible and to make it as cumbersome as possible."[36]

Even as early as 1952, two years before the *Brown* decision was handed down but in preparation for the possibility of an antisegregation decision by the Supreme Court, South Carolina voters had approved by two to one a referendum authorizing the closing of public schools to avoid integration. The move prompted *Raleigh News and Observer* editor Jonathan Daniel to comment that "South Carolina was not merely threatening to secede from the union, but from civilization."[37] Four years later, in what was dubbed by journalist William D. Workman Jr. the "Segregation Session,"[38] there were further steps to "impede and delay" integration. They included legislation authorizing the closing of public schools, the transferring of students to avoid desegregation, and the shutting down of a state park (Edisto) under federal order to be integrated. It even became illegal to be a member of the NAACP.[39]

Also gaining status and some notoriety at that time was the South Carolina School Committee, a panel created under Byrnes to combat desegregation and given formal status by the legislature in 1954 as a fifteen-member body to oppose the implementation of *Brown* "by all lawful means."[40] Its chairman, the venerable state senator L. Marion Gressette from St. Matthews, later contended that the committee's purpose was not to impede but to "prepare our state for the time when—if the court concluded that we should integrate—that we'd be prepared for it." Gressette noted that at the time, "You have people sounding off in Alabama [and other states] . . . and Georgia was pretty rough. . . . There was a lot of feeling that, among the people, this thing [school desegregation] would not be tolerated."[41]

Among those sounding off a day after the *Brown* decision was handed down was Georgia governor Herman Talmadge. He said the *Brown* decision "had reduced our Constitution to a mere scrap of paper, by issuing a bold political decree without basis in law."[42] Also sounding off was Mississippi senator James O. Eastland, who all but foreordained the violence that would wrack his state in subsequent years when he said: "The South will not abide by nor obey the legislative decision by a political court."[43]

Restrained Response to Desegregation Order

By comparison, a Columbia newspaper account the day following the *Brown* decision described South Carolina's position in restrained and measured tone. "[The state] has no plans for any precipitate action against yesterday's U.S. Supreme Court decision against separate public schools for whites and Negroes.

. . . Reaction from government and school leaders crystallized . . . into a wait-and-see attitude on the decision. . . . There appeared to be no plans to interrupt the state's multi-million dollar state school equalization program."[44] Governor Byrnes was quoted only as saying that he was "shocked" but that he urged South Carolinians to "exercise restraint and preserve order."[45]

Gressette believed that in South Carolina, "we didn't have a lot of people threatening to do this, that, or the other, or we didn't have street marches, meetings out in the open that would probably incite or encourage people to do things that they should not do. What we did was we went about it in an orderly fashion."[46]

Whatever may have been the intent of the Gressette Committee and the various other ploys South Carolina used—whether to delay, impede, or prepare—time was running out in those spring days of 1965 as Olin Johnston was laid to rest and Bob McNair became governor. South Carolina had escaped some of the bloodshed that accompanied school desegregation in other southern states, but so much time had elapsed that the state would be among the last to comply with the requirements of *Brown* and subsequent rulings and statutes. By 1965, Cyril Busbee said, the strategies of "delay and restraint" had run their course, and "it [school desegregation] became serious . . . it began to appear that action had to be taken."[47]

The clock measuring federal court leniency was not the only one at work in South Carolina at the time. Another chronometer was measuring the patience of black South Carolina as it witnessed the extraordinary machinations of the state's white leadership in forestalling implementation of the *Brown* decision.

Although the case bore the name of Oliver Brown, the African American welder who sued the Topeka, Kansas, board of education to gain admission to an all-white school for his daughter, Linda, the *Brown* case actually combined five suits, one of which had deep roots in South Carolina. Author John Egerton wrote, "I find myself wishing the title case had been *Briggs v. Elliott*—the South Carolina suit—or better yet, *DeLaine v. Clarendon County*, in honor of the Reverend Joseph A. DeLaine, of Summerton, South Carolina, the one individual above all others responsible for bringing the first of the five cases into court."[48] (In 2003, more than a half-century after his stance on behalf of school desegregation in Clarendon County, DeLaine was posthumously awarded the Congressional Medal of Freedom, a recognition initiated and carried out by South Carolina congressman James E. Clyburn.)

A Challenge to Segregation Itself

To black South Carolinians, the *Briggs* case—and ultimately *Brown*—was a showdown of major proportions. Initially brought in 1947 as an action by Clarendon County farmer Levi Pearson seeking equal school-bus transportation, the case emerged three years later under the names of Harry Briggs and nineteen other Clarendon County petitioners attacking not only the inequality of the separate school systems but the constitutionality of the separate systems per se.

"Before the proceedings could begin in the *Briggs* case, Judge J. Waties Waring privately let it be known that he wanted to try a case that attacked 'frontally' the entire 'separate but equal' doctrine." Clarendon County became a cause of special significance to national NAACP officials "because it came out of the Deep South and because it was an extreme example of separate and unequal," historian Barbara A. Woods has written.[49]

The suit, brought against Clarendon District 22, charged that Clarendon's black schools "were far inferior to its schools for white children." It was heard by a three-judge panel of the United States Court of Appeals, chaired by Chief Judge John J. Parker of Charlotte, who wrote the majority opinion upholding the state's segregated schools. Judge Waring cast the minority vote supporting the plaintiffs, and from that point *Briggs* became the first of the NAACP's five desegregation suits to reach the Supreme Court. It was combined with the Kansas suit, *Brown v. Board of Education,* in June 1952 and subsequently with three others from Virginia, Delaware, and the District of Columbia. And, "in order to make it clear that it was not just a Southern decision, *Brown* was put before *Briggs.*"[50]

Even before its eventual adjudication in 1954, *Briggs* was having a profound effect in South Carolina and—according to historian I. A. Newby—eventually led to Byrnes's advocacy of new funds to equalize school facilities. Newby wrote, "Political and educational leaders in white Carolina recognized that the *Briggs* suit . . . posed a fundamental threat, if not to school segregation itself, at least to school systems with gross inequities. Their decision was to equalize facilities of white and black schools."[51]

Black South Carolina waited and watched the state's delaying tactics with what was later described as characteristic caution, "an elementary fact about racial movements in black Carolina since World War II," according to Newby. "The NAACP determined the course those movements took," he concluded, "channeling them into cautious, limited programs in pursuit of moderate, pragmatic objectives. Depending upon one's point of view, this was the basic strength or chief weakness in the state. In a larger sense, maybe it was both."[52]

It was, in fact, according to Newby, black as well as white moderation that afforded South Carolina its peaceful early years of racial desegregation. He wrote:

In the 1960s, it became fashionable to praise white Carolinians for their moderation, for acceding to desegregation with more gracefulness than some other white Southerners. The praise was often deserved.

But if this be the reward for moderation, black Carolinians are more deserving than whites. Of the two races in South Carolina, whether in the civil rights protests of the 1950s or the activism of the 1960s, the black race was the less extreme and more responsible. Blacks never followed a leader whose views on racial policy were as extreme as those of Senator Thurmond.[53]

Thurmond indeed remained South Carolina's enduring symbol of a brand of conservatism that was traditionally, and increasingly, defined by race. Already something of a folk hero among many white southerners for his defiance of the 1948 Democratic presidential ticket and his race for president on the States' Rights (Dixiecrat) ticket, Thurmond was experiencing the benefits of a backlash to the civil rights movement that was propelling him and his newly adopted Republican Party to new popularity in the South.

In his 1964 race for the presidency, Barry Goldwater did only slightly better than Thurmond had done in 1948. But Goldwater's macho brand of no-nonsense conservatism suited Thurmond and his segregationist followers just fine, and the GOP became home to many traditional Democrats, including Thurmond, disenchanted with the civil rights initiatives of the national Democratic party. Thurmond's change of parties took place in the midst of the Goldwater campaign, September 15, 1964, only two years after the party had mounted its first statewide campaign of the century, a loss by conservative newsman Bill Workman to Olin Johnston. By 1966, Republicans would be fielding an almost full slate in the statewide races and would be garnering a majority of the white vote in some of them.

Civil Rights and the New Activism

In the spring of 1965, however, challenges to South Carolina's centrist leadership were coming not just from the political right. Emerging in the South to challenge and augment the cautious litigation strategy of the NAACP were activist elements of the left, particularly the Southern Christian Leadership Conference (SCLC) and the Student Non-Violent Coordinating Committee (SNCC), two organizations that by 1965 were already taking much of the civil rights movement out of the courtrooms and legislative halls and into the streets.

SCLC, organized in Atlanta in January 1957 under the leadership of a young Baptist minister from Montgomery, Alabama, named Martin Luther King Jr., became known for its use of large nonviolent public demonstrations, and by 1965, its protest movements in Albany, Georgia, and Birmingham, Alabama, had earned SCLC the reputation as the best-organized and best-funded of the modern civil rights organizations. Its leadership came largely from the southern ministerial ranks, including Andrew Young, Hosea Williams, Jesse Jackson, and Ralph Abernathy, but it was Dr. King who emerged as the articulator and the most enduring symbol of the civil rights movement in America.

SNCC, from its beginning in April 1960, was the aggressively contentious element of the civil rights movement. One of its founders and early leaders, John Lewis, since 1987 the congressman from Georgia's Fifth District, wrote of SNCC's spirit that "our revolt was as much against this nation's traditional black leadership structure as it was against racial segregation and discrimination."[54]

By 1965, Lewis's activist leadership was being threatened by a young Howard University student named Stokely Carmichael, whose advocacy of Black Power and Black Nationalism was pushing the organization even farther to the political left and chilling its relations with other civil rights organizations, particularly the SCLC. One of Carmichael's closest associates, Cleveland Sellers, a Howard University student from Denmark, South Carolina, had gained respect within SNCC for his organizational abilities and was moving into leadership positions as a Carmichael lieutenant.

On March 7, 1965—forty-six days before Bob McNair became South Carolina's governor—SCLC's Williams and SNCC's Lewis led about five hundred people, including Sellers, on a march intended to proceed from Selma, Alabama, to the state capitol at Montgomery to present a petition to Governor George C. Wallace protesting violence in voter registration earlier that year in the state. The march only got as far as the Pettus Bridge in Selma when state and local law-enforcement officers converged on the marchers. In the ensuing melee, dozens of marchers, including Lewis, were beaten and injured.

Two weeks later—on March 21—a second march was scheduled for Selma, and this time, some fifty thousand people from throughout the nation participated, including scores of well-known entertainers and most of the prominent civil rights leaders. It was peaceful and proved a powerful influence in the subsequent passage of the 1965 Voting Rights Acts by Congress later that year. It also proved, according to a writer cited by Lewis in a 1998 account, to be "the nova of the civil rights movement, a brilliant climax which brought to a close the nonviolent struggle that had reshaped the South."[55]

Later that same evening (March 21), civil rights volunteer Viola Gregg Liuzzo, a Detroit housewife, was murdered on an Alabama road. The murder, and the subsequent trial and acquittal of four Klansmen charged with it, provided, according to SNCC leader Lewis, "just one more reason to give up on this notion of nonviolence. . . . It was Selma that held us together as long as we did. After that, we just came apart."[56]

The dissolution of civil rights unity in the aftermath of the second Selma march would hold much significance for the course of racial strategies in the South of the late 1960s and would bear particularly on events in South Carolina. As Bob McNair took office thirty-two days after the murder of Liuzzo, the events of Selma seemed somehow remote and there was a setting of cordiality, of his inauguration ushering in an "era of good feeling."

Even as McNair took office, however, the restlessness of organizations like SCLC and SNCC was becoming increasingly apparent. Unwilling to wait out the courts' rulings and their long-deferred implementation, new militancy was replacing old moderation in the fragmenting civil rights movement. Leaders were following the impatient spirit of Dr. King, who had written in 1963 in his letter from the Birmingham jail, "The Negro's greatest stumbling block is not the White Citizens Council or the Ku Klux Klanner, but the white moderate who is more devoted to 'order' than to justice . . . who paternalistically believes he can set a timetable for another man's freedom."[57]

One of the signers of the letter to King urging restraint and setting off the civil rights leader's now-classic response was Paul Hardin Jr., resident bishop of the United Methodist Church of South Carolina during the 1960s. Bishop Hardin, under whose leadership the black and white conferences of the state's Methodist Church were merged in 1972, had been part of an ecumenical effort ten years earlier, in the wake of violence at Ole Miss in October 1962, to head off violence when Clemson desegregated with the admission of Harvey Gantt. The effort produced a statement, signed by 121 white ministers of thirteen denominations, which included this entreaty, "Let not the Sovereign State of South Carolina be disgraced by violence."[58] Similarly, James McBride Dabbs, a Coker College professor and Presbyterian layman who had been president of the Southern Regional Council between 1957 and 1963, called for peaceful acceptance of the Clemson desegregation, "urged the citizenry to maintain poise and balance," and predicted that South Carolinians would "have courtesy, pride and dignity."[59]

South Carolina had, in fact, been only on the periphery of the civil rights activism in the early 1960s and had been spared much of its violence. A report issued in 1966 by the Southern Regional Council and the American Jewish Committee of the Institute of Human Relations observed,

> The nation . . . has regarded violence as a characteristic of all the former Confederate states. This is an illusion. Violence has for several years been largely confined to the Deep South, and there generally to Alabama, Mississippi, north and delta Louisiana, and southwest Georgia.
>
> Occasional outbursts in the peripheral South, Texas, Arkansas, Florida, north Georgia, Tennessee, Virginia, North and South Carolina have been isolated incidents and not a manifestation of organized resistance.[60]

Part of that relative calm on the periphery was because much of the civil rights movement itself was initially concentrated only in certain areas. For James Forman, first executive director of SNCC, "It was Mississippi, that's all—for some just to say the name of the state is to tell the whole story . . . Mississippi, birthplace of the White Citizens' Councils—a white-collar version of the Ku Klux Klan. It was Mississippi, where years of terror, economic intimidation, and a grinding, day-in, day-out white racism had created a black population numb with fear and hopelessness."[61]

Others reasoned that the volatility of white leaders sounding off on racial matters constituted a tacit invitation to public misbehavior, and that it was in states where such leadership dominated that violence resulted. Atlanta editor Ralph McGill called it "an old lesson . . . [that] the white Southerner will not join mob violence unless he believes that laxity in law enforcement will make it possible."[62] Still others reckoned that it was all a matter of inherent civility among South Carolinians that distinguished them from other southerners. Clemson's first African American student, Harvey Gantt, a native of Charleston, wryly suggested that "if you can't appeal to the morals of a South Carolinian, you can appeal to his manners."[63]

For whatever the reasons—moderate white leadership, cautious black leadership, the influence of progressive churches, the targeting of civil rights campaigns elsewhere, inherent civility—South Carolina escaped the early waves of major violence that hit the South during the first half of the 1960s. Instances of attacks, abuse, and arrests had accompanied some of the early sit-in demonstrations across the state, but they were for the most part scattered and isolated and got little in the way of sustained public attention.

But, as John Lewis wrote, the nonviolent phase of the civil rights movement was coming to a close in 1965. Cohesion among the various organizations was becoming more difficult, and within organizations themselves disagreements over philosophy, strategy, priorities, and personalities were causing fragmentation. As the sense of common purpose yielded to narrower goals, frustration and rivalries set in, restraint weakened, and impatience replaced nonviolence as an operative motivator.

Even in white South Carolina, where political absolutes had been prevalent only two scant decades earlier, things were breaking apart into unprecedented pluralism. As Olin Johnston, the man who had made the last major stand for a one-party, all-white politics in 1944, was being laid to rest, the political system he had defended so stoutly was also dying away. South Carolina was not only being polarized into a two-party system, there were also shadings of diversity all along the political and philosophical spectrum. Localism and its alliances of regional interests were being replaced by coalitions defined by issues and doctrine. Even the once-unassailable allegiance to white supremacy and racial separation was finding its detractors and challengers.

The political transformation of the state was underway, but the strictures of its nineteenth-century political institutions were still in place and still in operation. For all the evidence of change in outlook and philosophy, in fact, South Carolina was still a place of racial and gender exclusivity. At the approach of the 1960s, within the halls of elective political power of the state of South Carolina, there were no blacks, no one identified as a member of the Republican Party, and no women. The 1965 *Legislative Manual* showed pictures and biographies of white, male Democrats in each seat in the House of Representatives, each seat in the Senate, each of the state's constitutional offices, each of the state's five Supreme Court seats, each of the state's sixteen circuit court judgeships, five of the state's six U.S. Congress offices (the Second District seat was vacant), and both U.S. Senate seats, even though Senator Thurmond switched parties in 1964.

Lying ahead for South Carolina were struggles involving minority citizens who had lain outside the political world for seventy years. Most of them were South Carolinians who had never held public office, had never cast a vote, had never registered to vote, and who had set foot in the halls of government only as bystanders and visitors.

As the Olin Johnston era of public service and political leadership came to a close in South Carolina on that Easter Sunday when the senator was laid to rest amid tributes and accolades, the political clock resumed ticking, faster this time and moving the state rapidly toward a rendezvous with some inescapable political realities.

Time had run out on the strategy of delay, and patience had run out among those clamoring at the gates for entry into the state's political system. The practice of political moderation, itself something of a novelty in the state that fired on Fort Sumter in 1861 and celebrated its defiance a century later by hoisting a Confederate battle flag atop its State House, would be tested by increasingly aggressive elements of political immoderation to the left and the right.

Political observers proclaiming McNair's ascendancy as an event ushering in an era of good feeling were basing their optimism at least in part on abilities he had demonstrated in functioning within the political processes of South Carolina's eccentric governmental systems and institutions. McNair, it was felt, could use personal skills and political moxie to overcome the realities of a system that regularly cast the governor as underdog in dealings with entrenched legislative power and authority.

But Bob McNair became governor as the pressures for change across a broad spectrum of unattended and unresolved issues were reaching the boiling point. Their collective forces would carry the state during the latter half of the 1960s to the brink of public and political chaos. The greater test for the new chief executive would lie outside the halls of the state's tradition-bound political and governmental settings. It would lie in confrontations with new political forces in the state arising from the streets and emerging from the ranks of the disenfranchised and disempowered. It would lie in the contest to determine whether South Carolina would find its political identity in the sometimes maddening pursuit of the ambiguities and equivocations of moderation, or whether the state would revert to the lure of its passionate past and the comforting certainty of its historic lost causes.

And ultimately, it would lie in the determination of whether South Carolina, amid the noisy upheavals of the 1960s, could sustain the political equilibrium necessary to mount public initiatives addressing the state's long-standing deficiencies in fundamentals such as public education, economic development, and human well-being. The new governor taking office on that April day in 1965 came to his tasks as no stranger to the realities of the state's condition, the multifaceted dilemmas it faced, and the root causes that lay at their heart.

2

Growing Up in Hell Hole Swamp

Bob McNair was born into a South Carolina stricken with grievous economic and political maladies. Unlike neighboring states to the north and south, where prominent homegrown industries built around tobacco, furniture, soft drinks, and textiles were providing some wealth and capital, South Carolina remained largely tied to the land.

The state's livelihood lay—as it had for 250 years—in the broad fields of agricultural enterprise that had defined its economy since the earliest days. Even after the abolition of slavery and the dissolution of the plantation system, South Carolina remained an aggressively agrarian state, rural in its political orientation and deeply committed to agriculture as its economic lifeblood.

In place of the wealth and opulence of antebellum plantation society, however, much of South Carolina in the 1920s was a place of cash-strapped dirt farmers eking out a living on small tracts of often marginally productive land. South Carolina's rural-based strategies of the 1890s, designed to "liberate" the state from Reconstruction and overthrow the "Bourbon" leaders remaining from the plantation era, had led the state down political and economic blind alleys. Slavery was dead, but most South Carolinians—white and black—lived in one or the other form of economic dependence as sharecroppers, tenant farmers, or mill workers.[1] And, while amendments to the United States Constitution in the post–Civil War era had guaranteed equal rights protection to the former slaves, most southern states had found ways by the start of the twentieth century to disenfranchise and segregate their black populations. In South Carolina, more than half the state's population was black, and it was a population that was effectively separated from the mainstream of the state's economic and political life.

It was into this troubled world that the newborn Robert Evander McNair arrived, the son of prosperous parents who made their home amid some of South Carolina's most poverty-stricken lands. They were prominent landowners in Berkeley County, a place where plantation wealth had once been extensive and where the state's latter-day rural poverty was most profound. The McNairs made their home in an area known as Hell Hole Swamp, a name traditionally traced to British cavalry officer Banastre Tarleton, who—in combat with General Francis Marion's patriot guerrilla forces during the American Revolution—reportedly told his Redcoat troops to retreat and "get out of this hell hole of a swamp."

McNair was born to Claudia Crawford McNair and Daniel Evander McNair on December 14, 1923, at the home of his mother's sister in the small Williamsburg County town of Cades. But from his earliest days, Bob McNair was a child of Berkeley County, growing up comfortable and secure on the vast reaches of a Santee River plantation called Ballsdam, a property whose origins could be traced to South Carolina's earliest settlement as a seventeenth-century British proprietorship. His father was a no-nonsense Scotsman from North Carolina who became active in local politics and raised his son to have a good knowledge of farming, a great love of the outdoors, and a keen sense of personal politics. His mother was a gentle countrywoman from nearby Russellville who was known for her church work and for helping neighboring families and who passed along to her son a sharp insight into the basic needs of impoverished people.

Growing Up amid Rural Poverty

The McNairs were comfortable and successful, but they were not detached from the harsh realities of their surroundings, as might have been the case with "old South Carolina" and its landed aristocracy. While they were landowners with farmhands and families dependent on them for their well-being, the McNairs were also part of the community, a community of large farmers and small, black and white, affluent and less prosperous, who worked the fields together and who worried together over things like rainfall, soil conditions, crop prices, and all the many factors that influenced how well the farm economy would go. Unlike cities and their racially divided neighborhoods, farmland was not segregated by race or economic condition. Blacks and whites were neighbors, and even in a society that deemed them unequal, they were partners in addressing the concerns and responsibilities of their community.

"My mother was very active," McNair recalled.

> She was the person in the area, if somebody was sick—be they black or white—people came to for help. If somebody needed to go to the doctor, particularly among the blacks, she was the one who would take them to the doctor and take care of them and be sure they had things.

My father ran the farm. We were involved in livestock operations. We were also in the crosstie business and we had timberlands. It was not big dollars, but it was to us, and it was for that area.[2]

In the late nineteenth and early twentieth centuries, old plantation lands were being valued for their forest resources, and as the Industrial Revolution spread across the eastern and midwestern states, it drew commodities from the states of the old Confederacy, among them petroleum from the Southwest, coal from Appalachia, and timber from the eastern seaboard. Particularly dependent on the forest resources was the booming railroad industry, which was clamoring for timber to be used for many purposes, including railroad ties for its ever-expanding shipping systems, as fuel for steam locomotives, and as building materials for the booming cities of the East and Midwest. Stripping away the long-standing forests with the efficiency of machinery and work gangs where cotton had been picked manually by slave labor only a few decades earlier, the rail and timber interests brought some new—if only temporary—wealth to the war-ravaged Carolinas economy.

Growing up in the special environment of hardscrabble Berkeley County in the 1920s and 1930s gave him special insight.[3] It was a view based on sharp contrasts and sensitivities to the economic and social implications of those contrasts. "I lived a very pleasant life," McNair observed, noting the creature comforts born of his father's success as a farmer and businessman. "We had an automobile and those things that were considered luxuries then. We never really wanted for anything, although we did not have what people in the city thought were essentials, such as electric lights or indoor plumbing. From the standpoint of the area that I lived in, I suppose that people looked at us and felt we had everything."[4]

"There was the hard side, too," he said. "There were the folks who lived in the tenant houses or small shacks. They really had no job and often had only a mule and a farm. They barely pecked out a living or they worked on the farms of others. They survived and that was all." That firsthand experience—the comfortable landowner's son amid the grinding poverty of 1930s South Carolina—would leave a lasting impression. McNair's world was racially mixed, and there were gaping differences between the haves and the have-nots. But it was a world defined more by the struggle to survive than by issues of civil rights or economic disparity.

There was very little racial tension then. . . . You did not have to worry about somebody breaking into your house and stealing things. That was unheard of.

Petty stealing, on the other hand, was not uncommon, but it was mostly stealing something to eat. People would steal chickens or pigs or watermelons out of the patch. They were doing it not to be thieves or criminals, but to get something to take home to the family to eat.[5]

The Influence of Parents

From his parents, McNair inherited traits and interests that friends would later recognize as being prominent characteristics of his emerging personal and political style. He formed early political interests watching Daniel McNair advise and consult with community members, and he saw his father become a leader of one of the county's political factions. The elder McNair was a powerful mentor for his son. "Coming along as an only child," he said, "I was one who knew what was normally going on. I was particularly close to my father. I can recall that I would get on the horse and ride with him when he would go out to round up the cattle. He would take me along and sit me on the front of his saddle. As soon as I got big enough, I would go other places with him. When he would go to Charleston to buy things, I would go with him. When he went to town to get equipment for the farm, I would go with him."[6]

Riding horseback across the farm remained a favorite McNair pastime over the years, and when he agreed to long-delayed hip-replacement surgery years later at age eighty-one, it was only after being told that he could no longer ride horseback without such a procedure. "That settled the issue once and for all," an associate said at the time.

It was also from his father that McNair inherited elements of a strong Scottish temperament. His father could be thrift-minded, particularly when it came to extending credit for customers of the McNair's country store, and son Bob became known for his tight and conservative, dollar-for-dollar budgeting as governor and chairman of the State Budget and Control Board.

McNair also inherited other Scottish tendencies. "He could be stubborn as a mule," good friend Robert S. "Bob" Davis later remembered. "If he made up his mind about something, it was very hard to change."[7] "On the other hand, he was a man that would listen," Davis said. Other friends recognized a sensitive and conciliatory side, which probably reflected the McNair family role in helping to solve problems among neighbors and families in the community. His political friends would later marvel at his negotiating and compromising skills and would see the more strident McNair only on rare occasions.

The senior McNair would also become the inspiration for his son's political interests. Daniel McNair assumed an ongoing role in local politics, chaired the school board, and became influential in a political faction of the county's rural leaders, often pitted against the courthouse insiders from Moncks Corner. Stocky and tough-minded, he had been a deputy sheriff in Robeson County, North Carolina, and he was known to carry a revolver in the glove compartment of his pickup truck.

The McNairs of Scotland

The McNairs were Highland Scots who had migrated from their home on the Kintyre peninsula of western Scotland in the mid-eighteenth century, settling in eastern North Carolina in places that still bear names from their homeland: Scotland County, Aberdeen, St. Andrews University, and Maxton.[8] One of their earliest settlements was called Campbelltown, presumably after the Kintyre town from which they embarked for America, but it was renamed after the Revolution for the French hero the Marquis de Lafayette, and it became Fayetteville.

McNair's ancestors, Duncan McNair and Catherine McCallum McNair, left Scotland in 1787, arrived at the port of Wilmington, North Carolina, and eventually settled in the Robeson County community of St. Pauls. Over the generations, Robeson County Scots became remarkably successful in the field of public affairs and produced a total of five governors in North Carolina, Tennessee, Alabama, and South Carolina.

The McNairs went into medicine, the ministry, railroad work, and teaching, among other things, and two direct ancestors, Duncan McNair and Evander McNair, were notable in the Presbyterian ministry. Robert McNair's father, Daniel, was born in 1875, one of eleven children, and grew up at the family home about ten miles north of Lumberton in rural Robeson County.[9]

At one point, Daniel McNair was a deputy sheriff under George B. McLeod, a fellow Scotsman who became a partner in the Shaw-McLeod Company. That firm eventually assigned McNair one of its new ventures in South Carolina. He arrived in Berkeley County around 1911–1912 to manage the Shaw-McLeod timber operations at Ballsdam Plantation. He was unmarried, in his late thirties, and for all his family's deep roots in American history and heritage just across the border in North Carolina, he was probably viewed as something of an outsider to some of the locals. They may have resented this newcomer coming into their territory to clear land and ship timber from what once had been an important part of the area's prominent past. Or they may have resented his family's attentiveness to the needs of their black neighbors.

Whether McNair was an outsider or not, one event sealed his determination to not return to the family security of Robeson County. He met and eventually married an outgoing younger woman named Claudia Lucille Crawford from the nearby farming community of Russellville. She was eighteen and he was forty-two when they were married on November 3, 1917, and she never referred to the stern North Carolina Scotsman as anything but "Mr. NcNair."

Claudia was one of four children born to Martha Susan Eatmon Crawford and Joseph Clark Crawford, both of whose families raised tobacco. Her father also preached at Russellville Christian Church and Betaw Christian Church in the Alvin community. While the McNairs had only one child, their home was regularly filled with family members and others being cared for by Bob McNair's mother. When her sister Leona's husband died, leaving six children, Claudia McNair invited the children to stay at Ballsdam while her sister farmed, kept a store, and obtained a teaching certificate. Another nephew was a regular visitor when illness struck the family of her brother, Roland.

Roland Crawford Jr. later recalled how "owning a large farm was a joint effort between husband and wife. Always frugal, Claudia took in boarders and sold milk and eggs to help make ends meet. [She] created an atmosphere of dignity, grace and love."[10]

Claudia McNair, the preacher's daughter, also made the church a centerpiece of her family's life. She taught Sunday school at the Jamestown Baptist Church and, Crawford recalled, "Mandatory attendance was expected for all visiting nieces and nephews."[11]

McNair recalled, "We felt they could not have a church service if we were not there. That is part of the heritage of growing up in the country. You find people with a rural background are more religious than folk who grow up in the city, where they have other opportunities. For us, community activities centered on the church and that was your social life, as well. Both my parents were very, very active."[12]

McNair's parents eventually moved their membership from Jamestown to the Macedonia Christian Church, where both were buried. Years later, their bodies were moved to the family burial ground, which McNair created at Ballsdam.

Daniel McNair was forty-eight years old when Claudia gave birth to their son, and they chose for him two McNair family names that were commonly used and reflected the Scottish tradition of using the same given name in every generation. Robert had most recently been the name of both Daniel McNair's father and grandfather, and Evander, besides being Daniel McNair's middle name, was also the name of an uncle who had achieve some prominence as president of Presbyterian College of Upper Missouri in the late nineteenth century.

The place Daniel McNair chose for their home was one of those faltering southern plantation properties that had declined conspicuously in the post–Civil War and Reconstruction days. He was able to purchase and rehabilitate the place into a working farm, and it would become the first home—and a lifetime residence—of Robert Evander McNair.

At Home in a Historic Cottage

McNair recalls the Gendron family as being among the earliest owners of Ballsdam, but recent history traces its development back to the Palmers, French Huguenots whose South Carolina roots went back to 1687. By 1835, two Palmer brothers had amassed holdings of 27,000 acres and four hundred slaves and erected a cottage a safe distance from the swampy and disease-infected banks of the Santee River. It was described as a "five-room, one-level compact house on higher ground, away from the river [which] became known as the Pineland house. . . . The location, relatively free from the fevers that so often plagued Lowcountry planters, would become the site of family activities from May to November, and was . . . everybody's favorite residence."[13]

More than a century later, the Pineland cottage, built by John Palmer as a summerhouse, would continue to be the favorite residence and focal point of activities for another family, the McNairs. The 1836 cottage would be the place where Daniel and Claudia McNair made their home and young Bob McNair grew up. Even after McNair completed his term as governor and established homes in Columbia and Myrtle Beach, the cottage at Ballsdam, known by then simply as "The Farm," was maintained and restored as a gathering place for family, friends, and business associates. The larger Ballsdam plantation house, built by John Palmer on the Santee River in 1842, fell into disrepair after the Civil War and was burned shortly after Daniel McNair acquired the property. The family never doubted that the fire was deliberately set by nearby whites who were upset that the McNairs gave help to their black neighbors.

It was from his father that Bob McNair gained some firsthand insight into practical politics and how the system could be maneuvered to produce tangible and specific benefits, a skill McNair would display to considerable advantage all through his public and professional career. Years later, he recalled one particular instance in which the senior McNair was pursuing an unorthodox means of bringing additional support to long-suffering public schools near Ballsdam.

Innovation in the Swamp

The Hell Hole Swamp area had already been a particular beneficiary of a state-level initiative of the 1920s abolishing one-teacher schools, but there was another particularly innovative measure of educational support that could provide some solid, cash-based assistance for the area.

Federal Depression-era legislation was leading to the acquisition by the United States government of vast tracts of South Carolina land for designation as national forests. More than half the state's 19.5 million acres—once dominated by plantations—had become woodlands,[14] and federal purchases for two major national forests—Sumter and Francis Marion—would total more than 580,000 acres. Of that amount, some 245,000 acres of Berkeley County land were identified as the Francis Marion National Forest, representing about a third of the total land area of the county (792,000 acres).[15]

Such acquisitions involved the purchase of timberlands from private owners, a transaction that traditionally was viewed with some consternation as taking property off the tax books and thus undermining the major source of funding for public education in the area. Such, however, was not necessarily the case in the schools of Hell Hole Swamp, thanks to the nifty political maneuvering by Daniel McNair on behalf of those schools.

Under policies in place at the time, the federal government was required to make an annual payment to the school district in lieu of property taxes, a measure designed to prevent revenue loss for the district. In the case of some of the rural schools, in fact, the purchase of the national forest land proved to be nothing less than a windfall for the community.

"In those days," McNair said, "property was valued so low. The houses and other properties were so small that they did not produce much income. So the district, the schools, got more money from the government than it would have gotten just from the raw timberland sitting out there. So, we had some of the benefits in that rural county."[16]

Macedonia, a school twelve miles from Ballsdam, was the major beneficiary of the funding windfall, but it took some politicking to swing the deal for the twelve-grade school deep in Hell Hole Swamp. According to his son, it was Daniel McNair who did the dealing. "My father became active in school affairs since I was coming along," McNair recalled, "and he became chairman of the local school board. . . . He was instrumental in getting that [the money], . . . and thus Macedonia got the bulk of the payment in lieu of taxes, because the school district was largely covered by the Francis Marion National Forest."[17]

Macedonia, in turn, became something of a model school of its time, according to McNair, boasting the luxury of "one teacher per grade." "It was a very progressive rural school," he said. "It had a very progressive superintendent and it had gained a good reputation."[18] The experience provided young McNair with some exposure to the world of practical politics at the local level, and it also instilled an understanding of the educational funding process and particularly the plight of rural public schools in South Carolina.

Going to School in Rural South Carolina

Bob McNair's first three years of schooling were at the Jamestown School, a two-teacher, seven-grade school two miles from Ballsdam. He remembered getting "a surprisingly good basic education" there in what amounted to a group teaching experience. "You just did not sit there with a group of five-year-olds [first grade age at the time]. You sat there with a group of older kids studying other things." Years later, McNair remembered two teachers at Jamestown in particular.

> Miss Lilly Bailey and Miss Stella Grady . . . were the two teachers that taught me in the beginning of elementary school, and [I remember] the influences from them because they were very stern disciplinarians.
>
> We hear today that "you can teach, but you can't make them learn." I have said later that Miss Lilly and Miss Stella not only taught us, they "learned" us, too. They made us learn. . . . They were also Sunday School teachers; you know, you usually went to the same churches, so they had a great influence on you.
>
> Back then, too, we had the old rule that if you got a spanking at school, you got one at home.[19]

Jamestown was a school he could reach from Ballsdam in a short buggy ride, and later, "I got big enough to ride my horse." Enrollment for his fourth year of schooling at Macedonia, however, meant a longer trip; it "was twelve miles from home, so I had to ride the bus twelve miles every morning and twelve miles back in the afternoon. Going to school was daylight to dark for me."[20]

Macedonia was a maturing experience, exposing McNair to the traditional academic subjects and engaging him in other activities such as debate. It was also at Macedonia where he developed a lifelong interest in sports, first as a participant and later as a strong supporter of the state's athletic programs. "We were taught the basics," he recalled. "Strong math, English and basic sciences, and those skills paid dividends later on. We also participated in the statewide tests and many statewide competitions. Not many rural schools did, but this was something that all the students at our high school did."[21]

Macedonia, at that time a small country school in a sparsely populated section of Berkeley County, also competed in statewide debate competition, sent its glee club to Charleston, and fielded athletic teams year round, although the conditions were sometimes challenging, McNair remembered. "We had athletics," he said, "and everybody participated. If it was football season, we all played football, basketball, . . . or baseball. There was track, not very much, but we did that, too. You would interrupt a baseball game to broad jump or high jump, or run a hundred yard dash, and come back and take your turn at bat in the baseball game."[22]

The model school left its mark on McNair and the community. "The parents there became more conscious of the need for education," McNair said. "Many of the children would work and go to school to prepare for college." The graduating class of 1939 only numbered between fifteen and twenty, but it included two lawyers, "one or two [others] who graduated from Clemson in engineering," and others who "got good jobs in Charleston at the Navy yard and places like that . . . and would commute back and forth."[23]

Poverty in Berkeley County

The McNair home in Hell Hole Swamp was something of an outpost of comfort in a remote area of Berkeley County whose name was later playfully attached to political natives of the area—McNair, First District congressman Mendel Rivers, Columbia mayor Lester Bates and longtime Berkeley County senator Rembert Dennis all claimed membership in what was dubbed "The Hell Hole Swamp Gang."[24]

For 1920s South Carolina, however, the area was also a "hell hole" in a different way for many of its residents. Berkeley County, historically for years a part of Charleston County and the site of some of the state's most affluent plantations, had fallen on desperate economic times in the wake of the Civil War. As the plantations were broken up, sold, or abandoned, many of the people remaining on

Berkeley County lands were former slaves, their families or descendants left to contend with the political and economic hardships afflicting black South Carolinians at the time. Berkeley County, in fact, was a place where some of the state's most dire economic and living conditions had evolved by the 1920s. Because it was the site of extensive plantation holdings in antebellum South Carolina, there was a high percentage of slaves in the pre–Civil War population of the area, estimated to be as much as 90 percent of the total population at the outbreak of the war.[25]

Much of the black population remained in the area and continued to be numerically dominant in the years subsequent to the Civil War and Reconstruction. Once granted the right to vote by the state's 1868 Reconstruction Constitution, blacks in the former plantation areas of what was then Charleston County became a source of significant strength for the state's emancipation-based Republican Party and a source of political irritation to the mostly white ruling party of Democrats. The racial divisions were such, in fact, that the present-day Berkeley County was split away from Charleston by the 1882 General Assembly, presumably to isolate the rural population and create what was dubbed South Carolina's "black county," distinct and apart from the urbanized precincts of Charleston.

The General Assembly took the extraordinary step of dividing Charleston County essentially along racial lines and establishing Berkeley County as something of a reservation of poor black people. "The main purpose," M. C. Orvin has written, ". . . was to keep the county and the city of Charleston in the Democratic fold. The act passed by the Legislature put in the new county practically all of the Republican or Negro population outside Charleston, and for several years, the Charleston papers delighted in referring to Berkeley as the 'Black County.'"[26]

The plight of South Carolina's "Black County" worsened fifteen years later, in 1896, when the state adopted a new constitution, which effectively disenfranchised its majority black population. Berkeley County Republicans had made something of a last stand in the governor's race of 1890 as one of two South Carolina counties, along with Beaufort, that supported the candidacy of Columbia attorney Alexander Haskell against the insurgent agrarianism of Benjamin R. "Pitchfork Ben" Tillman. Warning that the tendency of the Tillman movement "would be to remove such protection of the Negro race as had been provided under [former governor and U.S. senator Wade] Hampton, and his [Bourbon] successors,"[27] Haskell had forged a "fusionist" movement of blacks and white Republicans to head off the Tillman forces.

Ben Tillman and the 1896 Constitution

Haskell was prophetic. In what would prove to be the last major two-party race at the state level until 1962, Tillman swept into the governor's office by a vote of 59,159 to 14,828,[28] and shortly thereafter set about to remove his black opponents from political activity altogether. Attacking what he derisively called the state's 1868 "Ohio Constitution," a derisive term designed to reflect the anti-Reconstruction sentiment among white South Carolinians, Tillman pushed through a new constitution that not only disenfranchised most blacks through the use of literacy tests and property requirements, but also vested the state with an anti-city, anti-centralized government and anti-intellectual spirit that influenced South Carolina's development for the next century.

The constitution of 1896 was not the only bad news for South Carolina blacks at the turn of the century. In its *Plessy v. Ferguson* ruling of 1896, the U.S. Supreme Court upheld the "separate but equal" doctrine and set the stage for Jim Crow laws and separate educational systems among the states for the next fifty-eight years. It was not until the Supreme Court reversed itself in 1954 with *Brown v. Board of Education* that the racial policies established in the 1890s began to give way. Even so, Tillman's 1896 constitution was never repealed. It remained on the books as the twentieth century came to a close, altered significantly by amendment, or by federal law or judicial rulings that superceded some of its more racially onerous provisions.

Bob McNair's birth came about halfway between the racially restrictive events of 1895–1896 and the 1954 *Brown* ruling, which significantly accelerated the process of undoing the segregated society of the South. It would be McNair's fate to spend much of his political life and public career in a world whose issues and values would be largely shaped by the events of those two distinct periods.

His career would also be heavily influenced by economic developments that coincided with his birth and childhood in one of the South's most impoverished areas. Berkeley County, like most of the rural South, retained its dependence on cotton cultivation for economic survival and prosperity long into the twentieth century. Cotton represented 70 percent of the value of all crops in the state, and at the dawning of the decade the rest of the nation would call the "Roaring Twenties," South Carolina cotton prices hit a record high of 42 cents a pound, then collapsed and rarely got above 25 cents a pound for the rest of the decade.

A Firsthand View of Desperate Conditions

As cotton declined between 1920 and 1925, so, too, did the value of the state's farm property, which dropped by more than 45 percent. Only about half the state's 10.6 million acres of farmland lay in cultivation, and on average, the state's farmers—65 percent of whom were tenants—were harvesting crops from only about 25 acres of their property. The average farm was worth a little more than $3,000.[29] Farm life was characterized "by small cultivation units, too little diversification, low earnings and poor living standards."[30]

This was the desperation young Bob McNair was seeing firsthand among his neighbors in the rural remoteness of Berkeley County. It was the spectacle of a state that could no longer support itself and an economy that could no longer keep its people gainfully employed. Out-migration became the only option for many southerners, and during the 1920s, 1.3 million blacks left the South for other parts of the country, and another 1.5 million whites were abandoning the older parts of the South, many of them attracted by the oil-driven boom in the Southwest.[31]

In South Carolina, black out-migration was estimated at 204,000 during the 1920s[32]—about an eighth of the state's total population and a fourth of its black population. By 1927, out-migration of blacks was such that the state became majority white for the first time since 1810, a development that set off a near-celebratory observation from the state's white leadership. "This means a new freedom for South Carolina," an official state publication of the time observed. "It is the removal of a vague but always present shadow."[33]

In a less celebratory tone, historian I. A. Newby noted that "by 1930, one quarter of all native South Carolinians . . . were living outside the state, and 87 per cent of the expatriates were black."[34] For those who remained in the South, conditions deteriorated into such a state of dependence and poverty that the per capita income actually fell during the economic decline of the 1920s, the only region of the nation ever to have such an experience.[35] It had truly become what President Franklin Roosevelt would call "the nation's number one economic problem," and journalist Harry Ashmore, in visiting the South Carolina lowcountry in the 1930s, would describe it as "a desolate area in which time seemed to have stood still."[36]

In the primordial world of 1920s South Carolina, most politics were local, a reality in place long before it was applied universally by Democratic House Speaker Thomas P. "Tip" O'Neill in later years. Political scientist V. O. Key Jr. noted that even in one-party politics, there existed a wide range of regional and local political interests, loosely described as factions. If anything, Key wrote, factions within a one-party political culture tended to create political fragmentation, as opposed to the bipolar structure of a disciplined two-party system. Factions tended to develop from the grassroots up, in a process Key called "localism," or "friends and neighbors" politics.[37]

"In South Carolina," according to Key, "the small, rural county with a fairly homogeneous population probably offers the most fertile ground for 'localism.'" The characteristic also tended to create looseness and flexibility of positions and issues, and Key wrote, "whatever the explanation, localism tends to be associated with a multi-factional system, rather than with [a] dual division."[38]

The state, in fact, was a place of no-holds-barred politics. Key wrote that in the days before two-party politics returned in the 1960s and 1970s, South Carolina built its majorities from local to sectional to state levels, and for many years—before the cost of campaigning tended to winnow the field—statewide races were "a free-for-all among three or four principal candidates." During the 1930s and 1940s, the number of candidates rose as high as eight and eleven, and in the gubernatorial races of 1934, 1938, and 1946, eventual winners Olin

Johnston, Burnet Maybank, and Strom Thurmond, respectively, each polled less than 36 percent of the vote in the first primaries.[39] For all the perceived conformity within one-party politics, Key wrote, "factions in a one-party state are more fluid than parties, and such cross-currents as localism force alignments out of the patterns indicated by fundamental cleavages of interest."[40]

Factionalism and Localism in South Carolina

Unlike the orderliness of more-disciplined organizations elsewhere in the country, the fluidity of localism made rural South Carolina politics spontaneous, unpredictable, and highly personal. Leaders emerged who were skilled at patching together coalitions of factions, and in the absence of organizational brawn, they often prevailed with political deftness and quick-wittedness. Under the deceptive rubric of one-party politics, a breed of durable and contentiously individualistic figures arose—men like Olin Johnston, Edgar Brown, Marion Gressette, Solomon Blatt, Strom Thurmond, and Jimmy Byrnes—whose locally honed political skills would serve them well at higher levels and make them powerful figures in state or national politics for generations.

Localism was a phenomenon not limited to white political interests. In the political vacuum left by the disenfranchisement of most black voters by the constitution of 1896, localism was ostensibly the most practical form of political activity left to South Carolina's African Americans. Years earlier, their influence had reached a peak in South Carolina during the federal occupation and military supervision of the state's government. According to historian Orville Vernon Burton, "Blacks served in nearly every office at county and state levels [except for the governorship]; blacks won half the seats of the lower house of the General Assembly and held a majority in the House for six years . . . more land was distributed to former slaves than in any other state. During the years 1868–1877, eight blacks were elected to Congress and two became Lieutenant Governor. Afro-Americans served on the South Carolina Supreme Court, as secretary of state, adjutant general, secretary of the treasury, Speaker of the House and president pro tem of the Senate."[41]

All that began to change when federal troops left in 1876 and Confederate cavalry general Wade Hampton was elected governor in what was called by historians the movement of political redemption. The process of disenfranchisement of blacks, in fact, began soon thereafter with their exclusion from the Democratic primary in 1878.[42] Black political influence and participation was sharply diminishing long before the constitution of 1896.[43]

The constitution of 1896 was the ultimate blow, and it so effectively precluded black political participation that almost half a century later, in 1940, only 3,000 blacks, out of a total black population of 814,164,[44] were registered to vote. At a time when 42.8 percent of the population was black, only 0.8 percent of voting-age African Americans were on the voter-registration rolls.[45]

As black South Carolina bent to the imposition of political white supremacy in the early twentieth century, their political "powerlessness" took various shapes. Many blacks fled the state; others remained and were actively or passively resistant. Some resigned themselves to accommodation, and others sought refuge in the traditional black institution of the church.[46] The 1906 census reported that there were 394,149 black church members organized in 2,860 congregations, of which 55 percent were Baptist and 41 percent were various forms of Methodists (African Methodist Episcopal, or AME; AME Zion; Christian Methodist Episcopal, or CME; and Methodist Episcopal, or ME).[47]

The Black Church and Its Influence

The church, in essence, was becoming the black counterpart of the political localism taking place within the rural white communities. According to Newby, "Besides its religious duties, it [the church] performed important social, civil, and political functions. It was the agency through which black Carolina organized and expressed itself, undertook community projects, enunciated community goals, and often responded to white supremacy. It was . . . the institution which brokered power in the community."[48]

"The black church was the only institution owned and controlled by blacks," NAACP leader I. DeQuincey Newman would say in 1979. "The black clergy were the only ones who had the freedom of expression."[49]

Much of the political and philosophical debate centered around the differences between Booker T. Washington's utilitarian doctrine of self-help and industrial occupations for black Americans and the emerging intellectual approaches of W. E. B. DuBois. As the Washington-DuBois debates raised fundamental issues about the course of America's black population, South Carolina tended to favor the more cautious and conservative philosophies espoused by Washington. The state's black communities were described as places where "a mood of forbearance and faith cut across all classes."[50] Even so, the influence of DuBois grew in the years during and following World War I, and in 1917, the state established its first two chapters (in Columbia and Charleston) of the organization DuBois founded—the National Association for the Advancement of Colored People (NAACP). By 1919, four chapters were organized with membership slightly more than one thousand, mostly in Charleston, and by 1920, there were chapters in Aiken, Darlington, Beaufort, Florence, and Orangeburg.[51]

Amid the political stirrings in black South Carolina, a generation was emerging that would challenge the political status quo, and like their white counterparts, many of them would spring from rural South Carolina. Isaiah DeQuincey Newman, who would become South Carolina's first black state senator of the century in 1983, was growing up in 1920s Darlington County, grooming himself for the ministry. "My chief role model was my father, who was a preacher,"

Newman once said, and like McNair, he got his early political exposure from his father:

> He was traditional, very authoritarian, and he dabbled some in politics.
>
> He saw to it that I registered to vote, and—of course—black participation was limited to the general election and, he brought his influence to bear heavily on my first ballot. That was to vote for the person who was running on the Prohibitionist ticket, a man by the name of Upshaw from Georgia.[52]

Emerging Civil Rights Leaders

A sometime rival of Newman's within NAACP politics, Modjeska Simkins, was growing up in Columbia, the daughter of a middle-class family whose mother, Rachel E. Monteith, had been a member of DuBois's Niagara Movement even before a branch of the NAACP was established in Columbia in 1917. Simkins would become active in the founding of the State Conference of NAACP in 1939 and would be instrumental in many of the early phases of the *Briggs v. Elliott* school-desegregation case in Clarendon County.[53]

On a farm near Greenwood, South Carolina, Benjamin E. Mays was growing up picking cotton on his father's rented farm to earn money to attend South Carolina State College. He was inspired by stories of black leaders like Booker T. Washington, Frederick Douglass, and "the Negroes in the . . . legislature during the Reconstruction and post-Reconstruction years." Mays, who would become president of Morehouse College and mentor of young Martin Luther King Jr., remembered that the black South Carolina legislators "were the men held up in high school as being great men, and not the Negro-hating Benjamin Ryan Tillman and his kind, who strove so long and hard to deprive the black man of his vote."[54]

As the 1920s drew to a close, South Carolina remained economically damaged, politically divided by race, and officially reluctant to do much about either problem. Even as it was celebrating its newly discovered majority white status in 1927, the state was also defending agriculture as its economic base, suggesting that "it is only the lack of knowledge or initiative which prevents South Carolina from becoming as well-balanced an agricultural state as any other in the Union."[55]

Industry, according to entrenched southern attitudes, should be developed and maintained to manufacture only those goods associated with traditional farm products, such as cotton-based textile operations. Otherwise, some southerners fretted, "the best elements of the region's rural, agricultural way of life would be quickly destroyed as cities and manufacturing plants cluttered the landscape and Southerners forsook the farms for the dehumanizing regimen of the factory." Industrialization, they warned, threatened "the elements of Southern life most worthy of preservation."[56]

As the administration of Herbert Hoover sought to put in place limited relief measures to cope with the aftermath of the 1929 stock market crash, southern newspapers were on the attack, articulating familiar conservative themes that "it is not an obligation of government to furnish citizens with jobs" and arguing that "two objectives were necessary to put business back on its feet in this country: 1. Reduce the cost of government, and 2. Get the government out of business."[57]

In such a setting of economic and political laissez-faire, the likelihood of any type of state intervention to alleviate the plight of the poor was slim. It would not be until economic disaster struck the nation as a whole that relief efforts would get underway, and those came from federal, and not state, institutions in the form of Franklin Roosevelt's New Deal.

Lowcountry South Carolina was a prime prospect for New Deal attention, particularly rural Berkeley County. Poor, undeveloped, and with little in the way of economic prospects, the county was a place where political ideologies were less important than the practical prospects of jobs, income, and some economic security and stability. Newby observed about southerners, "On the farm, plain folk were among the unhealthiest groups of people in the United States."[58] In Hell Hole Swamp, survival was a day-to-day thing.

For many local residents, things seemed quiet, and the political clamor over the New Deal was far removed. Even communication with the outside world was difficult at times. Bob McNair recalled trying to tune an old-fashioned battery radio to pick up the 1934 heavyweight championship fight between Jim Braddock and Max Baer. "It would come and go," he remembered, "you could hear a little bit, and [just] when it got exciting, it would fade away."[59] Hours later, reception might return to tell listeners the actual outcome of the event.

On other occasions, it might take days to learn of incidents around the nation or world. For the huddled listeners at Ballsdam, the crackling static of faraway radio stations in places like Cincinnati or New Orleans (transmission from Charleston was too weak for the McNairs' radio) was an important measure of communication with an otherwise distant world.

In such isolation, even the weekly visit of the county farm agent became an occasion of major importance for learning of the events of the outside world. "The home demonstration agent was everybody's friend because she came around about every week and visited and had a cup of coffee or a piece of pie or cake," McNair remembered. "The real purpose was to bring information to let people know what was going on."[60]

The New Deal in Berkeley County

The New Deal came to Hell Hole Swamp in a big way, begrudging state politicians or not. McNair recalled in particular a significant infusion of public jobs from the Works Progress Administration (WPA) and the Civilian Conservation Corps (CCC).

> The WPA and the old CCC camps meant so much to our area and other areas like them because the programs put people to work. [They] dug drainage

canals and drained swamps and low, flat areas that were mosquito havens. They opened up land for cultivation by creating highly productive lands that before had been low swamp areas.

The CCC camps gave many young men an opportunity to see life. They came from the backwoods and other areas of the country and were put into those camps and worked in the forest and helped improve the forests. All of the programs were very, very meaningful to people, particularly in the area where I grew up.[61]

Jobs and forest enrichment were not all South Carolina got from the CCC experience. Hewn from the raw timberland acreage were clearings for recreational preserves equipped with picnic grounds, swimming ponds, shelters, hiking trails, and many other features to give South Carolina families a respite from their grim Depression-era ordeal. CCC workers did a lot of the structural work for what became state parks—grading and paving for roads and building the distinctive stone cottages still common to the older parks.

WPA and CCC projects also helped put people back to work on a temporary basis. But the New Deal's most lasting impact for rural South Carolina was bringing electricity to remote farming communities. In 1935, Congress appropriated $4.8 billion for rural power, and the Rural Electrification Administration was created by executive order.[62] Across South Carolina, 650 miles of power lines were put in place during the first year, serving 4,500 customers, and by 1941, the miles had jumped to 14,460 and customers had risen to 66,240.[63] Battery-powered radios and crystal sets gave way to radio sets powered by electrical systems that also brought lights and heat to rural homes. Electricity—public power—was what finally liberated the rural farmers of the South from their primitive living conditions and, in McNair's view, gave them the resources to develop economically.

It was not far from Ballsdam plantation, in fact, that one of the most ambitious New Deal projects of them all emerged, the Santee-Cooper power system. The state had long envisioned a means of providing transportation linkages between upcountry commercial centers and the port of Charleston. As early as 1913, the historic territory defined by the Santee and Cooper Rivers—in the heart of Berkeley County and not far from Hell Hole Swamp—began to gain attention as the possible site of a canal linking the two rivers to expedite steamship service between the inland state capital of Columbia and Charleston. It was the renewal of a project of more than a century earlier, in which a twenty-two-mile canal had been dug between the two rivers for similar commercial purposes. Initiated in 1793—only ten years after the Treaty of Paris concluded the American Revolution and twenty-two years before the Erie Canal was constructed in New York—the earlier Santee Canal was devised by plantation owners as an efficient means of getting their products to markets in Charleston or for shipping overseas.

The canal was never much of a success, however, due to design flaws and to weather fluctuations that left it flooded at times and dry at others. By 1840, it fell into disuse and was abandoned, remaining visible today at places like the Santee Canal Park near Moncks Corner, where the old canal flowed into the Cooper River above Charleston.

Revival of the idea more than a half-century later of a canal linking the Santee and Cooper Rivers sparked new—and expanded—interest in the sandy lowlands around the historic rivers, and by 1923, Charleston mayor John P. Grace was outlining plans for a hydroelectric plant using the Santee and Cooper Rivers that would "transform Charleston" into "a great commercial and industrial city."

The issue of public power caused some rethinking among South Carolina's conservative leaders. "Though I believed that power projects should normally be developed by private utilities," then–U.S. Senator James F. Byrnes wrote, "I also believed that when private capital could not or would not develop a necessary project, government might step in."[64] Historian Walter B. Edgar later concluded that in the Depression-weakened South Carolina economy, "The private sector was not capable of undertaking a project of such magnitude. Nor, was the State of South Carolina."[65]

The Santee-Cooper project cut across factionalized political lines in South Carolina, and the state's Democratic leaders, including Governor Ibra C. Blackwood, Charleston mayor Burnet R. Maybank, and Colleton state senator Richard M. Jefferies, were lobbying Roosevelt on behalf of the project as early as the party's 1932 convention. A 250-member committee of prominent citizens was organized to provide promotional muscle to the effort, and when a 64-member delegation journeyed to Washington to argue adoption of the Santee-Cooper scheme (a delegation that included a thirty-three-year-old state senator from Edgefield named James Strom Thurmond), the occasion was of such importance that the state's General Assembly suspended operations until the delegation returned and made its report.

Santee-Cooper got final approval from Roosevelt in July 1935, two years after the TVA project had been launched at Muscle Shoals, Alabama. All told, its magnitude was unlike any single project the state had ever experienced in terms of economic impact and geographic scale. Its $50-million price tag dwarfed the paltry value ($113,000) of the entire capital investment in Berkeley County and represented a healthy chunk compared to the entire capital investment in the state ($386 million). The two lakes created by the project—Moultrie and Marion—would cover 177,000 acres, mostly in Berkeley, and it would require the resettlement of 901 families and the relocation of ninety-three cemeteries containing over six thousand individual graves.[66] It would also submerge the land and buildings of some historic plantations, places like General William Moultrie's North Hampton and Captain Peter Gaillard's The Rocks.

Through the eyes of a teenage Bob McNair and his Hell Hole Swamp neighbors, the sheer scale would have been staggering. The project got underway with the logging of 200 million board feet of timber by some nine thousand loggers. On May 15, 1939, several thousand workers began excavation and construction of forty-two miles of dams and dikes, erecting in a matter of months a twenty-six-mile earthen dike that at its highest point stood seventy-eight feet above the surrounding land.

For the residents of Ballsdam and the surrounding territory, the massive project changed everything. "Santee-Cooper was built to provide power to rural South Carolina," McNair recalled. "It provided electrical energy through the area that I grew up in. It brought electric lights and all the other conveniences. Highways and paved secondary roads, which came along about the same time, made the area accessible. Improved roads also made it possible for people to get outside and get a job in order to earn a living."[67]

Santee-Cooper and the New Deal also changed South Carolina's political culture forever. For the first time, the state sampled the largesse of federal assistance on a grand scale, and—at least for a while—liked it. Writing later about the experience, Byrnes observed, "Certainly the President fulfilled his promise of action. Many had doubts about the future as a result of the methods employed, but the masses of the people, gradually recovering from the sufferings of the depression, were hopeful—and happy."[68] All told, Byrnes reported in 1936, New Deal benefits and projects in South Carolina totaled $242 million. It was a nice return on the federal taxes the state had paid over the same period, a grand total of $10 million in taxes.[69]

For all its New Deal jackpot, however, South Carolina leaders had turned against the FDR initiatives by 1938, some because of the so-called court-packing scheme by which the president had sought to increase the number of Supreme Court justices so that he could gain a majority of the seats. Others fretted over his reported softness on the topics of race and organized labor, the two biggest litmus tests for South Carolina political acceptability at the time.

The New Deal Backfires in South Carolina

Most blatant, however, were Roosevelt's efforts to purge uncooperative Democrats in the 1938 elections, specifically targeting Georgia senator Walter George and South Carolina's "Cotton Ed" Smith by supporting their opponents. In a state that cherished its political localism and its survival-of-the-fittest election free-for-alls, such outside influence was viewed as an intrusion and proved to be a kiss of death.

The 1938 South Carolina primary pitted the seventy-three-year-old Smith, seeking his sixth consecutive term, against former governor Olin Johnston and Edgar Brown, the powerful senator from Barnwell. As the *Winnsboro News and Herald* described it, the race involved "Old Dealer Smith," "New Dealer Brown," and "Super New Dealer Johnston."[70] Smith's subsequent election over his two pro–New Deal opponents was laid at Roosevelt's doorstep for his public support of Johnston. "Many of those who had intended to vote for Johnston resented the President's interference in the Democratic primary and turned to Smith, giving him a majority of 50,000 votes," Byrnes later wrote.[71]

The political misfire tended to obscure much of the positive impact of the New Deal in South Carolina and left for the sweeping federal aid program something of a mixed legacy. For others—particularly black Americans—there were political deficiencies of the New Deal as well. Southern support of the programs had been built on the tacit understanding that civil rights and racial equality would not be addressed by the New Deal.

As early as 1933, a White House meeting of prominent black leaders, including Walter White of the NAACP and college presidents Mordecai Johnson of Howard University, Robert Morton of Tuskegee Institute, John Hope of Atlanta University, and Charles Johnson of Fisk University, reached a consensus that "aid programs of the New Deal should come before desegregation, especially in the South." A governmental observer at the time noted, "We had no real doctrine, except that we were not to discriminate in the distribution of benefits. . . . In the South, we accepted the fact that Negroes usually lived in their own communities so we provided for them—Negro projects."[72]

"The majority of New Dealers," author Roger Biles has pointed out, "never cared deeply about the plight of blacks and considered the alleviation of racial inequality a low priority." It was the efforts of a group of "liberal New Dealers," Biles wrote, that later addressed the plight of black Americans and earned Roosevelt and the New Deal the reverence of black southerners.[73]

Other forces were at play in the 1930s that would prove influential in the South's later struggles with its economic troubles. On the same day that James F. Byrnes took his place as South Carolina's newest senator—December 7, 1931—a gangling, twenty-three-year-old Texan named Lyndon Baines Johnson was making his entry into Washington as secretary to Congressman Richard M. Kleberg, a conservative Democrat representing the Texas Hill Country's Fourteenth District. Kleberg, heir to the vast King Ranch domain in south Texas and a playboy who preferred polo and golf to management of his estate, believed that much of the nation's economic failure could be blamed on "government interference in business . . . and the expenses of maintaining those interfering agencies."[74] His young staff aide, the son of a cotton farmer/populist Democrat named Sam Ealy Johnson, would disagree, and three decades later, his presidency would produce successor programs to the New Deal under the title of "The Great Society."

Out of the torpor of the 1920s, new forces were being energized in the South Carolina of the Depression era. The New Deal was bringing new jobs and new comforts to much of the state, and new individuals and organizations were emerging to address the unattended issues of social, political, and economic unbalance that had left much of South Carolina divided and impoverished. The old economy had failed, and the old political order was wearing out. A new South Carolina was taking shape in Bob McNair's formative years, a South Carolina that could challenge human inequities, broaden economic horizons, and redefine individual opportunity in the state.

McNair was growing up in a neighborhood where he could see firsthand the human toll being taken by the state's impotent economy and its regressive racial policies and laws. He was learning from his parents the art of personal politics and the values of human concerns. He saw how government, in the form of New Deal initiatives, could prop up communities, undergird ailing economies, and fill the vacuum of human needs. He also got a firsthand appreciation of public education and the difference it could make in determining the long-term career success of its students. All these impressions and lessons would appear early and often in the career of a man who became a champion of public education and advanced the notion prominently that government, in many forms, could promote human well-being and economic progress. All these ambitions would be the focus of a man whose success, most people would contend, came about because of remarkable political skills, skills that could be traced to his early years in Hell Hole Swamp.

But much of America's attention to its economic and governmental needs would have to wait. As the decade of the 1930s was drawing to a close, the forces of Nazi Germany were annexing Austria and occupying Czechoslovakia. Japan was completing its conquest of China, and an Axis of fascist powers was encircling the globe. Conditions were leading the United States into a global conflict that would reach into Hell Hole Swamp and every other community in America. The war would bring its own set of reforms and transformations to South Carolina, and it would create its own momentum for accelerated change.

3

Coming of Age
War, Education, and Election

Halfway around the world and light-years away from the solitude of Ballsdam Plantation, Bob McNair observed his twenty-first birthday preparing to take part in one of history's largest military operations. General Douglas MacArthur was mobilizing the forces that would invade the Philippines and make good on the promise he had made three years earlier at the surrender of Corregidor—"I shall return."

Accomplishing MacArthur's return to the Japanese-held islands would require one of the largest amphibious forces ever mobilized, and on Christmas Day, 1944, elements of that assault force rendezvoused at the remote Pacific station of Aitape to finish loading and preparing for the invasion of Luzon, the main island of the Philippines. Shouldering key roles in the operations were the Navy officers who commanded the unwieldy amphibious vehicles that transported the men and equipment onto the beaches. Their vehicles were known by their initials— LST, LCI, LCM, and LCT—all designations for the vulnerable craft that plied the final few treacherous and dangerous yards of a beach assault.

One such commander was Lieutenant (j.g.) Robert E. McNair, a young officer who had risen quickly through the ranks in the rough-and-tumble campaign of island-hopping in the Pacific theater of operations. Originally an executive officer on one of the LCTs (Landing Craft, Tanks), McNair was given his own command after an officer-in-charge had run his vessel onto coral, causing heavy damage. "We'd never had any training on [how to operate] them," McNair recalled, "we were just sent clean out there to learn the hard way."[1]

Learning the hard way had meant heavy action in General MacArthur's major westward sweep toward the Japanese homeland in 1944 and 1945, a sweep that required island-by-island amphibious operations of coordinated Army and Navy units. As part of the Navy's Seventh Fleet, VII Amphibious Force, McNair commanded a crew of two officers and thirteen enlisted men aboard a vessel whose main purpose was to convey six tanks and other equipment and supplies ashore for use by Army combat forces. Along with various elements of the VII Amphibious Force, McNair's LCT saw action at various landings leading up to the Philippine invasion.

His was no ordinary duty, either. During one particular operation in the Leyte Gulf, McNair was instrumental in rescuing thirty-five crew members from a burning liberty boat while protecting his own vessel and crew. For that action, he was awarded a Bronze Star and recognized for his "outstanding courage, devotion and dedication to duty."[2] "There were numerous, smaller scale operations on other islands and around New Guinea," he recalled. "And, of course, there were the two big ones. We were in on the Leyte invasion, and then fully involved in the Lingayen Gulf invasion."[3]

The Lingayen Gulf invasion was a particularly harrowing experience. The coordinated Army-Navy operation landed almost 200,000 men and combat equipment along twenty miles of beach where sandbars, treacherous currents, heavy enemy resistance, and a typhoon stirring offshore made things especially dangerous. Many of the craft made it no closer than seventy-five or eighty yards from shore, striking shoals and sandbars, and McNair's VII Amphibious unit, whose job it was to deliver the two divisions of the Sixth Army's I Corps to the beaches, encountered both heavy fire and stormy seas. All told, the campaign was described as being "by far the largest of the Pacific war." A military historian has written: "It entailed the use of more U.S. Army ground combat and service forces than did operations in North Africa, Italy, or southern France, and was larger than the entire Allied commitment to Sicily."[4] The assault force itself constituted a single convoy over forty miles long.

By war's end, which was hastened by hard-won victories in the Philippines and the dropping of atomic bombs on two Japanese cities, more than 170,000 South Carolinians had entered military service, some 52,000 of them in the Navy.[5] Those who returned would find a world vastly changed from the Depression-era place they had left, and among them, Robert E. McNair would embark on a life significantly changed.

Returning to a Changed World

For one thing, an engaging, redhaired coed from Allendale, South Carolina, named Josephine Robinson had entered his life during the uncertain pre-service college days. Their impact on each other was so profound that she rushed to the West Coast—at some academic and family peril—to marry the Navy officer before he shipped out for his dangerous assignment in the Pacific.

McNair recalled:

Ordinarily, you finished your education first and talked about marriage later, but the war changed all that. It caused a lot of people to move ahead in their plans; I know we did. I had dated some [in college] and then started dating Josephine Robinson, who was an Alpha Delta Pi from Allendale. We had gone steady for a long time, and then—like others—had broken up, and then we started up again.

When I discovered that I was going overseas and would not have much time here in the country, we made a quick decision to go ahead and get married.[6]

The decision set off fireworks on both coasts. McNair was en route to the Pacific with a short stopover in San Francisco, and the decision to get married left both of them with long-shot logistical obstacles. The young female student from Allendale had to negotiate alone a cross-country train trip under restrictive wartime conditions, and Lieutenant McNair had to keep himself from getting shipped out as she rushed across the country.

We were all on standby, awaiting transportation to the Pacific theater. I wasn't even sure I'd be there when she arrived.

There was a list of everybody's name on a peg board at the Port of Embarkation, and we reported every morning to see if our name had been pegged. If it hadn't been, we were free for the day, and reported back the next morning.

Fortunately, one of my very close friends, Beecher Morton, who later became superintendent of schools in Aiken, was in my group and was in charge of pegging the names on the board. Knowing of my marriage plans and knowing that he was going to be my best man, he would not peg my name until Josephine arrived. I was in practically the last group to go, and that gave Josephine and me the opportunity to have about ten days together in San Francisco.[7]

Things happened so quickly that no family—Robinsons or McNairs—were participants, and Navy friends of McNair's were principals in the May 30, 1944, wedding.

Her mother was very upset because this was the last semester of her senior year in college and about two weeks before exams. So, Josephine had to rush a petition to all faculty members to take her exams late or to exempt exams in order to come to California for us to be married. As it turned out, she was able to return in time to graduate with her class, and that made her mother happier.

I do not think I was too popular for a while, though.[8]

Return to Civilian Life

McNair became a civilian again after a twenty-two-month tour of duty, a tour that had changed much for the young man from Hell Hole Swamp. "We grew up in a hurry," he recalled. "We had to. We matured almost overnight because we were confronted with decisions that were affecting our lives and our futures. Going through a marriage without waiting and not knowing what might happen to either of us—so many people did that—and then going into the service and getting into combat areas, and having the life-and-death responsibilities: that made mature men out of us almost overnight."[9]

It was a transformational experience that would leave an impact not only on McNair; it would change the cultural underpinnings of a state whose rural politics and economy had sustained for generations a tradition of isolation. In World War II combat, South Carolina soldiers, airmen, and seamen fought side-by-side with Americans of diverse ethnic, religious, and geographic backgrounds, some of them doubtless getting to know "yankees" for the first time. They also fought a war that had a clear moral dimension, against forces whose fascistic and genocidal worlds were viewed as antithetical to the principles of American democracy. As they returned home, many veterans, including McNair, carried their sense of liberating military mission into lives of public and political activity. Within the first two elections after war's end (1946 and 1948), a total of 59 World War II veterans were serving in the 124-member of House of Representatives, only 4 of whom had held office prior to the war.[10]

For many, World War II was an experience that probably raised some new questions for the young men and women from the heart of the old Confederacy and planted some doubts about the state's own rigidly enforced standards and practices of segregation and discrimination. And while the armed forces remained racially segregated throughout the duration of the war, some of the traditional premises of the Old South were being tested. In Walterboro, South Carolina, between 1943 and 1945, elements of the Army Air Force's Ninety-Ninth Pursuit Squadron—the black fighter pilots known as the Tuskegee Airmen —found themselves confronted with treatment that they felt made them second-class citizens, particularly in the presence of German and Italian prisoners of war who were being held at the town's Army airbase. "Walterboro was the place where we saw German POWs do things we could not do," one of the airmen, Chuck Dryden, recalled years later.[11]

There were more than one thousand of the Tuskegee pilots, and they flew 1,578 missions. According to recent accounts, they were the only such air group never to lose a single bomber under their escort, and they returned home with 150 medals for valor. "Their accomplishment in the air, with the most advanced machinery of the day, did much to allay the doubts and erase the ignorance of those who had questioned blacks' abilities to perform the task,"[12] one journalist observed in recent years.

One of those who trained with the Tuskegee airmen was a young Orangeburg native named Earl Middleton, a Claflin College graduate who eventually wound up serving in the Army and became something of a business pioneer when he returned to Orangeburg in 1946. Middleton rejected "preaching and teaching" as a profession and broke some traditional color lines by setting up a real estate and insurance firm serving black and white customers. In 1974, Middleton won election to the South Carolina House of Representatives, one of thirteen African American legislators elected to the House that year.[13] Four years earlier—in 1970—the South Carolina legislature had been desegregated for the first time since the advent of Tillmanism with the election of James Felder, I. S. Leevy Johnson, and Herbert Fielding to the House.[14]

A Changing Environment for Veterans

Returning veterans brought new energy for change to South Carolina, and they found much had changed in their absence. A 1944 Supreme Court ruling outlawing a set of Texas laws barring blacks from voting in the Democratic primary, *Smith v. Allwright,* had set off shock waves throughout the South, particularly in South Carolina, where less than 1 percent of black citizens were registered to vote and less than 5 percent of the total population even voted in the 1940 election. Such numbers were the lowest in the nation.[15]

At about the time that Bob McNair and his Navy, Marine, and Army colleagues were assaulting the beaches at Lingayen Gulf in the Philippines, South Carolina political leaders were taking steps to keep black people from voting in the Democratic primary and to avoid the effect of the Texas decision. At the behest of Governor Olin Johnston, the state's legislature convened to declare the Democratic Party a private organization and therefore not subject to the laws of the land.[16] "History has taught us," Johnston said, "that we must keep our white Democratic primary pure and unadulterated so that we might protect the welfare and homes of all the people of our State."[17]

The legislative action led to two major countermeasures in the state. One was the creation by black political activists in the state of the Progressive Democratic Party (PDP), an outgrowth of the 1939 organizing of a statewide NAACP conference in Columbia.[18] The second was the 1947 ruling by U.S. District Judge J. Waties Waring of Charleston that the Johnston-inspired legislative action was unconstitutional. "Negroes are voting in Texas and even in Georgia," where federal Judge Thomas Hoyt Davis had struck down the all-white Democratic primary in 1945, Waring said, in a decision that set off such bitter recriminations in his own state and city that he eventually left South Carolina permanently. "I cannot see where the skies will fall if South Carolina is put in the same class with these and other states," he said. "It is time for South Carolina to rejoin the union. It is time to fall in line with the other states and to adopt the American way of conducting elections."[19]

The ruling came too late to open the ballot to blacks in the 1944 and 1946 primaries, but it bolstered political energies that would fuel a generation of civil rights activism. South Carolina's emerging black political movement, with roots going back to the 1910s, gained organizational strength in the 1930s and would become a force of enormous influence as a party to the *Brown* decision of 1954. It would carry forward with even more power into the spirited and painfully volatile years of the 1960s, when Bob McNair as governor would become a focus of massive protests, demonstrations, and organized political disputes.

Powerful leaders such as Osceola McKaine, John Henry McCray, Reverend James M. Hinton, Modjeska Simkins, and Robert W. Mance were in the vanguard of the PDP movement, as well as a black Republican movement known as the Lincoln Emancipation Clubs. The efforts of these leaders in the 1930s were influential in raising questions about inequities in teacher pay and in bringing a young Thurgood Marshall into the state as an NAACP attorney to pursue legal actions. "In Columbia, black activities in the NAACP and several other groups made South Carolina stand out among the Southern states for the high level of its grassroots involvement in public affairs," civil rights historian John Egerton wrote. Hinton and Simkins, he noted in particular, as NAACP president and secretary, respectively, "were in the thick of every issue that enlivened the social agenda in that state."[20]

Undeterred by the snub from the white Democratic party, the PDP mounted its own slate of electors in support of President Roosevelt and ran McKaine against Olin Johnston for U.S. Senate in 1944. McKaine mustered three thousand votes, and claimed that white intimidation at the polling places had cost him another eight thousand.[21]

Other events were setting in motion forces that would change the racial climate and political landscape on a far wider basis. The brutal 1946 beating of a young black sergeant, Isaac Woodward, in Batesburg, South Carolina, opened the eyes of President Harry Truman and hastened his advocacy of major civil rights initiatives. "When a mayor and a City Marshall can take a Negro Sergeant off a bus in South Carolina, beat him up and put out one of his eyes, and nothing is done about it by the State Authorities," Truman wrote to a friend, "then something is radically wrong."[22] Woodward, en route home to North Carolina after his discharge in Georgia, was dragged off the bus by a white bus driver, cursed, and then beaten up and blinded by a local policeman. The black veteran was then locked up and charged with disorderly conduct.[23]

Economic factors were also at play, making postwar South Carolina a more ambitious and optimistic place than it had been ten years earlier. Former servicemen, with the newly won resources of the GI Bill of Rights, were buying homes and enrolling in college in large numbers. By 1947, veterans represented nearly 50 percent of all college enrollment in the nation, and in the four subsequent years, their income had risen by 40 percent. Before the program's end, 7.5 million veterans went on to college or received comparable post-secondary or professional education.[24]

For a region that had known two consecutive decades of economic distress, the war changed things drastically. "Southerners in 1940 were still the poorest, the sickest, the worst housed and clothed and fed, the most violent, the least educated, the least skilled, the most lacking in power," Egerton wrote. "And then came the war. Its impact was . . . incalculable. Between 1940 and 1945, federal involvement in war industries and military installations in the South exceeded $10 billion."[25]

It was to this land of inestimable change that Bob McNair and his wartime bride, Josephine, returned. McNair had completed his junior year in college when he was called to duty as part of the sizable Navy contingent being trained on the wartime University of South Carolina campus. "The University," wrote Daniel W. Hollis, "became a war community—from all outward appearance a naval base—functioning on a twelve-month basis."[26]

At various times between 1940 and 1945, the Navy operated four programs at USC: the NROTC, the Civil Aeronautics Administration War Training Service, the Naval Flight Preparatory Program (V-5), and the Naval College Training Program (V-12). At the peak of war-training activities (August 1943), there were 1,392 men engaged in Navy programs, as compared to a mostly female civilian student enrollment of around 1,000 between 1943 and 1945.[27] By war's end, it was estimated from an alumni survey that 5,463 former USC students had served in World War II, of whom 140 were killed or missing in action.[28]

McNair returned to a campus still bustling with military presence, but this time it was former servicemen, not trainees, who swelled the enrollment. Between academic years 1945–1946 and 1947–1948, enrollment doubled from 2,244 to 4,497.[29] By the end of that period, more than half (2,374) were servicemen.

From Jamestown to College

The University of South Carolina in 1946 was a far cry from the place where the young man from Hell Hole Swamp had enrolled six years earlier. In fact, USC had not even been his first choice. Most rural high-school graduates in South Carolina headed for Clemson, and McNair—even though he had already decided on a career in law—was no exception. "I opted initially to go to Clemson because that is where everybody went from my area," he said. "I do not think in the rural part of the state we knew there was any place other than Clemson."

It took McNair only one semester to discover that "Clemson was a . . . school which emphasized the sciences, engineering and agriculture. I did not plan to do any of that. I had made a mistake. The University was where I should have been to study law, so I transferred after one semester."[30]

He did stay at the upcountry institution long enough to explore an early and lifelong interest in athletics. At rural Macedonia High School, a place where a number of high-profile athletes would emerge and move on to success in college in the 1990s, McNair had been a multi-sport performer more than five decades earlier. He had also, however, incurred a serious injury. "I tore up a knee," he recalled, "one of those cartilages was totally dislocated. At that time, surgery was not what you did unless you had no alternative, because more often than not, you ended up with a stiff leg. So I passed up surgery."[31]

As an ambitious athletic teenager, McNair found the bad knee to be more than an inconvenience. It was limiting some interesting options.

> I had almost gone to Wofford on a football and basketball scholarship and probably would have gone had it not been for my knee. My family was more interested in me getting an education and they did not take well to somebody going off to school to participate in athletics.
>
> Going to Clemson, I played freshman basketball and then came to the university and went out for the team. After staying out for the year, I made the varsity and played one year there, but the leg got worse. It kept going out of joint. I played intramural football and tore it up terribly. So I had a choice between surgery or giving up athletics. I gave up athletics.[32]

As a disappointed athlete, McNair would become a lifelong fan of the state's college teams, especially USC. He would befriend coaches and athletes, none more so than 1960s–1970s basketball coach Frank McGuire, and he would support recruiting efforts to keep the state's highly sought high school stars in South Carolina colleges and universities. Son Bobby would become a stellar high school quarterback at Allendale and would go on to athletic success at Presbyterian College in Clinton. Around the governor's mansion in the late 1960s, high school Friday nights and college Saturday afternoons were always reserved by the family to follow Bobby's football career.

Studying at the University of South Carolina

For himself, young Bob McNair had reluctantly shelved his athletic career as he took up residence on the prewar USC campus and found other interests. It became a place of exposure to new ideas, intellectual stimulation, and influential faculty. It also became a place for a full range of social pursuits, a matter that required some adjustment for a young man who had spent most of his life on the isolated edge of Hell Hole Swamp.

McNair joined a social fraternity, Kappa Sigma, and became affiliated with the Euphradian Literary Society. As he was trying to nurse his bad knee back to competitive condition, he was finding social diversions, so much so that

> you first had to learn how to discipline yourself.
>
> I was fortunate to get involved in a lot of extracurricular activities in addition to athletics and that was difficult. I had to set aside time to study. Having grown up in the country in a rather sheltered atmosphere and going off to school where you had to make your own decisions, I had to determine to get up and be at class at eight o'clock.[33]

Professor Maude Hawkins taught an early morning English class and, if a student was absent three times during the semester, it resulted in dismissal from class. Her strict discipline reminded McNair of his high school teachers.

McNair's studies were far from traditional for a lowcountry lad growing up on a remote farm. He majored in English and in political science. He embraced literature and came to appreciate the works of nineteenth-century authors Tennyson and Browning. He also developed a closeness with Havilah Babcock, the colorful English professor who left a linguistic legacy with his course, and subsequent book, *I Want a Word.*

"I took everything Dr. Babcock taught at the University," McNair remembered. "I think we had a friendship because of his love for bird hunting. We both grew up in the country and loved to quail hunt."[34] From Babcock, McNair learned to appreciate the precision and subtlety of the language, and although he never pursued an interest in writing, he became a demanding editor of material submitted for his use or approval, insisting on terseness and crispness of language. It was J. Milton "Doc" Ariail, the popular Columbia College professor, who promoted his interest in the nineteenth-century English writers. Ariail taught on a visiting basis at USC because "the University didn't have anyone to teach these courses," according to McNair.

It was not unusual for Ariail to fill in at neighboring institutions during the lean Depression and wartime years, particularly for his close friend Babcock.[35] Babcock considered Ariail the "Dean of English Professors in South Carolina," and the Columbia College faculty member was a special master of poet Robert Browning, to whose lines "Ah, but a man's reach should exceed his grasp / Or what's a Heaven for?" he was known often to attach an "Ariail-style sermonette."[36] Far from the botany labs of Clemson and the plowed fields of Ballsdam, the young student from the lowcountry was probing a variety of intellectual curiosities, including history and English literature. "When you think about it," he said, "What's a young fellow from Hell Hole Swamp, South Carolina [doing] taking Tennyson and Browning?"[37]

Perhaps making an even more lasting impact was a relatively new academic discipline at USC, political science. "It was a developing department then," he said, "and it prepared us all a little better for the law and for public service." His studies exposed McNair to the political world around him, around the country, and around the world. "We studied the Russian Communist government, the Italian government, the Swiss government and the British government to form comparisons. It was particularly interesting because of the Huey Long days in Louisiana, the Share Our Wealth social reform and the other programs that he was espousing at the time. Political science gave us a chance to study communism against Americanism, or democracy, and to take a good look at what was happening in America and around the world."[38]

Postwar USC, its enrollment swelled by returning veterans, was a far cry from the small college McNair had known when he first entered in 1941. Struggling to recover from a Depression-driven decline of the 1930s, the university had grown to slightly more than two thousand students in 1939–1940, its highest enrollment since 1930–1931. The campus was little more than the old Horseshoe and the rows of buildings that flanked it along Pendleton, Pickens, and Greene Streets. Its president was J. Rion McKissick, a stern but engaging figure on campus, known for "his ever-present cigar in its cherry-wood holder, his slouch hat with brim pulled down over his eyes, or snapped up jauntily according to his moods," historian Daniel W. Hollis wrote. "On his strolls around campus, he often looked like a matured cub reporter covering his beat."[39]

McNair remembered McKissick and the atmosphere on the cozy Columbia campus similarly. "We knew everybody," he said. "You walked across the campus and spoke to everybody. Dr. and Mrs. McKissick knew everybody by name by the time they had been there a few months. He kept a very, very friendly atmosphere."[40]

Rion McKissick died on September 3, 1944, a little over four months before McNair and the VII Amphibious Force assaulted the beaches of Lingayen Bay in the Philippines. In a posthumous note found by an editor, he lamented that "the discharge of my duties has greatly lessened my contacts with and my knowledge of our students. . . . I have often wished I could go back to teaching here."[41]

McKissick also left a legacy of frustration with the state's higher-education system, sounding a warning in 1938 and noting that South Carolina was far behind its neighbors Georgia, Florida, and North Carolina in support for its state university. He mused rhetorically, "Shall the doors of hope and opportunity continue to be closed upon poor boys and girls of South Carolina by miserliness, false economy and by institutional competition and jealousy?"[42]

It was a theme that dated back to the post-Tillman days of institutional proliferation, and it was a challenge that McNair would address as governor. As the twentieth century ended, South Carolina lawmakers and educators would still be complaining, without resolution, that the state had too many institutions, had too much overlap and duplication, and was at a competitive disadvantage with Georgia and North Carolina.

Establishing Lifelong Friendships

Among his fellow students, the soft-spoken Berkeley farm boy became popular, making close friends who would remain important to him for life. Among them were Tom McCutcheon, a Kappa Sigma fraternity brother who became a prominent Columbia attorney; George Coleman, a circuit court judge; Robert Harper, an Andrews doctor; Jim Chapman, a former roommate who became an Annapolis graduate during the war and who retired to Myrtle Beach; and McLeod "Mac" Singletary, an attorney who would become a partner in the successful law firm McNair established after his governorship.

There was another friend of those prewar USC days who would leave a lasting imprint on the McNair career, a student from Barnwell known popularly as "Sol Jr." His father was Sol Blatt, the powerful Speaker of the House and one of the rural political barons who so firmly ruled the factional, localized politics of South Carolina in the 1920s and 1930s. Speaker Blatt was part of the celebrated Barnwell Ring, a term applied to "the unusual concentration of political influence in the hands of a small band of men from little Barnwell County."[43] At one time, in the early 1940s, Barnwell County could boast of Blatt, Speaker of the House; Edgar Brown, a longtime Democratic Party loyalist who was chairman of the Senate Finance Committee; J. Emile Harley, governor; and Winchester Smith, chairman of the House Ways and Means Committee.

"All of government was in Barnwell County," Senator Brown is quoted in a 1963 biography as saying. "But we didn't work together." Referring to the feud that characterized much of his dealings with Blatt, he said, "There was no community of interest, even back in those days."[44]

A quarter-century later, in 1965, only Brown and Blatt remained of the Barnwell Ring, and as the newly inaugurated governor, McNair would become one of the few political links between the still-feuding old politicians. By the end of his term five years later, McNair and Blatt would also have their differences over educational issues.

Changes in Postwar Experiences

The coziness of McKissick's prewar days on the USC campus had given way to the postwar boom by the time McNair returned in 1946 to resume his education, to get a delayed start on married life, and to probe further the curiosities of political life.

The McNairs set up housekeeping in small apartments, first on lower Main Street, near campus, and later in a larger place a few blocks away on South Pickens Street. To cope with the swell of veteran enrollments, USC went on a year-round, three-semester schedule and law school became a two-year, instead of three-year, proposition. That suited the McNairs, because of the unplanned arrival of a first son, Robert Evander Jr. "We had our first child while I was in law school," McNair said, "and that jolted us because Josephine was working, and that income meant a lot to us. So we were quite anxious to get through and get out and established."[45]

Like everything else at postwar USC, law school was crowded. Classes were twice the normal size, and many courses were taught by practicing attorneys, men such as Carlisle Roberts, Croft Jennings, Arthur Williams, and Charles Elliott. The dean was J. Nelson Frierson, who had joined the faculty in 1908 and became dean in 1920,[46] and the faculty included the noted legal scholar Coleman Karesh. "He [Karesh] was a brilliant fellow who taught wills and trusts and had been invited to [join the faculty at] just about every prominent law school in the country," McNair said.

He always declined the invitations because he had a love for South Carolina and wanted to stay and contribute here. He probably had more influence on all of us than most of the others on the faculty.

We got a good education. It was a practical education because we were taught by practicing attorneys. We learned how to practice law, as well as the theory part.[47]

The fast-tracking veterans were busy on other fronts as well. The USC Law School was becoming a hotbed of political activism, and McNair could number among his classmates three young Citadel graduates who would figure prominently in the state's political future.

There was Ernest F. "Fritz" Hollings, a Charlestonian fresh from thirty-three months in the World War II African and European campaigns, who would be elected to the state House of Representatives a year after his 1947 law-school graduation and who would go on to a political career that would include service as lieutenant governor, governor, and more than three decades as U.S. senator.

There was James R. Mann, a veteran of five years of wartime duty, who would graduate magna cum laude from law school in 1947, win election a year later to the House from Greenville County, and who would eventually move on to the United States Congress in 1968. Six years later, as a member of the House Judiciary Committee, Congressman Mann would cast a historic vote to proceed with impeachment charges against President Richard Nixon.

And there was John C. West, a five-year veteran of military intelligence service, who would graduate magna cum laude in 1948, move quickly into appointive service on the State Highway Commission, and enter elective office in 1955, first as a state senator from Kershaw County, then as lieutenant governor, and subsequently as the governor who would succeed McNair and usher in a new era of racial peace in South Carolina. In the administration of President Jimmy Carter, West would serve as U.S. Ambassador to Saudi Arabia.

Entering Politics

In the highly charged political atmosphere of that law-school environment, McNair made his own plans for public office, and—as with others in his law class—he did not wait for graduation to launch his first campaign. McNair filed in Berkeley County in the spring of 1948, his last semester in law school, as a candidate in the Democratic primary for the House of Representatives. It was a time when the county's two dominant political factions were squaring off, one headed by the scion of the county's most prominent political family, incumbent senator Rembert C. Dennis, and the other by Moncks Corner businessman Marvin N. Murray, who had been unseated by Dennis for the South Carolina Senate in 1942 after serving twelve years in that office.[48]

Murray was back for another run at Dennis, and, as McNair noted, "My father had always been aligned with the Murray group, and thus when I ran, I ran at odds with Senator Dennis."[49] McNair was also preparing to enter law practice with Marion F. Winter of Moncks Corner, a political rival of Dennis's who had served eight terms in the House and for three years (1944–1946) as Speaker pro tempore.[50]

The Dennis Faction in Berkeley County

"Mr. Winter was on the opposite political side from mine," Dennis later acknowledged, "[and so] naturally, Bob—as he entered politics and ran for the House of Representatives—was running on a different ticket from the one that I was supporting."[51]

Dennis had distinct advantages. He was descended from some of the area's earliest settlers, and his father and grandfather had served in the S.C. Senate for an almost unbroken span between 1894 and 1930. His grandfather, Captain E. J. Dennis, came to local political prominence as a Tillmanite Democrat who attended the 1895 constitutional convention that disenfranchised the state's blacks, and who had a legislative career that included three terms in the House and ten years in the Senate (1894–1903). His son, E. J. Jr., had already served two terms as a member of the House when his father died in office, and the younger Dennis—at age twenty-eight—succeeded him as Berkeley's senator in 1905. The conditions surrounding his assassination almost thirty years later remain a telling commentary on the state's political atmosphere in that era.

South Carolina was only beginning to recover from the political instability wrought by the Tillman-inspired statewide liquor monopoly known as the Dispensary State Board of Control and its successor county boards (1892–1915)[52] when statewide prohibition was imposed in 1915. The Volstead Act followed four years later, drying the rest of the nation for more than another decade. The subsequent illegal trafficking in bootleg liquor became a thriving and fiercely competitive business in the state, and particularly across the vast rural stretches of Berkeley County. What had been political factions grew into hot-blooded rivalries and feuds, and Senator E. J. Dennis Jr. escalated the bitterness when he sought to impose crackdowns on bootlegging in the 1920s, a period in which the lawlessness in Berkeley County was earning it a Chicago-like reputation in local circles.

It was in that kind of frontier atmosphere that Dennis, running for reelection to his fourth full term in the Senate (the previous three had been in 1911–1914, 1919–1922, and 1927–1930), was gunned down on July 24 on a Moncks Corner street by "Sporty" Thornley, a disabled veteran hired to assassinate him. Senator Dennis died a day later.[53]

"I had ambitions as a teenager to be a dentist or a doctor," recalled his son, Rembert Dennis, who was fifteen at the time of his father's assassination. "With the loss of my father and the loss of my older brother, I immediately felt it my responsibility to take up the political cudgel."[54] Dennis graduated six years later from Furman University, and in 1940 he graduated from the USC Law School, treading in the footsteps of his father and grandfather by setting up a law practice in Moncks Corner. By then, he had also followed his forebears into the South Carolina General Assembly, winning election to the House in 1939, followed by another House term two years later, and entering the Senate in 1942. By the time young Bob McNair entered the lists against the Dennis political faction in 1948, Rembert Dennis was well on his way to outdistancing his father and grandfather in political clout and acumen.

McNair recalled:

> I lost in a very, very close race. I really got caught up in my first introduction to real politics in that race and I thought I was going to win, even at eleven o'clock election night. I thought I had enough votes to win, but when the final returns were in, I had lost.
>
> It was a shock.[55]

It was also a shock later that year for Thomas E. Dewey, the Republican presidential candidate, who had also gone into the late hours of the 1948 election night thinking he had won. The downfall of Harry S. Truman, long-predicted by pollsters, pundits, and just about everybody outside the Truman camp, had not materialized, and the Democrat had won what was described as a "startling victory," "astonishing," and "a major miracle." "He had won," Truman biographer David McCullough wrote, "against the greatest odds in the annals of presidential politics. Not one polling organization had been correct in its forecast. Not a single radio commentator or newspaper columnist, or any of the hundreds of reporters who covered the campaign, had called it right."[56]

The Dixiecrat Element in South Carolina Politics

Also among those surprised by the outcome were the Dixiecrats, Democrats from the states of the old Confederacy who figured they could deny Truman enough of the 127 electoral votes from eleven southern states to throw the race into the House of Representatives. At the head of the Dixiecrat ticket was the redoubtable Strom Thurmond, who had been elected governor of South Carolina in 1946 as the moderate candidate, winning out over a field of eleven in something of a sweepstakes of the state's special brand of political localism. "Unlike other states, where party machines or the cult of personality—a Long in Louisiana or a Talmadge in Georgia—dictated politics," Thurmond biographer Nadine Cohodas wrote, "South Carolina was a kind of free-for-all; each candidate started with his solid home base and hoped to build on that with support from surrounding areas. Localism encouraged loyalty to individuals."[57]

Thurmond had been raised in politically volatile Edgefield County, and his father, lawyer J. William Thurmond, had been politically close to Tillman, serving once as his campaign manager and accepting the position of U.S. attorney that Tillman had obtained for him.[58] At age six, Strom met the aging South Carolina leader in what some described as the young Thurmond's first political handshake.

Like many postwar officeholders in the state, Thurmond was also a returning—if somewhat older—veteran. A much-decorated officer in the D-Day Normandy landings, Thurmond ran for governor at age forty-three, pledging a variety of postwar initiatives designed to stimulate the civilian economy, promote public education, and modernize state government. One of the outcomes of his reform effort, the State Budget and Control Board, remained a mainstay of managerial stability almost a half-century later.[59] In his May 1946 announcement speech, he said: "We dare not, we must not, fail to meet the challenge of the future. We need a progressive outlook, a progressive program, and a progressive leadership. We must face the future with confidence and with enthusiasm."[60]

Thurmond, in fact, lived up to his progressive tag in the early days of his administration. His lengthy inaugural address, drafted by Charleston attorney Robert McC. Figg and Spartanburg businessman Walter Brown, included calls for government reorganization, constitutional revision, improvement in workers' conditions, establishment of public kindergartens and nurseries, upgrading education for black students, and "equal rights for women in every respect."[61] As late as the fall of 1947, Thurmond was still in the Truman camp, saying on a Louisville, Kentucky, radio show, "We who believe in a liberal political philosophy, in the importance of human rights as well as property rights, in the preservation and strengthening of the economic and social gains brought about by the efforts of the Democratic Party . . . will vote for the election of Harry Truman."[62] Even essayist James McBride Dabbs of Mayesville was cheering the Thurmond governorship, telling him, "I am under the strong impression that the majority of people in South Carolina are ready for a progressive movement. . . . We who look to the future are proud to follow your leadership."[63]

All that changed within weeks after Thurmond's Louisville endorsement of Truman, triggered largely by the release of the report of the president's Committee on Civil Rights, entitled "To Secure These Rights."[64] The report, combined with elements of Truman's liberal economic program, formed the basis of two bombshells delivered to Congress in early 1948.

The economic reforms, articulated in a message to Congress on January 7, 1948, and a subsequent message less than a month later,[65] contained such items as a national health insurance program, a massive housing program, increased support for education, conservation of natural resources, and an increase in the minimum wage—themes that would become eerily familiar in political confrontations for the next five decades. On the civil rights front, Truman proposed voter rights protection, an end to poll taxes, the establishment of a Fair Employment Practices

Act to root out job discrimination action, the passage of federal antilynching legislation, an end to interstate transportation discrimination, and a charge to the secretary of defense to cease all discrimination in the military.[66]

The messages hit the political South solidly between its white supremacist eyes, and within weeks, rumblings were heard within the Democratic Party about possible defections. The momentarily moderate Thurmond, after an abortive effort to negotiate the Democratic National Committee away from the civil rights plank, embraced the resistance movement and became the standard-bearer of a states' rights party, dubbed the "Dixiecrats" by a headline writer of the *Charlotte News*.

The transition, to some, was remarkable: "it looked as though he was being shoved into a paradoxical position," early biographer Alberta Lachicotte wrote.[67] "By Southern standards, he was somewhat of a liberal; yet here he was leading the Southern States' Rights movement. . . . In the public eye, he changed overnight from a liberal to a conservative. . . . In later years, he would still adhere to his original concepts of government, but as the times steadily became more liberal, he was more and more pictured as an ultra conservative."[68]

There was not much liberal to the sound of Thurmond's attacks on the Truman civil rights proposals. He labeled them "the most astounding presidential message in political history" during a campaign in which he and Mississippi governor Fielding Wright crisscrossed the nation on behalf of states' rights and the thinly veiled issue of white supremacy. A political reporter covering the campaign in Kentucky wrote, "States' Rights is the issue only insofar as it concerns the right of states to solve—or refuse to solve—their race problems."[69]

The Dixiecrat dream of uniting the South against Truman never materialized, any more than the pollsters' predictions of Dewey's victory. Instead of carrying all eleven Confederate states with their 127 electoral votes, the southerners carried four states and 39 electoral votes—the home states of the two candidates, South Carolina and Mississippi, along with Louisiana and Alabama.[70]

On the national level, instead of the dire 44–31 percent advantage for Dewey predicted by pollster Elmo Roper two months prior to the November election,[71] Truman outpolled Dewey 51 percent to 46.5 percent. The Dixiecrats got 2.5 percent. Truman won the electoral-vote contest over Dewey by a margin of 333 to 189. By modern political standards, it wasn't even close, and as the Truman inaugural took place, biographer Lachicotte recorded that "the 1948 bolt of Southern Democrats came to an end."[72]

Well, not exactly.

The Dixiecrat Legacy

The Dixiecrats' rebellion would pass along a legacy of political, philosophical, and rhetorical symbols and strategies that would come to delineate southern conservative politics for years to come. They cloaked the raw, unvarnished ideas of Tillman and "Cotton Ed" Smith in the rhetorical ambiguity of states' rights and antifederalism, themes that would recur with regularity and frequency for the rest of the century.

Journalist Harry Ashmore wrote: "the Dixiecrats did have a considerable importance. Although they tried to be polite about it, it was quite clear that they were in fact the anti-Negro party. . . . The case they presented to the Southern [white] voter was a familiar one. They appealed to his prejudices and played upon his fears."[73]

Dixiecrat themes would recur in the 1964 campaign of Barry Goldwater, the "southern strategy" of Richard Nixon in 1968, and even in some of the antigovernment sentiments of Ronald Reagan, all political undertakings in which the old Dixiecrat warrior himself, Strom Thurmond, was front-and-center in a visible leadership role. Vestiges of racial exclusivity would continue to deny the conservative movement any substantial black political support, but the Dixiecrats' impassioned attacks, laced with biblical and constitutional rhetoric, on the federal bureaucracy would eventually blend with the subsequent more broadly based assaults on government in general by religious fundamentalists, populists, and disgruntled antitax conservatives, whose political disenchantment was not limited to the southern region.

Beyond its messages of defiance, the Dixiecrat effort would also leave territorial —and organizational—scars across the no-longer-solid South. In failing to unite the states of the old Confederacy against the two major parties in 1948, the Dixiecrats created political fissures along fault lines that would redefine the southern political terrain in many ways. It would validate a convenient separation between the Upper South and the Lower South, which would subsequently become something of a Dixie demarcation between the moderate South and the conservative South, the New South and Old South. As South Carolina struggled to recruit new industry to its borders and to establish itself as a progressive, economically significant state, it would also try to shake off identity with its Old South, neo-Confederate political partners.

The Dixiecrats left political scars within South Carolina as well. In his race for governor in 1946, Thurmond had chosen to assail the "Barnwell Ring" as a means of demonstrating his commitment to a platform of governmental reform. Although his ploy may have given some distinction to his race in the crowded primary field, it also amounted to an attack on Blatt and Brown—two Brahmins, two living legislative institutions in the state—and it represented to some an attack on the storied legislative domination of the state itself.

Thurmond was separating himself from loyalist Democrats, whose roots went back to the New Deal and earlier. He was dividing the aggressively segregationist ideology of the Dixiecrats from the practicing pragmatism of traditional Democrats who worked to accommodate change on an incremental basis. Such fissures sometimes had as much to do with style and strategy as they did with substance. As late as the 1960s, moderate South Carolina governors such as Fritz Hollings would dutifully proclaim allegiance to segregation as a public policy, but as a matter of practical politics, he labored mightily to bring about the peaceful desegregation of Clemson College by Harvey Gantt.

The Dixiecrats brought the divisions out into the open, paving the way for Thurmond to defeat Edgar Brown as a write-in candidate in 1954, leading to his defection to the Republican Party in 1964, and forming the fundamental, anti-civil-rights issues and differences that undergirded the emergence of the state's competitive two-party system less than two decades later. The Dixiecrats also energized the emerging power of black political interests by providing direct political opposition.

Exercising Options

For young Bob McNair, the defeat at the hands of the Rembert Dennis faction in Berkeley County bore no such cosmic political implications. But there were immediate and significant lessons and consequences. The defeat, surprising and stinging as it was, could be traced to factors that he felt may well have lain beyond his control, political divisions that went back to his father's activism in rural Berkeley County and his support of Senator Murray. The Murray faction, including Murray himself, McNair, and another returning veteran, Mike Newell, all went down to defeat, and Rembert Dennis and other members of the "ticket" were the winners.

"It was just pure politics," McNair said. "Families will align with different factions, going way back, and that alignment holds right on."[74] Given the politics of localism in the sparsely populated Jamestown area, there were not the numbers to counter a well-entrenched Moncks Corner faction such as the Dennises. But by then, politics had gotten deeply into the bloodstream of the young man from Hell Hole Swamp. He had reached a political moment of decision, the first of his career: remain out of the power loop in Berkeley County or explore other options. The options, as it turned out, proved appealing.

Visits with wife Josephine to her home and family in Allendale had begun to produce some interesting conversations with local business leaders. His law practice with Dennis's political rival, Marion Winter, had prospered, and McNair found himself heavily involved in real-estate work. "About 90 percent of my time was spent at the courthouse searching for records and closing loans," he recalled. "Also, I did a variety of other things from defending someone in magistrate's court to helping him [Winter] in a criminal case, to helping him defend the railroad in a crossing collision. Just about anything that came along."[75]

McNair was earning the healthy sum of $150 a month, enough to keep his young family comfortable in Moncks Corner. But the political dead end in Berkeley County kept him alert to other opportunities, the kind of opportunities his in-laws and friends were discussing halfway across the state in the town of Allendale.

The Allendale Frontier

If there could be a cultural, economic, and political opposite from crusty old Berkeley County, it was Allendale. Unlike sprawling Berkeley, to whose shores and riverbanks some of South Carolina's first European settlers came, Allendale was inland, compact, and relatively new as a political entity. McNair sensed the difference immediately. "I found the friendliest, warmest group of people I have ever run into," he said. "We never had a more pleasant life than we had in Allendale."[76]

Allendale lay on the western edge of lower South Carolina, bordering the Savannah River, the state's boundary with Georgia, about halfway between Savannah and Augusta. Largely a farming area with sandy, absorbent soil and a long growing season, Allendale had also attained some economic advantage as a stopover along a major north-south corridor, Highway 301, a route favored by truckers and long-distance travelers as a backcountry alternative to the busy north-south artery US 1. As the postwar travel boom stimulated auto traffic between the populous East and the emerging Florida vacation spots, motels, restaurants, and service stations sprang up along Allendale's portion of well-traveled Highway 301 and became a major source of the county's wealth and jobs.

Allendale County had been created as one of several new, small counties established early in the twentieth century after the revised constitution of 1896 to accommodate farmers with courthouses "within an hour's drive" of their homes. The town of Allendale and the neighboring farm communities dated back to English and German settlement of the eighteenth century, and the county's 435 square miles[77] were set aside as a separate county in 1919, only a few years after ten other counties had been similarly set up to serve the legal and political interests of the rural population of the state. The county to its north, and the place from which Allendale had been carved, was what amounted to the political capital of the state in those days, Barnwell.

Deciding to Move to Allendale

As the state's newest county, Allendale in postwar South Carolina was still looking for an identity apart from its older neighboring counties, Barnwell to the north and Hampton to the south. A group of business leaders, in fact, was openly recruiting some new professional and political leadership for the county, and Josephine Robinson's young lawyer husband from Berkeley County became a prime target. The Allendale group was not just looking for a new lawyer for their county, he soon became aware; they were recruiting someone who could run for the House in 1951 and who could bring Allendale some political stability. In the two previous decades, only one person had served as many as three consecutive terms in the legislature, and for two terms (1945–1948) the county was represented in the House by the son of the senator from nearby Hampton County, George Warren.

Besides Warren's influence, Allendale "had sorta been dominated by Senator Edgar Brown and Speaker Blatt," according to McNair. "Having been cut from Barnwell, Allendale was still the bump on the log, so to speak, in most people's minds."[78]

The opportunity to make something out of that bump on the log appealed to the politically struck Navy veteran. Even as he was settling into his new law practice in Moncks Corner, McNair took back to Ballsdam the idea of moving to Allendale and exploring the professional and political opportunities that lay there. He had been away from home for more than seven years in the service and college, but Berkeley was still his home. "My roots were there," McNair said, "and my father had such a strong interest in the county."[79] The move to Allendale would mean a clean break with his past.

As it turned out, the senior McNair, his son's political mentor and confidante, was all for it. "Surprising to everyone, he was supportive of my going to Allendale," McNair said. "He felt it was the best thing for me. He thought if I stayed in Berkeley, I would be caught up in a continuation of the political factionalism." By then, Daniel McNair had struck up a friendship with his old political rival, Rembert Dennis. "My father had acknowledged that Senator Dennis was doing a good job and was not playing the factional role in dealing with areas and people in the various communities. He became very fond of him, and they became friends in later years."[80]

By the end of 1948, the year in which Bob McNair and Tom Dewey suffered shocking defeats, the McNairs had departed Moncks Corner and moved to Allendale, all with the blessing of McNair's father, as well as with his assurance to continue financial aid to the young family. It was only a ninety-one-mile journey across swampy lower South Carolina from crusty old Berkeley to the state's newest county on the Georgia border, but for the aspiring young attorney, it was political light-years.

Developing an Allendale Identity

In his new home, McNair became known first as Bill Robinson's son-in-law, an introduction that helped him ease into business, legal, and political circles. The Robinsons were prominent and affluent; his father-in-law was a funeral director who "knew everybody and who had probably buried somebody out of every home in the county," according to McNair.[81]

Bill Robinson was also popular and served on city council in the small community, a situation that helped ease his newcomer son-in-law into the legal practice and politics. "He was one of the finest, most accommodating people you can imagine," McNair said. "Everybody just loved him." Like McNair's own parents in rural Berkeley County, Bill Robinson was known for helping people in the community. "Any of the old widow ladies around town that had a problem, they would go to him, and he would help them," McNair said.[82]

Being the son-in-law of a city councilman and funeral director gave McNair some early recognition. But being Bill Robinson's son-in-law did not erase the difficulty of getting a law practice started in a brand new town:

> It took longer than I had hoped to get established, because everybody had been so accustomed to going to Barnwell or Hampton when they had a major legal problem.
>
> We went through several years of pretty lean living and I was making a lot less than the $150 a month that I had been making in Moncks Corner. But my father helped us out. He gave me a continued allowance as he had done through law school and helped me in Moncks Corner.[83]

Part of McNair's problem was his decision to start his own law firm, a one-man practice. "I decided to do it the hard way," he said. "Others have tried it the other way, and people could never find them when they needed them." But the new law firm was a lonely vigil for a while. "I was determined I was going to make it work," he said, "so I went to the office every morning, and I stayed there all day. It was awfully difficult sometimes when the telephone wouldn't ring and nobody walked in."[84]

Allendale's newest lawyer got some help from an ailing older attorney named Thomas Boulware, who, McNair said, "took me under his wing." Boulware was suffering from emphysema, which made courtroom appearances difficult, so he recruited the town's new lawyer as an associate on some cases. "That was extremely helpful," he said. "We were lucky enough to get some good breaks, and to get some decent lawsuits, and to be reasonably successful."[85]

The McNairs also got some early financial help from a boarder, a law-school friend from USC, Vernon Sumwalt, who lived with the McNairs in Allendale and practiced law in nearby Hampton. Sumwalt was the nephew of Robert Sumwalt, engineering dean and later USC president. "We had been very close in law school," McNair said, "almost like brothers."[86]

Sumwalt practiced law in Hampton with Randolph "Buster" Murdaugh Jr., the solicitor of South Carolina's Fourteenth Judicial Circuit, which covered the entire five-county lower corner of the state—Beaufort, Jasper, Colleton, Hampton, and Allendale Counties. In later years, Murdaugh would become a political power in lowcountry South Carolina and a key McNair ally.

Sumwalt's rent payment of $50 a month, the continuing allowance from the McNairs of Ballsdam, and some furniture from the Robinson household got the McNairs started in Allendale. As the law practice began to pick up, McNair also recruited some secretarial help, a USC graduate in secretarial science named Josephine R. McNair. "We soon discovered," McNair said, "that was not a good idea."

I had seen it in Moncks Corner, where Mrs. Winter was a paralegal, one of a few at the time. She was almost as good as a lawyer, particularly at tax time. But Josephine did not have the time—we had one child and then a second—and it really was not a good thing to have my wife in the office.[87]

McNair turned to a part-time high school assistant in an office that he admitted was sparsely equipped. "We used Josephine's portable typewriter that she had in school for a long time, and I bought a desk from Vernon Sumwalt. Josephine's family had a set of old living room furniture which they loaned me, and I used that. I doubt if I had a hundred dollars invested in the office."

That much was clear to Allendale native Thomas O. Lawton, who had been persuaded by McNair to give up a law practice in Georgetown and to return to Allendale as more of McNair's time became committed to political activity. "When I got here," Lawton recalled, "his office was in a very small frame building on Railroad Avenue. There were two little offices; at one time, one had been a dentist's office and the other a lawyer's office. Each of them had two rooms with a central fireplace, an oil stove, and linoleum on the floor. Bob had one Royal typewriter and one file box that was a Campbell's Soup pasteboard box, stuck in a corner."[88]

Running for the House Again

From that setting, the twenty-seven-year-old McNair launched his second race for the House. He soon learned that Allendale, like Berkeley, was not without its factions. The county was split between two rival groups, one headed by businessman Martin Thomas, owner of the local Coca-Cola bottling plant, and the other led by farmer and grain dealer Ed Myrick. Unlike his experience in Berkeley, McNair—as the Allendale newcomer—chose neither faction. He worked both sides of the political street in the small town. The two factions, he noted, "swapped about every four years in the Senate, and Allendale had a history of never leaving anybody there for any length of time. There never really got to be a strong, permanent influence, and I made friends with both and crossed the factional line pretty well."[89]

In the seesaw politics of Allendale County, Thomas and Myrick had been bumping heads for more than a decade over the Senate seat, Thomas serving the 1939–1942 term, Myrick 1943–1946, and Thomas in 1947–1950. Thomas was being challenged again in 1950 by Myrick, and McNair was running for the House seat vacated by A. P "Dick" Williams, an automotive-parts jobber and farm-machinery dealer who had served the 1949–1950 term in the House.

Free of factions or alignments, McNair got little ticket support. That meant he had to scramble for votes, and in the days before smaller, single-member districts, all legislative candidates ran countywide. "I went from door to door out in the rural areas and in the towns," McNair said. "I do not think I missed a single house or a single person who was a voter at the time."[90]

These were also the days before extensive media campaigning, which meant that most politicking was done on a personal basis. "It was door-to-door, handshaking and sitting and talking with a lot of people," he recalled. "You just say hello and tell people who you were and what you were doing."[91] It was a punishing regimen, but one that remained a McNair campaign characteristic, even in statewide races. Media advertising, he would later tell candidates, cannot replace the punishment of working the streets on a personal basis. Face-to-face politics, whether campaigning or governing, would remain central to Bob McNair's style and strategy.

There would be no late-night shocks and surprises for McNair in this race. In June 1950, he was declared the winner of the Democratic primary. Six months later, he would steer his two-door Pontiac the seventy-eight miles to take his seat in the South Carolina General Assembly. He was no longer the farm boy from Ballsdam Plantation or simply Bill Robinson's son-in-law.

4

Learning the Ropes in a Rural State

There would not be much time for orientation or apprenticeship for the new House member from Allendale. As it was with the landing craft on the Pacific beaches, newcomers were expected to learn as they went along how to maneuver through the sandbars, floating mines, or typhoons without sinking. That much was apparent as the Eighty-ninth General Assembly convened on January 9, 1951.

South Carolina had a new governor, but James F. "Jimmy" Byrnes was a stranger to no one. Capping a political career that had led him through a remarkable assortment of prestigious positions—congressman, senator, U.S. Supreme Court justice, secretary of state, and consummate insider in the Roosevelt administration, among other things—Jimmy Byrnes was South Carolina's reigning political celebrity and rivaled the venerable John C. Calhoun as the state's greatest public figure.

Closing his political career by running for governor at age seventy-one, Byrnes was elected in 1950 in a virtual love-in; he garnered 80 percent of the vote in a three-way primary race.[1] If Jimmy Byrnes can't fix this racial segregation mess, most South Carolina voters figured, then nobody can.

And Byrnes came to office with a plan. Less than six years after he had sat elbow-to-elbow with Truman, Churchill, and Stalin at Potsdam to carve up postwar eastern Europe among the "Big Three" powers, Byrnes brought with him a reputation for craftiness and cleverness. He was a problem-solver, people figured, and, after the bluff and bluster of Thurmond and the Dixiecrats, maybe it was time for a diplomat. "During his long and lofty tenure in the three branches of the federal government," historian John Egerton wrote, "Byrnes had acquired the manipulative skills of a master politician and dressed them in the cool formality of a sophisticated diplomat."[2]

Byrnes's plan seemed to bear out that kind of assessment. Without coming right out and saying it, he conceded the point that South Carolina could not stand very firmly on its "separate but equal" legal justification for public-school segregation if its schools were not, in fact, equal. His approach seemed rational, enlightened, and even conciliatory.

"What the colored people want," he said in his 1951 inaugural address, "is equal facilities in their schools. We must see that they get them."[3] Implied, of course, but not admitted, was the gross inequality that had existed in South Carolina's public schools since 1896, when *Plessy v. Ferguson* gave the "separate but equal" concept judicial legitimacy. Tillmanism conferred with the clout of constitutional and Jim Crow statutory authority the further mandate that the state's actual policy would be white supremacy within a separate but unequal reality.

State spending on public education, in fact, favored whites over blacks by more than two-to-one as Byrnes took office in 1951, and even that imbalance represented a drastic improvement over conditions thirty-five years earlier, when the ratio was more than eight-to-one in favor of the white public schools.[4]

Byrnes was aware that there was a judicial clock ticking. On November 17, 1950—only three months before Byrnes's inauguration as governor—NAACP attorney Thurgood Marshall had gone before federal judge Waring for a pretrial hearing on a case that had developed in rural Clarendon County, sixty-five miles east of Columbia. In the summer of 1947, the chairman of Clarendon School District 22 and the school district's superintendent had denied a request by an AME minister, James A. DeLaine, for a bus to transport black children to school. Even after the black parents raised money to buy the bus, the district refused to maintain it.

Reportedly hesitant at first to pursue legal recourse, Reverend DeLaine was described as being inspired by a speech he heard later that summer in Columbia by the NAACP president, Reverend James M. Hinton. Hinton, among the founders of the State Conference in 1939 and one of those who challenged the all-white Democratic Party in 1944, called special attention to the lack of buses for black children, and DeLaine returned to Clarendon persuaded not to let the issue die. A subsequent NAACP lawsuit filed in the name of a black farmer recruited by Reverend DeLaine, Levi Pearson, was taken to court by Columbia attorney Harold Boulware and was dismissed on a technicality in 1948. But DeLaine and Pearson persisted. The following spring—in 1949—they met again with NAACP officials in Columbia, and this time the group included Thurgood Marshall.

Even as DeLaine and Pearson were confronted with economic reprisals at home, a group of twenty Clarendon County parents agreed to sign on as plaintiffs in a new suit. The first of the names alphabetically was a Navy veteran with four children, Harry Briggs, who worked at a filling station in the Clarendon farming town of Summerton, and it was Briggs's name that gave the suit its subsequent historical identity, *Briggs v. Elliott.*[5]

Byrnes later placed the timing of the NAACP suit as coming "after I had started our educational program," contending that the Clarendon County case "for equal facilities in a school district" had been abandoned and that a "new case asking the court to declare unconstitutional the laws requiring separation of the races in the public schools" was needed.[6] Technically, Byrnes may have been correct. The *Briggs* case on equalization of facilities was withdrawn, but only at the urging of Waring, who "was eager to see the larger case raised in his court."[7] The new case was filed a month later, which would have still come before Byrnes "had started our educational program."[8]

Byrnes's "Educational Revolution"

Whatever the chronology, Byrnes must have been sensitive to the nature of Hinton's contention and the Clarendon dispute when he presented at his inaugural the program he called an "Educational Revolution." Included in the revolution were provisions that would increase "by 50,000 the number of Negro pupils daily transported to school by bus."[9]

Besides the increase in busing, the heart of Byrnes's revolution was a massive bond program designed to upgrade the quality of school facilities across the state. The bonds were to be retired by revenue from South Carolina's first-ever state-level sales tax, a 3 percent imposition that came to be known as "Jimmy's tax." The three-cent tax outlived its bond-retirement purpose, becoming a major source of recurring revenue as the state assumed an increasing share of the financial responsibility from local governments for the financing of public education. Under McNair's gubernatorial leadership, the legislature would add a fourth penny in 1969 to Jimmy's tax in a comprehensive educational upgrading on the eve of long-delayed massive desegregation in 1970.

A lot of Byrnes's attention in 1951 went toward consolidating the state's rural districts. Reducing South Carolina's 1,200 school districts to 102, Byrnes could later also claim the elimination of "824 totally inadequate schools in rural areas." He would contend, "There was now at least one first class high school for colored students in every district, and in many instances, these schools were better than those provided for white students because they were newer."[10]

"Many of the new black schools became the schools used when we went to an integrated system," McNair recalled. "We had built all those good facilities [and] we had developed a statewide transportation system already." Had the effort been made after the *Brown* decision, he admitted, such support and funding from the all-white legislature, "would have been difficult."[11] Even coming as it did three years before *Brown,* McNair called it "a very courageous political thing to do."[12]

At that time people didn't visualize total integration, so the move that we were making to support a massive tax program to provide equal facilities—equal opportunity was the way it was put at the time—was looked upon by some as a very positive move and a major undertaking. Most of the money went to the improvement of black education in the state, the building of schools and the providing of transportation that the whites had always enjoyed.[13]

"It [the Education Revolution]," he said, "was a very positive thing for some. On the part of others, it was just another step in avoiding the time we would get to integration."[14]

> At the time, we all proceeded on the assumption that the state's position would prevail and that if we made the facilities equal, we could continue under the separate, but equal [system]. But we couldn't continue if we had inadequate facilities and if we didn't provide good educational opportunity.[15]

Byrnes's initiative in addressing the needs of black schools before the Supreme Court order was issued was a strategy not lost on McNair. Eighteen years later, as the state stood on the brink of the actual long-delayed desegregation of its public schools, McNair—as governor—would propose a tax increase to fund a major upgrade of public education, including state-funded kindergartens, before the actual desegregation took place.

Byrnes's plan, for whatever may have been the reasons, was appealing to the white political structure in 1951, and Byrnes was its master salesman. According to his longtime friend and admirer, Sol Blatt, "Jim Byrnes had the happy faculty of just putting everyone at ease. He was in charge." Blatt recalled an instance during Byrnes's 1950 campaign for governor when he was confronted by labor leaders who "began to ask him a few questions, how he stood about certain things."[16] Byrnes, known for his anti-union sentiments, executed a deft sidestep.

> I never shall forget how Jim took them away from the problems that they were considering and wanted him to talk about, and told them about Stalin and Russia and his visits over there, and how he was treated, what he thought about them, and everybody was just left with their mouths open.
> They forgot all about the damn questions, and he just got by with it.[17]

It was in that kind of atmosphere that Byrnes presided over what many thought would be an integration-proof strategy of improving black public schools. Of the $124 million in bond proceeds allotted to the "Education Revolution," Byrnes claimed the "Negro schools received two-thirds of the amount, even though Negro pupils comprised only 40 percent of the total."[18] Behind this kind of rationale, historian Egerton writes, Byrnes was "hoping desperately to ward off court-ordered desegregation."[19]

Expectations of Victory

A lot of the state's confidence had to do with the stature of its chief legal representative, the venerable Wall Street attorney, seventy-nine-year-old John W. Davis.

Friends with Byrnes since the two served in Congress in the 1920s, Davis had been solicitor general and ambassador to the Court of St. James under President Woodrow Wilson. Davis was the dark-horse Democratic nominee for president in 1924, losing in a landslide to Calvin Coolidge, and he subsequently gained a special reputation over the years for his success in appeals before the U.S. Supreme Court. A frequent vacationer at Yeaman's Hall in Charleston, Davis was called by Byrnes "the ablest constitutional lawyer of his time."[20]

Davis was a native of Clarksburg, West Virginia, who earned his undergraduate and law degrees from Washington and Lee University at a time when Robert E. Lee's son, Custis, was president of the institution. "It was a task for which his Southern upbringing and conservative states' rights orientation had prepared him both philosophically and jurisprudentially," wrote Sydnor Thompson, a longtime Charlotte attorney who was a Davis colleague in the Davis Polk firm at the time of *Briggs* and who worked on the five companion public-school segregation cases. The first *Briggs* brief was one "to which Davis gave more personal attention than was his custom."

"When Davis accepted the challenge of Governor Byrnes to represent South Carolina in *Briggs v. Elliott*," Thompson wrote, ". . . he was confident that the numerous precedents upholding the principle of 'separate, but equal' facilities in both federal and state jurisdictions, including the Supreme Court's 1896 landmark decision in *Plessy v. Ferguson,* would insure his success. The fact that the substantial forces of the NAACP were arrayed against him gave him little pause, despite that organization's record of successes in the United States Supreme Court since World War II."[21] Newsman Harry Ashmore later wrote, "Never, he told colleagues, had he taken a case to the Supreme Court with precedent so heavily stacked on his side. Segregation had been 'so often and so pointedly declared by the highest authorities it should no longer be regarded as open to debate.'"[22]

Heartened by expectations that Byrnes's initiatives would prevail, legislators viewed his Education Revolution as a win-win: blacks would get better schools, and segregation would be retained. For McNair, who remembered growing up in rural South Carolina, riding "to school on a school bus . . . while black children who lived in the area walked to school,"[23] the issue was not so much whether the program would be enacted, but how the monies would be allocated. McNair recalled the dire conditions in Hell Hole Swamp and the paltry economic resources available at the local level to support public education. He also remembered how Macedonia School had sprung to life with the new monies brought to the area by his father's political efforts, and he knew what a difference the model program had meant to him and his fellow students.

The legislative fight over Byrnes's Education Revolution program and its three-cent tax turned out not to be so much over racial issues or school desegregation. It devolved into the kind of big county / small county fights that characterized much of the South Carolina legislative wrangling in the days before single-member districts effectively diminished much of the countywide distinctions and interests.

> When it came to school transportation, we were all strongly for it because the rural counties— the small counties—were the ones that had less of it and could not afford it.
>
> When it came to funds for school construction, the big battle was over whether it would be based on enrollment or attendance. The small counties took strong positions for enrollment. While black children would enroll, they did not have good attendance, very often because of the long walks they had to and from school. Since the purpose of the program was to provide for them, we felt we had to provide the kind of physical facilities, and transportation, to encourage them to get into the school system, and to encourage them to stay and get an education.[24]

Navigating the Rural Legislative System

In that and other subsequent fights, McNair began to grasp the politics and tactics by which the traditional rural leaders maintained their influence on the state's purse strings and policies. In the case of Allendale and neighboring lowcountry counties, coalitions were built around the old Barnwell Ring, an alliance its members contended was overrated, but one that served good, symbolic purposes for neighboring small counties. "There was a Barnwell Ring, but we all laughed about it quite often, and said it was a lot bigger and broader because there were a lot of us [from nearby counties] who were probably members of it," he said.[25]

The leadership came from Blatt and Brown, and although they were often feuding personally over some things, "when it came to Barnwell County, they were together, and when it came to the lower state or the small county interests, they were together."[26] Blatt's practice of appointing only one House member from a county to a committee preserved small-county, rural dominance. Brown's control of the Senate Finance Committee and of the State Budget and Control Board provided additional assurance that interests of the few large, urban counties came second, if necessary.

As a freshman legislator, McNair took his place toward the back of the tile-floored, 124-member chamber in desk number 95, next to Walter B. Brown of Spartanburg, a classmate at USC. McNair regularly rode to sessions in Columbia with William L. Rhodes Jr., his legislative roommate in the Wade Hampton Hotel across the street from the state house. Rhodes was a burly lawyer from Varnville in nearby Hampton County who was an early McNair ally and member of the "extended" Barnwell Ring.

The 1951 House contained 123 men and one woman, a teacher and civic worker named Martha Thomas Fitzgerald from Columbia. All were white, and 55 of them, like McNair and Rhodes, were veterans of World War II. Also like McNair and Rhodes, 56 of them were serving for the first time, making almost half the membership in the body that year military veterans and freshmen. By comparison, only 29 of the 124 members had served more than two terms.

The 1951 House included Sam Boylston, who would become a longtime McNair ally and trucking lobbyist; Jim Aycock, a future chairman of Ways and Means during McNair's gubernatorial terms; future Columbia solicitor John Foard, with whom McNair would tangle during the 1970 USC campus uprisings; future South Carolina Supreme Court justices George Gregory, Lionel Legge, and Bill Rhodes; a future congressman, James Mann; and longtime Comptroller General Earle Morris, who also served a term as lieutenant governor. Speaker pro tempore that year was Ernest F. Hollings.

McNair learned to play the system early and began to refine a style of personal politics that would characterize his political and public career for years to come. He was gravitating toward the political center, and as a newcomer from one of the state's smaller counties, he was learning the ways of consensus-building through committee work and personal contact with other legislators.

> I've never seen an inflexible good leader. It just can't be done that way. If you ever find a dogmatic person who is just set in his ways and will not listen and will not bend or will not compromise, he's not going to be a good leader, and seldom does he ever get in a position to be a leader.
>
> I have found that what people say about politicians compromising is [a reference to] the strongest quality they have—to be able to compromise. I used to say quite often that there were three ways of doing something—your way, my way and the right way. And that wasn't always wrong because quite often when we compromised, we did get it the way it should have been done and the best way.[27]

The first step toward success in the oligarchic South Carolina legislature, McNair and his roommate Rhodes learned, was gaining the right committee assignments, and that meant either Judiciary or Ways and Means, traditionally the two most powerful committees in the chamber. Committee assignments, they also knew, were within the purview of Sol Blatt, the remarkable and impetuous Speaker who wielded the gavel in the South Carolina House of Representatives for a total of thirty years in two lengthy stretches between 1937 and 1973.[28]

McNair called on his law-school friendship with Blatt's son—"Sol Jr."—as well as his neophyte status as a member of the extended Barnwell Ring and made the rather bold request to be assigned to Judiciary, something of an elevated aspiration for a first-year legislator. Rhodes, at the same time, was making the equally long-shot request to be appointed to Ways and Means, sending a clear message that the newcomer roommates had their sights set high.

A Protégé of Speaker Blatt's

To their delight, Blatt honored both requests. The Speaker saw in them unusual skills, and also the opportunity to enhance the concentration of power within his small, rural power center in backcountry South Carolina. "I recognized in Bob a man of great ability," Blatt later said, "a courageous follow. He didn't play politics; he voted a statesman-like vote. I recognized his great ability, and [while] he was politically ambitious . . . he never sold his soul to get elected."[29] Rhodes, Blatt found, was also "a man of great ability, of great dedication." Within a short time, Blatt would help steer his two anointed protégés into the chairmanship of their respective committees, creating within three sparsely populated counties in western South Carolina a cartel of enormous political potency.

> Bob was a good talker and Bill Rhodes could make a crackerjack speech. They were the fighting kind when they were in the House. They were vigorous in their efforts to do the right thing. . . . The membership of the House recognized the fine leadership of Bob, his great dedication and his great ability and his fine character. Bob and Bill Rhodes would tell you the truth. There wasn't any question. When they told you something, you didn't have to go check on it.[30]

Rhodes and McNair also added muscle to Blatt's arsenal of political weaponry with which to protect small-county interests as well as to stand up to his rival, Brown, in the Senate, and the governor, too. "Those two [members] were the men upon whom I relied," Blatt recalled, "to a large extent, to help me with all programs that we thought were in the best interest of the state."[31] It was an alliance of political usefulness to all parties, and it typified the feudal-like, locally oriented political system in which small counties, particularly small counties in proximity to Barnwell County, were political winners.

A political loser only two years earlier, McNair had quickly become a fast-tracker in his new environment. He was also forming an alliance that would influence the rest of his political career. The son of an immigrant Jewish peddler from Russia, Solomon Blatt could be pugnacious, witty, feisty, brilliant, charming, or chilly, depending on his mood or the necessity of the moment. He had built a political career on his individual strengths and skills, ascending through a system where anti-Semitism raised some obstructions but where no one could deny his enormous energy, intellect, and determination. "In my early days," Blatt recalled, life "was right tough. It was in the days when the Klan was pretty active, and my being of the Jewish faith, they sort of stayed on me a little bit. At one stage of my life, in the practice of law, I suffered quite a bit, and so did my limited number of clients. They realized that I was not a member of the Klan, and the lawyers on the other side were members, and most of the jurors were. So that limited the amount of business I had. But I stuck to my guns, and I overcame the opposition, and they soon became very close friends of mine."[32]

73

Blatt and McNair were personal and strategic opposites. As Blatt himself described it,

> He's got that smile, which is a good thing for a fellow to have. I'm gruff and rough. I came up that way. I'm more of an in-fighter. Bob is a smiling fellow; he breaks you down with that smile and soft talk, and he has a way of doing it, and it's commendable.
>
> I took a more positive position; I would say, "No, right now." Bob would let it drag along for a few hours until he overpowered you, persuaded you.[33]

For his part, McNair acknowledged his inclination toward personal communication as a political style. He strove to develop

> a personal relationship . . . work hard . . . and be knowledgeable so that you could discuss the position informally with others. Debate was always available. I think most of us limited our standing up [at the podium] and speaking as much as we could.
>
> It did not take long to find out that the fellow who was always at the microphone accomplished very little. He really did not have that kind of influence; people got tired of the talk and soon quit listening. So you found that, if you were always getting up and trying to speak, you did not have much influence and people would not listen to you.[34]

Blatt agreed:

> We've got fellows in the House and Senate that start off and make a good speech, and then they get to speaking every day upon every subject that comes along and sooner or later they get to the point where the moment they get up, a group will walk out. They've heard him long enough and he's hurt himself. But if you've got sense enough to know when to talk and what to say and say it and sit down, they'll listen to you.
>
> I can remember when Bob and Bill Rhodes got up to speak that everybody would be quiet and listen. And when they got through and somebody else got up to say something, just talking, you couldn't hear what was going on.[35]

Blatt, like a stern schoolmaster in a rowdy country classroom, ruled the House with cunning, bluff, and bluster, imposing his will brashly through procedural ploys and strategic wiles that would often disarm his foes. He was an unchallenged master of the rules, an unashamed manipulator of power sources, and a fearless warrior in the face of a good fight. On those rare occasions when he took the podium himself, his emotional, high-pitched, tremolo voice was an intimidating force among those who had dared to cross his path. When all else failed, the Speaker could make eye contact with a friendly member and launch a rapid succession of self-activated parliamentary steps that would end with the gavel being pounded, the House being adjourned, and distraught members still screaming for attention and recognition—"Mr. Speaker! Mr. Speaker!"—to no avail.

It was also an affirmation of the expedient "family and friends" politics of the rural crossroads, a political arrangement that had grown up amid the state's recurrent economic distress of the early 1900s. As Blatt, McNair, and Rhodes were exerting small-county hegemony over the largely urban membership of the House, the Senate's dominant force was a triad of rural barons—Blatt's Barnwell rival, Edgar Brown; Brown's top lieutenant and McNair's one-time Berkeley County nemesis, Rembert Dennis; and L. Marion Gressette, the crisply assertive lawyer from tiny St. Matthews whose distaste for new legislation earned the Senate Judiciary Committee he chaired the nickname "Gressette's Graveyard." Arrayed with these small county legislative powers were governors such as Thurmond, Byrnes, and George Bell Timmerman, whose homes were rural (at that time) counties west of Columbia—Edgefield, Aiken, and Lexington, respectively.

It was no place for a city slicker, and McNair—with his Ballsdam upbringing and easygoing manner—fit nicely into the political ambience of the time. He also learned quickly that statewide legislative business was often secondary to local politics. Legislative delegations, dominated by the single senator from each county, enacted each year a county supply bill, which, in essence, was the county budget for the upcoming year. County business—everything from road paving to school construction—was under the direct control of legislators through the county supply bill. It was under that kind of financial authority that legislators exercised control over county business, which often constituted more in the way of real power and reelection opportunity than did the addressing of statewide issues.

Much of it was a throwback to Tillmanism and the constitution of 1896. Governors at the time were limited to one term, and the office was styled as little more than the state's chief magistrate. In addition to their budgetary preeminence, legislators controlled an assortment of appointments to local governing boards, often including school boards and county commissions. As a body, the General Assembly also elected members of statewide boards to preside over the state's colleges and universities, as well as key agencies that controlled public welfare, unemployment compensation, and the politically sensitive workers' compensation system, where lawyer-legislators were free at the time to represent clients before quasi-judicial officers they had elected.

Legislative authority in the state was such that John West, a protégé of Senator Edgar Brown in his early days as Kershaw County senator, recalled a comment by his mentor: "John, I hope you understand that I've served under eight or nine governors, and I've got a responsibility to keep running this state so they can't foul it up. Governors come and governors go, but senators serve on."[36]

In the days before a partial form of cabinet government was enacted in 1993, in fact, there were characteristics of the system that seemed almost parliamentary in nature. Besides there being considerable power vested in the legislative branch, there was the sense that legislative experience was essential in the preparation of a good governor, and that there was something of an unofficial line of succession that often led through the lieutenant governor's office and included time spent under the tutelage of Speaker Blatt.

Blatt's "School of the Gavel"

"All of us came through his 'school,'" McNair recalled. "Fritz Hollings was one of his young protégés and I came along as another one. People would talk [and say], 'You're too close to Sol Blatt,' or 'you're under the influence of the Speaker,' and those were the kinds of things you had to live with and deal with, but being a friend of the Speaker made it possible to get a lot more things accomplished than had you always been in opposition to him."[37]

For his part, Blatt looked upon his "School of the Gavel" as a prerequisite for higher political service. "If you want to become involved in politics as a future," he said, "serving in the House is the first step, working hard on a committee, learning government. [Too] many fellows serve in the House [and] serve on a committee just to be a member of the committee. But they don't study; they don't study the legislation; they don't know what's in the bill; and they don't acquire a knowledge that would help them formulate policies that are good for the state." Blatt's formula was to "work hard in the House, don't speak too often, but when you speak, know what you're talking about. Have knowledge of the subjects you're discussing, and then sit down."[38]

McNair agreed. "I found that my having served in the House, served as a committee chairman, served on conference and free conference committees on the state appropriation bill was just like going to school." He recalled that it "was a particularly good experience" when he later "became governor very suddenly."[39]

Graduates of Blatt's school were some of South Carolina's political elite, and some of the more notable among them would move on to become U.S. senators, cabinet members, congressmen, governors, lieutenant governors, constitutional officers, mayors, state Supreme Court justices, Democrats, and Republicans. Until antigovernment populism became a successful political device in the 1990s, Blatt's entreaty to learn government was accepted as a reasonable expectation of public officeholders.

Bob McNair's first term in the House would be the only one in which he did not chair a standing committee. His appointment to the Judiciary Committee placed him under the chairmanship of Lionel Legge, a sixty-two-year-old Charleston attorney who would move to a seat on the South Carolina Supreme Court two years later. "He was an outstanding person," McNair recalled, "a good lawyer, did a good job of running the committee, and when I say running it, the committee chairman literally ran the committee then. The chairman pretty well decided what bills were going to come up and in what order they would be considered."[40]

McNair on a Fast Track

By the next term (1953–1954), McNair would be chairing his own committee—Labor, Commerce, and Industry—replacing Charlestonian T. Allen Legare, who retired from the House to fill the unexpired Senate term of Charleston senator O. T. Wallace and to launch a twelve-year Senate career. In taking over Legare's committee, McNair inherited an issue that would quickly thrust him onto center stage among some of the state's most important and most powerful economic interests—the textile industrialists.

If there was one thing that haunted South Carolina's leadership almost as much as racial trouble, it was the specter of organized labor and workers' uprisings. Some of it may have gone back to the plantation days, when the threat of organized slave uprisings worried the minority white population. Similarly, as tenant farmers, sharecroppers, and cotton-mill workers began to comprise large elements of the population, the state's political community worried about order and control and often sided with profit-minded management and owners in labor issues and other disputes with workers.

Like its southern neighbors, South Carolina had marketed its ample labor supply as a major part of the strategy of recruiting new industry. Farm workers fleeing the weevil-infested, worn-out fields of the state's outmoded agrarian system made good and trainable candidates for employment in the transplanted cotton mills from New England in the early decades of the century. As the state's industrialization efforts stepped up in the post World War II era, the same strategies were in place. South Carolina boosterism usually included terminology such as "our workers will give you a good day's work for a good day's pay," which could often serve as a code to mean nonunion labor.

Obscured was the bloody history of the state's labor disputes. The union-organizing efforts and their attendant violence in the 1930s earned not a line in the authoritative history of the state produced by David Duncan Wallace in 1947. As recently as 1995, the state's widely known Educational Television Network refused to air an account of the state's Depression-era labor uprisings, even though a respected labor historian, Tom Terrill of the University of South Carolina, was one of the program's consultants.[41]

Labor unrest came to the South as early as 1929, when "management forced workers to work much faster and reduced the number of workers without reducing the amount of work required or increasing pay [a practice called 'stretchouts']." Work stoppages resulted, the most memorable of which took place in Gastonia, North Carolina, in 1929. It attracted national attention, inspired a substantial body of national literature, resulted in several deaths, and, according to historians Terrill and William Cooper, ended in "emotional trials, miscarriages of justice, and the complete defeat of the union."[42]

Encouraged by labor sections of the National Recovery Act (NRA), which guaranteed workers in the state a minimum wage of $12 a week ($13 outside the South),[43] southern workers joined the United Textile Workers Union (UTW) by the thousands. As the textile economy hit a mid-Depression slump, however, production cutbacks of 25 percent in 1933 and 1934 cut deeply into guaranteed wages, and workers rebelled. "Infuriated textile workers from the South forced the UTW to call the General Strike of 1934 and by September 10 of that year, ten days after the strike was called, 43,000 South Carolina workers, about half the textile labor force in the state, were refusing to work, and half the state's mills were closed," according to the account provided by Terrill.[44]

The Legacy of Labor Violence

Violence erupted as militia and other security elements were called to quell the strikes and subsequent demonstrations, and in a precursor of the civil-rights-related tragedies of the 1960s, seven people were killed, six in a particularly brutal episode in Honea Path, near Anderson.[45] Ten thousand people attended the funerals in Honea Path, and it was the made-for-television account of that event—produced for a national public-television audience—that was rejected for showing to South Carolina audiences sixty years later by the state's ETV leadership.

Southern congressional leaders were arrayed against the worker-protective Fair Labor Standards Act, and South Carolinian "Cotton Ed" Smith was among the most vocal opponents, calling it an attempt "by human legislation to overcome the splendid gifts of God to the South."[46] Most southern political leaders were also solidly in favor of the postwar Taft-Hartley Bill (1947), a measure adopted over President Truman's veto[47] and generally acknowledged as giving "several advantages to companies resisting collective bargaining, including the right to file charges of unfair labor practices against unions."[48] It gave to southern management leaders the one prize above others they had sought. It empowered southern legislators to pass right-to-work laws, which would ban closed shops requiring all members of a company workforce to pay union dues once the union had won an organizing election.

If there was an assignment made to order to give a young, small-county legislator seeking statewide exposure, it was the management of the state's right-to-work bill, and the assignment fell to an eager Bob McNair as chairman of the Labor, Commerce, and Industry Committee. Like Br'er Rabbit of southern tales, he recalled, "I was put into the briar patches in a hurry and given a difficult assignment."[49]

The legislation gave McNair statewide exposure for the first time and tested his developing political skills. It also challenged his ability to moderate a dispute between two groups important to his electoral base—the corporate community and organized labor. "The big battle was to be fair to all sides and to give everybody an opportunity to be heard," he recalled. "I felt good coming out of that with the friendship of labor. I don't know that I had their strong support, but I had their friendship and respect, and in later years, when I got into statewide politics, I think that's one of the things they would say: 'We didn't always agree with him, and he certainly didn't always support the things we wanted, but he was always extremely fair and gave us a full opportunity to present our position.'"[50]

A Political Score with "Right-to-Work"

If McNair salvaged some credibility with labor leaders in the right-to-work experience, however, it was with corporate executives and industrial developers that he scored the biggest hit. Organizations such as the State Chamber of Commerce, and the Textile Manufacturers' Association, powerful forces among the state's anti-union institutions, began to pay attention to the Allendale attorney and to regard him as a reliable ally.

Between 1947 and 1954, every southern state except Kentucky and Oklahoma passed right-to-work laws, believing that such open-shop statutes sent a clear message to management that the South was, indeed, a good place to do business. "Southern development officials lost no time in incorporating their right-to-work statutes into their professional arsenals," author James C. Cobb has written, referring to claims in Arkansas and Mississippi about the relationship between economic growth and open-shop labor laws.[51]

Typical of such promotional claims was that of Daniel International Construction Corporation, the Greenville-based construction giant whose longstanding chairman, Charles E. Daniel, was a major force behind South Carolina's industrial expansion. In a speech to his hometown Elberton, Georgia, Chamber of Commerce in the mid-1950s, Daniel said: "we [in the South] are eager to produce; eager to give a fair day's work for a fair day's pay because few of us—white or Negro—ever had the real opportunity before to produce and earn fair wages. Our working people do their own thinking. Consequently, it is no accident that the 11 states of the old Confederacy have all passed right-to-work laws—laws fundamental to the Southern philosophy that, while a man may join a union if he wishes, there is no power on earth that should force him to do so before he can get a job, or hold a job, and make a living for himself and his family. To do so is to destroy freedom, and the South is a great believer in freedom of choice."[52]

In so many words, Daniel articulated what would become a credo for southern economic development, promoting the right-to-work as a part of a solemn southern heritage linked to the eleven states of the Confederacy and acknowledging as an almost parenthetical assumption that henceforth the term *worker* applied to white and black, male and female alike.

Charles Daniel and a Dictum of Racial Enlightenment

Daniel became even more explicit in a speech in Bill Rhodes's rural home county of Hampton. As Daniel's biographers, "Red" Canup and Bill Workman, wrote,

"On one controversial issue, Daniel shows outspoken liberalism. . . . At a festival in the town of Hampton, he told startled listeners, 'The desegregation issue cannot continue to be hidden behind the door. . . . We have a definite obligation to increase the productivity of our Negro citizens, to provide them with good jobs at good wages and to continue to assure them of fair treatment. By raising their educational and economic status, we would raise the economy of the whole state.'"[53]

In the emerging dawn of post–World War II South Carolina, the voices of industrial moguls such as Daniel were countering some of the race-centered rhetoric of earlier decades and were challenging some of the state's long-held assumptions. Fair treatment and good jobs for Negroes, he was saying, "would raise the economy of the whole state." History and politics aside, racial equality was simply good business, leaders were beginning to contend.

The 1950s and 1960s were decades in which South Carolina was enthralled with the energy and excitement of industrial development. The Daniel Company itself, Daniel's biographers have estimated, was responsible for influencing the location of 250 major industrial plants in South Carolina and 400 throughout the twelve southern states where the company operated.[54] With that kind of record, it was only natural that he and his industrial colleagues would merit the close attention of public leaders, whatever their political stripe. In the years ahead, right-to-work laws and racial peace would be the company line from South Carolina's corporate community. And Bob McNair would be an increasingly prominent figure in that emerging strategy.

It was late in the 1954 legislative session—McNair's second term in the House—that the *Brown v. Board of Education* ruling was issued by the Supreme Court. Eight-column banner headlines in the *State* newspaper of May 18, 1954, proclaimed, "Supreme Court Outlaws School Segregation." The headline also speculated, "Long Delay Seen before Decision in Effect."[55]

It was correct in both instances. The Court, some of whose members had been colleagues of Byrnes when he served on the Supreme Court for sixteen months in 1941 and 1942, rendered his Education Revolution useless as a tool against school desegregation, addressing in some specificity the question of equal facilities.

In *Brown* the Court opined,

> We come then to the question presented: Does segregation of children in public schools solely on the basis of race, even though the physical facilities and other "tangible" factors may be equal, deprive the children of the minority group of equal educational opportunities? We believe that it does.
>
> To separate [black students] from others of similar age and qualifications solely because of their race generates a feeling of inferiority as to their status in the community that may affect their hearts and minds in a way unlikely ever to be undone.[56]

In so many words, the decision took away the basis on which much of South Carolina's political order rested. From Ben Tillman to Olin Johnston and Strom Thurmond, racial segregation was not only the law of the land, as validated by *Plessy* and the 1896 constitution, it was the bedrock of the racially imbalanced principle on which public policy was based. In its absence, the traditional political dynamic of the South was altered and destabilized, and the ensuing uncertainty created widely varying responses and strategies. In South Carolina, where many were shocked that their seemingly integration-proof strategy had failed, however, the disappointment among white leaders was measured and tempered, particularly as compared with those of other states.

Postwar South Carolina was a place where the themes of the past were still present and powerful. The *Brown* decision reached deeply into the traditional philosophical fabric of the state and became an issue of enduring significance to the state's political makeup. But by then, there were other themes competing for attention and support. Unlike the 1920s and the 1930s, when the state either took a laissez-faire attitude toward the economic condition of its citizens or waited begrudgingly for federal assistance, postwar South Carolina accepted economic well-being as a legitimate part of the political agenda of the state.

Racial politics were still appealing to many South Carolinians, but in the atmosphere of postwar court rulings, the zeal of economic growth, and the open-mindedness of returning World War II veterans, race was no longer a political imperative in South Carolina. There were options and shadings to the state's strategies, and in the fluidity of racial politics, there were variables and room for negotiation. In that setting, there were no immediate answers or solutions to the state's racial dilemmas. But there was maneuvering room in which skilled negotiators and consensus-builders could find strategies and steer midstream courses. Bob McNair's political star was on the rise as the state pondered the promise and the uncertainty of its future.

5

A Circuitous Route to the Governor's Office

The big news around the State House in 1955 was that Solomon Blatt might step down as Speaker of the House and run for election to the S.C. Supreme Court. Fifty-nine years old and a veteran of fourteen years as the House leader, Blatt was making it known that he would be a candidate in 1956 for the associate justice seat to be vacated by Taylor H. Stukes, who was expected to be elected chief justice.

The reports set off shock waves across the state. South Carolinians had grown accustomed to stability in their political leadership and Blatt, the Barnwell attorney who was first elected to the House in 1933, was a part of it. Blatt had served two stints as Speaker, 1935–1947 and 1951–1955. His iron rule of the House gave comfort, particularly to those business leaders who were clamoring for economic development and were worried about things like fiscal responsibility of government and labor unions. Blatt, as they had seen in stubborn budget showdowns and in the fight for right-to-work legislation in 1954, was their champion.

The longtime Speaker had actually toyed with the idea of running for the Supreme Court two years earlier when the resignation of Associate Justice Edward L. Fishburne in 1953 created a vacancy. According to biographer John K. Cauthen, Blatt considered the Supreme Court as "the highest honor that can come to a lawyer" and was giving the matter "my most serious consideration."[1]

In South Carolina, state judges, including Supreme Court justices, are elected by the General Assembly. Given Blatt's long-standing power in the legislature, his election to the high court would have been considered something of a given. Cauthen wrote,

Although many people had promised their support to the Speaker in running for the Supreme Court . . . perhaps an even larger number of friends, legislators, businessmen [including Cauthen and his powerful textile colleagues], farm leaders and others . . . urged Blatt to sacrifice the honor and sanctuary of the Supreme Court for what they regarded as the more vital service in continuing as Speaker at this critical stage of South Carolina's forward surge in economic development.

Blatt chose not to run on that occasion, saying, "I am happy in my position as a practicing lawyer. After careful consideration of all factors involved I have come to the conclusion that I will not be a candidate for the present vacancy."[2]

Two years later, however, his intentions to seek a Supreme Court seat were judged to be serious enough to set off a series of moves within House circles to fill the prospective void of Blatt's presence at the top of the chain of command. Tracy Gaines, a legislative veteran serving his eighth term from Spartanburg County, had been elected Speaker pro tempore earlier that year. He announced his plans to run for Speaker to replace Blatt.

McNair, as Blatt's protégé, also began to take soundings about his own chances to assume the Speaker's robe should Blatt discard it. The soundings were encouraging, and McNair recalled, "I was able to put together with Rex Carter, who was from Greenville, something of an upstate / big county – lower state / small county combination. The two of us felt very firmly that we both had enough votes for me to be elected Speaker and for him to be elected Speaker pro tempore."[3]

Then came Blatt's second withdrawal from contention for the Supreme Court. "I think Mr. Blatt had been such a stabilizing influence in this state . . . strong fiscal responsibility, always very pro-business . . . that they [business leaders] felt very comfortable with him," McNair said. Blatt worried, too, that he would miss the rough-and-tumble legislative life in favor of what he might have viewed as a more cloistered life on the bench. "I think it was the fact that he was undecided, too. . . . He had some strong questions in his mind whether he wanted to go on the Supreme Court. Mr. Blatt like[d] his friends. He like[d] people. It began to weigh on him that on the Supreme Court you lived a more isolated life, and you couldn't really be with your friends. It would not be active. It would not be the kind of involvement that he had enjoyed in the House, and thus he decided that just wasn't for him."[4]

Looking Statewide from a Small-County Base

For McNair, Blatt's decision foretold his own inclination, as well. It was "probably the same kind of decision I made when I opted not . . . to seek a judgeship and not ever to have any interest in being a judge. I just never felt that was my thing. I never felt my personality and disposition and temperament . . . suited that."[5]

For the moment in 1955, however, McNair was discovering that his personality and disposition were suited to something new in his political career, a statewide race. The brief campaign for Speaker had whetted his appetite for bigger things and had given him reason to believe that a House member from a small, lower-Savannah River county could have statewide ambitions. "Being from Allendale, one of the three smallest [counties]," he said, "you just didn't get into statewide politics. Our area had the fewest people of any section of South Carolina. You had all the odds—all the political odds—against you. I just wasn't sure that somebody from one of the three smallest counties could get elected to statewide office."[6]

Hollings's vaulting from the Speaker pro tempore of the House into a statewide race for lieutenant governor in 1954 and governor in 1958 cleared up at least two of McNair's misgivings. He witnessed that rarity of twentieth-century South Carolina —a lowcountry governor—and he also saw a House member move directly into a successful statewide race. Even so, McNair viewed things cautiously, noting that Hollings had come from Charleston with a base of support from a big population center. The arithmetic was undeniable: in 1960, Allendale County had a population of 11,362; Charleston County totaled 216,382.

For the short-term future, however, the flurry of activity in the House of Representatives over Speaker Blatt's decision about running for the Supreme Court in 1955 left at least one victim and one clear winner. Once Blatt decided not to run for the Supreme Court, McNair withdrew and remained chair of the Judiciary Committee. Gaines, however, chose to run for Speaker pro tempore against Rex Carter, and with McNair and colleagues supporting Carter, Gaines lost by a large margin.

The immediate winner in all of it was Carter, a young Greenville attorney who was serving his second term in the House in 1955. The experience would launch for Carter an extended career of House leadership, serving under Blatt as Speaker pro tempore from 1957 until 1973, getting serious consideration for a lieutenant governor's race in 1966, and eventually succeeding Blatt to serve four terms as Speaker.

Brown v. Board of Education and Its Aftermath

For the moment, things returned to normal within the hierarchy of the House, but things were far from normal as the state moved through the last half of the decade of the 1950s. Tension and recrimination in the wake of *Brown v. Board of Education* were stirring public anxiety, and black pressure for the implementation of the desegregation order began to build almost immediately. Within a year after the issuance of the decision, a petition signed by fifty-seven black parents in Orangeburg called on the white school board in 1955 to transfer their children to white schools.[7]

In the furor that followed, "more than half the petitioners withdrew their names as the result of pressures which were chiefly economic, including loss of jobs, termination of loans, denial of credit, and refusal of white banks and wholesalers to do business with the petitioners," according to historian I. A. Newby. Blacks responded with a boycott, and students at South Carolina State joined in, prompting the legislature "to authorize an investigation of NAACP activities at the college, and [to] direct the State Law Enforcement Division to place the campus under surveillance."[8]

The administration of the college clamped down on protesting students and faculty, and in the ensuing months of boycott and counter-boycott, "both sides grew weary of it, and each eased its position somewhat. The boycott dissipated, but the grievances which produced it remained."[9] By 1959, frustrated that the decision had lain unenforced for five years, Clarendon County blacks resumed their fight. They filed petitions in August of that year for the reassignment of seventy-six black students to all-white schools, an exercise that was turned down but that provoked promises from the NAACP at its annual meeting for action "elsewhere in the state to break down racial barriers."[10]

Across South Carolina, white citizens' councils were organized to carry on the fight for segregated public schools. Historian Ernest Lander reported, "In some cases . . . the citizens' councils used means of doubtful legality, all of which gave encouragement to the more radical Ku Klux Klan. Threats, intimidation, and outright violence broke out."[11]

Reverend J. A. DeLaine, the black minister at the heart of the Clarendon County suit that led to *Briggs* and *Brown,* had his home and church burned in 1955 and fled the state to escape arrest after he fired from his home on a carload of white men. Several white ministers relinquished their pulpits under pressure, and *Florence Morning News* editor Jack O'Dowd, whose paper advocated compliance with *Brown,* left the state after he was "subjected to threats and attempts to force his car off the road." "Other incidents," according to Lander, "included the beating of a Greenville Negro, for which confessed Klansmen were sentenced to prison, and the bombing of a Gaffney physician's home, apparently because his wife spoke openly for moderation."[12]

For its part, the South Carolina General Assembly was an ever-present force for racial intolerance. In its "Segregation Session" of 1956, the legislature authorized the closing of schools to avoid integration and even empowered sheriffs to transfer pupils from one school to another "to prevent riots or trouble."[13] The General Assembly also saw fit to close Edisto State Park in response to a lawsuit seeking to open it to blacks, a step that would eventually lead to the closing of all South Carolina state parks in the 1960s. And, to make matters even more divisive between the races, the legislature made it unlawful for any state employee to be a member of the NAACP.[14]

The Advent of Industrial Recruitment

For all its racial regression of the 1950s, however, South Carolina was beginning to look ahead on at least one front. Starting with Governor James F. Byrnes, the state was examining its economic condition and exploring potential strategies for growth, particularly with the recruitment of new industry. Although later governors considered economic development among their more prominent responsibilities, Byrnes, in fact, found it something of a curiosity. "It was surprising that I should be called upon to give so much time to the effort to obtain industries for the state," he wrote. "But it was rewarding. A prudent businessman moving a plant for any reason makes a careful survey before deciding on a new location. I recall working with one prospect for three years before he reached a decision. In fact, he did not actually start construction until my term had expired. This effort to 'sell' the state as the best place for the location of an industry provided some interesting experiences."[15]

As Byrnes was leaving office in 1955, South Carolina was still dominated by the textile industry. More than one in every two industrial jobs in the state was in a textile mill, and by 1957 textiles accounted for almost $2 billion of production in the state and more than 130,000 jobs. The state was lagging behind its neighbors in the recruitment of new industry, and one report noted that among the southern states, North Carolina and Georgia had each acquired more than $195 million in new industry in 1957, while South Carolina's new acquisitions amounted to some $114.7 million, trailed only by Arkansas and Mississippi.[16]

Even so, the state was beginning to sample the taste of economic prosperity. Using some of the techniques developed in prewar Mississippi to lure industry with tax incentives, South Carolina had by 1955 attracted a handful of new industries, which represented a breakthrough of sorts in helping the state move away from its dependence on textiles. Notable among them were the $75-million DuPont Orlon plant on the Wateree River near Camden and the $60-million Celanese synthetic fiber plant on the Catawba River at Rock Hill. In 1955 alone, historian Lander reported, "25 new factories were begun, each of whose investment was $1,000,000 or greater or whose working force was 100 or more."[17] "Dwarfing all else," he noted, "was the Atomic Energy Commission's gigantic plant at Aiken. This enterprise alone cost over $1.4 billion . . . [and] in 1956, it was employing 8,500 workers."[18]

Lander contended that South Carolina had five major inducements in attracting new industry: (1) a friendly reception from business-minded governors and a state policy favorable to new industry;[19] (2) ample natural resources, including timber, stone, clay, gravel, and water; (3) a plentiful supply of cheap labor and well-recognized antilabor sentiments; (4) an adequate supply of power including hydroelectric plants and steam-generating electric plants; and (5) an improving system of transportation and communication, including major overhauls at the port of Charleston.[20]

Death of "King Cotton"

It was, in short, a far cry from the modest statement of Bernard Baruch three decades earlier urging only the diversification of crops to bolster the state's economy.[21] By the late 1950s, agriculture was in retreat as a major sustainer of South

Carolina's economy. "King Cotton," according to Lander, was in "his death throes,"[22] and cotton production had dropped from an annual average of 824,000 bales during the Depression decade of the 1930s to around 300,000 bales in 1958. Total farms were down from 157, 931 in 1930 to 124,203 in 1954, and total farm acreage was down from 4.9 million acres in 1940 to 3.1 million acres in 1958.[23]

All that made for fresh, new political fields to plow for ambitious young public figures, particularly for those with an emerging reputation for probusiness sentiments. For the World War II generation of political leaders in South Carolina, economic development was the made-to-order issue. It cast the newcomers as solid political progressives and gave them a new foundation from which topics—in particular, public education—could be viewed. While there was an element of the state's leadership espousing the termination of public education for racial considerations, others had a new platform from which to neutralize race as an issue and from which to view public education in its more utilitarian role as part of the emerging package for an economically aggressive South Carolina.

It proved to be the perfect political forum for Bob McNair. Although he was neither the first nor the only voice articulating that message, he was beginning to acquire some special credentials around the legislative halls. McNair had stood shoulder-to-shoulder with Blatt on the litmus-test business issue of the 1950s, the right-to-work law. And it was McNair, after all, who had been anointed by Blatt to be his successor as Speaker in 1955. Such an endorsement opened doors and created credibility, and it was no coincidence that McNair shortly began to attract attention from some of the same forces that had persuaded Blatt to remain as Speaker. In McNair, they were seeing a Blatt protégé who was twenty-seven years younger than the Speaker and without Blatt's rough edges.

McNair was emerging as a prominent political newcomer who did not have a lot of political baggage. He moved easily among the various political factions and seemed comfortable with all of them. It was hard to assign him a place in either the political left or right, and he seemed equally at home in most elements of the traditional South Carolina rivalries: upcountry versus lowcountry and big county versus small county. If it was difficult to find his philosophical center at times, however, it was not difficult to find his tactical center. As issues, ideology, and regional and factional interests carved the state up into feuding political camps, McNair was more likely to be working the aisles of the legislative chambers in search of a settlement rather than striding to the podium to extol opinions and dogma. He was finding among his colleagues that "compromising is the strongest quality they have . . . quite often, when we compromised, we did it the way it should have been done and the best way."[24]

Capturing Business Attention

McNair became a particular favorite among business interests hoping to move the state toward a more expansive economic future. They were neither looking for ideologues who could stir public passion, nor were they advocating a radical boom-town approach that could disrupt some of the state's essentially cautious financial philosophies. They were looking for accelerated gradualism, moderate, controlled change at a pace that could close the gap between South Carolina and the rest of the nation but still be absorbed within the norms and tolerances of the state's own sense of comfort. In McNair, they found a man who seemed suited to the times. Amid the rancor and combat of legislative fights, he seemed to keep his head and keep things moving toward settlement. His ideologies sometimes seemed obscured by his sense of political pragmatism, which impressed those who were paying more attention to information contained in legislative journals than to headlines in the daily newspapers.

The question then became how quickly the new prospect should move into the statewide political arena. Some pushed for an early arrival.

Things had destabilized somewhat within the Democratic ranks and the unofficial order of succession seemed to be growing looser. George Bell Timmer-man Jr. had come out of World War II to serve two terms as lieutenant governor (1946–1954) and moved on to the governorship in 1954, to be succeeded as lieu-tenant governor by Hollings. As things began to shape up for the 1958 contests, Hollings's candidacy for governor was known, and he would be pitted against popular University of South Carolina president Donald Russell, a Byrnes protégé who was something of a political neophyte. Among those emerging as prospects for lieutenant governor was Burnet Maybank Jr., son of the popular former gover-nor and U.S. senator from Charleston, who as a legislator had served three terms with McNair in the House. From all the postwar shuffling, it was becoming evi-dent that service in the S.C. Senate was no longer a leading prerequisite for state-wide recognition. Candidates for lieutenant governor and governor were coming from a variety of backgrounds—Thurmond from military service and a judgeship, Byrnes out of retirement, Timmerman out of military service, and Hollings and Maybank directly from the House.

There was some talk, in fact, of a McNair candidacy for lieutenant governor in 1958 against Maybank, and some balloons were floated. Successes and popularity within South Carolina's legislative and political community had elevated the ambitions of the small-town attorney who had once believed his career would never go beyond the local level. For the first time, statewide office seemed more than a distant ambition for McNair; it was a possibility that was being openly dis-cussed and suggested by some of the state's business and political leaders.

Then reality set in. It was one thing to work the aisles of the House chamber lining up votes for the Speaker's position; it was another thing to stump the state in quest of the tens of thousands of popular votes it would take to gain statewide office. It was also one thing for Fritz Hollings to step into a statewide race for lieutenant governor in 1954 from a traditional population and political base like

Charleston and another thing for a candidate from one of the state's smallest counties, Allendale. For all the appeal that statewide office held for the energetic young legislator, the decision realistically boiled down to two essential components: name recognition and money. Outside the corridors of the State House and the circles of influential insiders, McNair had enjoyed little public exposure. And aside from the few hundreds of dollars it took to run for the House from Allendale, McNair had little in the way of a political war chest and had never raised the big money it took for a statewide contest.

Resisting an Early Ambition

There were conversations and some public speculation. There was also some stern evaluation of prospects and certain political realities. One such assessment came from a meeting in Speaker Blatt's office in Barnwell, McNair recalled. The meeting included statewide leaders such as John Cauthen of the Textile Manufacturers, Hugh Agnew of the Farm Bureau, John Floyd of the State Chamber of Commerce, and Walter L. "Buck" Edwards of Southern Bell. Others, McNair said, were "several of my good friends from Allendale, a banker and a couple of large farmers and . . . some of the political leaders from the House."[25]

Speaker Blatt also recalled the meeting: "one afternoon we had about . . . twelve, or fifteen, sixteen fellows meet here in my office. They were pushing Bob to run, and we talked about everything. . . . I said, 'Well, gentlemen, the first thing let me ask you is, it's going to cost money. . . . You're going to have to have some money and I would not run for Lieutenant Governor . . . until you first put fifty thousand dollars on the barrelhead. [You'll get] promises, but a promise is no good for money in a political campaign. . . . You can't run unless you've got the money and you can't run on pledges. You've got to run on cash.'"[26]

McNair had ambitions, but he was not given to gambling, and this one was beginning to look like a long shot. "I toyed with the idea," he said, "[but] we concluded that it was not the time to run and that I should not entertain the idea further at that time." The seed had been planted, however, and the process of statewide exposure had begun. "Because of the mention of my name in 1958, the possibility of my candidacy continued to be in the forefront of those who were thinking about the office, or considering a campaign."[27]

Building a power base from tiny Allendale, however, would take what amounted to a four-year campaign across the state. The campaign, he said, would be "a physical endurance test."

> I had many, many obstacles, [and] there were more obstacles than just name recognition. The lack of name recognition is always a shock to anybody who gets into politics, and thinks he has been in the public eye. Coming from one of the three smallest counties in the state, I had no big voter base. I worked

hard in Charleston and Richland and Greenville and Spartanburg and many other areas like them—Florence and Anderson—for example. I targeted some of those larger areas and spent a lot of extra time there to try to get recognition and to get voter support from those areas.[28]

Along the way, he recalled speaking to groups that ranged from automobile dealers to education groups, and there was a particular interest in civic clubs. "I did not decline the chance to speak to a civic club luncheon meeting, and I believe I spoke to almost every one of them in South Carolina on at least one occasion."[29]

His business-oriented backers were exposing McNair to a wide range of audiences. McNair recalled that "all of the support of the legislature and business and agricultural leaders . . . together with the backing of the small business people, who then worked with the State Chamber of Commerce . . . gave me a very broad political base."[30] McNair was also getting "almost unanimous support" from fellow House members, who had been ready to elect him their Speaker only a few years earlier. "The House members," he said, "were not only for me, [they] actively promoted me back home and had me attend functions all around the state. House members introduced me and, in the early stages, many of them endorsed my candidacy."[31] That kind of support tapped into the organized political elements at the local level, the so-called courthouse crowd.

Although Americans were seeing the early stages of modern political techniques in the early 1960s—innovations such as high-profile media campaigns and televised debates between presidential candidates Richard Nixon and John Kennedy —McNair remained essentially a practitioner of the "friends and neighbors" politics he had learned and cultivated in the small county settings of Berkeley and Allendale Counties. For him, South Carolina was a patchwork of hundreds of communities, crossroads, neighborhoods, mill gates, main streets, and shopping centers where voters were influenced by personal contact, word-of-mouth impressions, and local tickets as pieced together by the political power brokers. It was old-fashioned "shoe leather" campaigning, a throwback to the state's rural and political past. "Local support was the key to the Lieutenant Governor's race," McNair said. "Most of the time, nobody running . . . was even known in most of the state. If somebody who was respected in the community was strongly for you, you really did well, because that is the way people would normally make up their minds."[32]

While McNair was selling himself to local political leaders with the same one-on-one style that had won him a leadership role in the House, he was also conveying a message that was essentially a nonthreatening one, and one that gave comfort to his business backers. "The issues focused on the need for an aggressive economic development program in South Carolina," he said. "The themes were improved capital investment, more jobs, and better education. All of those actually work together."

There also began to be injected into the McNair political agenda a lesson from his earliest days in Hell Hole Swamp and Macedonia School, a lesson that there was a direct linkage between public schools and economic success. "I especially sought a recognition that we really had to do something broader in public education than we were doing," McNair said. "We could not continue just to go along the same way we had in the past, that we had to do something with early childhood education and that we had to do something about the dropout rate." Campaign themes, he recalled, were economic development and more jobs. "Since I came from an agricultural area," he added, "I talked about and focused attention on agriculture, as well."[33]

1962: McNair Runs for Lieutenant Governor

Things went well, and by 1962, a strategy meeting of McNair backers similar to the 1958 gathering was convened. This time the outcome was different. "We went through the same exercises," McNair recalled, "and generally decided to go forward."[34]

South Carolina's political sands had shifted again by then, particularly with regard to Burnet Maybank Jr. The son of former governor and U.S. senator Burnet Maybank Sr., the younger Maybank had been elected lieutenant governor in 1958 by a comfortable 35,000-vote margin. At age thirty-six, two years younger than his father's age when he became governor nineteen years earlier, Burnet Jr. seemed destined to follow his father's path. But questions were being raised about his political potential, and, McNair said, "It became obvious that Burnet was going to have trouble getting elected [Governor]. There were questions about his leadership ability [and] even members of the General Assembly showed some real concern . . . and began to talk to me." McNair's business backers were among those "concerned about the leadership of the state for the next four years [who] strongly persuaded me not to commit myself to the Lieutenant Governor's race unalterably. [They wanted me] to stay open and flexible because it may well have developed that I should go ahead and take the chance and run for Governor in 1962."[35]

Such speculation heightened McNair's status and confidence as an emerging leader in the state's political community. "In those days, it would have been a very big step and one that people did not normally take. I was apprehensive about it [and] I continued to focus on the Lieutenant Governor's race. However, I did begin to look at the governorship . . . you could not withstand it, you were flattered, so you began to look at the opportunity."

The shift in attention to the governor's race was almost a disastrous one. It interrupted the momentum of the campaign, created indecision among advisers, and sent an unfriendly message to Maybank supporters, some of whom had been in the McNair camp for lieutenant governor. "That caused some of Burnet Maybank's close friends, notably Allen Legare [the state senator from Charleston], who had been a strong supporter of mine, to get offended. He and a few others . . . got very upset with me because I was toying with the idea of running against Burnet for Governor. So they started looking actively for somebody to run for Lieutenant Governor to force me to make a decision."[36]

Legare, whose decision to run for the Senate in 1953 had opened the door for McNair to become chairman of the House Labor, Commerce, and Industry Committee, was part of a small but influential group of state senators who also owned property on Kiawah Island, then an undeveloped sea island that contained only one small enclave of modest houses. Other members of the Kiawah group were John West, then a state senator from Kershaw County; Earle Morris, House member from Pickens County; John Martin, state senator from Fairfield County; and Marshall Parker of Oconee County, serving his first term in the Senate.

Parker, described by McNair as a "very good Senator [who] moved very quickly in the Senate and . . . had strong support from the business community also," was the choice of the group, and Kiawah friends West and Legare agreed to run his campaign. The Parker campaign, in fact, became so quickly organized that he beat McNair to the punch in announcing his candidacy. "By holding back," McNair recalled, "I sort of generated opposition . . . I had to announce later on, and that gave him [Parker] something of a head start."[37]

A Race with Long-Term Impact

What ensued was what McNair called "one of the toughest races for Lieutenant Governor . . . that has been run in this state," and one that drew political lines of demarcation within Democratic Party circles for some years to come. Parker, with the support of upcountry industrialists Charles Daniel and Roger Milliken, quickly put together a campaign managed by Crawford Cook, a newsman who left his post at United Press International to accept the position. Cook later recalled:

> John West came to me one day and said, "Crawford, we want you to run Marshall's campaign for Lieutenant Governor." I said, "Well, what am I going to do, John, if Marshall doesn't win? I have a wife and two kids. I have to make money."
>
> He said, "Oh, we'll find something." So to show you how irresponsible I was, I ended up doing the damned thing. When the campaign was over, I actually got a job with the state Municipal Association as their legislative representative and their Vice President for Public Relations.[38]

"Crawford Cook masterminded the campaign," McNair said, "[and] he is now nationally recognized as a campaign professional. Although it was his first real political venture, Crawford was very tough. They played . . . hardball politics . . .

[and] dealt in a hard-nosed way and organized extremely well. We found ourselves in a dogfight that we had not anticipated."[39]

Political campaigns in 1960s South Carolina were not fought in television debates or large-scale media campaigns, particularly in a traditionally low-profile race such as that for lieutenant governor. More often, they were fights waged between population centers, regions of the state, or political factions. With McNair and Parker, however, most of the traditional assumptions did not apply.

Neither had much of a population base. Parker's home county of Oconee had a population of around forty thousand, much larger than Allendale but small compared to other significant metropolitan areas such as Richland, Greenville, and Charleston. For that reason, both candidates worked each other's territory, and neither could lay claim to a regional edge. "Both of us tried to avoid the Upstate/Lower State thing," McNair said, "because our support bases were partly reversed. I had strong support up in the Greenville-Spartanburg area and in his home area. He felt that he had Charleston and strong support down in that area."[40]

One of the most intriguing fights, in fact, took place in Charleston, where McNair had hoped his Berkeley County upbringing would tilt the nearby county in his direction. He realized early, however, that Parker's key ally, Charleston attorney Legare, was a member in good standing of the so-called Broad Street Gang, a political mechanism named for Charleston's elite business and law-firm address, and one that traditionally had the city's strongest political ticket. Parker, it quickly became clear to McNair, was the Broad Street choice. "Well, I almost panicked," McNair said, "because I was familiar with Charleston County politics."[41]

Taking on Broad Street in Charleston

The Allendale candidate was not ready to concede the area, however, and he adopted two strategies: (1) break up the Broad Street Gang and (2) build an anti–Broad Street organization of his own. For the first part, he solicited his friend from the old-time Hell Hole Swamp Gang, L. Mendel Rivers, by then serving his eleventh term in the United States Congress and chairing the House Armed Services Committee, to make an incursion into the Broad Street group. Rivers, himself a member in good standing with the Broad Street powers, made known his support of McNair in the lieutenant governor's race, and he was joined by other influential members, including Hugh Lane Sr., president of C&S National Bank; realtor Joe Riley, father of mayor-to-be Joe Riley Jr.; labor leader Cecil Clay; contractor Bob Russell; North Charleston businessman Allen Carter; developer J. C. Long; Y. W. Scarborough; and educator Gordon Garrett, a member of an informal and improbable assemblage of public-school administrators that came to be known as "The Dirty Dozen." "We ended up putting together the first non–Broad Street gang," McNair recalled. "The [McNair] committee put ads in the paper with fifty names of just about everybody that you would want in Charleston . . . and that let everybody down there know that I had the support. Parker did not."

It was the Hell Hole Swamp Gang, or Dirty Dozen, versus the Broad Street Gang, and the outcome, McNair believed, "broke up the Broad Street gang." It also introduced into Charleston politics a significant business element from industrial North Charleston, including Allen Carter, a feisty realtor who later served two terms in the S.C. Senate. "Allen Carter, who had never been active in politics in the North Area," McNair said, "got out and worked harder for me than he ever worked for himself. [He] decided, like others, that it was time for the people to have a voice [and] they ended up . . . two years later, running a separate group and winning against the Broad Street crowd."[42]

Charleston was one of the few places, in fact, where McNair did not have the inside track with the local political leadership from the beginning. His years of cultivating fellow legislators and local business and political leadership left him with a distinct advantage with the courthouse crowd, and it was a major and deliberate part of his overall campaign strategy. "We worked very hard to get the courthouse crowd . . . [and] I think we had almost unanimous support. It was . . . based on my time in the legislature and my work with them on legislative reform and the other things you needed to do."[43] The courthouse crowd never had a precise definition, but the term generally applied to governmental functionaries, political bosses, and officeholders at the local level. For McNair, it meant everything from mayors to probate judges to funeral-home directors to automobile dealers to good friends and their families.[44]

Politics before Television Campaigning

It was strictly a down-home affair, and probably one of the last such personal campaigns South Carolina would see in a major statewide race. Red-white-and-blue-clad "McNair Girls" from Allendale—housewives and young mothers who were friends of Josephine McNair and high school friends of the McNair daughters—fanned out across the state as goodwill ambassadors and gained what McNair called "more name recognition than anything else at the time. They went into every small town, went up and down every street, and went into every shopping center and covered the towns completely."[45]

While McNair was winning votes two and three at a time, Parker's campaign was going for high media exposure, at least what passed for high media exposure in the low-budget, low-technology days of the 1960s. In the insider language of the twenty-first century, McNair was practicing "retail" politics, Parker the "wholesale" strategy. Cook recalled,

> We did anything we could do to get Marshall's name in front of the people. A
> day didn't go by that I didn't put out a press release. One of the things that I

learned at UPI was about all the news cycle, when the best times to file releases were, which radio stations had real news activities and which ones had news directors who came in at various times. So I was really able to maximize free press.[46]

With its early start, the Parker organization also gained a quick edge on what was then a major campaign commodity—billboards. "We spent more money on billboards than anything else," Cook recalled. "We put billboards in every nook and cranny in the state. It raised his [Parker's] name recognition very quickly."[47]

"He had the state plastered with billboards," McNair said. "I could not—literally could not—get a billboard and had trouble getting slots on television because they had absorbed what was available."[48] The McNair camp countered with an innovation. "Somebody gave me a bunch of plywood, and we had someone else fix us up some signs to put on a sheet of plywood. We put up plywood all over South Carolina, and it attracted a lot of attention. I think I got more recognition because of my plywood billboards than I would have gotten had we had the regular, huge ones."[49]

The campaign lurched along largely as a contest of personalities and name recognition, the down-home style of McNair against the media orientation of the Parker campaign. "As it got down to the bottom line," McNair said, "there were issues about who could do the best job." There were also emerging anxieties about the outcome, and while instruments such as polling were little used and were imprecise for measuring or predicting outcomes in the 1960s, there was a sense that things were close and that it might all boil down to the last month of campaigning.

Cook, in fact, believed that Parker and McNair were even as they headed into the final month. "We actually caught Bob McNair," he said. "In about the last three or four weeks of that race we had about pulled even."[50]

That's when things got hot. Thundering down the homestretch, both candidates were looking for something that might give them a last-minute edge. The contest, which had been waged for name recognition on billboards and at mill gates and shopping malls, was about to gain some fire and substance as election day neared. Both candidates set their sights on the annual meeting of the state's Municipal Association in Myrtle Beach as offering that opportunity.

Like most other entities of local government, South Carolina cities were creatures of the state and were financially dependent on shared state revenues, called kickbacks, for much of their operating funds. In the economically meager 1960s, much of South Carolina's state spending was going into public education, and cities were feeling the pinch of urban growth without commensurate revenue to expand services to accommodate that growth. Because of his strength with the courthouse crowd and because of cities' dependence on friendly legislators, the Municipal Association was considered a stronghold of McNair support.

Sales-Tax Increase as a Campaign Issue

Knowing of McNair's popularity with municipal leaders, Parker sought to make some inroads into the McNair fortress and addressed himself to the cities' financial woes. Along the way, he made reference in a friendly and supportive way to a proposed one-cent sales tax. From that point on, stories differ as to what he actually said. There was no news coverage the next day, and because each candidate was invited to address the conference separately, neither heard directly what the other said. According to McNair, "He was trying so hard to get their support that it got to him. . . . He had a little tendency to get carried away sometimes anyway and go overboard on a position that he wanted to take. . . . He got a little carried away down there and, according to them [Municipal Association members], advocated the possibility of a fourth cent on the sales tax with the cities getting half of it."[51]

Crawford Cook's recollection of Parker's comments to the Municipal Association was somewhat different: "Marshall made a speech to the state Municipal Association [that reflected] discussion in the legislature about increasing the sales tax by a penny. In that speech what he said was that if the state enacted a sales tax increase, that he would support earmarking a portion of that sales tax for the state's municipalities. Bob's people got hold of it and the way they depicted it was that Marshall was advocating another penny sales-tax increase. They did a great job of selling through radio and newspaper ads, word of mouth, press conferences, etc. It wasn't long before Marshall Parker was the guy who was proposing a sales tax increase."[52]

McNair admitted he got some inside help in sticking Parker with the sales-tax issue. "Some of my friends called me about it," he said. "Fortunately, Jim Covington, who was then with WIS [-TV]—bless his soul—taped it and finally—with much persuasion—let me hear it." What McNair found on the tape were not just references to the sales tax. He also found what he considered a shift in Parker's style and aggressiveness. "He had begun to jump on me personally," McNair said, and it represented what he considered a turning point in the race, "a pretty good break in the campaign."[53]

In a matter of days, the McNair-Parker race had gained some passion and bitterness, and the two candidates began to lose some of the civility of the earlier months. "[When] I felt I was out front . . . my policy had always been . . . to run my campaign, my race, and never make a reference to my opponent. My attitude was, if his name is going to get recognized he is going to have to do it. I am not going to do it for him."[54]

Those niceties began to fade, however, and McNair recalled that the campaign became tough at that point. There were three major campaign events remaining, he said: one in the upcountry, where he needed support, and the other two in Columbia. In all three events, the candidates got their fair share of personal shots at each other.

Things Get Rough

It was at the upcountry rally in Spartanburg on June 1 that McNair first accused Parker of advocating a sales-tax increase, claiming that "he was saying one thing in one area and another thing in another area."[55] Under the headline "Lt. Governor's Race Erupts Over Taxes," one newspaper account of the Spartanburg rally called it "one of the harshest stump battles of the campaign" and reported, "McNair accused Parker of being inconsistent about the tax and Parker said McNair knew 'very well' that he has not been inconsistent."

McNair was quoted as saying that Parker had predicted a 4 percent sales tax during a speech at Myrtle Beach. Parker responded that "only one of us has ever voted for a sales tax, and that is not me," referring to McNair's 1951 support of the 3 percent sales tax for public education.[56] McNair contended that "he [Parker] was saying what he thought the automobile dealers wanted to hear and then what the farmers wanted to hear and then he had gone down to the mayors at Myrtle Beach and advocated—or talked about—the four cent sales tax, sharing a different view with them in order to get their support."[57]

The attack, McNair said, provoked Parker's ire, as well as a counterattack in which he "lost his cool." "He got up . . . and lambasted me. [He said] I was dishonest . . . [and] I was not fit to hold public office." Parker's outburst fit a later reference to him by newsman Hugh Gibson, who described him as "a chisel-chinned ex-Marine lieutenant with a temper and a tongue to match."[58]

The outbreak in the upcountry was the fifteenth of eighteen scheduled stump meetings in the 1962 primary. Five days later in Lancaster, in the next-to-last gathering, the pair squared off again, and the press reported, "The sizzling lieutenant governor's race exploded in a kind of spontaneous combustion." Parker was reported to have called McNair "dishonest" and accused him of "deliberately trying to mislead," and a headline confirmed that a "Distortion of Truth Is Charged."[59] It was on that occasion that McNair made known his secret weapon, the Covington tape of Parker's comments to the Municipal Association at Myrtle Beach, but he was saving its actual use until later.

The tape was produced on June 7, two days after the Lancaster exchange, on Columbia television. The station had requested that presentations by the candidates be prerecorded, but McNair insisted that he go on live to preserve the element of surprise. After several references to the heated exchanges between the two candidates and what McNair called attacks on his "integrity and honesty," the tape was aired. "Rather than quoting my opponent, I preferred to let them hear my opponent," McNair recalled. "I played the tape . . . [and it] was worse than I thought it was. And that really, everybody says, had a damaging effect on his campaign."[60]

Two days later, the candidates squared off for the final time before a crowd of three thousand at Columbia's Township Auditorium. McNair had worked up a head of steam and attacked Parker on several counts. He contended that Parker's billboards "proclaiming [himself] a dairy farmer were misleading" and charged that "in fact, he not only does not own an acre of land. He does not own a milk cow, and he never has owned one."[61] For good measure, McNair got in a parting shot at Parker's North Carolina background: "[I] served the people of South Carolina for over 12 years in the State House of Representatives—that's about as long as he [Parker] has lived in South Carolina."[62]

Whether Marshall Parker owned a milk cow, an acre of land, or spent most of his life in North Carolina or not, however, Bob McNair had let observers in South Carolina know something about himself politically. He had shown backers and foes that he had resilience and durability in a statewide race and that he could get tough and deliver a knockout punch.

A One-Sided Win for McNair

Four days after the Township Auditorium meeting on June 12, McNair dispatched Parker in a race that was not even close, garnering 191,429 votes (58 percent) to Parker's 138,463 (42 percent).[63] He won a majority in thirty-seven of the forty-six counties. It was a moment of rare—and somewhat uncharacteristic—exuberance for McNair. A winner in his first statewide race, a battle that had developed into hand-to-hand combat in the final days, he called the victory "an overwhelming experience."

McNair campaigners and backers spilled out onto Main Street from their head-quarters next to the old Wade Hampton Hotel at the corner of Main and Gervais Streets and celebrated a victory in which he was declared the winner early in the evening. There were still some moments of special glee, however, as the evening wore on. "When we saw we were running better than two-to-one in Charleston, we pretty well knew we were in. When I saw that in Anderson—which was next door to Parker [Oconee County]—I was doing extremely well."[64] McNair was also beginning to see the real strength of Olin D. Johnston, the incumbent who was in the process of defeating challenger Ernest F. Hollings for the U.S. Senate. Along the way, Johnston was also providing some indirect help to McNair in his fight against Parker.

It was in the upcountry counties like Anderson where the Johnston influence was felt. McNair noted that "the Johnston help really came in. I got a good vote in Pickens County, even though Earle Morris [then a state senator] was tacitly for Parker. The courthouse, the sheriff and the auditor and people like that were for me."[65]

The crowning blow came when McNair carried by a wide margin Johnston's home county of Spartanburg, giving him almost a clean sweep of the upcountry, where Parker lived but where Johnston was the political kingpin. Parker carried Greenville County by a narrow margin, but when the Spartanburg and Charleston results came in, the race was conceded, and the state's fiercest lieutenant governor's race in memory was history.

The McNair-Parker fight was only part of the political fireworks of 1962, the last year in which the Democratic primary would serve as the main election for statewide office. There was a critical contest involving the state's old-line political heavyweight, Johnston, and young challenger Hollings, fresh from a term as governor in which he had gained significant attention for his racial moderation and aggressive economic development activities. Donald Russell was making his second run for governor against Burnet Maybank Jr.

The Johnston-Hollings race was the headliner, pitting the old master against the new contender in Democratic circles, and its fallout had significant effect on the undercard. For McNair, Johnston's candidacy was producing an unexpected campaign boost, which turned into a longer-lasting political alliance. Although he was almost two years younger than Hollings, McNair had begun to be identified with some of the Democratic Old Guard, owing probably to his closeness to Blatt, his familiarity with the courthouse crowds across the state, the wide tolerances of his ideological beliefs, and the general pragmatism that marked his approach to politics. There were some natural likenesses among the styles and strategies of Johnston and McNair, and McNair recalled, "We seemed to gravitate together. We seemed to have some of the same base support, and he [Johnston] was very kind and friendly."

The McNair-Johnston Linkage

"As the race progressed, I began to pick up . . . an awful lot of Johnston support across the state," McNair recalled; "in fact, I think I got most of it."[66] For all his tradition of racial politics, Johnston had also begun to attract significant black support in his postwar races, particularly against Strom Thurmond in 1950. According to a 1992 report, the black weekly *Lighthouse and Informer* "urged its readers to work for the defeat of 'Dixiecratism,' endorsed the Senator [Johnston], several days before the primary, and later claimed that 60,000 black votes provided Johnston with his margin of victory."[67]

Johnston's support among blacks was explained thus: "All things being equal regarding segregation and the public stance of the majority of southern politicians, black voters looked for a candidate who, once in office, would support policies which improved the welfare of the black community. It did not require much reflection to determine that the New Dealer and the Fair Dealer [Johnston], with strong roots in the upcountry working class, was more likely to support beneficial federal programs than the candidate of the corporate boardrooms who talked of cutting the federal budget."[68]

Most South Carolinians also recognized that Olin Johnston was the unchallenged master of personal campaigning in the state, and he had the record to prove it. It was Johnston who had defeated political legends "Cotton Ed" Smith and Thurmond in statewide races for U.S. Senate, and his contest against Hollings was viewed by many as giving the senior senator a chance to nail yet a third major political scalp.

The Johnston-McNair friendship had several points of common interest, including a preference for courthouse politics, pragmatism, and ideological flexibility. Like Johnston, McNair had also gotten a firsthand look at the ravages of poverty in 1920s and 1930s South Carolina, and he had seen firsthand how the infusion of federal dollars had helped bring to life some of the otherwise dormant economy of rural Berkeley County. If Bob McNair had gained legislative strength through his identity with Speaker Solomon Blatt, Olin Johnston was providing a similar type of associative power for McNair as he stepped into the statewide political arena for the first time. And while no one would have mistaken the stooped older senator for the energetic young House member, it was no coincidence that their names probably came up in the same conversations around the courthouse offices and water coolers. They both liked personal campaigning; they both found their source of power at the local level; and they both seemed to gravitate toward an elusive and ever-changing pragmatic centrism in South Carolina politics. And while Johnston would not live long enough for a formal political alliance to arise between the two, traces of his style and members of his political family would be an unseen presence within the McNair political and governmental organization for some years to come.

Scars within the Democratic Party

As often happened in the wake of hard-fought campaigns, however, the 1962 primary left some scars within the Democratic Party. McNair's competitive battle with Parker left bitterness among supporters on both sides, some of which did not subside for years. "Those who know the two men are well aware that the old wounds are unhealed," a newsman wrote some years later. "At best, a kind of armed truce marked by cool politeness has characterized their relations."[69] And after Hollings's stunning defeat at the hands of McNair's ally Johnston, there developed an intra-party rivalry that also lingered for years. Even though they never ran against each other for public office, it was clear to most Democrats that there was within their party a distinct McNair wing and a distinct Hollings wing.

In the aftermath of the 1962 Democratic primary (there was no general-election opposition for McNair in November), there were definite winners and losers. McNair passed his first statewide test with flying colors, and there was little doubt that his next goal would be the governor's office. For Burnet Maybank, it was the end of a political road, which left him one step short of the governor's office, and he would never offer for statewide office again. Hollings was the odd man out in the 1962 sweepstakes, going into a forced retirement, which would take him out of public office for the first time in fourteen years. It was Donald Russell's first election victory of any kind, and the onetime USC president had reason to think that his political star might be on the rise.

Civil Rights Storms Gathering

There were other issues looming for South Carolina as the dust settled on the Democratic primary contests of 1962, however, and a series of events was foretelling the state's not-very-distant future. A year earlier, a group of some two hundred black demonstrators marched on the State House in Columbia, singing "Down, Down with Segregation" to the tune of the "Battle Hymn of the Republic" and carrying placards that read, "You may jail our bodies, but not our souls." Among those arrested for obstructing traffic at the corner of Main and Gervais Streets was NAACP field secretary, the Reverend I. DeQuincey Newman.[70]

Forty miles away in Orangeburg, unrest continued in the wake of the unsuccessful 1955 black protest against segregated schools. By the fall of 1963, mass demonstrations were calling for an end to segregation of more than public schools. Among the institutions targeted were the local hospital, public accommodations, and the United Fund campaign. There were calls for "equal treatment of customers in retail stores, equal job opportunities, and equality of blacks before the law and the local government."[71] Students and faculty from the two Orangeburg colleges, Claflin and South Carolina State, played a prominent role in the demonstrations and began learning the "techniques of activism and pressure."[72] There were eventually some concessions made in downtown Orangeburg, but "the changes were grudging and incomplete, and the fundamental issue—the desire of black Orangeburg for a desegregated equalitarian city—was not resolved."[73] As the demonstrations abated, "open hostility was replaced by a gnawing feeling of racial unease."[74]

The nation was feeling the full force of demonstrations, freedom rides, and desegregation incidents, and violence was erupting in places like Oxford, Mississippi, and Birmingham and Montgomery in Alabama. A "March for Jobs and Freedom" brought some 200,000 demonstrators to Washington, D.C., in August 1963, producing what was called "the largest public demonstration ever held in the nation's capital" and generating pressure for passage of President John F. Kennedy's proposed civil rights bill.[75]

America in the early 1960s lingered in the fading glow of postwar confidence. Kennedy was standing up to cold war foes and was speaking with eloquence about New Frontiers and sending men to the moon. Babe Ruth's home-run record of sixty in one season fell to another New York Yankee, Roger Maris, in 1961. Across the nation, Chubby Checker, a South Carolina lowcountry native, was urging people to "Do the Twist," and a threesome of Arnold Palmer, Jack Nicklaus, and Gary Player was bringing professional golf to its greatest-ever height of public popularity.

South Carolina's Gamecocks were enjoying the exploits of a young quarterback named Dan Reeves, and spring break was still a time for expeditions to Ocean Drive. Donald Russell and Bob McNair advanced almost automatically from primary victory in June 1962 to general-election triumph in November to become South Carolina's next governor and lieutenant governor. There was a sense among more than a few that the state and the nation were indeed in the midst of an era of good feeling.

For McNair, however, there was something of an adjustment from the day-to-day combat of the campaign and from the frenetic pace of activities in the House of Representatives. The Senate was a stern, formal place where things moved slowly and where seniority determined the pecking order and the allocation of power.

Adapting to the Life in the Senate

"You had to be very cautious," McNair said. "The Senate is a different organization. They do not like meddling from anybody, including the Governor, as everybody knows, and they do not like for a Lieutenant Governor to meddle in their legislative affairs. Their general view was 'your job is to preside, not to tell us how to handle issues. You can help us run the Senate, but you do not even do that. We run it. You preside.'"[76]

When McNair arrived as the chamber's new presiding officer in January 1963, there were six senators with twenty or more years of service. The ruling moguls were Edgar Brown, a veteran of thirty-four years who had for the previous twenty years been president pro tempore and chairman of Senate Finance, and Marion Gressette, chairman of Senate Judiciary, who was second in seniority with twenty-six years of service.

McNair's old Berkeley County nemesis-turned-friend, Rembert Dennis, was a top lieutenant in the Finance Committee and was completing his twentieth year. Small-county senators Lawrence Hester of McCormick and Wilbur Grant of Chester were in their twenty-second and twentieth years, respectively. A colorful lawyer and popular orator by the name of James P. "Spot" Mozingo was in his twenty-fourth year of serving Darlington County.

In the chamber also were Marshall Parker, the vanquished lieutenant governor candidate from Oconee, and John West, his campaign manager from Kershaw County. Parker was still smarting from the campaign and would continue to distance himself from McNair and eventually the Democratic Party itself. West, a political healer who could bridge most roiling waters in the party, was testing out statewide waters himself and would work to patch things up in the ensuing years. Coming to the Senate in 1965 would be a strong McNair ally, Fairfield senator John A. Martin, who had broken with the Kiawah Island group to support McNair in the 1962 lieutenant governor's race. It was, in essence, the prototypical South Carolina Senate, with power in the hands of senators from places like Barnwell, Calhoun, and Berkeley Counties and with senators from populous Greenville, Richland, and Charleston Counties still occupying back- or middle-row seating in the chamber.

Modeled after the office of U.S. vice president, South Carolina's lieutenant governor is *in* the Senate, not *of* the Senate. With only one official duty, to preside over the Senate, the lieutenant governor votes only in cases of a tie. Otherwise, he or she bangs the gavel, announces votes, recognizes speakers, ratifies acts, keeps an eye on the rule book, and serves to referee squabbles. He or she also succeeds to governor if there is a vacancy in that office.

The trappings of the job were minimal. "It was a part-time job," McNair recalled. "There was no driver, no car, no special expense allowance. I did get the same per diem and salary as a state senator, plus a thousand dollars to be Lieutenant Governor. [I] was also provided a secretary then for six months of the year."[77]

Building Alliances Senate-Style

There was plenty of time and opportunity, however, for McNair to turn his attention to the kind of activity he liked best—mixing with the legislators themselves on his own terms. "Because of my friendship with many senators, I developed a good working relationship with the entire Senate—especially with Senator [Marion] Gressette, Senator Rembert Dennis, who was then the young comer with the Finance Committee, Senator Brown [and] Senator John Martin, and the others, who were then coming over [and we] developed a good working relationship."[78]

In the process, McNair created something new for the old Senate, regular Tuesday-morning leadership meetings. "I would invite all the Senate committee chairmen," he said.

> We would meet with them and the leadership to determine what they wanted to accomplish that week. Then I could be helpful. . . . We did not just go blindly with no plans and no organization.
>
> It worked pretty well. It worked effectively enough to cause me to follow through in the Governor's Office with the same kind of meetings on a weekly basis.[79]

McNair was most effective in working breakfast or lunch sessions, where he could use time efficiently and maintain an informal setting. He was not a cocktail-party operative, and if he did choose to invite colleagues on social outings, they were more likely to be in the outdoor settings where he was most comfortable—hunting, fishing, or boating. Once he was elected governor, it was a rarity that alcoholic beverages were served at the governor's mansion, an unwritten policy largely influenced by Josephine McNair.

The leadership meetings gave McNair what Russell had not provided—a role in the legislative process. It was an informal and restricted one, and unlike his work in the House, he could not work the aisles. "[The Lieutenant Governor] should not go around lobbying and buttonholing the senators and trying to change votes and that sort of thing," he said.[80]

The new role also gave him the opportunity to cultivate further the friendship of people like Brown, Gressette, and Dennis, and to build in them the kind of confidence that would stand him in good stead not only in legislative affairs but also in future political considerations. Together with his ongoing friendship with Blatt, Rex Carter, and other members of the House leadership, McNair was able to build a power base around that rarest of legislative commodities—House-Senate cooperation. He was able to set the stage for a race for governor in which the membership of the General Assembly—with a few exceptions—would be a veritable McNair campaign committee. "As lieutenant governor," a newsman wrote, "he presided over the Senate with a hand so gentle that few ever saw or felt the iron."[81]

Working the State

The part-time nature of the lieutenant governor's job gave him the opportunity to pursue other avenues of campaign importance. For all the attention given to the fiery final days of his race with Marshall Parker and for all the impressive vote totals, Bob McNair was still a lawyer from the town of Allendale, and political success was a fleeting thing. What name recognition he had gained through his campaign of billboards, stump speeches, and limited advertising could easily slip away over a four-year period without constant renewal. If McNair was going to exploit his many old and new friends in the General Assembly, he would have to do it the same way he conducted his race for lieutenant governor. It would have to be a four-year campaign carried out at the local level and pulling together his by now remarkable coalition of legislators, courthouse politicians, and business backers. It would be another marathon campaign of shoe leather, civic clubs, mill gates, and shopping centers.

Journalist Charles Wickenberg captured the pace of the McNair campaign strategy in an April 7, 1963, article in the *State* newspaper, in which he reported: "Lt. Governor Robert E. McNair spoke at a convention of Future Teachers in Columbia Saturday night, at a booster's club in Elloree the night before, and tonight at Ware Shoals to a meeting of Presbyterian men."

The Ware Shoals speech was his thirty-fifth speaking engagement in fifty-eight working days (with time off Saturday and Sunday for family), Wickenberg observed, and he went on to publish McNair's March 1963 travel and speaking schedule:

March 2, South Carolina High School League;
March 5, Clemson Community College;
March 8, Limestone College at noon, Gaffney Chamber of Commerce at night;
March 11, Medical seminar, Columbia;
March 14, Chamber of Commerce banquet, Jasper County;
March 15, Sumter Elks Club;
March 17, S.C. Coin Operators Association, Columbia;

March 18, Wesley Memorial Methodist Ladies' Night;
March 19, USC Young Democrats;
March 21, S.C. Student Legislature at USC;
March 22, attendance at teachers' luncheon, Greenville;
March 25–27, New York City industry trip;
March 28, Kiwanis, Florence;
March 29, State Employees Meeting, Greenville.[82]

A typical McNair visit would include more than a speaking appearance. He would usually pay a visit to the local newspapers and radio stations, particularly in small towns where such journalistic outlets might often be thought of as an extension of the courthouse crowd. It was a practice that he continued through his gubernatorial days. Even as tension developed for him with some members of the capitol press corps in Columbia, he continued to enjoy the small-town press, relaxing and showing them the outgoing personality that reporters in Columbia rarely saw. McNair was most comfortable with the press when he could consider its members as part of his extended political universe and network. It was a strategy that often worked at the local level, but one that would prove risky with the state's larger dailies and regular radio and television reporters.

While McNair worked to create tasks for the lieutenant governor where not many existed by constitution or statute, there was a certain inescapable powerlessness about the whole thing. "I said [at the time], 'Well, the best way I can describe it is that I had more power as a legislator, particularly more power as chairman of the [House] Judiciary Committee, than at any other time. I had more fun and just enjoyed being Lieutenant Governor because you did not have to make decisions to any great extent and you were able to work with people and try to coordinate and travel around and make appearances.'"[83] He recalled: "You really did not accomplish a great deal other than in a quiet sort of way in trying to influence legislative leadership."[84]

1963: Suddenly It All Begins to Change

Elsewhere, however, things were not so quiet. An assassin's bullet jolted America on November 22, 1963, ending the life of President John F. Kennedy and a presidency often described as "Camelot." Racial conflicts were growing more frequent and more violent, and sentiment was building among the nation's younger generation against a war in the Southeast Asian nation of Vietnam.

There was also evidence that changes in the political condition of South Carolina were accelerating. Even before the Voting Rights Act of 1965, registration of black voters in the state had risen by more than 50 percent between 1958 and 1962. It was still a small percentage of the black population of almost a million, but it constituted enough numerical strength to have a distinct influence in statewide races.

South Carolina Republicans mounted their first statewide candidate of the century in 1962 when journalist William D. Workman Jr. took on Olin Johnston for the U.S. Senate in the general election. Even though he lost, the showing was respectable and encouraging to the GOP faithful.[85] Republicans also elected their first state legislators in modern times: Charles E. Boineau of Columbia in August 1961 and G. Fred Worsham of Charleston in August 1962.

An article by Bill Mahoney in the January 2, 1962, *State* painted a dire picture for Democrats. "I looked around for my party and couldn't find it," Mahoney wrote, quoting a "leading Democrat in the wake of news that the Republicans were grabbing the grassroots by the roots":

> It all results from the one-party system. When you have no political enemy, you don't have to have the finely drawn ward organization. . . . The . . . GOP has done what Democrats might never have done without opposition—organize.[86]

From Hell Hole Swamp to the Governor's Office

Then, on a spring day in 1965, South Carolinians began to learn that the condition of their senior senator was declining seriously. Reports revealed that Olin Johnston's health had been failing since earlier that year. Johnston's brother Bill told of the senator's mounting ailments—a cancerous tumor operation in January and another operation in early April to correct a blister aneurysm of the aorta. Most recently, viral pneumonia had set in, and his fever had reached 103 degrees. Thursday, April 15, was, according to Bill Johnston, "his first really bad day from either of the two operations, but both his personal physician and the surgeon have just assured me he is making good progress and they feel he will continue to do so."[87]

McNair recalled that Senator Johnston's health had not been much of a discussion topic until he entered Providence Hospital in Columbia. "His health had been declining some, but he had managed to carry on his duties. . . . When he entered the hospital . . . the general feeling was that Senator Johnston's health was not good at all."[88] Two days later, Bill Johnston reported that his brother "is not responding to treatment," and newspapers on Sunday, April 18, were carrying stories describing the senator's condition as "extremely grave."

Even so, McNair remembered feeling shock when he heard the news on his car radio as he and Josephine set out for the sunrise service in Allendale on Easter Sunday that Johnston had died during the night. The newspapers on the following Monday carried the story, one of them reporting, "Death on Easter morning ended the stormy political career of U.S. Senator Olin D. Johnston, a career that knew early defeat, but which closed in consistent triumph."[89]

Within days, the lives of men with whom Johnston had been closely bound politically for years would be changed forever. His political friend Bob McNair would be summoned to Columbia to discuss an arrangement with Governor

Donald Russell that would elevate Russell to the U.S. Senate to replace Johnston on an interim basis until the next general election. For that to happen, Russell would resign as governor, setting off the constitutional succession process by which the lieutenant governor would assume the office of governor.

The agreement was sealed, and within days South Carolina had a new governor. He had arrived by way of such unlikely places as Hell Hole Swamp and Allendale County. But on April 22, 1965, Bob and Josephine McNair became South Carolina's first couple. So that the children of the McNairs and Russells could complete their school years in Allendale and Columbia, respectively, both families stayed home for another month, and the McNairs did not occupy the governor's mansion until June. With speaking engagements remaining on his busy lieutenant governor's schedule as well as the commitments made by Russell, Bob McNair hastily took office, appointed Russell to the U.S. Senate seat, and turned over the reins of the S.C. Senate presidency to the man who had run things for years anyhow, Edgar Brown, the president pro tempore.

McNair's immediate duties were to wrap up things in the lieutenant governor's office, assume executive control of the state, finish up commitments with his still-busy law firm in Allendale, attend to new living quarters for his family, and, amid what one reporter called "a day of confusion with purpose,"[90] remember that the ultimate goal for most of his career had just been achieved—and ahead of time, at that. In another year, he would also be reminded, he would be required to run for that office again.

6

Preparing for the Showdown

Within weeks after taking office as governor on April 22, 1965, Bob McNair received a letter from Henry H. Hill, a school-desegregation troubleshooter from the Center for School Education Studies at the George Peabody College for Teachers in Nashville, Tennessee. Hill wrote:

> During the past few months, I have enjoyed serving as consultant to the Public Education Committee of the General Assembly [the "Gressette Committee"], and I am performing some services for the Greenville School System and Greenwood. I have been particularly pleased that South Carolinians in general kept their shirts on in regard to desegregation.
>
> It has been a wonderful thing for South Carolina that the last two Governors [Hollings and Russell]—and I am sure it will be true in your case—have had a quieting effect on the emotions that exist or are aroused in this regard.[1]

Hill's letter foreshadowed the coming storm of public-school desegregation, which would dominate—more than any other single issue—the administration of Robert E. McNair. From virtually his first day as governor until he left office almost six years later, the dismantling of the racially separate public-education system in each of the state's more than one hundred school districts was a constant, contentious, and often volatile companion for the young chief executive. Each school district dealt directly with Washington in developing and carrying out its own desegregation plans, but for many of them, the office of the governor became a place of consultation, liaison, and, at times, refuge.

McNair's role in school desegregation thrust his new administration—billed as ushering in an era of good feeling—into an unexpectedly active, and as he called it, a delicate situation. It had been eleven years since the Supreme Court had ordered the abolishing of the state's dual school system, and South Carolina was among the very last to begin stirring toward compliance. The state's belated moves to comply coincided with McNair's unexpected arrival in the governor's office, a coincidence that would place in the hands of a man who had not been elected governor the responsibility of overseeing one of the most dangerous and provocative political assignments of the century.

> In that interim period [the completion of Donald Russell's term as governor], we were really in a delicate situation because we were trying to . . . finish Donald Russell's term [April 1965–January 1967]. I felt we had to carry on what he had started.
>
> At the same time, we had to deal with the very delicate problems that had begun to arise. The voting rights legislation came along [1965], and we had the beginnings of real integration in the public schools.
>
> We had been talking about it [integration] up to then, and we had done some "spot-type" integration, but we were getting into freedom of choice, and that was the beginning of that period [of racial integration].
>
> We had all the normal problems that Alabama and Mississippi and others had brewing around the state. We were trying to keep the support of the public while at the same time trying to move into some of these things and deal with them—of course—with the knowledge of what had happened in Alabama and Mississippi.
>
> In those states, there was total resistance.[2]

For South Carolina, "Total Resistance or Accommodation"

There is, in fact, some contention that South Carolina gave serious consideration to joining those states that chose the stance of total resistance. Historian John G. Sproat suggested that "Byrnes and his successor George Bell Timmerman, Jr., tried mightily to weld a Southern front on the issue [defense of segregation], but with little success."[3]

"Timmerman kept South Carolinians preoccupied with the 'race question' throughout his term as governor [1955–1959] and very nearly took the state down the road Alabama and Mississippi were traveling at the time to ultimate civil disorder."[4] South Carolina avoided bloodshed in the 1950s, at least in part, Sproat argued, because during Timmerman's term there were no court-ordered efforts by blacks to integrate the universities or the public schools.[5] "That no such effort was forthcoming at the time," Sproat wrote, "may have been due to a perception among NAACP strategists that at least some of South Carolina's white leaders were working behind the scenes to dampen the appeal of the more fiery racists and move the state toward some form of accommodation, however slowly."[6]

Such accommodation was part of a larger condition in South Carolina at the time that tended to resist extremism of either the political left or right. There was at work in the state, Sproat believes, "a determination among established white leaders to put social stability above all other considerations: to insure that relations among classes and between races should never 'get out of control.'" This tendency, Sproat wrote, could be traced back to the "Bourbon"[7] overthrow of Radical Reconstruction in 1876, and it reemerged after the excesses of Tillman and Coleman Blease as "an instrument of control within the white community during the desegregation crisis."

"In a sense," Sproat contended, "the bizarre spectacle furnished by the race-baiters of an earlier day spurred white leaders in the years after the Second World War to prevent, almost at all costs, any revival of such populistic outbursts."[8] The white leadership's desire for control, he believed, was complemented by "the essential conservatism of South Carolina's black people."[9]

Even so, the 1950s were dangerous times in South Carolina. Instances of violence were not uncommon, and J. P. "Pete" Strom, chief of the State Law Enforcement Division (SLED), estimated that there were as many as ten thousand members of the Ku Klux Klan in the state at the time.[10] Signs bearing the exhortation "Impeach Earl Warren" littered the countryside, and in 1962, eight years after the issuance of the *Brown* opinion, South Carolina hoisted a Confederate battle flag over its State House in celebration of the one hundredth anniversary of the state's secession from the United States. "We were coming through the political period when we really isolated ourselves in the South, both as a region and as states," McNair said. "We took the position that we did not want federal involvement in state government. So we resisted federal support for education and other activities on the theory that federal support brought federal control."[11]

Treading the Middle Path

South Carolina in the mid-1960s was caught squarely between its past and its visions of the future, and somewhere along the way something had to give. Any aspiring political figure emerging in South Carolina had to make a choice between the state's traditions and the state's ambitions, and McNair trod cautiously a middle path that eventually bore to the left.

> We were in an evolving stage, and at a turning point on that issue. We were becoming more a part of the whole national system again, politically and governmentally.
>
> I came at a time when we were reaching the conclusion that we not only should but we also needed all the help and all the support we could get, and we sorta stepped out front. We were going after the federal dollar. We were going to utilize it to help build and develop South Carolina.[12]

Acceptance of federal dollars, and especially the aggressive pursuit of those dollars, signaled surrender, many felt, on the issue of segregation, particularly in public education. "It was part of the same old . . . political problem: civil rights. I think the civil rights issue was at the foundation of so much of the resistance to federal programs and federal control," McNair felt. "Most of the fear and resistance stemmed from the education issue; federal support for education meant federal control of education." The southern rallying cry, he recalled, was "we do not want federal involvement or federal control or federal interference in what we are doing and how we are doing it."[13] *Federal,* in the vernacular of the 1960s South, simply meant the implementation of racial desegregation.

All those uncertainties did little to prepare the state for the biggest change in its way of life since Appomattox and the Emancipation Proclamation. Black South Carolina and white South Carolina, in fact, still barely knew each other. Although federal courts and the Congress were dealing blow after blow to the nation's segregationist processes, most of South Carolina remained essentially divided into black and white worlds into the mid-1960s.

In the absence of articulated policy to address desegregation, and in the absence of substantive communication between the races, it fell to each governor, mayor, school superintendent, police chief, shopkeeper, and college president to devise policy and improvise approaches on an incident-by-incident basis. In the early days of sit-in demonstrations, those decisions often rested in the hands of local law-enforcement officers, and justice was meted out largely on a stern, law-and-order basis.

Lester Bates and Orchestrated Peace in Columbia

It was not until Columbia mayor Lester Bates took control of the city's handling of lunch-counter demonstrations in the capital city in August 1962 that racial desegregation incidents were elevated to the policy level and achieved broad community attention. Bates, like McNair a product of Berkeley County's politically fertile Hell Hole Swamp, set in motion an elaborately orchestrated scheme in collaboration with his own council members and black community leaders that not only desegregated lunch counters but established new city policies for hiring and employment.

The Bates plan had three major elements: (1) interracial cooperation; (2) business-government alliances; and (3) sensitivity to South Carolina's evolving distaste for public conflict. Believing that too much public attention could invite violence, the planners of the Bates peace strategy clamped such tight security around the events that even the local daily press agreed to keep things quiet for a couple of days, a decision that provoked professional scorn from journalistic peers for years thereafter.[14]

Except for a few white demonstrators who complained that businessmen were surrendering principles for profits, the Bates plan worked, and South Carolina's first encounter with racial issues at the policy level was carried off virtually without incident. Coming as it did at a time when violence accompanied desegregation incidents elsewhere in the state and throughout the South, the Columbia lunch-counter strategy left some South Carolinians believing their state might have an approach that could help them avoid the distress of other more volatile southern states.

One of those peace advocates was Edgar Brown, the senior surviving member of the Barnwell Ring who still wielded significant influence within the state's Democratic Party and its drift toward political moderation and centrism. Like Bates, who had lost in earlier gubernatorial contests, Brown had been a loser on the statewide political stage, most recently being denied his ambition for the U.S. Senate as the victim of Thurmond's 1954 remarkable write-in victory. Remaining to him as sources of major influence were his chairmanship of South Carolina's Senate Finance Committee, his traditional role as national committeeman to the Democratic Party, and his lifetime membership on the Board of Trustees of Clemson College.

Doing the "Right Thing" at Clemson

It was in that latter role that Senator Brown emerged as an architect of the state's response to its next major racial challenge, the desegregation of Clemson in January 1963, five months after Columbia had integrated its lunch counters. In the intervening months, violence had broken out in Oxford, Mississippi, with the admittance of James Meredith as the first black student at Ole Miss. Three were killed, hundreds wounded or injured, and it took sixteen thousand National Guardsmen to restore order to the campus—all amid the public defiance of a federal court order by the state's governor, Ross Barnett. "The terrible business in Mississippi did make it easier to do the right thing in South Carolina," Brown was later quoted by biographer W. D. Workman Jr. as saying, "but many of us had determined to do the right thing for law and order, no matter when we faced the issue in this state."[15]

The right thing was another orchestrated event, which involved the collaboration of Clemson president Robert C. Edwards; industrialist Charles Daniel; two of the state's former governors, Hollings and Russell; Greenville newspaperman Wayne Freeman; Brown; and the lobbyist for the state's powerful textile industry, John K. Cauthen.[16] "Johnny Cauthen came to see me," Brown recalled. "He said he thought peace could be preserved if business people took the lead at the right time, taking politicians 'off the spot.' Johnny summed it up by saying that politicians and educators were in a 'hell-if-you-do-and-hell-if-you-don't' predicament, but that business people might take a public position when the time came with the help of newspapers, building up sentiment for law and order and breaking the ice so that South Carolina could do the right thing."[17]

Preparing South Carolina to do the right thing had another interesting wrinkle. As Edgar Brown stated, "Don't ever forget that all of this [peaceful desegregation] was contingent upon using up all the courts."[18] At a time when men like Governors George Wallace and Ross Barnett were intoning their warrior-like exhortations in Alabama and Mississippi, official voices in South Carolina were muted, and opinion expressed by various officials was generally circumspect. Leaders were trying to find a middle path through the political thicket of desegregation that would spare the state bloodshed and at the same time protect the political flanks to the right of vulnerable decision-makers. The strategy of using up all the courts seemed to fill that need, casting South Carolina in a suitably conservative and combative fight-to-the-finish mode but sustaining what was becoming for the state the businesslike image of peaceful behavior and civility. At a time when many parts of the South were mired in political extremism, it gave South Carolina Democrats the political center and won praise around the country for the state's peaceful behavior. In crisis times, as McNair and others were proclaiming to the approbation of moderate and liberal political observers that "we have run out of time, and we have run out of courts," they actually meant just that. The state, they were contending, had lived up to its end of the tacit agreement with conservative whites to exhaust all legal remedies, and it was calling on the citizenry as part of the deal to keep the peace and obey the law.

It was a strategy that proved at least temporarily effective in sustaining a tenuous peace as the state moved toward its belated encounter with the realities of desegregation. It also created something of a precedent. While there was no policy in place other than the oft-articulated devices of defiance to guide the state's decision-makers, there was emerging an unwritten pact of prudence, albeit a short-term one, among South Carolina's moderates. It could trace its lineage back no further than the governorship of Hollings, but in that brief period, South Carolina was finding itself uncharacteristically restrained and quietly challenging for the first time in generations the institutional grumpiness with which the state had greeted any loosening of its ancient rules of racial separation. A modest legacy of moderation, based on the strategy of using all the courts, was emerging from the likes of Brown, Hollings, Russell, John Cauthen, and Bob Edwards. It was offering the state for the first time a viable alternative to the longer tradition of racial inflexibility, a tradition that could trace its lineage back through men such as Thurmond, Johnston, "Cotton Ed" Smith, Coleman Blease, and Ben Tillman.

A Two-Party System Defined by Race

GOP conservatives were developing a basic strategy of adhering to the tenets of South Carolina's traditions of defiance. They were challenging the emerging moderates by questioning whether all legal remedies had been exhausted, and whether the desegregation process was, in fact, inevitable. By challenging the moderates, and by confronting the ruling political oligarchy in the state, the GOP, McNair felt, was threatening the social stability that had emerged from the tumultuous 1950s and the tacit truce by which white and black leaders had sought to keep the state's racial passions under control. This fundamental conflict gave much of the definition to the state's two-party system and shaped the policies and platforms of state and local candidates. Five and a half years later, it was the issue that would still dominate the final weeks and months of the McNair administration.

As early as 1963, Governor Hollings was employing the theme of using all the courts in the call for moderation he made in his farewell address to the South Carolina General Assembly. "If and when every legal remedy has been exhausted," he said, "this General Assembly must make clear South Carolina's choice, a government of laws or a government of men."[19] Hollings's comments were specifically directed toward the peaceful admission of Charleston architectural student Harvey Gantt as Clemson's first black student, an event that took place on January 26, 1963, nine days into the term of Hollings's successor, Donald Russell. Russell, the former USC president, also oversaw the peaceful desegregation of that campus on September 10, 1963, by three black students—Robert Anderson, Henri Monteith, and James Solomon.

"By 1963," Leon Panetta wrote some years later, "the pattern of courage or accommodation, leadership or cautious tagalong was centering more and more on civil rights. What politicians would have the guts to follow conscience and not political expediency? Especially in the South?"[20]

The report card for South Carolina would probably have found some leaders earning good marks for courage and leadership. But while the state was avoiding violence and gaining some public attention for its peaceful stances on civil rights, not all South Carolinians went gladly or swiftly toward the desegregation mission or even the "use-all-the-courts" strategy. Beginning with the 1956 General Appropriation Bill and continuing into the 1962 fiscal year, the General Assembly, and subsequently the Budget and Control Board, were empowered to close any public schools submitting to desegregation court orders.[21] A subsequent U.S. Supreme Court decision nullified that ploy in 1964 when it ruled that the closing of public schools in Prince Edward County, Virginia, violated the equal protection clause of the Fourteenth Amendment.[22]

South Carolina also lost a bid in the Supreme Court in 1965 to keep major provisions of the Voting Rights Act of 1965 from being enforced on the grounds that they "invaded states' rights to set voter qualifications." The Voting Rights Act, introduced March 17, 1965, in the wake of violence in Selma, Alabama, gave the U.S. attorney general the right to send federal examiners to supervise voter registration in states that had literacy or other "qualifying devices" in place on November 1, 1964, and where fewer than 50 percent of voting-age residents were registered or voted in the 1964 election.[23]

The act was signed into law by President Lyndon Johnson on August 6, 1965, and within days, the Justice Department swung into action, filing suit to strike down the poll tax in Mississippi, Alabama, Texas, and Georgia and suspending literacy tests and other devices in Alaska, Georgia, Louisiana, Mississippi, South Carolina, Virginia, and parts of North Carolina and Arizona.[24]

Claudia Crawford McNair. Courtesy McNair Family

Daniel Evander McNair.
Courtesy McNair Family

Robert Evander McNair,
age 3. Courtesy McNair
Family

Athlete Bob McNair (front left). He played basketball and other sports at Macedonia High School, Berkeley County. Courtesy McNair Family

Scholar Bob McNair. After high school, he chose Clemson, then USC. Courtesy McNair Family

Lieutenant. (j.g.) McNair aboard the landing craft he commanded in the invasion of the Philippines. Courtesy McNair Family

As Sol Blatt's protégé, Representative McNair fast-tracked to House leadership jobs. Courtesy Robert E. McNair Papers, South Carolina Political Collection, University of South Carolina

Lieutenant Governor McNair was one of few who could deal with both Senator Edgar Brown (left) and Speaker Blatt (right). Courtesy McNair Family

Donald Russell (left) sworn in as U.S. Senator with Senator Strom Thurmond, Mrs. McNair, Senator Russell Long, Vice President Hubert Humphrey, Governor McNair, and Senator Mike Mansfield. The McNairs had become First Family of S.C. only days earlier. Courtesy McNair Family

Campaigning in 1966 in S.C. mills was still hand-to-hand. Courtesy Robert E. McNair Papers, South Carolina Political Collection, University of South Carolina

The electorate was changing. Thousands of black South Carolinians registered to vote in the 1960s. Courtesy Bill Barley Papers, South Carolina Political Collection, University of South Carolina

Black leaders such as the Reverend I. DeQuincey Newman held powerful political influence. Courtesy Bill Barley Papers, South Carolina Political Collection, University of South Carolina

The McNairs were big winners in 1966. Courtesy Robert E. McNair Papers, South Carolina Political Collection, University of South Carolina

The McNairs celebrated with a formal ball in 1966. Courtesy Robert E. McNair Papers, South Carolina Political Collection, University of South Carolina

Democrats were still in control in the 1960s. Congressman L. Mendel Rivers, Jr., Governor McNair, Senator Ernest F. Hollings, Lieutenant Governor John C. West, and Congressmen W. J. Bryan Dorn and John L. McMillan. Courtesy Constance Schulz, History of South Carolina Slide Collection *(Sandlapper Publishing Company and Instructional Resources Corporation, 1989), I-109*

Tourism became big business under McNair-launched initiative. Courtesy Robert E. McNair Papers, South Carolina Political Collection, University of South Carolina

Industry grew and diversified as S.C. went international. Courtesy Robert E. McNair Papers, South Carolina Political Collection, University of South Carolina

The executive staff: Jim Konduros, Wayne Corley, Bob Alexander, Wayne Seal, Katherine Wolfe, George Fender, Harry Coker, Phil Grose. Courtesy Robert E. McNair Papers, South Carolina Political Collection, University of South Carolina

The First Family. Claudia, Corinne, Robin, and Robert Jr. with their parents. Courtesy Robert E. McNair Papers, South Carolina Political Collection, University of South Carolina

A monument at the Capitol Complex commemorating McNair's leadership role. Courtesy Robert E. McNair Papers, South Carolina Political Collection, University of South Carolina

The First Lady was a pioneer in developing and renovating the Governor's Mansion. With Mrs. Herbert (Lilla) Hoefer. Courtesy Robert E. McNair Papers, South Carolina Political Collection, University of South Carolina

An LBJ insider, McNair (with Bob Alexander) was a leader of Democratic Party moderates. Courtesy Robert E. McNair Papers, South Carolina Political Collection, University of South Carolina

Off the cuff with the newsmen Doug Mauldin, Lee Bandy, and Wayne Freeman. Courtesy Robert E. McNair Papers, South Carolina Political Collection, University of South Carolina

Coffee-cup diplomacy. Reporters Ted Shelton, Thom Billington, Dwayne Walls, and Bill Mahoney with Bob Hickman. Courtesy Robert E. McNair Papers, South Carolina Political Collection, University of South Carolina

Orangeburg under siege. National Guardsmen at a street blockade. Courtesy Bill Barley Papers, South Carolina Political Collection, University of South Carolina

Aftermath of shootings. A student victim is carried away as bonfire smoulders. Courtesy Bill Barley Papers, South Carolina Political Collection, University of South Carolina

South Carolina State students protest the Orangeburg shootings at the State House. Courtesy Bill Barley Papers, South Carolina Political Collection, University of South Carolina

Hospital workers protest during a hundred-day strike that crippled Charleston. Courtesy Bill Barley Papers, South Carolina Political Collection, University of South Carolina

Southern Christian Leadership Council leaders Reverend Ralph Abernathy (left) and Andrew Young were strike leaders from a national level in Charleston. Courtesy Bill Barley Papers, South Carolina Political Collection, University of South Carolina

Bill Saunders (left) and Reverend Esau Jenkins were among local leaders and Saunders helped settle the strike. Courtesy Bill Saunders, Charleston, S.C.

The young governor. Courtesy Robert E. McNair Papers, South Carolina Political Collection, University of South Carolina

The outdoorsman with friend Bobby Rigby. Courtesy McNair Family

The battle-weary governor. Courtesy Robert E. McNair Papers, South Carolina Political Collection, University of South Carolina

A last farewell. Speaker Sol Blatt applauds his one-time protégé as McNair delivers his final state-of-the state address in 1971. Senator Edgar Brown is at right. Courtesy McNair Family

McNair in 2003 at his home place, the 1836 cottage at Ballsdam. Courtesy Jim Covington

A New "Image of Compliance"

South Carolina's suit in resistance to the Voting Rights Act challenged what the state considered the unfair application of the act, which prohibited literacy tests in South Carolina but allowed them "in places like New York and elsewhere." At the same time, McNair was quick to insist publicly at the time that the suit "does not represent any desire on our part to deny the franchise to any South Carolinian."[25] The suit was a test case, McNair said, and the decision dismissing the South Carolina challenge was unanimous.[26] Years later, he would recall the experience as a critical one for the state's new political moderation.

> We were trying to establish a new image for South Carolina. One of compliance, not defiance. At the same time, we realized that, if we were going to do this, that we had to maintain the confidence of the public. Unless we maintained that confidence, we could not accomplish anything.
>
> There had not been a single violation presented at any of the Congressional hearings as far as South Carolina was concerned. [Our feeling] was one of resentment at being included among those states in that target group when there was no reason for it. We thought it was unconstitutional to single out one section of the country and impose on it certain particular voting rights requirements that did not apply to the nation as a whole.[27]

Attorney General Daniel R. McLeod, who filed the suit on behalf of the state, believed the Voting Rights Act "had a profound effect here in South Carolina.[28] In McLeod's view, it forced people to "straighten this thing up and do it right. If you don't, you're going to have the whole federal army floating in here with observers and so forth. I got an idea that they're going to have to quiet a good bit of 'that stuff,'[29] and it is pretty well demonstrated by the fact that this is about the first time they ever had any prosecution for violation of election laws."[30]

McNair, he recalled, was "not a person to try to keep up anything wrong about any election procedure . . . the vast majority of people in this state don't want the federal people coming in . . . but he recognized that if we got a failure on this, it's got to be cleaned up ourselves, or we can't really complain."[31]

McNair, who developed a close working relationship with McLeod, recalled:

> We [joined] in testing the constitutionality of the [Voting Rights] law, and we felt by doing this, we could demonstrate to the public that we were not retreating and rolling over and playing dead. We were going to legally exercise all recourse and remedy available to us, but we were going to comply with the law, whatever that might be.
>
> We were trying to figure out that delicate way of maintaining their confidence and at the same time [establishing] South Carolina's posture of being one which is going to comply rather than defy the law.[32]

Avoiding "Adventures in Futility"

Months later, in his first State of the State Address to the 1966 General Assembly on January 12, McNair articulated the moderate theme as something of a preamble to what would be his most important policy speech to date.

> "The responsibilities of public trusteeship have placed new and unusual burdens on all branches of our government in recent months," McNair told the legislature, "but challenging and perplexing problems such as school compliance and the voting rights law have failed to deter the strength or the momentum of our forward movement.
>
> "Our people have wisely avoided adventures in futility, choosing instead to rely on the recourse of the law."[33]

Helping to craft the remarks, McNair later recalled, was USC dean of business administration James A. Morris, a McNair insider who was called upon for help in the days before there were such things as full-time staff speechwriters. "They were brief remarks," McNair later recalled, "but the tone was important, and Jim Morris helped prepare the speech."[34]

In newspaper coverage of the speech the next day, major attention was paid to other matters addressed in the speech, among them a recommended "War on Reckless Driving" and other proposals related to education at the adult, college, and elementary levels. Reporter Thomas N. McLean of the governmental affairs staff of the *State,* however, picked up the significance of McNair's admonitory reference to the coming civil rights transition, calling it "unmistakably a reference to sociological changes sweeping the nation." For the most part, the address got routine attention. "As a whole," according to McLean's account, "the speech was received with less enthusiasm. . . . Some [legislators] dismissed it as a 'journeyman speech' or merely shrugged when asked for comment."[35]

But in the nicely turned—and almost unnoticed—phrase about "adventures in futility," McNair had elevated the scheme of using all the courts, developed during the Clemson experience, to full-fledged policy status. For the first time, South Carolina had something besides ancient historic and legal precedent to guide its actions in dealing with the realities of imminent civil rights changes. McNair thought it was well suited to the times. "I was really pleasantly surprised at the reception and the reaction to it," he said. "I think it helped set a tone. I think it told the people that we were going to exercise our legal remedies in instances . . . but we were not going to defy the law. Therefore, when it came later to moving into integration of the schools, the same thing applied. We were going to comply, not defy. . . . I believe the statement became a guide for events leading up to the time when final, total integration had to take place."[36]

A well-intended theme or policy was one thing. Its application was another. As McNair sought consensus on a theme of moderation, the state was braced for the concurrent impact of two federal mandates that would change forever the racial aspects of two of the most fundamental aspects of the state's life—voting and public schools. The Voting Rights Act of 1965, with its provision for federal registrars, would complete the process of opening the ballot box to the state's black citizens and would change forever the political balance in the state. The Civil Rights Act of 1964, with its provisions for the cutoff of funds, would force what no amount of judicial orders had done—the desegregation of the state's 107 public-school districts. Of the two mandates, the educational challenge was by far the more daunting.

A Civil Rights Commission report issued September 30, 1963, found that "almost ten years after the 1954 Supreme Court decision holding officially segregated schools unconstitutional only 8 per cent of Negro school children in the South were going to school with whites. It found 'no evidence' that resistance to integration 'is dissipating.'"[37]

Putting Teeth into the *Brown* Decision

All that changed, however, with the adoption by Congress of the 1964 Civil Rights Act and the powerful provisions of Titles IV and VI of the act. Title IV, among other things, provided that the Department of Justice could file suit against any school district "in which there was a complaint by children or their parents that equal educational opportunity was being denied."[38] Title VI barred discrimination under any program receiving federal assistance and provided for a cutoff of federal dollars to any program found not to be in compliance with the provisions of the act.[39] Title VI, in essence, put the legal teeth into the enforcement of the *Brown* desegregation requirements, and it sent South Carolina and other southern states—after years of indifference toward the *Brown* requirements—into sudden and frenzied activity.

"It was Title VI which enraged so many politicians," wrote Leon Panetta, civil rights chief under President Nixon and budget director in the Clinton administration. "It said that no federal assistance could be extended to any activity in which there was discrimination on the grounds of race, color or national origin. That meant no Washington money to schools segregating by race in defiance of the law as laid down in the *Brown* decision; such school districts would have to desegregate to get and keep their federal money." From that time on, Panetta noted, Title VI "became a North-South battleground as well as a liberal-conservative one."[40]

Panetta's forecast of political turmoil was an accurate one. As the implementation of Title VI got underway, local school districts and federal Department of Health, Education, and Welfare (HEW) officials clashed in a war of wills so bitter that it sometimes overshadowed the issues over which they were fighting. When Alabama governor George C. Wallace, in his race for president in 1968, belittled the Washington establishment as being comprised of "pointy-headed bureaucrats," much of his invective was directed toward the HEW stalwarts whose job it was to determine whether school districts had achieved sufficient compliance with Titles IV and VI to avoid a cutoff of federal dollars. Ideologically—as Panetta described—there were North-South and conservative-liberal face-offs.

But there were other anomalies, as well. The process pitted quarrelsome, small-town southern lawyers against grayish Washington careerists, a cultural mismatch that left both sides suspicious and frustrated. For southern states, which had fought at the loftiest levels of the nation's legislative and judicial systems to retain their much-cherished systems of racial separation, there was some ignominy in the fact that their ultimate fate had fallen into the hands of nine-to-five functionaries.

"School District #19 thinks it is being harassed!" Board Chairman Daniel I. Ross Jr. of Blackville complained in a September 10, 1965, letter to Governor McNair. Contending that the district had submitted four plans of compliance to HEW, "two [of which] were practically written by people from the Department of Health and Education and Welfare," Ross fumed that "the school district has been getting the runaround from the very beginning": "The Federal Government is taking control of the school system in South Carolina. . . . For a small percentage of our total school expenditures we are giving up local control."[41]

Ross's letter typified the lament of South Carolina districts, many of which were confronting for the first time the 1954 Supreme Court decision requiring that the state's dual public-school system be dismantled. It also—perhaps unintentionally—suggested where the state's real vulnerability lay. Ross's contention that the state had at stake only a small percentage of total school expenditures constituted a serious misreading of the state's dependence on federal moneys. Among all the states, in fact, South Carolina was one of the heaviest users of federal dollars in public schools. For the school year 1965–1966, fully 17.3 percent of the state's revenues for public and secondary education came from federal revenue sources, the fourth highest such percentage in the nation and more than twice the national average of 7.8 percent.

At the time, most of the money for public education in South Carolina came from the state level, a condition largely the result of the 3 percent sales tax that had been instituted in 1951 as a last-ditch effort to make its dual school system truly separate but equal. The 3 percent tax, initially designed to meet the capital needs for upgrading facilities, survived as a recurring source of support for public education. By 1965–1966, state funds provided 58.9 percent of all support for public schools, the eighth highest in the nation. Local moneys, coming largely from property tax millage, amounted to less than 28 percent.[42]

The reliance on state dollars reflected a basic South Carolina governmental premise. Property owners, mostly white, were placated by low ad valorem taxes at the local level, while control of state dollars, largely supported by the broad-based and regressive sales and income taxes, was vested with the legislative barons in Columbia, not just for education but for most functions of state and local government, as well.

Formal governing authority of schools and other governmental entities was dispersed across a wide variety of marginally empowered public boards and commissions. The legislators reserved for themselves the real power of budgetary control over school districts, state agencies, and—to a great extent—local governments. In some cases, they even had a prominent role in the selection of many local governing boards and officials, including school districts.

Most South Carolina school districts in 1965, even though they were statutorily governed by local boards, were thus actually beholden to state government and the federal government for more than three-fourths of their annual operating dollars, and therein lay a dilemma that made them—as it evolved—answerable to conflicting masters. The state was ordering them, per legislative enactment of 1956–1962, not to desegregate. The federal government, as of the *Brown* decision in 1954 and the Civil Rights Act of 1964, was telling them just the opposite. Caught squarely in the middle was Bob McNair, the newly installed governor who had been looking to use his interim term as an opportunity to consolidate his political strength in preparation for the 1966 election. He found, instead, an impending political firestorm that potentially could wreck his long-term gubernatorial aspirations.

"Saving Public Education" in South Carolina

Welcome or not, the residue of ten years of inattention to school desegregation lay conspicuously and unavoidably on the doorstep of the new governor as he took office. Implicit in the looming court orders to desegregate was the question of whether South Carolinians would support a racially desegregated public-school system. "At the time, the challenge was not simply to comply with desegregation orders," McNair later recalled, "it was to save public education in South Carolina."[43]

On both counts, the task was formidable. At best, South Carolina had traditionally evinced something of a lukewarm attitude toward the concept of universal public education. It was a state where antebellum culture had once viewed education as a privilege reserved for the landed gentry, many of whom were privately tutored or dispatched outside the state for the socially refining educational experience of Europe or the Ivy League. At the same time, state and local laws forbade literacy among the state's hundreds of thousands of slaves, deeming it potentially dangerous to the orderliness of things in a place where slaves outnumbered whites in some areas by as much as four to one. With that kind of heritage, South Carolina was late, even recalcitrant, in coming to the notion of public schooling for everyone. The provision for free public schools at the state level, in fact, was first enacted by the black-dominated Reconstruction General Assembly in the years of federal occupation after the Civil War, appearing in the state's egalitarian constitution of 1868. Remarkably, even as most of the racially temperate provisions of that document— such as broadly based voting rights—were abandoned in the constitution of 1896, public education somehow survived the ravages of Tillmanism and remained a part of the state's basic governmental framework.

Over the years, however, public education did not fare well in South Carolina. The state's decades of post–Civil War ordeals—economic distress, racial separation, political turmoil, and even the time-consuming accommodations for spring planting and fall harvesting—took their toll on public schools. As the era of desegregation dawned, South Carolina stood near last in many important rankings of achievement and financial support. In the early 1960s, at a time when most American adults went through life with at least a tenth-grade education, South Carolina's median attainment was 8.7 years, the worst in the nation. More than one in twenty South Carolinians were illiterate, and more than half the students who entered the ninth grade dropped out before they graduated, both classifications also the worst in the nation. Perhaps most telling of all, more than 56 percent of all South Carolinians who registered for the draft in 1964 failed preinduction and induction mental requirements.[44]

At least part of the dismal record could be attributed to the weak financial support public schools received. As the state with the nation's next-to-last ranking in per capita income, South Carolina ranked dead last in per capita spending for education, and its spending per pupil was only 65 percent of the national average. Classroom teacher salaries were forty-eighth in the nation, and only slightly more than two out of one hundred of them were earning the national average of $6,500 per year.[45] As the threat of a federal funding cutoff loomed, it was, in short, a time when informed leaders knew that South Carolina could ill afford to lose any of its scarce moneys for public education, whatever the source.

The school districts' financial vulnerability and dependence on federal money came in programs that were especially popular in the state at the time. South Carolina, for example, was among the largest recipients of federal funds from Titles I and II of Public Law 89-10, a program that provided moneys to support a wide range of school activities, including libraries, kindergartens, and—most notably— free or reduced-price lunches. In 1965–1966, all but 5 of the state's 104 school districts were receiving money from Titles I and II, and during that year, they spent $24.2 million of the funds that were allotted to them. Compared to state-appropriated dollars going into public education at the time, and contrary to some popularly held opinions, the federal outlay constituted a substantial amount of the state's cumulative budget for its public schools. Total state-generated expenditures for public education in 1964–1965 were $116.8 million, and a year later, that amount was increased to $126.5 million,[46] meaning that the federal government was providing more than 16 percent of the combined state-federal outlay for public education in the state.

So ingrained, in fact, had the federally funded school lunches become in South Carolina that a survey in 1964 showed more than 56 percent of the state's students receiving hot lunches under the program, fourth highest among the states,[47] and by 1967, the percentage had risen to 65.4 percent, still fourth in the nation.[48] For all the bluff and bluster of unhappy white politicians, therefore, it was unlikely that South Carolina was about to jettison a popular program that was helping to feed some 400,000 of its elementary and secondary students every school day.

Nor was there likely to be much enthusiasm for imposing new taxes—estimated to amount to thousands of local property tax mills—to replace the federal dollars. South Carolina at the time had the lowest per capita state and local tax collections in the nation.[49] According to figures made available to the McNair administration for the 1965–1966 school year, in fact, South Carolina counties and school districts would have had to double their tax millage to compensate for the loss of the Public Law 89-10 dollars. In Dan Ross's Barnwell School District #19 in particular, it would have taken a millage hike from 75 to 148 to offset the loss of the $100,694 the school district was using in Title I and Title II moneys in 1965–1966.[50]

There was, in short, far more than a small percentage of school operating funds at stake in South Carolina in the combat over compliance with Titles IV and VI of the Civil Rights Act of 1964. From a practical point of view, the state was not only running out of time and running out of courts, it would also be running out of money to sustain its public schools even at the current modest level if it lost federal dollars under Title VI. The moment of truth was arriving, and it would be on Bob McNair's watch. More powerful than all the constitutional, legal, and legislative barriers the state had thrown up over the years to safeguard its traditions of segregation, South Carolina was learning that there was, truly, no such thing as a free lunch. "It was a very trying period in the life and history of the state," McNair said, "a very difficult period politically and socially and every other way, and particularly in education."[51]

It was only a matter of months after taking office that the new governor received a report from the state Department of Education entitled "Pupil Integration." It revealed what most people by then at the federal and state levels already knew: South Carolina had scarcely begun the process of desegregation.

Long-Delayed Desegregation

For the school year 1965–1966, fewer than half the state's school districts—forty-eight districts in twenty-eight counties—had made even the first steps toward integration, and what steps had been taken were largely of the token variety. Most of them—like Daniel Ross's Barnwell District #19—had made little or no effort to comply with the eleven-year-old Supreme Court decision. Out of the state's 660,154 students enrolled in the state's public schools that year,[52] all but a relative handful were still attending racially segregated schools. Only 2,121 black students had been enrolled in previously all-white schools that year, a gesture that in most districts amounted to less than 4 percent of the total enrollment. For the same school year, only eighty-two black teachers had crossed racial lines to teach in previously all-white schools.[53]

It was hardly what the Supreme Court had in mind when it declared in 1955 that the desegregation provisions of *Brown* would be carried out "with all deliberate speed." McNair recalled, "Most people at the time felt that 'with all deliberate speed' meant that we have taken a hundred years to get where we are, and it will take us another hundred years to get from where we are to where we ought to be."[54] Cyril Busbee, state superintendent of education during the massive school desegregation of the latter 1960s, said later that in terms of "sheer human rights, to say nothing of civil rights, there was no other decision [than *Brown*] you could come up with." The nature of the decision, he said, however, left indecision as to impact and timing. Even the "all deliberate speed" language of *Brown v. Board of Education II* (1955), Busbee said, was interpreted to mean "Well, take your time . . . but begin to look to see if there's something you can do."[55] McNair recalled:

> There was stalwart opposition to . . . doing anything, regardless of the approach, including actual secession. There were the interposition resolutions, the total opposition [and] . . . the creation of the private school program. . . . There was even strong support, fortunately not in numbers, but strong vocal support for closing the public school system.
>
> We had to stand up to that. South Carolina had a constitutional mandate to maintain a free public school system for all children, and that we had to do.[56]

It was, for McNair, something of a defining moment, and for all his professed reluctance to advance beyond finishing Russell's term, he was not bashful about advancing his own concepts of public education. To him, the challenge of school desegregation and the problems of the state's woeful educational deficiencies were, in fact, not separate issues at all but were elements of an overall educational and economic malaise that had plagued the state for decades. Their solutions, in turn, were bound together in a strategy that recognized that a unitary system could do things that the separate systems could not do, particularly as a means of tying South Carolina's economic future to its ability to get out of the nation's educational basement. A lot of it came from his experience in two of the state's smaller and poorer counties—Berkeley and Allendale. McNair said:

> I came [to the Governor's Office] with a strong commitment to education. I had seen the benefits of a good program with my father as chairman of the consolidated board of trustees in Macedonia where I thought we had, with limited resources, as good a faculty as you could find anywhere. When it came to the basics, we got a good education.
>
> [In] Allendale . . . we saw the positive effects of bringing schools together into one district with one consolidated school program. With progressive, enlightened leadership, it was amazing what they could accomplish there.

In those rural settings, many of them with majority black population, McNair saw desegregation and consolidation as companion processes that afforded what he called "the base" on which to build "and to really improve the quality of education." In rural settings, for generations plagued by out-migration, he saw the opportunity "to reach more people and to retain more people."[57]

The Damage of "Avoidance Steps"

Along the way, he observed, certain things damaging to public education had been done to preserve the racial separation of schools. One of them had been the repeal of the state's compulsory school-attendance law, a step taken by segregationists supposedly to avoid forcing white and black people to go to school together.

"We had taken all kinds of avoidance steps," McNair said. "I was committed to reinstituting the compulsory attendance law, and I recall my reason was that I did not want to raise another generation that we had to support through public welfare. It was a lot cheaper to educate people and find them jobs than it was to support them on welfare or in the corrections system."[58]

Avoidance steps littered the educational landscape in South Carolina, as did structural eccentricities with which the state had organized the final defenses of its "separate but equal" segregated public-school system. Most notable of those structural eccentricities was the Educational Finance Commission, a powerful agency created by the 1951 General Assembly to oversee the management of the proceeds of the 3 percent sales tax adopted that year. So urgently did Byrnes and his legislative colleagues view their eleventh-hour effort to live up to the grievously abused "separate but equal" contention that they chose not to entrust the task to the state's superintendent of education, an elective position that had changed hands only once in the previous forty-two years.

The incumbent in that position was seventy-three-year-old Jesse T. Anderson, who had held that post since 1947; his predecessor as state superintendent was James H. Hope of Newberry, who had held the position from 1923 until 1946 before retiring at age seventy-two.[59] Rather than deal with the vagaries of such entrenched administrations, the legislature chose to create a new entity and to empower it in four specific areas it considered the school system to be the most vulnerable and inequitable: (1) school district organization; (2) school buildings; (3) transportation; and (4) textbooks.

Not all of South Carolina's educational difficulties were race-related, it had become clear by that time. As early as 1947, the legislature had authorized a study of the state's school system, and a year-and-a-half later, results of that study told a grim story of the condition of public education in the state. According to long-time state auditor Patrick C. "Pat" Smith, who was chief financial officer of the State Department of Education at the time, "The state was more disorganized than organized."[60]

Smith recalled that the South Carolina Constitution of 1896 "prohibited the creation of a school district of more than 49 miles in area or less than nine square miles." As a result, he said, the state had some 1,680 school districts in 1947. "You could drive down the road, light a cigarette, and before you finished, you had passed through three or four school districts," he wryly observed.[61]

Smith's view from the perspective of the white educational establishment was shared by historian I. A. Newby, who wrote, "The [public school] system was hardly a system at all. It was a conglomerate of independent districts which were often more concerned with local autonomy than educational quality. The state did little more than help finance this arrangement and certify its uneven results. Local all-white school boards made most fundamental decisions and held the real power in the state."[62]

Two hundred of the school districts no longer operated any schools, Smith recalled, under a provision that left up to each individual school district the decision of whether or not to operate schools. "There were four thousand schools . . . with less than four teachers [and] there were over two thousand one-teacher schools in South Carolina," he said.[63] The cost of such an overhaul would have come to more than $12 million of state funds, an amount that "was a substantial sum" at the time, according to Smith. "For that reason, probably as much as anything else, none of the recommendations was immediately effectuated."[64]

Pearson and Briggs Challenge the Status Quo

It was about that time, in 1947, that Levi Pearson, a black farmer in Clarendon County, filed suit for equal bus transportation for his children. Three years later, Harry Briggs and nineteen other petitioners in Clarendon County District 22 filed their suit broadly attacking the overall inequality of the state's school system. Knowing of the state's educational deficiencies and sensing the likelihood of judicial and public examination of racial inequities, Governor James F. Byrnes mobilized the state's legislature to address the inequities and to live up to the then-operative mandate of *Plessy v. Ferguson* to deliver a "separate but equal" system.

In South Carolina, Smith recalled, "separate was not equal [and] what had to be done was simply to . . . rebuild the school system for blacks."

> My recollection at the time is that white school property in 1950 was valued at about 700 million dollars, and Negro schools were valued at about $70 million, about ten per cent [of the white value]. . . . The population proportions were roughly 60 per cent white and 40 per cent black.[65]

It was in that atmosphere that the 1951 General Assembly enacted the 3 percent sales tax and created the State Education Finance Commission to carry out the overhaul of the state's schools sufficiently to achieve the separate but equal status in facilities it considered necessary to withstand potential scrutiny and challenges to the dual school system. Historian Newby reported that between 1953 and 1957 the value of school property for black schools in South Carolina rose from $19.7 million to $107.4 million, and that the number of elementary schools for blacks dropped from 2,975 in 1950 to 393 in 1960. During the same period, he reported, there was a reduction in the number of one- and two-teacher schools from 1,434 to 16 and an increase in the number of accredited high schools from 80 to 145. "It was not equality," Newby wrote, "but it was certainly progress."[66]

The formidable Education Finance Commission was still in place when McNair became governor in April 1965, as was the South Carolina School Committee, known as the "Gressette Committee" for its longtime chairman, Senator L. Marion Gressette of St. Matthews. The Gressette Committee, formed under Governor Byrnes's administration in 1951 and abolished at its own request in 1966, was acknowledged by most as a mechanism to forestall the desegregation of South Carolina public schools.[67]

By 1965, both entities had outlived their original purpose and had adapted their roles to evolving conditions within the state. Historian John Sproat credited the Gressette Committee with absorbing much of the state's pent-up anger and frustration over desegregation. "When it closed its books in 1966, the committee could claim fairly that during its tenure, no school had been closed because of racial incidents, no one had died or suffered from racial violence in the state's schools and colleges, and no federal troops or marshals had ever turned fixed bayonets, tear gas guns, rifles and tanks against the people of South Carolina."[68]

For its part, the Education Finance Commission, in carrying out its mission of upgrading facilities, equipment, and systems, had become something of an emissary of the white educational establishment into the state's long-neglected black schools. Until then, the gulf between the state's separate black and white school systems was so wide that as pressure began to build for desegregation in the early 1960s, State Superintendent Anderson felt the need to create a liaison position for relations with black schools, which he gave the remarkable title "State Agent for Negroes." Prior to that time, the most significant acknowledgment of black educational interests had been the appointment in 1951–1952 of Mrs. Sylvia Poole Swinton as state supervisor for black elementary schools, the first black South Carolinian to attain a statewide supervisory position.[69]

A "State Agent for Negroes"

Anderson's choice to become state agent for Negroes was a white Tennessean named Jesse A. Coles Jr., a graduate of Austin Peay University who had helped to work his way through graduate school at George Peabody College (now part of Vanderbilt University) by playing bass for country-and-western bands in Nashville. Taking advantage of both his music and educational skills, he came to South Carolina in the early 1960s as a combination high school principal and band director in the Pee Dee tobacco town of Mullins. Coles, who later rose to prominence as a deputy state superintendent of education under Busbee and executive director of the State Budget and Control Board, recalled that it was common practice for district school superintendents to consider their duties as being limited to the white schools in their respective districts. "I soon found out that at the local level," Coles later recalled, "the superintendent primarily took a hands-off attitude toward black schools, and the principal in the black school was a position of significance in the community."[70]

One of Coles's early assignments was to bring to the attention of the state's white educational leadership the reality of conditions in the state's black schools. An example Coles cited was Northfield, a black high school near Norway in Orangeburg County. "I had a list that said there were 80 or 90 kids in an English class," Coles said. "So, I went to the superintendent's office and said this was totally unacceptable—30 kids max."

After the superintendent questioned the actual attendance in the class, Coles recalled, "I said, 'Let's go see.' We went; every kid was present. They were sitting three to a desk in those little desks." With support from Anderson and the State Department of Education, Coles said, two teachers and two portable classrooms were added later in the school year.[71]

In his role of bringing such conditions to the attention of the white power structure, Coles functioned with a two-person staff, and the physical limitations of such token operation were obvious. But Coles was also developing alliances with the Education Finance Commission staff, a group of hand-picked professionals who were systematically attacking some of the fundamental inequities and weaknesses in the state's dual school system.

"By creating the Education Finance Commission," McNair remembered, "we took a lot of the politics out of it [upgrading the black school system]. That was a group of very, very strong people who were determined to use this money [the increased state revenues occasioned by the 3 percent sales tax], and they were the ones who had to approve the utilization of it for the construction of schools."[72]

In the waning years of Anderson's tenure as state superintendent of education, the Finance Commission was like a separate education department for the state, and its critical tasks were assigned to some of the state's top educators. Among the notables were Ryan Crow, former superintendent of schools in Sumter; Pat Smith, the veteran financial officer from the State Department of Education; Ralph Durham, brought out of retirement to build a transportation system from the old "Jitney" routes; and Cecil Tucker of the University of South Carolina, whose assignment was to reduce 1,200 school districts to 105.

It was, in retrospect, a remarkable moment. As Sproat observed:

Never before, not even in the days of Radical Reconstruction, had white South Carolinians been asked to spend tax dollars to benefit black people . . . and [it] marked a slight, but significant, change in the tone of racial politics. It indicated as well that the Governor and his advisors recognized both the inevitability of change and the vulnerability of South Carolina to federal action in support of change. The massive school building program that followed did not prevent desegregation . . . but it had the salutary effect of providing the physical base for a subsequent general improvement of education in the state.[73]

In terms of salvaging the segregated public-school system, it was indeed far too little, far too late. But the Education Finance Commission and its staff built the facilities and the systems upon which much of the unified school system would be based in the latter half of the 1960s. Also from the commission in subsequent years would come some of the educational professionals who would shape a rejuvenated State Department of Education as a major force in seeing the state through the stormy days of massive school desegregation during that pivotal last half of the 1960s.

Jesse Anderson's plans for retirement in 1966 opened the door for new leadership at the helm of the agency that represented the state's public education establishment. As an elective position, the office would also be something of a political barometer of sentiment in South Carolina as the state neared its long-delayed date with desegregation. By then, Bob McNair recognized that much of the success or failure of his administration—were he to be elected governor in 1966—would depend upon the effectiveness of the new superintendent and the compatibility of a McNair administration with that of the new public-school leader.

McNair also realized that what lay ahead in desegregating the state's public-school system would be far too massive to permit the fine-tuning and orchestration that had accompanied desegregation of Columbia lunch counters, Clemson, and the University of South Carolina. Whereas only a relative handful of people had been involved in those events, statewide public-school desegregation would involve hundreds of thousands of students, teachers, and administrators and would—in one way or another—reach into the homes of virtually every South Carolinian. Maintaining peace on such a broad scale would require a united front of political leadership, which, if it could not sell South Carolinians on the merits of desegregation, could at least make the case for the strategy of using up all the courts. In so doing, it might also tap into the state's unusual proclivity for control and order in its public life and its conditioned distaste for demagogues.

Republicans as the Party of Resistance

To challenge that strategy would be the newly energized Republican Party. Fired by the conservatism of the new GOP icon Barry Goldwater and given credibility by the switch of Senator Strom Thurmond to the Republican ranks, it was offering a political home and haven for disenchanted white South Carolinians who believed Democrats were not fighting hard enough to resist desegregation. Republicans were also offering an almost full slate of candidates for the impending 1966 general election to challenge the evolving centrism of the Democrats and to provide an aggressively articulated alternative to McNair's plan of accommodation. The GOP, for a while little more than a support group for popular individual candidates, was growing as an organization, even beyond the status that Thurmond provided.

McNair believed it took more than Thurmond's switch to build the Republican Party:

> When Senator Strom Thurmond switched parties, that was the birth, the real birth, of the Republican Party [but] . . . the fact that Strom Thurmond was an independent kept the party from really becoming instantly established. . . . He would never endorse or support anyone else. He never let the Republican Party build around him. He kept that independence because he leaned heavily on the same people we did, the county courthouse crowd, and he avoided being the South Carolina Republican, a "Mr. Republican," as some others did.
>
> So it [the Republican Party] really emerged in South Carolina that way with Thurmond. It [later] grew up as a resistance to integration.[74]

The redefining of politics in South Carolina applied not only to parties and organizations, but also to terminology itself. It was the period, according to McNair, "when conservatism and liberalism began to take on new meanings":

> Up until then, conservatives were fiscally conservative people, and liberals were free spenders. Therefore, we were all conservatives in the South. Franklin Roosevelt and [presidents after him] battled the conservative South, [but it was a South] that was identified as being conservative on fiscal policies.
>
> Conservatism began to take on new meanings [in the 1960s]. It became how you felt about civil rights. . . . The integration question emerged as . . . the more dominant factor in determining whether somebody was a conservative or liberal. We had to coin the phrase "moderate." So then, we became the moderate Southerners. It did not have a thing to do with fiscal matters, other than as it related to programs to do something for less fortunate people. I still think the conservative-liberal identification was almost exclusively built around the civil rights movement at that time.[75]

The McNair campaign for governor in 1966, therefore, would be fought on new political terrain with new political organizations and even newly minted political terminology. It would also be the most aggressively contested fight over racial issues and values the state had seen since the 1890s. For McNair, whose twenty-one months in office had been intended as a completion of the initiatives of Donald Russell and as a time to build consensus toward his own gubernatorial ambitions, things had been unexpectedly accelerated. The 1964 Civil Rights Act and 1965 Voting Rights Act had driven the state out of its post-*Brown* inertia and had drawn political lines that forced the state's leaders to take sides. Thurmond and the nascent Republican Party had emerged as champions of resistance; McNair and his Democratic colleagues had chosen various forms of centrist moderation.

McNair as the Candidate of Compliance

The McNair candidacy in 1966 thus had something of a built-in agenda, an agenda of implicit accommodation with federal requirements, and the implicit assurance to the state that such compliance would be built around the strategy of gradualism. It was a strategy that offered to detractors clearly visible targets for attack and left for supporters what were often complicated and difficult positions to describe.

Centrism in South Carolina in the 1960s, in fact, was neither easily explained nor facilely pursued. It was an awkwardly articulated strategy that required more than single champions or heroes; it needed a broad range of supporters who could defend a sometimes ambiguous position against the political left or right and maintain working relationships across a wide variety of governmental and political levels and jurisdictions. "It may have looked awfully good to be able to go out to the football stadium and have everybody stand and cheer and wave the flag for you when you said we were still going to fight until the last," McNair once said, "but we knew we could not win."[76]

In short, for his strategy to succeed, McNair needed more than an election victory for himself as governor. He needed political and philosophical friends in positions of power throughout the state's eccentric governmental structure, and that meant his interests in the 1966 races extended beyond his own candidacy. Besides the critical role of the state superintendent of education, McNair needed allies who could bring the necessary political and philosophical cohesion to the state's new centrism. He needed peacekeepers at home, power in the legislature, strength in the courts, and firm relations with Washington. If ever McNair needed a "we" strategy, it would be in 1966.

Critically important in that first line of defense was the oligarchy of legislative leadership—Brown, Blatt, and Gressette—all by then established and skilled manipulators of the various instruments of gradualism and peaceful accommodation. They were politically secure, and they were the heirs and executors of the state's tradition of political control. They were not only McNair allies in the effort to ward off potential disruptions, they were the prime beneficiaries of the credo of "stability at all costs" that bound together the state's traditional rural leaders.

McNair also needed key operatives within other politically sensitive positions. Aside from the crucial office of superintendent of education, there were also the attorney general, who would guide the state's legal strategy and serve as the governor's top-ranking lawyer, and the lieutenant governor, who could become a key legislative supporter for the governor. Also critical would be a uniquely South

Carolina creation known as the State Budget and Control Board, a legislative/executive hybrid that oversaw most of the important central governmental management functions. Established in 1951 as the major part of a postwar governmental restructuring initiative during Thurmond's term as governor (1947–1951), the five-member board comprised the chairmen of two key legislative budget committees—Senate Finance and House Ways and Means—along with the state's two elected finance officers, the state treasurer and the comptroller general. The governor served as chair of the unusual five-member political conglomerate, but had only one of five votes on any major decision.

Under South Carolina's decentralized system at the time, most of the agencies were governed by citizen boards and commissions and there was little in the way of central management of state government. But in a system in which the office of governor had not been accorded much power by the 1896 constitution, the state Budget and Control Board did have the one authority critical to a chief executive office. It proposed the annual budget to the state legislature, and that document more than any other defined the state's policies and priorities.

Building the Team of Moderates

State senator Edgar Brown, who had been chairman of Senate Finance since 1942, was a fixture on the board, and the House Ways and Means chairman was Jim Aycock of Sumter, a Blatt ally who could be expected to be friendly to a McNair governorship. But with the retirement of longtime comptroller general E. C. "Dusty" Rhodes, and with the unexpected death on August 18, 1966, of the state's highly regarded state treasurer, Jeff Bates, two of the board's five seats were open and would be filled by newcomers in the November election. Rhodes, Bates, and Brown had been original members of the board when it was created in 1951, and the 1966 election—in which a new comptroller general and state treasurer would be elected—would represent the first major interruption of the board's original leadership. A sweep by Democrats favorable to McNair's centrist, moderate position—along with the ongoing harmony McNair held with rural legislative bosses Brown, Gressette, and Blatt—would give the new governor not only a mandate of popular support for his strategy in support of civil rights and racial peace, it would also put in place the kind of power figures who could deliver political support at critical, bumpy stages of what promised to be a stormy ride. Anything less than a sweep, however, could seriously hamper a man whose major strength was viewed as his ability to organize a "we" mentality across a broad range of political and philosophical fronts.

Lining up for those key races was a combination of veterans and newcomers, and at least one of them was a one-time McNair adversary. John West, a Camden attorney and three-term state senator, had been a key supporter of Marshall Parker in the 1962 lieutenant governor's race, and McNair acknowledged that the "Parker campaign divided us . . . [it] caused very strained relations":

It put me in a position that if Rex Carter had wanted to run for Lieutenant Governor, I had let everybody know that I had an obligation to him and intended to carry that out because I felt I owed him one.

Carter, however, "got busy building in his law practice and working as Speaker Pro Tem," according to McNair, "and this let John West, who was aggressive and hustling and hardworking, just go out and outwork him." Carter's decision not to run, McNair said, "left us sitting there with no choice."[77]

In West, however, McNair found a comfortable political ally. "We all knew his capabilities," McNair said. "He was articulate and bright and good." West was a close friend of Senator Edgar Brown's, and in comparing him to Carter, McNair said,

John was probably more of an idealist.

[He] was more aggressive and probably more liberal. . . . John's views had come from his upbringing and his background and politics in Kershaw County. He had to battle almost the strongest Ku Klux Klan–type of activity of anybody in the state, and he never won by more than five-to-ten votes in Kershaw County.

Camden is what everybody identifies [in Kershaw County], but then you get out into other parts of that county, and it is tough. It is two different types of people [and] John was always looking for the Utopia.[78]

Incumbent attorney general Dan McLeod, a member in good standing of the powerful McLeod political clan of the Pee Dee, was a salty veteran of the state's political wars who brought a quick legal mind, a keen sense of humor, and a well-honed appreciation of political pragmatism to his job. He was a nephew of Governor Thomas G. McLeod of Bishopville (1923–1927), and a veteran of naval service in World War II, when he spent much of the war decoding secret messages in Europe, many of them from Franklin Roosevelt to Winston Churchill.[79] He was also a two-term incumbent as attorney general.

Like West, McLeod was no McNair insider and admitted that he came to know McNair initially only as a close friend of Speaker Blatt's and found him "a decent fellow and not a conniver."[80] He admired McNair as being "moderate, open-minded . . . a Grade A Governor,"[81] but he confessed that he found the 1962 McNair-Parker race for lieutenant governor "just a powder-puff campaign . . . like a couple of people running for president of the student body."[82]

The 1966 race brought two newcomers to statewide politics in the Democratic camp. The sudden death of Jeff Bates left a vacuum in the state's fiscal leadership and a glaring hole in the Democratic Party ticket. Emerging as a candidate for the vacant treasurer's office was a young attorney from the textile town of Calhoun Falls named Grady Patterson, who had caught McNair's attention while serving as assistant attorney general on loan to the fledgling McNair staff during the interim governorship. Patterson would be involved in a four-way primary race for the office. Comptroller General Rhodes's seat was up for grabs in a four-way primary that included among the candidates a popular former highway patrolman, Henry Mills, who had served as a member of the House from York County for one term and had been sergeant-at-arms of the House during McNair's years of service there.

Completing the Team: Cyril Busbee as Education Chief

But while candidates like West, McLeod, Mills, and Patterson gave McNair some key allies at the party's center, it was the position of superintendent of education that was at the heart of the strategy. Although in South Carolina's bifurcated system, the state superintendent had no direct control over the local school districts, the position in the right hands could be of profound importance in exercising the kind of consensus-building so critical to McNair's effectiveness. The position, in fact, was so critical to McNair that it was not entirely left to chance. The "Dirty Dozen," the informal advisory group of the state's major school superintendents, had come together to discuss major public-school issues, especially desegregation, and McNair utilized the group for guidance and advice as he formulated his own policies and strategies. Included in the group were ten superintendents from large districts and Henry White of Allendale, who had been McNair's superintendent in Macedonia. The group met regularly with McNair, and as time drew near for the choice of a successor to Jesse Anderson, the Dirty Dozen was asked to select the man they thought could best lead the state through the stressful times of public-school desegregation.

The consensus choice, McNair recalled, was Cyril Busbee, the superintendent of Brookland-Cayce schools across the Congaree River from Columbia in Lexington County. From a professional perspective, Busbee had impressive credentials. He not only had the backing of his fellow administrators (he had served as president of the state's School Administrators Association); he also had two other important bases of support, classroom teachers and the sports community. Busbee had been president of the South Carolina Education Association, the statewide teachers' organization, and he had also served as president of the state's High School League, the sports association. Few administrators could claim such broad-based support among organizations that were often feuding with each other.[83] Busbee had also come to McNair's attention through Columbia businessman and trusted insider Bob Davis, and although McNair had not met Busbee at that time, he trusted the judgment of the Dirty Dozen and Davis that Busbee was the man needed to see the state peacefully through the ordeal that lay ahead.[84]

A native of the Aiken County town of Wagener, Busbee had a reputation for decisiveness and no-nonsense operation of the Brookland-Cayce district in Lexington County, which bordered Columbia's Richland County District One on the west side of the Congaree River. He also had the kind of down-home practical liberalism common to rural South Carolinians who—like McNair—grew up amid the impoverished conditions of the 1920s and 1930s. Living for most of his later life in Lexington County, which would become a bastion of Republican Party conservative strength, Busbee later described himself as "not necessarily a conservative. I've done some mighty unconservative things and gotten away with them."[85]

Busbee himself attended one of the state's one-teacher schools—Neeston Elementary—then fast-tracked his way through school so that he finished Wagener High School at age fifteen. By the time he was nineteen, he had graduated from the University of South Carolina and was embarking on his first teaching job at Homersville, Georgia. Denied the opportunity to pursue a banking career because of the economic conditions of the times, Busbee was superintendent of two South Carolina rural school districts before arriving in 1943 at Brookland-Cayce (later Lexington District Two) at age thirty-five.

Like McNair, Busbee's career was interrupted by World War II service in the Navy, and he returned to Brookland-Cayce to oversee major postwar consolidation of the districts, including the merger of seven feeder districts with Brookland-Cayce in 1949, two years prior to the Byrnes overhaul and the major statewide consolidation of 1951. The 1949 mergers in Lexington County were accomplished largely through the political initiative of Busbee. He recalled half a century later—still strong-minded and feisty at age ninety-two—that one of the mergers required approval from a three-member school board, two of whom were illiterate, "even to the extent of not being able to sign their names."[86]

Jesse Coles, who later became one of Busbee's deputy superintendents in the State Department of Education, attributed Busbee's candidacy for state superintendent in 1966 to Davis, a longtime member of Richland District One Board and a major mover-and-shaker in Columbia as president of the R. L. Bryan Company. "He and a bunch of people who really were trying to bring about peaceful change absolutely got behind Cyril Busbee and convinced him to run and backed him," Coles remembered.[87] Busbee acknowledged Davis's role. "The person I would have to blame for my being state superintendent of education—or credit—whichever way you want to put it—would be Bob Davis. I had known him casually, just socially a bit, and we always considered . . . each of us as friends of the other. He was an astute businessman, and he was loaded with common sense."[88]

Asked if he interpreted Davis's encouragement for his candidacy as coming with McNair's knowledge, Busbee said, "Yes, because I know they were close." In urging him to run, Busbee recalled Davis as saying, in effect, "We can't think of anybody who could do a better job in the situation that you're going to face." As a superintendent, Busbee said, "I knew what situations we were going to face because I figured . . . I was here and we had the same problems as every other school district had."[89]

As was often the case in races for an open statewide seat, candidates emerged from various geographic bases of support around the state. Busbee was the

Midlands candidate; from the upcountry came Townes Holland of Spartanburg and Bill Royster of Anderson. Ed Eaddy of Georgetown was the Pee Dee/low-country candidate. Of his three opponents, Busbee's most serious contender was Royster, a respected professional in the State Department of Education who had the support of elements of the educational community, including Coles. Later hired by Busbee for a key role in his administration, Coles remembered confiding in Busbee, "I'm going to have to tell you I worked for your opponent," to which Busbee fired back, according to Coles, "You think I didn't know that? I didn't ask about your politics; I asked you to help me reorganize the department."[90]

1966: A Political Sweepstakes

Getting elected in South Carolina in 1966 was an especially difficult affair for Democrats. As a holdover from the one-party days, the Democratic primary was still a stern statewide test, particularly for the vacated seats of comptroller general, treasurer, and superintendent of education. Awaiting the primary winners in the November general election, however—for the first time in the twentieth century—was almost a full slate of Republican candidates, many of them former Democrats who carried to the GOP not only name recognition but a high degree of experience and individual prominence. In an unusual twist of events, both U.S. Senate seats were being contested in the same election. That quirky development came about because the interim service of Donald Russell as successor to Olin D. Johnston, which began April 22, 1965, lasted only until the next general election, 1966.

It was a political sweepstakes if there ever was one. Associated Press newsman Al Lanier wrote in mid-October, "Except for an aging handful with recollections of Reconstruction, nobody in South Carolina can remember a political year like this one. The state Republican Party, for 75 years a minuscule organization remote from the public pulse, is now riding a wave of anti-administration sentiment that could conceivably sweep the GOP into control of the state capital and the Congressional delegation."[91]

All Senate and congressional seats were up for grabs, as were those of the governor and all the state constitutional officers and 174 legislative seats. And all the state's political heavyweights at the time were engaged. Hollings was challenging Russell in the Democratic primary for the Senate in a renewal of the bitter 1958 governor's race won handily by Hollings. Awaiting the winner of that contest was Marshall Parker, still smarting from his 1962 loss to McNair in the Democratic primary and contending in his conversion to the GOP that he had been a Republican "in his heart" since 1952, and that he wanted "no part of the Negro vote."[92]

Although there had been strong South Carolina sentiment for GOP presidential candidate Dwight Eisenhower in 1952 and 1956, much of the Republicans' success in South Carolina had been spasmodic until Goldwater's race in 1964 and Thurmond's switch to the GOP later that year. The newly energized party, recast in the philosophy of Goldwater conservatism and molded in South Carolina around the issue of school desegregation, emerged in 1966 not only with almost a full slate of statewide candidates but also with an aggressive, crisply packaged case against Democrats, incumbency, school integration, and government in general. Notable national figures such as Richard Nixon and Gerald Ford visited the state for fund-raising events, and a combative internal organization headed by former Thurmond aide and future Nixon staffer Harry Dent was proving to be downright irksome to some entrenched Democrats and an absolute delight to news-hungry capitol reporters.

Typical of the frontal attacks of Republican candidates was the blast by Joseph O. Rogers, McNair's opponent for governor, in the fall general-election campaign: "Lyndon Johnson's candidates in South Carolina are dependent on some Negro leaders, union leaders, and Democratic faithful to deliver their sizable chunk of bloc vote."[93] As the race evolved, there would be oft-repeated GOP charges designed to keep race, organized labor, and Johnson as ongoing issues of visibility and contention.

The Republicans were also hammering away at McNair and others on whether the state had indeed "run out of time and run out of courts" in its resistance to desegregation. The state could "slow down to a crawl" federal intervention in public schools and hospitals, Rogers said, by hiring a staff of "skilled attorneys and specialists" who would work directly for the governor "to take on federal officials," thus diminishing the role of the state's elective attorney general in such determinations.[94] Rogers was also among those who did not "feel that withdrawal of $10 million in federal funds now going to the state's school system would have much effect on educational progress."[95]

For statewide newcomers Busbee and Patterson, the Democratic primary proved a particularly severe test. Busbee recalled that for all the anxiety over school desegregation, the primary was relatively free of racial discussion or debate, to some extent because "I think we all knew" of the impending desegregation of the school system. The state superintendent's race, he said, "was not hot" and was influenced "by forces not related necessarily to education."[96] For whatever may have been the issues, however, the Busbee-Royster race went down to the wire, and in a runoff, Busbee won by 108 votes.

Grady Patterson's candidacy was perhaps the most improbable of them all. If there was one unassailable political presence in South Carolina in 1966, it was longtime state treasurer Bates, from the lower Richland community of Wateree. Bates, sixty-nine, had been generally credited with stabilizing the state's finances after the disastrous Depression years and had served with no political opposition since assuming the office on January 15, 1941. His credibility was such that neither party offered opposition to the longtime Democrat.

When Bates collapsed suddenly and died from a heart attack in August 1966, the shock waves were profound. Retired state auditor seventy-four-year-old James

M. Smith was appointed by McNair to fill out Bates's term, and the Democrats set about to organize a primary to nominate a replacement on the ballot for Bates. Democratic attorney general McLeod ruled that by not filing in April to oppose Bates, the Republicans had lost their right to place a candidate on the ballot. A subsequent request by the GOP for a special session of the legislature was denied by McNair, who responded curtly by letter to Republican executive director Harry Dent by asserting that a cost of $200,000 would be incurred "to remedy your neglect and failure to follow the statutory procedures."[97] Dent called McNair's letter "snide," and the best the GOP could do in that race was to mount the unsuccessful write-in candidacy of W. W. Wannamaker of Orangeburg in the general election.

Patterson, in his first political race, was pitted against three other Democrats in the August primary, Mason T. Motes of Laurens, William Garrett of Spartanburg, and Tom E. Elliott of Richland County.[98] Patterson wound up in a runoff against Elliott and easily defeated the Richland County treasurer and longtime Democratic leader by 31,080 votes to 18,593.[99]

As primaries gave way to general-election campaigns, and as the grueling South Carolina summer gave way to an only slightly cooler autumn, the state braced for the biggest two-party showdown in its history. Hollings had dispatched Russell handily again in the Senate primary and was taking on Parker; Thurmond was pitted against a popular state senator named Bradley Morrah from Greenville. Morrah was trying to hedge his bet by running at the same time to retain his seat in the South Carolina Senate. McNair was matched against Rogers, and West against Aiken attorney Marshall Cain. Except for the Thurmond-Morrah race, they all figured to be close, with most observers not certain just how strong the fledgling Republican Party organization would be in the top races.

An Aggressive Opponent for Governor

Joe Rogers was new to statewide campaigning and lacked the name recognition and overall experience that McNair brought to the contest. Fellow Pee Dee native Dan McLeod described him as "a very fine fellow . . . an exemplary person. You couldn't throw any bricks at his character or anything of that nature. He's just a plain Republican and an ineffective campaigner. . . . I don't think he expected to be elected because he's too much of a realist."[100]

Rogers came across, however, as one of the new breed of aggressive GOP candidates who would leave a lasting impact on South Carolina politics for decades to come. A Manning attorney and a veteran of three years' service in World War II with the Army Corps of Engineers, Rogers was elected to the House in 1955, served four terms there with McNair, and said that he voted for McNair in the 1962 lieutenant governor's race against Marshall Parker. "I always thought of him as a friend," Rogers said of McNair.[101]

Besides being attorneys, USC graduates, and World War II veterans, McNair and Rogers had other similarities. They both came from small counties, and both had benefited from the favor and support of Speaker Blatt during their years in the House. Rogers served from 1955 to 1966, and prior to his decision to run for governor as a Republican, he was described by Charleston journalist Hugh Gibson as "one of the most influential lawmakers in the Lower Chamber . . . and almost certain of promotion if he remains a Democrat." Gibson's article went on to observe, "Rogers was a favorite of Donald S. Russell during the latter's tenure as governor [1962–1965]. House Speaker Solomon Blatt thought highly enough of the tall lawyer to name him to the Senate Reapportionment Study Committee last year."[102] During his legislative career, Rogers supported a number of major causes, including the state's technical-education system, a limited mandatory school-attendance law, and a tuition-grants program to encourage South Carolina students to attend private colleges.

McNair and Rogers also enjoyed English literature, but there the similarities ended. Among McNair's favorites were light, hopeful romantics like Tennyson and Browning, and one of his favorite lines was Browning's "Ah, but a man's reach should exceed his grasp / Or what's a heaven for?" By contrast, Rogers preferred the stern, authoritarian voice of the Puritan John Milton, and he kept with him for years a paper he had written during his college days at USC on the seventeenth-century English poet. "In God's decision to allow the forces of hell to remain powerful and launch an attack on the earth," Rogers wrote, "Milton saw, not Earth's destruction, but rather an opportunity for man to prove his worth. This concept is the basis for everything we do today."[103]

The literary comparison gave insight into the two men. McNair was conversational and compromising; Rogers tended to be stern and absolute. Their differences, in fact, were much deeper, particularly when it came to public-school desegregation. Rogers—whose home county of Clarendon was the site of the original *Briggs v. Elliott* school-desegregation suit—reminded voters that he had been a member since 1956 of the South Carolina School Committee (the so-called desegregation watchdog known as the Gressette Committee), an experience that he said was instrumental in his decision to run for governor.[104] It gave him strong standing and credibility to attack the McNair administration in the pursuit of its strategy of moderation and compliance with federal court orders.

In announcing his change of parties, Rogers believed it was the Democratic Party and not he who had changed positions in adopting the moderate stance. "I have had no change of heart or change of philosophy. . . . The Republican Party's philosophy is more closely related to Clarendon County feeling, and I believe to South Carolina feeling among the masses, rather than the National Democratic Party."[105]

For all the perceived ideological advantages the GOP may have felt, however, there were several factors that worked against the newcomers. While the Republicans seemed to have staked out the traditionally popular South Carolina position against desegregation and seemed to be aggressively beating their Democratic foes to the punch in media coverage, the Democrats were still the bosses when it came to local races, and the 1966 political contests seemed to turn on more than ideological debates or media battles.

A reapportionment order aimed at rural Democratic leaders, for example, may have provided an unexpected short-term benefit to statewide Democratic candidates. In a movement fraught with historic irony, McNair called a special session of the General Assembly on December 14, 1965, to deal with a federal order requiring reapportionment of the state Senate. The order was based on a one-man, one-vote suit filed on September 23 by South Carolinians Dexter and Hazel O'Shields of Spartanburg, who contended that a Senate majority (52 percent) was elected by only 23 percent of the voters.[106]

Last Hurrah for the Old Guard

The three-judge federal panel upheld that position, ordering that the Senate be reapportioned on a one-man, one-vote basis, a ruling that spelled the beginning of the end for South Carolina's traditional rural-based power structure. As writer Bill Rone of the *State* reported on the special session, "Hanging over the whole scene was the thought in the minds of many small county senators that they might be setting forth to legislate themselves out of office."[107]

For Edgar Brown in particular, the dissolution of the old rural power base was distressing. As noted in Rone's account, "A member of the Senate since 1929 and long its most powerful member, Brown lashed out at the . . . rulings that forced reapportionment on the General Assembly. At one point, Brown, noting a covey of photographers clicking away, quipped, 'I hope no one objects to the taking of what may be your last picture here.' He was half-serious: 'We've got to keep our humor, I guess. But this is the most dangerous short period in the history of our government.'"[108]

While the reapportioning of the Senate would have the long-term effect of diminishing the power of rural, traditionally Democratic senators[109] and creating a new corps of suburban, largely Republican senators, the short-term impact of the reapportionment was probably beneficial to the Democrats. Unlike the usual procedure by which half the Senate seats were up for election every two years, the reapportionment plan required that all seats be filled in the 1966 election. This meant that all Democratic incumbents choosing to run to retain their office would be activating their organizations at the local level, generating more than the usual Democratic turnout.

Another disadvantage for the insurgent Republicans was the fact that 1966 was an off-year election, meaning there was no presidential race that year. Not since the days of Franklin Roosevelt had Democrats in South Carolina felt any kind of boost from their presidential candidates, and in the case of Dwight Eisenhower and Barry Goldwater in particular, South Carolinians had clearly rallied around Republicans. But while those coattails may have been instrumental in the rise of the party, the absence of a popular presidential candidate at the top of the 1966 Republican ticket in South Carolina probably weakened the GOP impact. For all their demonizing of incumbent Democratic President Lyndon Johnson, South Carolina Republicans still could not vote against him in 1966, and the best Republican strategists could deliver was a message of guilt by association about Democratic candidates at the state and local levels.

The GOP pursued this strategy aggressively and persistently, making the president a scapegoat for everything from Vietnam policy (Thurmond called LBJ a "traitor")[110] to coloring books. Rogers became particularly exercised over a coloring book he found in public schools in which a small child was depicted as asking President Johnson in person for assistance in the state's beautification program. "Brainwashing," Rogers fumed. "Why tell our children that in order to clean up South Carolina they must go to Lyndon Johnson for help?" he asked, calling McNair "the candidate of control of direction and thought—brainwashing if you will." McNair did not respond directly to Rogers, saying instead, "If Mr. Dent and company want to keep up the campaign at the kindergarten level, that's all right with me."[111]

McNair, whose honeymoon with state Democrats was still such that he had no opposition in the 1966 primary,[112] spent much of the campaign parrying from a distance with media-oriented Republicans. In the days before television debates and heavy electronic concentration on political campaigns, the Democrats and Republicans lobbed long-range shots at each other and rarely made direct contact. Democrats tended to keep to themselves, work their longstanding local organizations, and concentrate on logistical items such as voter turnout and personal political followings. Republicans, without the decades of organizational strength at the local level, resorted to high-density news-media strategies, issuing press releases and some fifteen to twenty position papers with great frequency and regularity. As the campaign neared its conclusion, McNair snappishly attacked what he called "a political propaganda machine at Five Points in Columbia [location of state GOP headquarters], that grinds out news releases faster than the newspapers can print them."

The variables and complexities of McNair's moderate positions on civil rights and education were not easily disseminated or digested by daily political reporters and often found more analytical attention on the editorial page. One such favorable treatment came from the friendly *Florence Morning News,* whose editor, Jim Rogers (no relation to Joe Rogers), was an avowed McNair supporter. Rogers later wrote that his paper and the *Greenwood Index-Journal* were the state's only two liberal newspapers. In an open defense and explanation of the state's position on school desegregation, the newspaper itemized eight principles of McNair's program, listing them as "Quotations from the Governor."[113]

As the campaign wore on, McNair said that he "is proud that [the] campaign consists primarily of people all over the state who believe in me and my record" and that he "doubts that many people will be convinced of his [Rogers's] new-found wisdom by any amount of cure-all policy position papers. . . . South Carolinians have always rebelled against the kind of campaign of distortion the opposition is waging."[114]

McNair's reaction was, in part, to a GOP publication known as *Had Enuff? News,* some 200,000 copies of which had been distributed by party headquarters in an effort to "depict Democratic Governor Robert McNair as the candidate of Negroes and the national Democratic administration." A press report said that the publication's "front page . . . has a picture of a smiling McNair shaking hands with Negro attorney John McCall at a Democratic rally in Cheraw."[115] In that publication, which reprinted articles from various newspapers in the state, Rogers was quoted in a *Charleston News and Courier* article as saying that the country was "under a mad spell of civil rights. . . . Aside from the racial question in such areas as housing, medicine [and] schools, congressmen seem to be in a state of mass hysteria when the President sends anything down with the heading of civil rights."[116]

For their part, the Republicans were described in press reports in the waning days of the campaign as having "written off about one-fifth of the votes to be cast in the November 8 general election." The report cited estimates by the Republicans of some 80,000 to 100,000 Negroes expected to vote out of a total anticipated turnout of 425,000 to 500,000. "I will have to have 80,000 to 100,000 [white] votes to start off even on election day," Senate candidate Marshall Parker was quoted as saying.[117]

A lot had changed in four years. The low-key campaigns of 1962 had given way to blockbuster races of 1966. The stakes had changed, too, and voters were being asked to decide through their ballots how the state would approach the most momentous half-decade of the twentieth century. They would decide whether the state would stand with their traditional colleagues of the Deep South in defiance of federal law and court order or whether South Carolina would opt for compliance with the law and a compromise of its racial traditions.

For Bob McNair, the vote would also be a referendum on the new politics of moderation that had been fashioned through the twenty-one months he had served as South Carolina's surprise governor.

7

A Full Term and a Mandate for Moderation

In its next-day coverage of the 1966 elections, the *State* newspaper headline of November 9, 1966, contained precisely the message Bob McNair had hoped would be the outcome of that eventful day: "Democrats Sweep State Offices."[1]

Not only did the incumbent governor carry South Carolina convincingly to gain his own four-year term, the team he considered essential to carrying out his plans for racial moderation and economic advancement had also gained an unquestioned mandate of voter support. McNair's margin, as announced in the newspapers' reports, was 58 percent to 42 percent, almost precisely the same as that by which he had defeated Marshall Parker in the 1962 Democratic primary for lieutenant governor, and his support was spread evenly across the state—upcountry, lowcountry, small counties, large counties, and urban and rural areas. Final totals gave McNair a margin of almost 72,000 votes, 255,854 to 184,088.[2] Only four counties chose the Republican, and those were by narrow margins—Clarendon, Rogers's home county, by 34 votes; Lexington, by 782 votes; Aiken, by 256 votes; and, ironically, Barnwell County, by 160 votes.[3]

John West's victory margin over Republican Marshall Mays in the lieutenant governor's race was by a margin comparable to that of McNair's (250,041 to 185,042), and Cyril Busbee had an only slightly smaller cushion in his victory over the GOP's Inez Eddings in the contest for state superintendent of education (233,623 to 196,963).[4] Grady Patterson polled 78 percent against write-in candidate W. W. Wannamaker for state treasurer, and Henry Mills was elected comptroller general without opposition. Democrats carried four other statewide constitutional offices without opposition, and Fritz Hollings won a comparative squeaker over Marshall Parker for the U.S. Senate, 223,790 to 212,062. Strom Thurmond, running for the first time as a Republican, won overwhelmingly over Bradley Morrah, 271,297 to 164,955, for the GOP's most notable triumph.[5]

For the rest of the Republican candidates, however, it would be the end of their elective lives, although Rogers told an interviewer three months after the election that he was "slamming no doors" on future political opportunities. "It would be foolish to say I wouldn't have any interest in returning to politics," he said.[6] Rogers's opportunity to return to public life would come August 11, 1969, in a non-elective position when he was sworn in as U.S. attorney in South Carolina in the Nixon administration, an appointment confirmed by the U.S. Senate "over protests by the National Association for the Advancement of Colored People, who objected to Rogers's civil rights stance."[7]

Rogers subsequently was nominated for a federal district judgeship, but as the opposition from civil rights groups intensified, he withdrew. In a news release dated December 18, 1970, he said, "It has been approximately six months since my name was proposed [for the judgeship]. Since that time, many reports and rumors have appeared in the press. To date, there is no indication that the matter will be resolved without further delay. For this reason, it is necessary to my personal and professional plans that I return to the private practice of law."[8]

An Emerging Political Star

Charleston News and Courier columnist Hugh Gibson observed some days after McNair's 1966 victory over Rogers: "With returns official now, the affable Allendale lawyer stands as the S.C. Democratic Party's top vote-getter, and second only to Republican Sen. Strom Thurmond for the state championship." McNair, Gibson wrote, "looms as a powerful figure who must be taken into account in any assessment of the state's political future."[9]

The political journey from the Berkeley County defeat of 1948 to the overwhelming statewide victory of 1966 was complete for the Hell Hole Swamp farm boy. At age forty-three, he had beaten the odds, coming from a small county on the Georgia border to win two statewide races, and in the process he had not only built a significant personal following, he had established through a convincing ballot-box mandate the legitimacy of South Carolina's new racial moderation.

Two months later, as he was inaugurated to his own full, four-year term, McNair would hail the event as "the happiest and proudest day of my life."[10] In the inaugural address delivered on the State House steps to an assemblage of six thousand people that included Alabama governor George C. Wallace and his first wife, Lurleen, he would also offer a brief personal reminiscence. "I give you my firm commitment to responsible forward movement," McNair said.

> I would like to believe it is the same kind of commitment my parents must have felt some 40 years ago in a small farm community in Berkeley County.

The efforts by my father and others to put as much quality as their resources would allow in a three-teacher schoolhouse near Jamestown gave me opportunities for which I have had many reasons to be grateful.

Proud as I know my parents were of the benefits they were able to provide, I regret that their life span was not long enough to share with me this greatest honor of my life.[11]

It was a far cry from the short, tone-setting address he had delivered to the General Assembly twenty-one months earlier upon assuming office to fill out the uncompleted term of Donald Russell. Having his own victory in the governor's race under his belt and bolstered by the wide margin of victory, McNair was expansive and aggressive. He also knew, as did most Democrats, that their power base had shifted significantly with the infusion of significant numbers of black voters in the brief months following the passage of the Voting Rights Act of 1965. He was aware that his 72,000-vote margin over Joe Rogers had been bolstered by the estimated 90,000 black votes among the total of some 350,000 who had gone to the polls in November.

An Inaugural of New Racial Harmony

McNair did not miss the opportunity to call attention to his black support and to celebrate what he viewed as the state's new racial harmony. Taking a giant step beyond Donald Russell's biracial barbecue on the mansion grounds four years earlier, the McNairs staged a full-blown inaugural ball, the state's first in two decades, with invitations for both races. Don Fowler, longtime state and national Democratic leader, recalled:

> No Inaugural Ball had been held since 1947 because of fear of racial problems associated with such a social event. Governor McNair asked me, as head of the S.C. Young Democrats, to chair the event, to create apart from his official inaugural a separate "private" social event.
>
> Dolly Hamby, Cora Graham and I did it. [Graham and Hamby were Columbia advertising executives who handled the media aspects of McNair's gubernatorial campaign.] There were three thousand-plus people at the Township and it was a great event. Blacks attended without incident and almost without comment.

It was an example, Fowler said, "of McNair's care and wise approach to breaking with the past and creating positive innovation."[12]

McNair's convincing victory also gave him the opportunity to articulate what he now viewed with some certainty and security as the state's evolving centrist position on racial issues. He said in his second inaugural address, "perhaps the greatest tribute to the people of South Carolina is the reputation we have established as a state whose citizens are dignified, fair-minded and respectful of the law."

I firmly believe that we can have no finer purpose than to uphold that reputation. Convinced as I am that this purpose is supported by a large majority of
our people in every station of life, I intend to use all the authority and influence
at my command to see that the good name of our state is not tarnished—either
by infringement of human rights or by flagrant disregard for law and order.

I plan to discourage at every opportunity any attitude or suggestion that the
law can be treated as a matter of personal convenience. Until laws are changed
in our system of representative government, it must be assumed that they represent the will of the majority. We cannot engage in selective enforcement and
maintain respect for the law. As law-abiding citizens, we are obligated to give
full support to our local and state enforcement officers in their efforts to carry
out their duties. To do otherwise will instill doubts in the minds of our children that we truly believe in the legal system and the constitutional form of
government to which we pledge allegiance.[13]

Building a Professional Staff

The speech's rhetoric and polish reflected the addition of a key staff member who
brought to the new administration a wide range of skills and a good dose of credibility. Bob Hickman, a popular Columbia television newsman, was sought out by
McNair and personally offered the position of news secretary early in the interim
term, and by 1967 he had become a fixture in State House circles. A graduate of
the University of Missouri's journalism school, Hickman was well liked in the
State House corridors, where he had worked as a newsman. Leaders such as Sol
Blatt were comfortable with him; the sometimes crusty Speaker called him "a good
fellow [and] a good speech writer."[14]

Hickman's appointment also broke the longstanding practice of hiring news-
papermen for press-relations jobs. Dating back more than two decades, men like Alex
McCullough, John Cauthen, Charles Wickenberg, and Fred Sheheen had come
from newspapers to serve governors in key executives positions, including the day-
to-day responsibility for contact with reporters. McNair changed the job title from
"press secretary" to "news secretary" to give the position broader definition; hired a
recent Miss South Carolina, Adelaide "Tootsie" Dennis, one of the Dennis clan
from Berkeley County, as Hickman's assistant; and turned the press office into an
upbeat gathering place for State House reporters. At Hickman's departure to head
the newly created Parks, Recreation and Tourism Department, an early McNair
initiative, the governor tapped another television newsman, Wayne Seal, as his successor and replaced Dennis with Becky Collier, a Charlotte native who maintained
the upbeat tone in the press office. Hickman and the press office were the most visible signs of a major source of McNair's political effectiveness, his professional staff.

Staffing, in fact, would become a significant departure from the past for the
McNair administration, it was later observed. "It was really McNair who first

addressed the issue of professional staff hired across a spectrum of different professional skills," noted Luther F. "Fred" Carter, president of Francis Marion University, who also logged time as chief of administration for Governor Carroll A. Campbell and chief of staff for Governor Mark Sanford. "With McNair, you also see the first governor who begins to layer in that staff in ways that not only gave it scope, but real depth with regard to specialization."[15]

"I worked hard to get people at the staff level who were top-level people, who could really implement what we were trying to accomplish, and who were the kind of people the department heads would work with," McNair said. "Our staff had to be made up of people that the state agency heads respected and would cooperate with as a part of making the whole thing work. We had different staff people who had various areas and activities that they were responsible for coordinating."[16]

Key to that assemblage was Katherine Wolfe, a holdover from his lieutenant governor's office who had served with Hollings during his governorship and who had become McNair's insider and trusted confidante in most matters of political or governmental importance. A native of Easley and a niece of longtime House clerk Inez Watson, Wolfe had an office adjoining McNair's, making her gatekeeper and scheduler. Wolfe was also the acknowledged boss of the staff, and she sustained a remarkable and unchallenged authority over the operation of the office, including monitoring such style items as the length of men's hair and the shortness of women's skirts during the iconoclastic 1960s.

Wolfe kept things running smoothly, and it was not always an easy task keeping on schedule a governor whose very style was that of protracted personal conversations. It was not all that unusual for a McNair day to begin at 7:00 or 8:00 in the morning and for each meeting to last ten to fifteen minutes longer than scheduled. Staffers or others hoping to catch the governor at the end of the day would often be disheartened to find McNair's 5:00 appointment entering the office around 6:30.

Other staff appointments reflected McNair's broad governmental interests and political linkages. True to his friendship with Senator Olin D. Johnston, he chose two aides from the late senator's Washington organization, James S. Konduros of Anderson and Robert Alexander of Columbia. Konduros, who was a major force in setting up the machinery to carry out one of Johnston's last legislative priorities—the multistate economic-development instrument known as the Appalachian Regional Commission—joined McNair's staff as executive assistant with responsibility for relations with larger state agencies. Alexander, as federal-state coordinator, handled the federal liaison job and coordinated program and grants assignments in Washington, as well as carrying out some of the delicate relationships with the U.S. Office of Education during the stormy school-desegregation days. Unlike other states' federal coordinators, however, Alexander remained in Columbia and functioned as an ongoing member of the executive staff.

As early as 1965, McNair chose a former House colleague, Henry Lake of St. Matthews, to serve as legal assistant, a job that combined the tasks of general counsel, bill drafter and tracker, legislative liaison, and maintainer of ongoing relations with law enforcement agencies. Lake, a former highway patrolman, had served as first vice chairman of the House Judiciary Committee during McNair's chairmanship of that committee, and he maintained friendships in the House as well as with his powerful St. Matthews colleague, Senator L. Marion Gressette.

Lake later left the staff to become director of the Legislative Council, the General Assembly's staff of bill-drafting attorneys. He was replaced as legal assistant first by retired Marine general Lewie G. Merritt, and subsequently by O. Wayne Corley of Lexington, who had served on the staff during the completion of his work toward a law degree at the University of South Carolina.

In staff selections, McNair would also affirm his longstanding friendship with members of the Municipal Association, bringing on board several former mayors for key assignments. Woody Brooks of Andrews became a federal-funds coordinator; Reg Wilson of Chester was heavily involved in the shaping and creation of the state's ten planning districts; and David Traxler of Greenville became a coordinator of federal housing programs.

By design, McNair's staff was virtually devoid of persons coming from the election campaign staff, and for the most part staff members kept a low public profile. They were generally expected to be seen and not heard, and their role was to serve as extensions of the governor, not independent operators. Statements to the press bore the governor's name, and at least one reporter insisted that he would deal only with the governor and not the staff. It was considered bad form and unacceptable political etiquette for a staff person to engage in public exchanges with legislators or other public figures whose status was considered comparable with that of the governor. Staff members were a cohesive group, close-knit and comfortable in their roles.

Longtime state auditor Pat Smith, a McNair insider and a de facto power behind the throne as chief executive of the Budget and Control Board, said, "His [McNair's] office staff was a most loyal group. They were all loyal to him, and they all worked together. There was a very wholesome relationship . . . between him and each member of the staff and among the staff members themselves. I don't recall any evidence of discord at all. Everybody was working for the same objectives. There was cohesiveness and congeniality to the group that I think impressed everybody who was in a position to observe them."[17]

The emergence of the Great Society programs of the Lyndon Johnson administration—and the complexity of delivery systems required by that massive initiative—put new demands on states, and in the case of South Carolina it created the enormous predicament of navigating the state's decentralized and entangled bureaucracy. As never before, it became the task of the governor's staff to assume some of those navigation responsibilities. Staffers reached into the various communities and constituencies considered necessary for the effective functioning of the office—the agencies of government at state, local, and federal levels, other elected officials, the press and public in general, and most prominently, the legislature.

Quiet Strategies for Desegregation

Few if any governors ever enjoyed a stronger bond with the state's often cantankerous legislature than McNair, and there was an unwritten understanding within the McNair professional and political family that the "we" relationship with the General Assembly was the uppermost priority in day-to-day operations.

In return, the General Assembly accorded McNair some extraordinary liberties. When he declared publicly his intention to appoint black South Carolinians to state boards and commissions, there were no immediate acclamations of enthusiasm from the traditionally conservative legislature. But there was also the quiet agreement that certain legislatively elected board and commission positions would be left vacant when the General Assembly adjourned, allowing the governor to make recess appointments in the interim. Those appointments would quietly become permanent when the General Assembly later confirmed them.

It was through that mechanism that McNair was able to desegregate without much attention several state boards and commissions, including those of Mental Health; Public Welfare; Probation, Parole and Pardon; the Criminal Justice Academy; and South Carolina State College, the state's historically black college in Orangeburg. The State College Board had been all-white since the establishment of the institution in 1896, but with the unspoken concurrence of the legislature, McNair was able to desegregate the board in 1966–1967 with the appointment of I. P. Stanback of Columbia and Samuel Bacote of Kingstree.

McNair also desegregated the governor's staff in 1967 at the administrative level. At the recommendation of Daisy Dunn Johnson of the Urban League, another McNair insider in the days of quiet racial diplomacy, McNair appointed Johnson's secretary, Margaret Percell, to his immediate staff, where she remained for the rest of his term. Percell stayed on with Governor West until she joined the newly created Governor's Advisory Commission on Human Relations (later the State Human Affairs Commission) in 1972, where she remained until her retirement more than thirty years later.

Centrism: Law, Order, and Compliance

The 1967 State of the State Address, McNair's first as elected governor, was a resounding affirmation of the two nicely balanced cornerstones of the state's new Democratic Party centrism: (1) law and order, a theme popular with traditional white conservatives, and (2) peaceful compliance with civil rights statutes, an article of faith with the emerging black electorate. It was an appeal to the state's sometimes warring factions to the left and right to bury the hatchet and to join hands against what McNair perceived as the real enemy—extremism. "Today's South Carolina has no room for obsession with either 'black power' or 'white backlash,'" he said.[18]

The statement gained some additional symbolic credibility from the fact that it was delivered in the presence of George Wallace, who had earned a national reputation as the champion of defiance three years earlier by standing at a schoolhouse door to articulate to a nationwide television audience the state's rejection of federal school-desegregation orders. McNair's inaugural statement in Wallace's presence was taken to be the deliberate separation of South Carolina from its Deep South confederates and a clear identification of the state with the moderate elements of the New South. McNair remained on good terms with Wallace and other Deep South governors, and during the heated years of civil rights transition South Carolina became something of a demilitarized zone through which political leaders of Upper and Deep Souths, liberal and conservative, Old South and New South, could find communication linkages.

In his inaugural address, McNair had upbeat things to say about prospects for improving the state's downtrodden economy and public-education system, and he did not shy away from identifying South Carolina with the politically moderate and economically progressive elements of the South. "Your generation and mine have created a new and diversified economic base. We have ceased to imitate and begun to innovate. We are creating new jobs and new hope for those who show their willingness to help themselves. We are setting the pace for a vibrant New South."[19] The speech was hailed as representing the "thrust of a 'new' McNair personality," and the inaugural address—as well as the subsequent State of the State Address—were called "his hardest hitting yet. The general public had rarely seen such a display of political confidence from McNair."[20]

The change, it was noted, was a reflection of McNair's newly felt security in having been elected to his own term as governor, as compared to the interim status of twenty-one months in serving out the term of Donald Russell. "When one comes into the office by vote of the people, you feel that is an expression of approval," he told a reporter. "You feel more secure in what you're doing. . . . I listen a lot. . . . Now, I've begun to talk more."

"The speeches," he said, "included things that needed to be said. And it was the right time. . . . The speeches were a result of my 16 years in state government, including two as governor." It was a change in tone and strategy that did not go unnoticed, and even those who had known McNair over the years were caught off guard by the "new" McNair. "McNair did not advocate any startling new programs or positions in his Inaugural or State of the State address," it was reported in one of the state's dailies. "But the political force, conviction and confidence which he conveyed surprised many, especially those who had labeled him 'colorless' and 'wishy-washy.'"[21]

A Practicing Political Scientist

During what some viewed as the lackluster twenty-one months of his "interim" service, McNair had actually been occupied with behind-the-scenes building of an organization structurally and politically that could withstand the anticipated racial and civil rights pressures of the 1960s and could address the state's desperate economic and educational condition. The election of West, Busbee, Patterson, Mills, McLeod, and other key elected officials gave him a solid external base of political allies who could join in support of such initiatives. The continued leadership of Blatt, Brown, Gressette, Dennis, and others in the General Assembly also made possible the sustaining of his remarkable friendship with the House and Senate and offered an ongoing partnership of remarkable proportions between the legislative and executive branches of the state.

Those partnerships, and their extraordinary linkages into the power sources of the state's political community, would serve many purposes during the next four years. Outwardly and most visibly they would buttress the state's emerging policy of moderation on racial and civil rights issues. But withstanding the arrival of civil rights changes and sustaining civil peace and order scarcely constituted the sum of ambitions for the McNair administration. The newly elected governor, who apprenticed under Sol Blatt, honed his leadership skills as presiding officer of the eccentric Senate, and painstakingly built a political team across a broad range of jurisdictions and disciplines, was preparing himself for another long-overdue task of governance in South Carolina: modernization of government.

McNair had emerged from his years of legal education and political seasoning as that rarity among modern public leaders: a politician who understood and appreciated the inner workings of government. The years he had spent at the University of South Carolina engaged in the new field of political science had made him a lifetime student of government and its various structures, powers, and patterns. Just as he had mastered the art of personal politics in Blatt's "School of the Gavel," McNair applied himself vigorously to the world of governmental agencies and departments, their stress points, and their potential points of linkage. In the days before it was politically chic to demonize bureaucracies and their functions, McNair studied the machinery of governmental operations and mastered its mechanics and behavioral tendencies.

"He was kind of a tinkerer," recalled staffer Jim Konduros, who served from the earliest days of the administration. "He picked this up in years and years as a legislator, and then as chairman of the Judiciary Committee, where he got a lot of high traffic, and then afterward as Lieutenant Governor. There wasn't any one subject which ruled him totally. He was most curious about government. He was truly a governmental man of all seasons."[22] Scholar and college president Fred Carter said, "By training, he may have been an attorney, but by inclination and interests, he was really an organizational theorist. Anybody who sat down and had a discussion with Bob McNair of any length quickly came to the appreciation that he really looked at ways to examine complex organizations from a very, very academic [and] very analytical perspective."[23]

Like most of his colleagues and allies, McNair had watched firsthand the transformation wrought by the New Deal on the state's impoverished areas, and he believed that government—and sometimes only government—could address the needs of his economically downtrodden state. He was also aware, however, that the state's government was built on a nineteenth-century model that afforded neither the structure nor the philosophical underpinning to support the kind of ambitions McNair had for the state. Earlier governors of the New South variety—Hollings and Russell—had advanced specific issues and causes such as technical education and industrial recruitment, and the notion of such innovative initiatives had set well with the generation of Depression survivors and World War II veterans who were assuming public-policy leadership roles in the state. Governors, because of their limited authority under South Carolina's fragmented governmental system, were understandably cautious in treading much further into the totality of governmental operations and raising the kind of jurisdictional considerations that might be viewed as matters of legislative prerogative.

McNair, however, because of the extraordinary partnerships he had forged among constitutional officers, legislative leaders, and others of influence in the political hierarchy, could afford to look beyond single-issue initiatives or piecemeal strategies. He could do something that had not happened in South Carolina since the administration of Governor Richard I. Manning (1916–1919) and the initiatives he took in furthering the Progressive movement. McNair could examine the inner workings of state government and develop comprehensive systemic approaches to meeting the evolving needs of modern South Carolina in an orderly and rational manner.

Manning, using the impetus of the Progressive movement that had reshaped the nation's state and local governments in the late nineteenth and early twentieth centuries, carried out the first management initiatives in South Carolina government in the twentieth century in the course of his two two-year terms as governor during and after World War I. Manning's initiatives led to such fundamental steps as the creation of the first state budget and the establishment of the state's tax commission and highway commission. He also championed humane causes such as the improvement of conditions in state prisons, the doubling of state support for public education, and the adoption of a number of other measures designed to improve public health and the care for the mentally ill and others dependent on the state for support.[24]

Three subsequent studies of the state's governmental structure carried out during the ensuing three decades[25] recommended further major changes in the structure of state government, but the state resisted such organizational overhaul, at least partially because of the reluctance of the traditionally dominant legislature to cede authority to the governor. What evolved over the first half of the twentieth century was something of a headless executive branch, populated by agencies whose governance came not from a central authority, but from part-time, unpaid citizen boards whose members were chosen variously by the legislature, the governor, or some combination thereof. Between the Manning administration and McNair's assumption of the governorship in 1965, some twenty-six such agencies were created by the General Assembly for tasks ranging from bank regulation to juvenile corrections to soil conservation.[26]

Leading without Structural Power

The only major organizational change that took place during that time was the creation in 1950 of a conspicuously hybrid agency known as the Budget and Control Board, whose membership was comprised of three constitutional officers—the Governor as ex-officio chairman, the state treasurer, and the comptroller general—and two legislative powers, the chairman of the Senate Finance Committee and the chairman of the House Ways and Means Committee.

In time, the Budget and Control Board evolved into the major central management agency of state government, handling such state-level matters as budget, personnel administration, property management, retirement systems, information technology, and surplus property. In a state whose executive-branch organization was scattered and fragmented, the Budget and Control Board had virtually the only semblance of central authority, and to Bob McNair it became the ideal instrument for launching major governmental initiatives. Surrounded by allies such as Treasurer Grady Patterson, Comptroller Henry Mills, Senate Finance Chairman Edgar Brown and, Jim Aycock, a Blatt insider who chaired the House Ways and Means Committee, he could not only exploit the political leverage of the board's authority to develop the annual state budget, he could also marshal significant front-end support for whatever other management initiatives he might pursue. It was the ultimate tool for building the "we" coalitions he sought and nurtured so diligently. In South Carolina government of the 1960s, it was as close as one could come to the "friends and neighbors" politics of rural Berkeley County.

For all the state's organizational eccentricities, however, McNair never believed that structural change was necessary for a governor to exercise effective power in South Carolina government. "I think historically, it [the boards and commissions system] . . . served us well. It provided more stability and more continuity in government because [most of] the boards are appointed by the governor. Some are elected by the General Assembly. . . . Historically, they were on staggered terms so that no governor could change the whole direction and complexion of what was going on."[27] Don Fowler later observed: "McNair was a clear and open defender of the boards and commissions form of government in sharp contrast to changes in the 1990s. He had such good relations with the legislature that he could get most of what he wanted indirectly and didn't require direct control."[28]

The loose governmental structure, which would baffle and frustrate many a subsequent South Carolina governor, was simply another opportunity for McNair to exercise his personal political skills and powers of persuasion to build coalitions. "What I did was begin to work not only with the heads of these agencies, but with the chairmen of the boards," he said. "I found that is where you really could have some influence immediately. You could sometimes get things started a lot faster if you pulled in the board chairmen and even the full board on occasion to get their support and enlist their involvement in what was going on. There was your policy-making group. When you ran into a difficult director, who was just so set in his ways, sometimes through the board you could persuade him to be more cooperative."[29]

"The key to getting things done was having a good board chairman. That was something I focused in on fairly early. . . . [I took] a look at these boards and commissions and tried to bolster them and strengthen them. [I tried] to get people . . . who I felt would not be just political appointments. I wanted individuals who would take an interest or who had a reason or had some background to serve on a board or commission. [Then I set out] to find some chairman who would devote some time and effort and who would exercise some policy-making authority," he said.[30] "So we started by pulling together what we called interagency councils of related agencies, both in broad groups, for example in health and welfare . . . and then under that umbrella, specific groups from various agencies . . . [could] deal with a specific problem."[31]

Creating such agency combinations was usually done by the governor's executive order, a practice, he later admitted, may have been on some dubious legal or constitutional ground. Speaking to a group of governmental executives in the late 1990s, McNair said,

> I had heard all about how little power the governor has, constitutionally and otherwise, and if you read [the constitution] looking for what it said the Governor could do, it was very little. . . . But I took the position of calling the Attorney General [Dan McLeod] and saying, "I want you to look in the constitution and see if you can find anything that says I *cannot* do thus and so because it does say I'm the Chief Executive Officer."
>
> Lo and behold, Dan came back. And when I'd ask him a question if I *could* [do something], can you find something that says I *can*, he'd come back and say, "No, I don't see anything that says you *can*." I wouldn't ask him the rest of the question about whether I *couldn't* do something.[32]

"We found," McNair said, "that the interagency approach worked a lot better [than other ways to structure government]. . . . Other states created divisions of administration within the Governor's Office, and they grew into monstrous operations themselves. State agencies and state departments began fighting with them, so you really just got another layer of government. More and more of the federal dollars were peeled off to support administration. That new money was kept away from doing the things you intended to be done. I had a normal, natural resistance to that. Although we established some new agencies, I had a normal resistance to building more layers. I wanted to tear down those layers and get more into the direct administration of programs."[33]

Gradualism and Functional Stability

There was another dimension to state-government operation that influenced relationships among the various major components of government structure in the 1960s. As a holdover from its days as a rural-dominated oligarchy, South Carolina especially valued stability and equilibrium within its political and social structures. It was a characteristic, it could have been argued, that might have suppressed some of the vigorous growth initiatives emerging in other southern states, but it was also a trait that moderated some of the more extreme sentiments present in the state.

In that context, the McNair "we" administration was more than a tacit partnership between a constitutionally limited governor and a powerful legislature. It was a "we" that extended into the world of agency operations, and despite the appearance of disorder among the structurally decentralized agencies, agency heads and legislators were no strangers to each other and legislative leaders made it their business —particularly through the standing committee system—to know and understand the nature of programs and services they oversaw and to understand the implications of their decisions. The boards and commissions system, because it was detached by at least an arm's length from the elective process, fostered longevity of service among its leadership, both board members and executive staffs. And while critics liked to describe the phenomenon as spawning entrenched bureaucracies, long-serving officials also tended to learn their jobs well and to become skilled professionals in their fields.

The long-serving agency leaders matched up well with their long-serving counterparts in the General Assembly and created a kind of collegiality that did not show up in organizational charts. Most agencies and the constituencies they served had their legislative champions, often coming out of joint House-Senate committees designed to study and familiarize legislators with specific issues or problems. Such committees often created—or filtered—proposed legislation germane to their areas of interest and also produced advocates within the General Assembly for those respective programs.

The annual appropriation bill was frequently the result of swaps and deals among the various legislative agency or program champions and thus represented something of a consensual statement of the state's priorities from year to year within the confines of an established but unspoken protocol. In the days before

Watergate and Freedom of Information laws, state government insiders were regularly formed into coalitions of legislators, agency leaders, lobbyists, and other advocates around central issues. It made possible a setting in which personal politics could hold sway and in which a practitioner such as Bob McNair could be especially effective and persuasive.

What government critics and detractors would later describe as a scattered and unaccountable array of service delivery agencies actually functioned as an informal but resilient series of political and operational cliques that valued organizational constants and operational stability. Critics and scholars who sought the purity and symmetry of paper charts and solid chains of command failed to take into consideration what was essentially an unspoken operational ethic among the various components of the state's government at the time. It was an ethic that was undeniably rooted in the past and its enduring principle was the continuity of the various aspects of governmental operation at a predictable level from year to year.

Such an ethic, popularly dismissed in later years as a slavish allegiance to the status quo, was essentially the belief that governmental policies and practices were determined with some permanency by the statutes and missions that established the state's agencies and programs. As such, the tendency toward incremental budgeting was an affirmation of the state's commitment to those statutory mandates, and they needed no year-to-year commitment as later proclaimed by advocates of such costly management tools as the so-called zero-based budgeting and other requirements that diverted funds away from direct service delivery and into expensive exercises in service and program justification. As other such "accountability and performance-based" budgeting practices caught the attention of the state's leaders later in the century, the state's spending priorities tended to be reshaped, and funding support for many longstanding programs and services became erratic.

Grabbing the Tourism Initiative

Even in what could have been viewed as the static nature of state-government operations in the 1960s, there was room for maneuvering as certain opportunities and imperatives emerged, particularly in the hands of a political operative like McNair. One such opportunity developed early in McNair's gubernatorial service in 1966 and—as later generations could attest—it turned out to be something of a blockbuster development that anticipated and helped to shape a multibillion-dollar segment of the state's economy.

Until the 1960s, out-of-state tourism in South Carolina was largely flow-through traffic en route between the major cities of the East and the beaches of Florida. Travelers might spend the night at a roadside motel along Highways 1 or 301, perhaps buy a meal or two, fill up with gasoline, and stock up with a few firecrackers, cigarettes, and pecan rolls. South Carolina's beaches were remarkable for their beauty, but they were also sweltering places for much of the vacation season and were largely for use by families from North or South Carolina renting cottages or spending weekends at mom-and-pop beachfront hotels. The state's largest single tourist attraction for years was the South of the Border complex in Dillon County just south of the North Carolina line, well-known to travelers along the eastern seaboard for its countless "Pedro" billboards.

Then two major developments took place that changed things forever: the completion of the interstate highway system and the popularization of air-conditioning. Suddenly, South Carolina was closer by hours along Interstate 95 to New York, New Jersey, Pennsylvania, and—most strategically—the populous eastern provinces of Canada. In addition, Interstate 26 and, later, Interstate 77 opened vast territories of the Midwest, particularly Indiana and Ohio, to vacationing families. None of it would have worked, however, had the technology of air-conditioning not converted the state's torrid barrier-island beaches into vacation paradises. As the comforts of chemically and mechanically cooled air became readily available, the mom-and-pop beachfront hotels gave way to the high rises of Myrtle Beach, the condominiums of Hilton Head and Kiawah, the historic inns of Charleston, and the glamorous second homes all across the state's eastern sector. By then, visitors could arrive in air-conditioned cars, making it possible to seal themselves almost entirely from the heat and humidity that had made South Carolina summers so notorious only a few years earlier. "Tourism," McNair later said, "was a sleeping giant in this state. . . . We had a tourism study done by [a] California group, and they just put it right out there for us. We were all shocked to find out that, with no effort, tourism was then producing and contributing an equal amount to the economy as agriculture was."[34]

As early as 1966, McNair put together legislation that would create a super-agency to develop and promote tourism in the state. It involved the merging of three entities: (1) the state-park system, developed under New Deal initiatives in the 1930s and managed by the Forestry Commission; (2) the state's independent Recreation Commission; and (3) the tourism-promotion division of the state's economic-development agency, the State Development Board. The new agency would be known as the Department of Parks, Recreation and Tourism (PRT), and it would be designed to move South Carolina aggressively into potential new markets never imagined a decade earlier.

Addressing the Liquor Laws

There remained, however, one more issue to confront before South Carolina's tourism package would be fully marketable. For all the benefit the state would realize from the comforts of air-conditioning, the convenience of interstate highways, the enlightenment of desegregated state parks, and the aggressiveness of promotional work by a new PRT agency, a visitor still could not buy a mixed drink legally in South Carolina. It was one of the holdovers from the quirky history of the state's liquor laws and practices.

From 1892 until 1907, the state sold liquor through its dispensary. That institution fell in disorder and scandal, and eight years later, in 1915, the state enacted its own prohibition of alcoholic beverages, preceding by four years the Volstead Act and national prohibition, which kept the nation legally dry from 1919 to 1933. Upon the lifting of prohibition, South Carolina legalized the sale of beer and wine, and two years later in 1935, it became legal to sell unopened bottles of liquor so long as there was no consumption on the site.[35] That was essentially the situation as McNair began his tourism initiative. Restaurants around the state sold beer and wine with meals, but there were few establishments that resembled anything like a bar or tavern.

Except in Charleston. As a port city and a place that was beginning to attract large numbers of tourists, Charleston was a place where liquor laws were flaunted, for the most part with impunity. As McNair addressed the mixed-drink problem, the resolution of which many felt was essential to the state's tourism success, he therefore found two obstacles: the religious fundamentalists, including his fellow Baptists, who wanted the law stringently enforced, and Charleston, which wanted no enforcement.

In time, the illegal serving of mixed drinks spread to Myrtle Beach and Beaufort. When a supper club in Columbia began the practice, there was a crackdown, and its owners tested the constitutionality of the existing provision. When the Supreme Court upheld the 1930s statute, the entire issue of the state's liquor laws and drinking practices came to a head. McNair crafted for the 1967 General Assembly a proposal he hoped would fit within the limited constitutional provisions without the necessity of a public referendum and would also fit between the two contending forces doing battle over the issue of liquor in the state: fundamentalists and the tourism business community. Known as the "Brown Bag Law," McNair's proposal provided that adults could bring their own liquor into hotels, motels, and restaurants in a "brown bag." In hotels and motels, guests could drink in their rooms, and in restaurants patrons could have their liquor checked and served at their table. At the completion of the meal, the unused liquor would be returned to them to take home.

McNair carried his proposal to the two opposing camps with different strategies. He spoke directly to the State Baptist Convention in Columbia with one of the most carefully constructed speeches of his administration. Authors and contributors to that oration included McNair's own pastor at First Baptist Church in Columbia, Dr. Archie Ellis (later state commissioner of social services), along with Jim Morris from USC, textile industrialist John Cauthen, and staffer Bob Hickman, who would become the first executive director of the new PRT agency.

"I said to them from the beginning that I knew how Baptists felt because I was one of them," McNair said. "I went on to say that they had to recognize that I was not only governor of the Baptists, I was governor of all the people of South Carolina." McNair won some of the Baptists to his cause and gained support from prominent Methodist minister Wright Spears, the president of Columbia College, as well as "the real strong, open public support from the Bishop of the Episcopal diocese."[36]

To the tourism business community, his message was one of toughness, and a promise to enforce the law. "I had to satisfy the public first that we were going to enforce the law, whatever it was, and if they became comfortable with that, we were going to try to change to a more moderate position on liquor and alcohol."[37]

It was one of McNair's tougher stances. John West, then lieutenant governor, recalled a breakfast meeting involving those senators likely to oppose the brown-bagging bill. "Bob McNair really laid it on the line," West wrote in his personal journal. "He said that if we refuse to relax the law [adopt the "brown bag" bill], he would expect the legislature to set the example with no more drinking, even in hotel rooms. He also said, privately, that he would put SLED agents in the counties where the delegations voted against the law to make sure the laws were enforced to the letter. I believe he changed a good many votes."[38]

A week after the meeting, the "brown bag" bill came up for a deciding vote in the Senate, and West, as presiding officer in the Senate, wrote in his journal: "No one is sincerely opposed, but a few of the ministers have put terrific pressure, especially upon the Piedmont senators who feel obliged to oppose it. The question is whether or not a roll call will be had. Finally, it was agreed that five members would not ask for a roll call, and, sure enough, they didn't. [Greenville senators] Dick Riley and Harry Chapman demanded it, but I could never see more than three or four hands, so I put the question and brown bagging passed [by voice vote]."[39] Legislation creating the Parks, Recreation and Tourism Commission gained final passage on March 30, 1967, and the "brown bag" statute was adopted eighty-two days later, on June 20.[40] In keeping with the organizational patterns of the time, the new PRT agency was created with an eleven-member governing commission comprising four ex officio members from state agencies of similar interests and seven appointed by the governor. The first PRT board was like an all-star team of McNair friends and business leaders, including Pickens businessman Dwight Holder as chairman and McNair's close friend Robert Rigby of Columbia as vice chairman. Among its other members were Spring Mills executive William Close, Hilton Head developer Charles Fraser, Greenville newspaper executive Ned Ramsaur, Myrtle Beach developer Edward Burroughs, and banker James McNair of Aiken.

With the new agency, the new liquor law, and state parks desegregated, McNair was ready for full ignition on the state's new tourism initiative, and the economic impact was almost immediate. Travel-promotion shows in places like Montreal and Toronto lured Canadians to Myrtle Beach and led to the institution of Canadian Days along the Grand Strand, complete with Canadian maple leaf flags and, more practically, the use of Canadian dollars in business establishments. South Carolina sold itself to its northeastern customers as a place where travelers could get two extra days of vacation time by not traveling all the way to Florida and back—and the cost in South Carolina was much lower.

Reports indicated that travel-related spending in the state, estimated at $130 million in 1954, rose to $307 million in 1967, the year PRT was created, and to $355 million the following year.[41] By 1971, the figure rose to $405 million,[42] and the trend continued in subsequent years. Between 1972 and 1976, total travelers from outside South Carolina increased from 26.8 million to 38.6 million, and by 1976, visitors who were making South Carolina their point of destination represented almost a third of the state's travel business. Money spent in South Carolina by travelers passed the $1 billion mark in 1975, a tenfold increase in twenty years, and by the end of the century, tourism spending in the state had passed the $6.5 billion level.[43] South of the Border and its billboard mascot, Pedro, remained, but its importance to the state had long been surpassed by places known worldwide such as Hilton Head Island, the Grand Strand, and Charleston. In the Grand Strand area alone, eighty golf courses were beckoning visitors from Asia, North America, and Europe.

With his remarkable and almost intuitive sense of how the pieces of government could fit together and function, McNair had created an agency that for decades would be a model of how government could energize and activate the private sector. What ensued was the investment of billions of private dollars and the creation of thousands of new jobs in an industry that would eventually be recognized as the state's number-one economic engine. The creation of the Department of Parks, Recreation and Tourism was pure McNair, practical, farsighted, and low-key.

For all its immediate and long-term impact, however, the tourism initiative—like earlier efforts to create a job-enhancing technical-education system and modernize the state's industrial-recruitment strategies—was a single-issue adjustment. Those actions, as bold and imaginative as they may have been, were essentially designed to help the state do a better job of marketing and developing itself as it was. And as it was, South Carolina was a pleasant enough place, reminiscent of Charlestonian DuBose Heyward's "Summertime" lyrics in the Gershwin opera *Porgy and Bess*. It was a place where "the living is easy." But it was also a place whose organic limitations in public education and human development had chronically restricted its potential for economic development. If left unattended and unaddressed, they would also doom the state to self-imposed mediocrity in the fast-paced economic surge of the last half of the twentieth century.

A Blueprint for South Carolina

Bob McNair's confidence in the strength of his moderate coalition was leading him to think big thoughts as he headed into his full term as governor. The emerging alliance of newly registered black voters, centrist Democrats, and the remnants of courthouse crowds that still controlled local politics had withstood the first wave of Republican frontal attacks in the 1966 elections. There was a sense that the overtly racial political appeals that had been so successful in the past had failed and that the state was preparing itself for something of a political Renaissance of historic proportions.

Old-timers like Gressette, Brown, and Blatt were loyalists whose stake in the Democratic Party outweighed whatever appeal may have remained in the Republicans' conservative positions. The arrival of young reform-minded senators like future Governor Dick Riley of Greenville, John Drummond of Greenwood, and Nick Zeigler of Florence brought some new energy and perspective to the chamber. They formed the core of what would become a "Young Turk" brigade, which was irksome at times to the traditionalist McNair, but that seemed to pave the way for continuity of the Democrats' domination. The power of the new black vote, scarcely visible in the State House but inestimable in its long-term potential, seemed numerically to have been for the Democrats a good swap for the loss of some rural and suburban white votes to the Republicans.

These were good times to be a Democrat in South Carolina. The optimism over the apparent racial peace, the expanding economy, and the new political harmony within the party was encouraging to McNair and emboldened him to cast his eyes with a new and more ambitious vision on the state he now governed. With what he viewed as a clear public mandate, an unprecedented degree of favor with the General

Assembly, and the support of a new black electorate, he could address what might have been politically unthinkable only a few years earlier.

Taking a Candid Look

McNair's world had grown politically and ideologically. It was a world that included the dirt farmers with whom he had grown up in Berkeley County, not just as a part of his personal experience but also as a part of the political realities of a South Carolina he now felt empowered to address. McNair's world included municipalities whose support had always been solidly his, upcountry textile people of Olin Johnston loyalties, manufacturers who had cheered his antiunion stance, and black citizens liberated politically by the Voting Rights Act of 1965 and earlier court rulings. McNair's was also a world where memories of the New Deal in the 1930s reinforced his belief that in places like South Carolina, where private wealth was scarce, it took government to intercede to fill gaps in the state's economic, educational, and social fabric. McNair's world was also one of the Great Society, that latter-day New Deal of the 1960s woven together by the Lyndon Johnson administration, which brought into being such phenomena as Medicare and Medicaid and changed the arithmetic and vocabulary of state government to include the terminology of matching-funds programs.

Through it all, McNair escaped ideological branding. He was, after all, still a member in good standing of the conservative Barnwell Ring, and he was making friends with the New Left of the state's political community, including black political leaders such as Matthew Perry and I. DeQuincey Newman. No man in South Carolina could better span the left-to-right political spectrum than McNair. And given the studious tinkering with which he could address the inner workings and mechanics of state government, no man was better equipped to target and focus the state's efforts in priority directions than McNair. It was the perfect convergence of opportunity and inclination.

The South Carolina renaissance McNair envisioned, however, would never be identified as such. It was not the style of a man known to his friends as cautious and close-mouthed. There would be no abrupt shift in the state's political equilibrium. McNair was not given to broad-brush, publicly proclaimed visions or concepts. His language was plain and deceptively ambiguous at times. He often spoke with gestures, referring to "this" or "these" with motions to denote opposite or contrasting views. He was most comfortable in casual and conversational settings, and he commented often that much of his work had been accomplished in telephone conversations and informal meetings for which there was often no printed or written record.

McNair approached the job of executive leadership in ways that were reminiscent of Speaker Blatt's description of McNair's legislative leadership. "He could break you down with that smile," Blatt had recalled, and senior staff executive Jim

Konduros had similar recollections of his own experiences in McNair's meetings with agency professionals:

> How do you describe subtle leadership? How do you define someone who is not going to impress his will immediately on a group of professionals and people who feel as dedicated as he is to government and to helping people?
>
> His way of running a meeting was to guide, to let the discussion take place and to nudge gently into the areas of interest that he wanted to pursue. At the end of the day, it's as if he's impressed his will on people. [He would say] you're not really serving me, you're serving the school children, or whatever else may have been the topic, and he would work that conversation around to where—by changing some part of their attitude or plan—they were serving a greater good.[1]

Even McNair's language could be filled with generalities, indirection, and occasionally misdirection. The appearance of a book in the late 1960s by Beaufort doctor Donald Gatch describing hunger conditions in the state peeved the governor and prompted his public criticism. But all the while McNair was working vigorously to bring food stamps, school lunches, and other nutritional programs into the state and to give them political credibility. He was not comfortable with terms such as *poverty* or *hunger,* and he rarely made direct references to racial identification. He preferred to talk about "all the people of the state" and to do so with sufficiently emphatic gestures to get across just what he meant by the term. He once told a reporter, "I would rather talk about something after I've done it, not before."[2]

Through it all, it was difficult to locate a clearly definable McNair public persona or a visible political ego. "He had probably the greatest humility of any sitting governor I have ever known," said Konduros, whose work in government, the legal profession, and nonprofit work spanned four decades of the state's history. McNair's low-key style fit well the tasks he set out for himself in reshaping South Carolina's governmental direction in the 1960s. But it left much of the work of his administration either ill-defined, unrecorded, or institutionally obscure in later years. An oral-history project conducted between 1979 and 1983 was an attempt to address that historical deficiency, and this manuscript draws heavily from material from that project. Early in the twenty-first century—decades after McNair left office—veteran newspaper reporters were surprised to learn that the state's first major post-*Brown* educational reforms were not introduced in the Education Finance Act of 1977 or the Education Improvement Act of 1984. They came during the administration of Bob McNair in 1969 as part of a comprehensive governmental overhaul known as "The Moody Report."

A Not-So-Modest Proposal

It was typical of the McNair style that the vehicle that would contain the expansive vision he had for the state of South Carolina would bear neither his name nor the inflated promises of a glorious tomorrow often associated with such projections. It would not be billed as a New Deal, or a Fair Deal, or a Great Society.

It would announce itself modestly in the document's official title as *Opportunity and Growth in South Carolina, 1968–85,* and it would quickly become known as the Moody Report, after the Wall Street bond-rating company that had been a partner in the study. But its content was anything but modest or simple. From the day it was released in the fall of 1968 until the final gasp of its legislative proposals two years later, the Moody Report became the crucible for South Carolina's progressive, post-segregation ambitions. Its 446 pages resonated with a richly documented—and at times painfully explicit—examination of the full range of the state's activities: education, transportation, health, recreation, and tourism. Apropos of the participation of Moody's, the report came not only with an itemized price tag attached to its proposals, but with an entire section analyzing the state's fiscal condition, its potential, and the expected returns on investments for the various proposals made in its programmatic sections. With the kind of detailed financial explanations and justifications befitting McNair's Scottish thriftiness, it accounted for virtually every dollar to be raised and spent, as well as the long-term benefits to be anticipated.

The Moody's consultants, in fact, put a fiscal spin on most of their findings and recommendations. Although he was once serenaded at a public function with a rendition of the popular *Guys and Dolls* song "Hey, Big Spender," McNair took a remarkably conservative approach to the study. He later recalled that the original charge to the consultants was to survey the state's needs and determine how much it could afford. He asked Moody's, "Would you agree to come in and serve as the financial consultants to us, to take a hard look at South Carolina, to take a look at all those needs that we have outlined and help us determine whether we could afford to do these things? If so, tell us how we can do it and not jeopardize the state's credit rating."[3]

By couching social and educational recommendations in terms of their fiscal impact on the state, McNair could also avoid the dreaded tag of "do-gooder" or, worse yet, "liberal." Besides, McNair needed no convincing that there was a direct connection between the state's human condition, its educational condition, and its economic condition. He had seen enough of that growing up in Hell Hole Swamp. The Moody Report itself launched into its recommendation section with an affirmation of the education-economic linkage. "South Carolina must improve its elementary-secondary education in order to produce the human talent required for sustained economic growth," the report stated. "Its educational system now lags in both quantity and quality; in the numbers graduating from high school and moving on to higher education and in the caliber of the education they receive while in school. Specific negative factors are the very high proportion repeating first grade, the large numbers of educationally disadvantaged children, a low level of in-service improvement of teachers, and, despite recent improvement, the comparatively low level of teachers' salaries."[4]

More than half the content of the report, in fact, was dedicated to education. It was a compendium of McNair's education beliefs, tracking the successive phases of the learning process from early childhood to higher education and beyond. It addressed the gaps, the inadequacies, the systemic eccentricities, and the blind alleys. It also addressed, without saying so, the clearly discernible reality facing South Carolina in the years immediately ahead: racial desegregation of its public schools.

McNair knew, as did any enlightened educator in the state, that the ultimate success of desegregating the public-school system would not be measured by the political or social acceptance of a biracial learning process. It lay in the knitting together of two school systems that were not only inherently unequal but traditionally unrelated to each other in any meaningful way. Success lay in forging a new system that damaged neither of the older systems and created bridges and new common grounds from which a unitary mentality could emerge. McNair also knew that the long-term well-being of the state lay not in perpetuating the "three C's" of the state's traditional economic base—cheap land, cheap water, and cheap labor. It lay in making the emerging unitary system better than either one that it replaced and in making the public-school system the first step in developing a skilled and intellectually competent workforce that could meet the demands of the sophisticated economy that lay just around the corner.

Preparing for Public-School Desegregation

The Moody's consultants put the report in a language that gave it a businesslike tone, a language that made it politically palatable in conservative 1960s South Carolina. They used the vocabulary and the arithmetic of accountancy, and McNair later recalled that kind of logic. "Look," he recalled the Moody's consultants saying, "you have got a certain percentage of first grade repeaters. If you can cut that down by a certain amount, you can start your pre-school, and your reduction there [measured by fewer repeating first-graders] will pay for it there. So it is not really going to cost you any money, except start-up."[5]

There was also the language of educators anticipating the desegregation of public schools and foreseeing some of the adjustments and modifications that might ease that transition. The Moody recommendations observed, "A pre-school and kindergarten program is particularly appropriate in South Carolina, where the existence of a high proportion of educationally disadvantaged children is attested to by such measurements as educational attainment of adults, literacy and numbers of families officially categorized as living in poverty."[6] It was a direct assault on the inequities of the state's separate but unequal school system, and it became identified as such in the ensuing political and legislative debates.

For all the mathematical savings to be realized from the reduction of first-grade repeaters, McNair also knew that the repeating rate of black first-graders was twice that of white first-graders. A preschool and kindergarten program, he realized, would go a long way toward leveling the racial inequities of the traditional dual school system at an early age and would set the stage for more extensive effort at student retention later in the educational process.

McNair chose his 1969 State of the State Address to convey the recommendations of the Moody Report to the General Assembly. It was strategically important in that it would be the opening of the final two-year session of the General Assembly during his governorship, and while the fresh new faces of urban senators populated the Senate, the old guard was still firmly in control. For whatever advantage such a setting may have carried, however, the Moody Report had sparked controversy long before lawmakers arrived in Columbia that chilly January.

For one thing, much of the early work on the study had been conducted on a confidential basis, a practice not uncommon for Moody's in its normal business practices but a strategy that irked some of McNair's allies in the legislature and elsewhere. "They [the Moody's people] did not want a lot of political involvement and political interference," McNair recalled. "They were going to do a report; they were going to do a study; and they were going to explain it to us. . . . Then, as far as they were concerned, they were through with it."[7]

"It [the confidential nature of the early stages of the study] got a few people riled and feathers ruffled because they did not feel they had had enough input into it," he recalled.[8] Among those irritated were McNair's mentor and usual ally, Speaker Blatt, and his close friend John K. Cauthen, who was executive director of the Textile Manufacturers Association. Agency directors also complained, "it is not ours, and we did not have enough input," McNair recalled, and critics had derisively zeroed in on the report's references to "quantum leap" as stuffy consultant language.

At that point, McNair called agency heads together for two days at the Santee Cooper preserve at Pinopolis on Lake Moultrie and brought legislative leaders to Columbia to examine what had become by then—in Speaker Blatt's terms—the "now infamous" Moody Report. It was about then that McNair also revealed that the Moody Report had a price tag.

Packaging and Marketing

"It was not simply a tax increase program," he contended. "We went to the legislature with a program for South Carolina that was essential to the state, and then we said, 'Now here is the way we recommend you pay for it.' That was the package. It became easier to support the full package than it had been before. It became more difficult to be against it because if you were opposed to it, you were not supporting preschool education; you were not supporting the upgrading of vocational adjunct education and all those kinds of things we had built into it [our recommended package]."[9]

For whatever may have been the nuanced differences as intended in the package strategy, "McNair Asks $64.5 million in Tax Increases" was the eight-column headline in the *Greenville News* that greeted the proposals the day after he delivered his recommendations to the General Assembly. In its coverage of the 1969 State of the State speech, the upcountry paper's lead sentence called his proposed tax increases "whopping."[10] By then, Speaker Blatt had targeted the public kindergarten for his "adamant opposition."

Even so, the state's thoughtful journalists were taking analytical looks at the Moody package. "Gov. Robert E. McNair's bold 1969 legislative program reveals his . . . budget options and calls for $64.5 million in new taxes. [It] was meticulously crafted with the precision of a fine watch," wrote Charleston's Hugh Gibson.[11] Charlotte's Jack Bass acknowledged that the Moody Report "basically is a study that coordinates and analyzes South Carolina and its economic problems and potential. Many of its recommendations can be implemented without legislation. Some already have been."[12]

In the State of the State Address McNair made no mention of the Moody Report by name, and he chose to replace the devalued term "quantum leap" with its more straightforward counterpart, "a great leap forward."[13] He cloaked the tax recommendations as "a rejection of the status quo." In those days before tax policy was used as a social vehicle to shift wealth from one level of income to another, McNair's proposals were downright egalitarian. His plan came in two parts: (1) a $47 million revenue increase by raising the sales tax from 3 to 4 percent, and (2) an additional $17 million in revenue from a supplemental program that tapped several sources, namely, an increase in the cigarette tax from 5 to 8 cents per pack, an increase in the corporate income tax from 5 to 6 percent, and an increase in the beer tax from .5 to .6 cents per container.

It was the state's biggest tax-increase proposal since Jimmy's Tax, the initial 3 percent sales-tax levy recommended by Governor Byrnes to ward off public-school desegregation seventeen years earlier in 1951. In terms of the level of state spending in fiscal 1969–1970, the tax package represented an almost 13 percent increase in the annual general revenues of the state. It was clearly a proposal that would test as never before the cozy relationship McNair had maintained with the General Assembly.

Much of the Moody recommendations, as Bass noted, could be adopted without either legislation or additional funding. The big-ticket items were (1) an $800 salary increase for teachers to draw South Carolina close to the southeastern average; (2) $8 million for a state match to expand Medicaid programs and services in the state; (3) monies to cover the equalization of state employees' salaries under a new compensation and classification plan; and (4) funds to implement the proposed kindergarten system and to reduce the average size of classrooms.

The governor told the General Assembly:

It is never easy to recommend new taxes. We have never found one yet that was popular.

I would ask, however, that those who oppose these steps consider the alternatives and judge whether our state can afford indifference and timidity at this stage of [its] development.

In South Carolina, we are shortening the distance between today and tomorrow. Fulfillment of our future is within reach. Let us resolve that we will seize this opportunity. Let us work together to reshape our future. Let us in the years ahead develop a renewed confidence in ourselves and invite the rest of the nation to follow our lead.[14]

If there was some rhetorical overkill in the text, it could be charged to McNair's breaking in a new speechwriter who had been on staff less than three months. A respiratory infection further dampened the event and reduced the governor to speaking in "hoarse tones."[15] The speech got lukewarm responses from the likes of cautious legislators like Edgar Brown and Sol Blatt. Marion Gressette withheld any comment at all.

The recommendations, in fact, came at a time when South Carolina was enjoying some success in its new role as an economically progressive and politically moderate state and was beginning to enjoy some momentum in that transformation. Overhaul of the State Development Board as an industry-recruiting agency and the creation of the state technical-education system had given the state something of a head start on its southern neighbors in bringing industry from other parts of the country. It was a version of the old BAWI (Balancing Agriculture with Industry) program of prewar Mississippi, but without so much emphasis on tax incentives. South Carolinians believed that industries could be lured just as well—and perhaps better—with the offer of a workforce trained by the technical-education system at state expense.

It also helped that the state had recruited two North Carolina professionals to head the programs: Walter Harper, a savvy industrial recruiter who became director of the Development Board, and Wade Martin, a veteran of North Carolina's vocational training and community-college programs who became director of South Carolina's technical-education system. Harper had learned the ropes of industrial recruiting at the North Carolina Conservation and Development agency, where he developed a close association with the Romeo Guest Construction Company of Greensboro, the firm that originally proposed the development of the Research Triangle Park to North Carolina governor Luther Hodges. Martin had come to South Carolina because he liked McNair's position of keeping technical education separate from community colleges.

The tandem of Harper and Martin had already built a record for itself in South Carolina by the mid-1960s, and—unlike Governor Byrnes fifteen years earlier—

McNair saw nothing unusual about the role of the governor in being an industrial recruiter for the state. That role, by then, had become customary for southern governors such as Carl Sanders of Georgia, Luther Hodges and Terry Sanford of North Carolina, and Hollings and Russell of South Carolina, who served as supersalesmen for their states. McNair, in fact, found the role a particularly comfortable and appropriate one.

Developing Economic Momentum

Capital investment in the state during the years 1964–1966 amounted to $911 million, nearly double what it had been the previous three years,[16] and per capita income had leaped from $1,376 in 1960 to $1,897 in 1965, an increase of 38 percent.[17] Conspicuously, the annual investment of foreign capital in the state, what McNair called "reverse investment," rose from $40.2 million in 1963 to $152 million in 1966.[18] In the decade of the 1970s, that number would swell to more than $1.7 billion.

Industrial announcements were the political plums of the 1960s, and they were welcomed with the enthusiasm usually reserved for the recruitment of prize athletes to play for Clemson or South Carolina. As plants with familiar names like General Electric, Monsanto, Owens-Corning, and Allied Chemical began taking up residence in the state, there was a certain celebrity about it all, particularly as they were joined by overseas companies with names like Michelin and Hoechst.

Among South Carolinians, there was a sense of collective interest and approval, and the state seemed to be enjoying a shared pleasure and optimism about its successes. A survey conducted by Louis Harris and Associates and released in 1971 found that almost 70 percent of South Carolinians polled felt that economic conditions had improved during the previous ten years, and 30 percent of them found things to be "a great deal better."[19] They attributed those conditions largely to the influx of new industry, the creation of more jobs, and the presence of state-sponsored technical and vocational training programs. Another 83 percent said good race relations in the state were either "very important" or "somewhat important" in the state's pursuit of economic development.[20]

For a number of reasons, McNair believed it was now or never for any major programmatic recommendations he might wish to advance to the legislature. His full term in the governor's office was passing the halfway point, and the clock was ticking on his opportunities to advance major legislative proposals. As civil unrest was developing across the nation and in South Carolina, as well, it was becoming increasingly likely that his last years in office would be devoted almost simultaneously to two intensely complex activities, coping with civil unrest and turning the Moody Report into reality. The convergence of these powerful forces gave the McNair administration a certain historical uniqueness, the pursuit of major educational and governmental reform against the background of relentless public upheaval.

No document of its time would more profoundly argue the case for public investment as an agent for economic growth than the Moody Report. It was a watershed of post–World War II optimism, and it captured the essence of a generation of Depression-era leaders who believed that the state's quality of life could be sustained and improved only by discreetly fashioned governmental initiatives and moderate leadership.

Men like Bob McNair, who had been impressed by the transforming effect of government programs such as rural electrification, Santee Cooper and others, were applying their strongly held beliefs in the inseparability of public and private interests in the state. They remembered unhappily the laissez-faire indifference with which many of the New Deal initiatives were met politically by South Carolina's ruling white oligarchy in the 1930s, and they associated the state's recent gains with the newly wrought activist posture of state government.

Partnering Public and Private Interests

In that context, the Moody Report argued a cause-and-effect relationship between government and business. A well-run and well-financed array of publicly supported educational programs would produce a skilled and competent workforce with which private business and industry could successfully and profitably operate in South Carolina. Similarly, a modern system of publicly financed roads, bridges, highways, ports, and airports would provide the infrastructure the private sector required. Achievement of the public-sector goals would lead to private-sector success. Under such a premise, government success would directly influence business success, leading to the shared benefits of jobs, higher incomes, increased purchasing power, enhanced property values, and overall economic stability. As partners, business and government had a common stake in each other's success—profits for business, revenues for government, and stability for both.

The partnership, in fact, was more than a philosophical or political theory. It became a highly individual and personal activity in which the state's business leaders were recruited into service on key state boards and commissions. In addition to the notable executives serving on the Parks, Recreation and Tourism board, a number of private-sector leaders brought business perspective to other policy boards.

The Higher Education Commission was conspicuously endowed with strong business leadership and its membership included John H. Lumpkin Sr, CEO of the state's largest bank, South Carolina National, businessmen Robert S. Russell of Charleston and E. Craig Wall Sr. of Conway, and textile executives Robert Vance of Clinton and John Cauthen. Elsewhere, men such as W. G. Edwards of Columbia, Joe Riley Sr. of Charleston, Ellison S. "Bubby" McKissick Jr. of Easley, Alester Furman of Greenville, Hugh Lane Sr. of Charleston, Jim Chapman of Spartanburg, Buck Mickel of Greenville, and Boone Aiken of Florence were among those who bridged the business-government gap with service on various state boards and commissions. McNair had come to the Governor's office with the support of, and as a champion of, the state's business interests, and his administration became a fertile place for promoting the common interest he believed existed in a cooperative relationship between the two sectors.

None in that coterie of public-minded business VIPs was more prominent than W. W. "Hootie" Johnson, the Greenwood native who grew his small State Bank and Trust into the statewide Bankers Trust, among the state's largest, and chaired the State Ports Authority during its expansion years under McNair. Johnson was often an influential leader in McNair's push for moderation and peace in racial issues, even chairing the finance committee of Columbia attorney I. S. Leevy Johnson in his successful bid to become one of the first black legislators to be elected to serve in the S.C. General Assembly in the twentieth century. In retirement, Hootie Johnson became nationally known as chairman of the board at Augusta National Golf Club, home of the Masters Tournament, and he and McNair remained close friends over the years.

When McNair later defended the boards and commission system and praised the working relationship he developed with board members and their chairmen, he was talking about more than a political or governmental strategy. He was often talking about the bond that had been forged between business and government, and the buy-in that private sector leaders had in the success of public-sector ventures.

The public-private partnership, in fact, was not a radical or a particularly new idea. The notion that good public service led to a good business environment had become virtually institutionalized not just in South Carolina but elsewhere in the region in the postwar era. It was the same kind of premise that had suggested earlier that peaceful and harmonious race relations were also good for business. Neither premise was proven empirically, but both sides seemed satisfied with the inherent and—to them, undeniable—political and economic logic of the hypothesis. The convergence of so many negative statistical indicators—poor health, low life expectancy, weak educational achievements, low per capita income, and more—must be more than coincidence, they reasoned. Their remedy lay, as had Roosevelt's New Deal a few decades earlier, in the infusion of public dollars to create conditions under which the economy could grow. Unlike the New Deal, however, the Moody plan did not call for the direct expenditure of governmental dollars in creating jobs in public-works projects. But the underlying principles were similar: public expenditures for the expansion of the private-sector economy.

For South Carolina, the 1960s represented a remarkable and, as it turned out, a somewhat ephemeral moment. Twenty years earlier, the state's leaders had passionately defended white supremacy with lawsuits and legislative action designed to forestall racial desegregation and to blunt the extension of full civil rights to minorities. Twenty years later, the War on Poverty of the 1960s evolved into a war on poverty programs as conservative-led governmental downsizing and wholesale tax cuts dismantled many initiatives of the 1960s in a wave of populist antigovernment fervor.

The 1960s, however, belonged to the ideological moderates, the economic progressives, the political pragmatists, and the societal centrists who championed the cause-and-effect theory of public/private partnerships. McNair, the ultimate centrist, was charting some new territory, but it was across a terrain that had been smoothed by the new political, racial, and economic realities of the state. The Moody Report hardly seemed radical; if anything, it appeared to be another step on a linear progression of the state's movement from its racially separatist, economically impoverished past to a level of economic success and racial harmony of undetermined magnitude. Strategically, its provisions were presented as being inseparable, and McNair, the consummate insider and inveterate centrist, found himself presenting to his legislative allies, in essence, what amounted to an all-or-nothing proposition. "We cannot emphasize too strongly," read the language of the Moody Report, "that these recommendations have intricate inter-relationships, and that they are designed to give the state and its economy a quantum leap forward. They are not presented as a cafeteria assortment from which to pick and choose; rather, failure to implement some will seriously jeopardize the thrust of the others."[21]

Such a strategy of interdependence among components depended on the confidence the legislature had in McNair himself and their basic belief that the notion of a public/private partnership was a valid one. The report, most recognized, was largely the product of McNair himself, and its contents originated as much from Columbia as they did from Colorado Springs, Colorado, the home of Campus Facilities Associates, the Moody's-related firm that produced the final report.

The "McNair Report"

Fred Carter later speculated rhetorically:

> Was it the Moody Report that really influenced Governor McNair's views on what needed to be done to move the state forward, or was it Governor McNair's views that truly produced the Moody Report? I think by the time you get to '69 and '70 . . . Bob McNair's stock for what's beginning to emerge as a lame duck governor was still enormously high with that General Assembly. Not to be trite, but how many consulting reports have ever been given the serious consideration that the Moody Report was given by our General Assembly?
>
> The Moody Report was embraced because the Moody Report was, in truth, the McNair Report.[22]

Senior McNair staffer Jim Konduros, who coordinated much of the Moody Report work, recalled, "He [McNair] felt at the time that he was looking at South

Carolina as being one of the poorest states, and [he wondered] how was it going to get to another level." The answer, he was convinced, was through public education. "He just had a natural feel for and curiosity about education," Konduros said. "If there was any one thing that in terms of something that he loved to deal with, was fascinated by, kept his hands in, and learned beyond anything I knew, it was education." A typical meeting with the consultants, Konduros recalled, would involve reports from the researchers exploring South Carolina's educational system, and McNair's determination to direct them toward his goals. "You know the state doesn't have a kindergarten," McNair would regularly remind them, and "if those kids aren't ready to learn by the time they get to the ninth grade, you're going to have a hard time graduating them."[23]

McNair remembered the meetings as being joint efforts and had high praise for Warren Rovetch, the Campus Facilities Associates president who coordinated the project. "He was one of the most brilliant planners and programmatic people I have ever known," McNair said. "Warren and his people ran through many discussions with us about all of our concerns. We talked about everything from the need for preschool, how to cut down [the number of] repeaters, how to cut down the dropout rate [the retention rate was terrible]—to what could be done to build an adjunct education program. We talked about how to broaden and expand the adult literacy program, about how to develop the TEC [technical education center] schools and really accelerate that program statewide, but to make them technical education centers, not colleges."[24]

Whatever may have been the various versions, recollections, and contentions, the recommendations transparently reflected McNair's own vision and issues and positions in four major categories.

Elementary and Secondary Education

McNair believed the stress points in the public-school system lay at the first grade level, with the frequency of repeaters, and at grades 9–12, where the dropout rate was high. As remedies, he proposed the first state-supported preschool and kindergarten programs for four- and five-year-olds. He also advocated a loosely defined series of initiatives called "Adjunct Education" to provide a combination of counseling and alternative-education programs for potential dropouts, bridging the secondary and post-high-school years for high-risk students. A major part of the report's proposed "quantum leap" was a substantial hike in teacher salaries, designed to bring the state close to the southeastern average.

Higher Education

Disorderly governmental planning and budgeting was nowhere more visible than with respect to the state's splintered post-high-school education system. Annual free-for-alls among the separately governed institutions, McNair believed, were not only disorderly but also wasteful. The Moody Report proposed a three-tiered system: (1) to establish a level of senior research institutions at the University of South Carolina, Clemson College, and the Medical College; (2) to create a four-year college level, which would include existing colleges at South Carolina State, Winthrop, and the regional campus of the University of South Carolina at Florence, as well as the addition of the College of Charleston to the state system and the creation of new four-year institutions in the Piedmont and Midlands areas; (3) to separate two-year regional campuses administered by USC and Clemson and administer them as a third tier of the new system. Authority of the existing Higher Education Commission would be strengthened; a new board to govern the two- and four-year colleges would be created; and Winthrop would be made coeducational.

The report also upheld a long-held McNair belief that the Technical Education Centers should remain in their technical, job-related function and not be expanded into community colleges. It was a position he had held since taking office in 1965 and publicly disagreeing with his predecessor, Donald Russell, over converting TEC into a community-college system. McNair believed that preserving the separate status of the technical system was critical to the state's continuing economic development success.

Health

Almost overlooked in the flurry of education-related recommendations was one that lay in the area of public health, but it created something of a political minefield for South Carolina legislators. The proposal called for the "strengthening of the Medical College at Charleston in a number of ways, the condition precedent to which must be affiliation of the Medical College with the University of South Carolina."[25]

While the 1969 General Assembly stepped gingerly around the recommendation and the topic of medical education, it was an issue that it would revisit subsequently and with explosive results. The creation of the Medical School at the University of South Carolina during John West's term as governor was still provoking Charleston-based opposition as late as the turn of the twenty-first century.

Infrastructure

Other Moody Report recommendations dealt with improvements to the state's transportation capabilities, the core of which called for issuing $85 million in bonds for highways and $71.7 million for ports improvement through 1985. Transportation should be closely coordinated, the report said, through the creation of a McNair-styled Inter-Agency Council.[26]

Analyzing Financial Capacity

While the Moody Report's most controversial proposals were increases in annual taxes, one of its most enduring recommendations put the state on a scheduled debt-retirement program that significantly increased its capital-funding capacity. In past years, much of the state's capital projects had been paid for "in cash" from unspent operating funds at the end of each fiscal year or from specifically appropriated moneys for debt retirement. Moody's suggested that the state formalize and formularize a program of long-term debt and build in a legislatively prescribed debt-retirement ceiling as something of an automatic part of each year's annual appropriation.

No scorecard was kept on the Moody Report wins and losses, and any assessment of the outcome would have required years to determine. For all the wide-ranging issues that were raised in the comprehensive study, however, the Moody Report was at its core about public education, and that scorecard could be tallied on the basis of legislative responses during the 1969 session. It turned out, predictably, to be a testy, race-oriented battle, and it was one that required the full force not only of McNair's persuasive power but also the strength of his remarkable legislative alliances.

Kindergartens, church-based and privately sponsored, had been a part of the South Carolina educational experience for generations, but they were largely available to the affluent middle classes, and most of them were white in 1969 South Carolina. "We needed [public kindergartens] primarily for the children coming from the low-income families and from the rural areas who were not exposed to the environment that kids in the city were exposed to, and, therefore, we had to have a state-supported kindergarten program," McNair later said.[27]

Kindergartens and Racial Implications

That kind of initiative touched off racial sensitivities and ugly legislative bickering in what was still an all-white General Assembly. "[Race] was a very big issue," McNair said, noting that it took on personal and anecdotal tones like "my little grand-daughter sitting in there with you-know-who" and "at that tender age," a barely disguised reference to the prospect of young white children sharing bus rides with older black children. Such references had come early in the fight from Speaker Blatt. "The stronger filibuster and the biggest fight was over the compulsory school attendance law [recommended separately and two years before the Moody Report] and the kindergartens," McNair recalled.[28]

Two years earlier, in his 1967 State of the State Address, McNair had successfully tackled the racially sensitive issue of compulsory school attendance, stating, "We must have new laws and new programs to keep more of our children in school. If we discourage literacy by ignoring this need, then we are paving the way for a welfare state."[29]

Even years earlier, when he was running for governor in 1966, McNair recalled, "people reminded me and some of the polls showed that my biggest problem was with mothers of school-age children, particularly at the elementary level, because they identified me with integration and the fact I was out there forcing their children to go to school together and in the younger ages."[30]

Blatt and McNair had a rare disagreement over the kindergarten provision, but by mid-January Blatt had moderated his stance and said he felt that he and the governor had "common ground of agreement" over the Moody proposals.[31] Two weeks later, the Speaker acknowledged that he would "take a good, hard look" at the kindergarten proposal, although his support of the proposal would subsequently fall short of supporting the 175 kindergartens envisioned in the McNair plan.[32]

Even though he was in the midst of civil rights scuffles throughout the spring of 1969, including the lengthy and tedious Medical College Hospital strike, McNair worked the legislature hard for the key Moody proposals, and by session's end, he had attained some measure of success. Contained in the House-Senate compromise version of the State Appropriation Bill for 1969 were critical elements of the governor's tax-raising proposal (the 1 percent sales tax had passed under separate legislation), and the provision for a modest start on public kindergartens (a $500,000 appropriation).[33] The conference committee, reminiscent of McNair's first year in office in 1965, in which the two houses were in such harmony that no conference committee was necessary, ironed out their differences in only two days. Longtime McNair ally Senator Edgar Brown, who chaired the committee, said that the six conferees had "forgotten everything on the outside for two and a half days and [had] done in two and a half days what it usually takes two weeks to do." Brown said he had never worked with "a more knowledgeable, more agreeable, more conscientious or more dedicated group."[34] His comments were also an acknowledgment that his longtime friend Bob McNair had not lost his touch with the legislature.

A Declaration of Victory

Nine days later, the Associated Press noted that "Gov. Robert E. McNair's love affair with the South Carolina Legislature may have cooled somewhat since 1967. But he still commands an impressive batting average in dealing with the House and the Senate." The AP report went on to say that

> McNair, a state representative for 12 years, has had remarkable rapport with the General Assembly for the past three years. He had spectacular success in 1967 when the legislature approved all but one of his major proposals.
>
> When McNair went before the General Assembly last Jan. 15 [1969], he presented some sobering fiscal facts and recommendations: the state must raise $63 million in new taxes if it is to move ahead in the mainstream of American life.
>
> Afterwards, individual legislators took issue on this point or that, but it was their consensus that the 45-year-old governor had displayed courage in making specific, and probably unpopular recommendations for raising taxes.[35]

McNair lost some of his battles that year, including the recommendation that the Medical College in Charleston be affiliated with USC. His pleas for a three-tiered higher-education system overseen by a strong Higher Education Commission also went unheeded. McNair scored a partial and temporary victory with the creation of a State College Board of Trustees to oversee two new four-year state institutions, Francis Marion in Florence and the College of Charleston, a two-centuries-old liberal arts institution that became part of the state system. Regional politics soon prevailed in each instance, however, and the schools attained their own boards shortly thereafter. Winthrop College did become coeducational in the administration of McNair's successor, John West, and the state's four-year system was expanded to include Lander College in Greenwood, another ailing private institution taken over by the state.

But the scorecard for the Moody Report recommendations would not be measured simply in political wins and losses. Coming as it did while the state stood at a crossroads over public education, and coming on the eve of massive desegregation of the schools, the Moody Report, and the 1969 McNair legislative recommendations, offered the state an opportunity to affirm or deny its commitment to public education under the pressure of impending desegregation.

Those portions of the report that gained approval—tax hikes to upgrade teacher salaries and to cover other items and, most notably, a first step toward public kindergartens for the low-income and rural students—spoke loudly that South Carolina was passing through its crisis over public education and was fitfully putting aside the notion that racial considerations should dominate the public discourse over education, economic development, and other matters vital to the state's future. The battle for South Carolina's political soul was still in full force, but the outcome of the 1969 General Assembly gave Bob McNair another victory in easing the state toward a consistent and politically sustainable position of consensual moderation.

9

The Gathering Storm at South Carolina State

For a consensus-minded governor, the 1960s were difficult times to carry on political business as usual. McNair's complex economic and educational reform proposals would have been major political chores under ordinary circumstances. But as it turned out, they would be fought out against a backdrop of increasing civil unrest and public anxiety that not only drew attention away from the legislative and governmental business at hand, but also created political divisions of their own.

South Carolina's tenuous racial peace was giving way to the risky business of public demonstrations. As the state entered the latter half of the decade, the civility of courtroom fights over civil rights was yielding to the hostility of street confrontations, and the adult leadership of organizations such as the NAACP was giving way to impatient youth whose allegiance was more to a cause than to an organization. The comfort zone of orchestrated desegregation events earlier in the decade was being replaced by the uncertainties of spontaneous emotional outbreaks, and South Carolina was finding itself treading the hazardous path of human conflict and face-to-face encounters.

In some instances, the governor's office became a round-the-clock operation, carrying out legislative and administrative business by the day and addressing civil rights and law enforcement matters in the evenings and on weekends. For all the pioneering work of Fritz Hollings, Donald Russell, and others in shaping a moderate role for South Carolina's racial policies, McNair's experience was one of unprecedented pressure and challenge. For his last three years in office, there was a virtually unbroken string of major incidents that brought students, workers, and public-spirited reformers into the streets and brought South Carolina to the brink of political anarchy and public chaos. While Bob McNair's political skills were being measured in the halls of the legislature in terms of educational and economic-development achievements, the stiffer tests were coming in the streets of places like Charleston, Orangeburg, Lamar, Denmark, and Columbia, where he would be tested as diplomat, peacekeeper, and protector of public safety. It would be in the latter category that much of his historic destiny would be determined.

As the pace of civil rights activism accelerated in the years following the *Brown v. Board of Education* decision, much of the energy and attention of black South Carolina became concentrated in the city of Orangeburg and on the campus of South Carolina State College. It was a place where the erratic and edgy nature of race relations in the state was in clear evidence, and where much of the frustration of the state's black population had been visibly experienced and expressed over the years.

From its earliest days, in fact, South Carolina State was an institution entangled in ironies and contradictions. Its establishment came during the most improbable of times, the mid-1890s, when the white-supremacist doctrine of Tillmanism was sweeping the state, depriving virtually all blacks of the right to vote and exiling them economically into segregationist isolation. The same white-dominated political force that adopted the discriminatory Constitution of 1896 also created the institution that for generations would be a rallying cry for black identity and for black economic and professional aspirations.

Some contend the college was established to break the domination of black college education in the post–Civil War South by white church missions in the North. South Carolina's first two black colleges—Claflin (Methodist) and Benedict (Baptist), both established in 1869 were among many such church-related institutions in the region. Other scholars believe that the creation of South Carolina State was part of a compromise with black political leadership that had lost virtually all its powers in the Constitution of 1896. As such, it was part of a three-college package (also including Winthrop and Clemson) as proposed by Governor Ben Tillman, who disliked the University of South Carolina and the Citadel and believed that the older institutions were elitist. (See endnotes 2, 3, 4, 5, 6, and 7 for the present chapter.) "The story of South Carolina State College," historian William C. Hine wrote in 1991 in describing the apparent anomaly, "is the story of rural black people attempting to build an institution to provide them with the knowledge and skills necessary to survive in a society that until recently regarded them as second-class citizens who did not deserve a first-class college."[1]

Saddled with a Limited Mission

For whatever the reasons, the college emerged from the 1896 General Assembly with the ponderous name, the Colored Normal, Industrial, Agricultural and Mechanical College of South Carolina, and with a distressingly limited mission.

Historian I. A. Newby called it a school "established by white Carolinians to serve their purposes. Its function was to segregate blacks, provide them with an 'acceptable' education, and fit them into the social order of white supremacy." From its earliest days, South Carolina State fought against that limited mission and did so with a chronic lack of funding support from the state. When its doors were opened for business for the year 1896–1897, the school enrolled 960 students, "an astonishing total . . . which indicated the pressing need for public schools in black Carolina, [and which] overcrowded the school's facilities, a condition that existed throughout its history." The college also inherited an awkward governing arrangement. While its president and faculty were required by its enabling legislation to "be of the Negro race,"[2] its governing board was all white. Its first president, Thomas E. Miller, retired under pressure because he opposed the election of white supremacist Cole Blease in the election of 1910.

South Carolina State did not award its first bona fide bachelor's degrees until 1924–1925.[3] For much of its early life, in fact, it was scarcely a college, in the current usage of the term. Along with other black institutions in the state, it offered mainly elementary- and secondary-level programs. Newby reported, "By 1910, Claflin had granted a total of 79 bachelors degrees, and Benedict 26. Through 1911, the state college had graduated 533 students, most of them educated through about the seventh or ninth grade level."[4]

One of those who enrolled in the high school program at South Carolina State in those days was the son of a Ninety Six cotton farmer named Benjamin F. Mays. He enrolled as an eighth grader in 1911, graduated four years later from the thirteen-grade high school program, and recalled, "It did my soul good in 1911 to find at State College an all-Negro faculty and a Negro president. They were good teachers, holding degrees from Benedict College, Biddle College [now Johnson C. Smith University], Lincoln University in Pennsylvania, Fisk University and other colleges. President Robert Shaw Wilkinson was a graduate of Oberlin. His wife, Marian Birnie Wilkinson, was one of the finest women I have ever known. She fought racial injustice and discrimination, and the white merchants who sold to the school paid her the unusual tribute of calling her *Mrs.* Wilkinson."[5]

Wilkinson presided over the college until his death from pneumonia on March 12, 1932.[6] He saw the institution through some important developments, including the establishment by the college of extension activities into the rural communities of the state and the significant acquisition of philanthropic moneys to help the institution survive the impoverished Depression years of the 1930s.[7]

By the post–World War II years, South Carolina State was still suffering serious funding shortages and lagged far behind the state's white institutions. The college's 1947 appropriation for its 1,697 students was $523,000, or $306 per student, as compared to Winthrop ($996 per student), the Citadel ($797 per student), Clemson ($790 per student), and USC ($595 per student). The funding shortage was also reflected in the sparse allocation to the institution in a college bond bill of 1937. South Carolina State received a total of $75,000 out of a total amount of $13.5 million, with the rest being divided up among the four white institutions.

The lack of dormitory space would deny many returning black veterans immediate access to the college education guaranteed most of them by the GI Bill of Rights. In 1946, the college was forced to adopt a policy of accepting five hundred applications and placing another five hundred on a waiting list. Even when the 1947 legislature proposed spending $7.5 million for higher education, only $350,000 was initially authorized for South Carolina State, and the institution's undergraduate program was further damaged by requirements that a graduate school and a law school be established to avoid the desegregation of the state's other institutions.[8]

Choosing a President "Not Sympathetic to Desegregation"

By 1950, South Carolina's white political establishment was more worried about the possibility of racial desegregation than it was the chronic funding shortage at South Carolina State. When the State College Board met in the office of Governor Strom Thurmond to elect a new president in 1950, "the trustees made it clear that they did not want a president sympathetic to desegregation."[9]

Their choice was Dr. Benner C. Turner, a Harvard graduate who had come to the campus in 1947 as dean of the newly established law school. He was a man described as "quiet, dignified, and intelligent . . . an able administrator who worked well with the trustees and the state's political leaders."[10] Turner's mandate to resist desegregation, however, was evidence to many that things had not changed much politically in half a century. It was reminiscent of the presidency of Thomas Miller in 1896 and the mission "to segregate blacks, provide them with an 'acceptable' education, and fit them into the social order of white supremacy."[11] It was also a mandate that put Turner on a collision course with the powerful forces of change looming in the very near future, forces that would make him a target for an increasingly impatient civil rights community, much of whose leadership would come from the State College student body.

His first test came on July 31, 1955, two months after the U.S. Supreme Court had handed down its *Brown II* decision ordering that school desegregation be implemented "with all deliberate speed." Under the leadership of the local NAACP chapter, fifty-seven black Orangeburg residents signed a petition calling for the school board "to take immediate concrete steps leading to an early elimination of segregation in public schools."[12] The petition, one of some sixty such actions taken by local NAACP chapters across the South, set off a firestorm of boycotts and counter-boycotts, economic reprisals, student demonstrations and strikes, threats to close the school, student and faculty expulsions, and a spate of legislative investigations into "subversive elements" on campus.[13]

The protest earned the title "The Ugly Battle of Orangeburg" in an Edward Gamarekian article in the now-defunct publication the *Reporter,* which detailed the bitter boycott fights, the anti-NAACP actions, and the emergence of the White Citizens Councils as not only a local anti-desegregation effort but also a national movement sufficiently significant to warrant the promise from President Eisenhower that he would "thoroughly examine" the discriminatory allegations.[14] The 1955 conflict stretched out over a year, during which time President Turner was unwilling to support the NAACP effort and held the firm line on student and faculty discipline. By the time the effort finally disintegrated in 1956, Turner's actions had earned him the gratitude of white leaders and the acrimony of students, who registered a vote of no confidence in his leadership.[15]

His next test came four years later, in 1960, as South Carolina State and Claflin students joined the sit-in movement that had been initiated earlier in the year in Greensboro, North Carolina. Despite Turner's admonition that "the college could not and would not protect them, and that future demonstrations would risk possible disciplinary action," two marches, involving four hundred and one thousand students, were planned, and the school's white board of trustees was on record as prohibiting "demonstrations which involve violation of laws . . . or which disrupt the normal college routine."[16]

As with the 1955–1956 protests, the administration's actions did not stop the students, and when the second march was ended by fire hoses and mass arrests of four hundred students, the sometimes aloof black community of Orangeburg rallied to their support and assisted with bail and legal defense. Among those arrested in the March 1960 Orangeburg marches were James E. Clyburn of Sumter, a future congressman, and Charles McDew, of Massillon, Ohio, who would become chairman of the Student Non-Violent Coordinating Committee (SNCC) from 1961–1964. Clyburn was quoted in a *State* newspaper account of March 20, 1960, as testifying in the breach-of-peace trial against the demonstrators "that he was apprehended while en route with others 'to petition city officials for denying us our rights of peaceful assembly.'" Also present at the trial was NAACP president I. DeQuincey Newman, who was quoted in the *State* account as telling newsmen that "fees for the . . . four Negro defense attorneys are being paid by 'volunteers,'" and that the NAACP would step in if further help was needed.[17]

Three hundred seventy-three of the students were convicted, tried in groups of fifteen and sentenced to a $50 fine or thirty days in jail. One of the presiding magistrates, D. Marchant Cullers, told students convicted in his court, "What you did could have caused violence. . . . It was a very dangerous situation. This must stop."[18]

The demonstrations did not stop, and the convictions did not stick, either. Three years later, the U.S. Supreme Court agreed with the nineteen-year-old Clyburn that the students had the right to demonstrate peacefully and overturned the conviction of the 373 students.[19] By then, the Orangeburg demonstrations had persisted and escalated, and in September 1963 some 1,350 students from Claflin, South Carolina State, and the all-black Wilkinson High School were arrested in what became known as "The Orangeburg Movement."[20]

Under the leadership of the local citizens committee, however, the Orangeburg white community successfully resisted the pressures for voluntary desegregation of the city's public accommodations, and the ten years of vigorous activity brought little visible change. Orangeburg remained racially divided, and the president of South Carolina State College remained at some distance from his students and faculty. A section of the student handbook gave students the dire warning that those "whose examples or influence is found detrimental to its [the college's] welfare may be dropped at any time without obligation on the part of the officers of the College to state specific reasons for requesting the withdrawal." Similar provisions applied to faculty, including those without tenure.[21] It was in that uneasy and simmering condition that Orangeburg lay as Bob McNair became governor in 1965, and it would be in Orangeburg, amid a decade-long buildup of racial resentment, hostility, and alienation, that he would find civil rights challenges that would shape much of the long-term image and perception of his administration.

Early McNair Contacts with Black Leaders

In his campaign for lieutenant governor in 1962, and particularly in the racially charged governor's race of 1966, McNair had become acquainted and friendly with some of the state's black political and civil rights leaders, particularly those connected with the NAACP. "I developed a good relationship with the black leaders who were emerging at the time . . . [and] I have said there were two reasons. One is they had no other choice when I came along because my opposition in the governor's race in the general election [Joseph O. Rogers, 1966] was sort of the leader of the resistance movement in the legislature. . . . I sort of fell heir to that [black political support]. But at the same time, I had developed communications and—I think—a chemistry with Matthew Perry and then with Reverend [I. DeQuincey] Newman and some of the other leaders."[22]

Chemistry was the critical element, and as with most of Bob McNair's dealings, politics was a personal thing, whether it was in legislative scuffles, campaign strategies, press relations, or civil rights disputes. McNair was not comfortable in a highly public or confrontational setting. His political effectiveness lay in his ability to engage his adversaries in quiet settings with pleasant conversations.

Civil rights, however, was becoming a matter of life and death in many parts of the South in the early 1960s. South Carolina's racial experience—while not as visibly brutal as elsewhere—had its elements of violence, bitterness, and mistrust. The events in Orangeburg were symptomatic of the deep gulfs that still separated the races and the combativeness that both races brought to issues of civil rights. The state's heritage of chilled race relations had only begun to thaw as McNair became governor, and it was clear that he would have difficulty practicing his style of personal politics in a setting where the parties involved were so distant from each other.

For decades, the NAACP had dominated the state's civil rights movement, and it was not known as a friendly rival by its white adversaries. "Before the emergence of the new black civil rights organizations of the mid-1950s and the 1960s, the NAACP was the most militant regional spokesman for black civil rights, and the southern establishment hated it," wrote historian Barbara W. Aba-Mecha (Woods) in a 1981 paper. "By 1956, members of the NAACP were forbidden to work in any agency of the state government. Attempts to disband the NAACP in the South continued until the Southern establishment directed its attention to the more radical elements of the young revolutionists."[23]

The southern establishment had good reason to dread the NAACP. It was that organization more than any other that had dismantled the segregated school system, the Jim Crow laws of public accommodations, and the white-supremacist electoral process in the South. Its South Carolina members and chapters were often in the vanguard of those efforts.

The organization had been transformed in 1939 from locally based chapters to a statewide association dedicated to restoring full rights to the state's black citizens, particularly in the areas of public education and voting. At the core of its aggressive leadership were strong-minded and forceful people such as Reverend James Hinton, Levi Byrd, Osceola McKaine, John McCray, and the indomitable Modjeska Simkins. Simkins had brought fire and passion to the NAACP's leadership, and along the way her "caustic and . . . abrasive style" stirred concerns among not only white conservatives, but also among moderate elements of the civil rights movement. "She was for many years a target for conservative whites who regarded her as a bleeding-heart liberal agitator—and a Communist," wrote journalist Charles Wickenberg in her 1992 obituary.[24]

It was not only whites who worried about Simkins's leftist political leanings. Her alleged friendship with members of the Communist Party had not only earned her a file with the U.S. House Committee on Un-American Activities, it had also earned her an uneasy relationship with the national office of the NAACP, which was worried —among other things—about its tax-exempt status with the Internal Revenue Service at a time when McCarthyite politicians were finding reddish tint to elements of the civil rights movement. Things came to a head in 1956 with the issuance of a press notice that Simpkins would appear along with singer Paul Robeson "at a rally for convicted black Communist leader Benjamin J. Davis, a longtime friend of hers."[25] She later agreed not to attend the controversial meeting in New York "because she did not want the NAACP to be attacked because of her participation," but she fired off a shot at NAACP leader Roy Wilkins, telling him that "the NAACP did not have the only answer to the problem of discrimination against blacks."[26]

Simkins's break with the NAACP came in 1957 over what was considered by some as further evidence of her alleged Communist connections. She believed, however, that she "was not returned to office . . . because of a deal made between the power structure and the president of the South Carolina NAACP Conference, James M. Hinton. She cited the fact that soon after her ouster, Hinton stepped down from his own post."[27]

Newman and the Transformation of NAACP Leadership

In his 1992 obituary of Simkins, Wickenberg observed that she "was suddenly removed and replaced by the Rev. I. D. Newman," a transition described as leaving "a bitter taste" with Simkins.[28] For whatever may have been the reason, the accession of Newman to the leadership post of the NAACP represented a major stylistic shift for the organization. It would prove to be a fortuitous development for McNair, who would find in Newman a kinder, gentler adversary than Simkins and something of a silent partner in addressing the civil rights issues of the 1960s.

To McNair, Newman had the "unique ability to represent the position and represent the movement but at the same time to be able to sit down and talk rationally and reasonably about the problems that we were all confronted with." Newman became McNair's inside man on racial matters, an adviser and counselor in private while remaining a staunch adversary in public. It was an element of racial communication that enhanced South Carolina's quest for peaceful settlement to its civil rights issues, and it gave McNair something that may have been lacking elsewhere in the South. "The thing that brought us through that period [civil rights] was the communication . . . and the leadership from the black community. Rev. Newman, Rev. Holman [NAACP leader Alonzo Holman] and Herbert Fielding [later to become a member of the S.C. House of Representatives and senator from Charleston, 1971–1973 and 1983–1985] . . . stepped forward and took a leadership role and kept it from becoming open hostile confrontation. . . . We had it [confrontation], but it wasn't the type it was in some other places."[29]

In the style of the 1960s, however, resolution did not come in a direct way. Things were orchestrated. "You could not have press conferences . . . and announce change and show how progressive you were moving," McNair recalled. "Everything that we did . . . with rare exception, was discussed with the black leadership. They did not always agree, but I cannot recall many instances when they were caught by surprise. Now, quite often on television, they would express great dismay and displeasure and come down on me pretty hard, but they normally knew what was going to happen, and there was . . . an understanding. They had to keep their position and maintain their credibility and their image, also. We operated that way, but we tried very diligently to communicate. . . . They were honest enough to tell us when they were going to have a disagreement."[30]

It was a role for which Newman had been especially well prepared. Unlike Simkins, who came from a comfortable urban background, Newman was a product of South Carolina's rural poverty of the 1920s and the rough-and-tumble economic and political conditions of the times, and like McNair, he learned his early politics from his father. Born in Darlington County, Newman remembered his father as being "a 'Tieless' Joe Tolbert Republican," referring to the patronage broker who had been a key South Carolina GOP leader dating back to the days of the presidency of William Howard Taft. In the days of the all-white Democratic Party, the Republican Party was the only outlet for black political participation, and it was, according to Newman, "not much more than a conduit for patronage . . . when there was a Republican President."[31]

Newman worked his way up through the ranks of the black political community, logging time as a minister in small rural churches; he recalled that his first cash salary, in 1932, was "sixty cents, a quart of peaches, a quart of whippoorwill peas and a piece of hog jowl."[32] He was also on the circuitous journey blacks were taking to political power in South Carolina, first as Republicans, later as members of the Progressive Democratic Party (PDP) of the mid-1940s, and finally as Democrats in the 1960s.

The PDP experience provided Newman an early exposure to the black political conditions in South Carolina, and he recalled being inspired by two of the PDP's early advocates, John McCray and Osceola McKaine. "I'd heard about it [the PDP]," he recalled, "read about it in the *Lighthouse and Informer,* and I was inspired. . . . I was present for the first organizing convention and was what you might style as the junior partner in the undertaking—I was elected fourth vice-president . . . [and] we were termed radicals. We were described by I. S. Leevy, the old black Republican patriarch, as 'strange cats in the woodpile.'"[33]

Newman's politics followed the shifting national inclinations of black Americans at the times. "I voted for Truman in '48, Stevenson and Sparkman in '52, Eisenhower and Nixon in 1956, and Nixon again in 1960. . . . As late as 1960, there were any number of strong black leaders who were members of the Republican Party [including one-time House member Earl Middleton of Orangeburg]. I supported Mr. Nixon in 1960 not so much because I thought he was a better man than President Kennedy, but because I had gotten to know Nixon."[34]

Newman in many ways was a bridge between the passive past of South Carolina's black political experience and the activist strategies of the 1960s. He was a product of the traditional mix of church and politics by which black South Carolinians sustained political localism during the days when their legal political status was minimal. It was a time, Newman would later say, when the civil rights leadership and the black ministry were almost interchangeable. "The black church is the only institution owned and controlled by blacks," he told an interviewer in 1979. "The man in the pulpit was the spokesman and easily identified as a leader. He was the leader of a flock which gets together on certain occasions. He was accepted as the leader of the community because of his exposure and opportunities to mold opinion. . . . The black clergy were the only ones that had the freedom of expression."[35]

Newman was also working his way up the NAACP ladder, holding leadership roles in such key counties as Orangeburg and Sumter. "[When] the transition [of NAACP leadership] took place," recalled Isaac "Ike" Williams, a Newman protégé and later field secretary of the NAACP, "'Deak' Newman already had a statewide base from two points. One is the United Methodist Church [at that time an all-black denomination], because he had pastored in every nook and cranny in the state. And then he had an NAACP base. . . . Since the churches were our inroad, the United Methodist Church and the Baptist leadership . . . and the rest of them came together . . . to provide whatever core you needed for the support of the NAACP."[36]

Newman recalled his evolution from local to state leader. "I had been branch president [of the NAACP] in Orangeburg," he said in an interview. "I was very active in the executive committee of the Sumter NAACP branch and somewhere along about 1948 or 1949 I had become vice president of the NAACP conference and the heir . . . to Mr. Hinton [Reverend James Hinton], the fearless leader of the NAACP during most of the 1940s and 1950s. I was elected president of the NAACP conference in 1958 and went on to become Field Secretary in 1960."[37]

By the time he became field secretary, Newman was almost fifty, no longer a young man and finding himself amid youthful men and women who were energizing the civil rights movement. But Newman conceded little in the way of energy or initiative. His arrival as field secretary coincided with the initiation of sit-in demonstrations protesting segregated public accommodations, and he had been on the job only a matter of weeks before mass demonstrations took place in Columbia and Orangeburg and he found himself in jail for the first time. "I was not fearful of any bodily harm," he said, "but it was uncomfortable and inconvenient, and served to steel my determination."

It was a time when the NAACP was taking off the gloves and turning its attention to activities outside the courtroom as well as inside. Newman brought to that transition an unusual quality, that of a middle-aged minister who was almost a father figure leading his young charges into the hazards of public demonstrations. There was a certain sense of reassurance, particularly for parents of demonstrators, that Newman would conduct things responsibly, would protect the demonstrators from physical harm, and would take care of things if the protestors got into legal trouble. By then, Williams recalled, the NAACP had also developed a network of people who "would not get out there on the picket lines . . . but who put up bail bond money and . . . would mortgage property and all that."[38]

For all the organizing and planning for contingencies, however, demonstrating and protesting in the 1960s was hazardous business, for the demonstrators and for Newman himself. "It was not always peaceful on the part of those resisting change," he once told a reporter. "There was some police brutality. A demonstrator was attacked with a deadly weapon at a sit-in [at a local store] and almost killed. In one of the marches toward the State House, one of the demonstrators was ganged up on by people who were opposed to the demonstration . . . [and] he was beaten up."[39]

Newman, in fact, liked a good fight and sometimes had to be restrained. "We were going from a period of litigation to confrontation," Ike Williams recalled,

> and "Deak" Newman was a believer in confrontation. His hands were sorta held by Matthew Perry, who was the brilliant lawyer, but quite a conservative when it came to confrontation. I can remember "Deak" Newman saying so many times to Matthew Perry, "Well, they pay you to law, and they pay me to field direct."
>
> And—needless to say—afterwards in a meeting when Matthew Perry would counsel "Deak" that it would not be wise to do this and wise to do that, he [Newman] would say, "Never go to a lawyer when you want to discuss direct action. You go to the lawyer after you take direct action."[40]

For his part, Newman took seriously both roles, insider and outsider. Later in life, there was some criticism that he may have abandoned his civil rights agenda for the security of high-level governmental jobs when he accepted a position with the State Department of Social Services. Newman said at the time, "I don't want to stick a pin in anybody's balloon, but [in] my being a party to things—however privileged—there was some method to it. . . . I have never passed up an opportunity to open the door a little wider if I thought for a moment that I could use my position as Executive Assistant to Dr. Ellis [Social Services Commissioner Archie Ellis], or working for Governor West, or Governor Edwards, or Governor Riley. I would have been content being the shepherd of a flock as a minister, but being quietly on the inside, I was in a better position to serve the ultimate purpose of improving the political, social and economic status of black people in the state."[41]

It was the multidimensional aspect of Newman's role that suited McNair best and made them allies. As a consummate insider himself, McNair valued not only the confidential nature of his relationship with Newman, he was also comfortable with the pragmatism and practicality of the NAACP chief. McNair accorded Newman broad access to his office, to his staff, and to law enforcement leaders, including SLED Chief J. P. Strom. It was often, however, a back-door access to keep their communications out of the public eye. Disclosure of such meetings, McNair felt, would have been damaging to both sides and could have limited the range and candor of their discussions.

As things heated up yet again in Orangeburg in 1967 for what would be the first serious civil rights challenge of his administration, McNair had formed friendships with the triumvirate of NAACP leadership at the time—attorney Matthew Perry, State Conference president Alonzo Holman of Aiken, and Newman—and in Newman, he had a particularly valued ally. With all three, he could practice personal politics and could feel some security in the sense that across the table from him were leaders who also believed in the fine art of negotiation and compromise. For all the public disagreements reported among them, there were private meetings taking place in out-of-the-way places that were designed to address the not incompatible agendas of the two—racial peace for McNair and racial progress for the NAACP leadership.

It was a partnership that had great potential. McNair had come through the 1966 election with impressive numbers, a strong centrist position among Democrats, and a good election day showing with black voters. For his part—in the days when white leaders tended to think that there could be a single spokesman for all blacks—Newman came as close as anyone to fulfilling that unreasonable expectation.

South Carolina State Students and Administration on a Collision Course

Bob McNair was less than a month into his elected term of office when things at South Carolina State began stirring again. The immediate issue this time was the college's decision not to renew the contracts of two popular white professors—Thomas Wirth and Anthony Fanning—who had come to South Carolina State under a Woodrow Wilson grant designed to "help small struggling colleges upgrade themselves."[42] The students, concerned that Wirth's and Fanning's departures signaled an academic retreat by the administration, also still harbored resentment against what was considered a distant and white-oriented administration. President Turner's declaration that the college "could not and would not" protect demonstrators in the 1960 protests remained something of a legacy of discontent on the campus, and the unhappiness of Wirth's and Fanning's treatment only aggravated some already painful sentiments.[43]

Unrest turned into protest with a demonstration at a women's dormitory in mid-February 1967, and a week later it flared up as "a raucous late night sit-in on the lawn of Turner's campus residence."[44] A student occupation of the Student Center until dawn the next day led to the suspension of three student leaders—Joseph Hammonds of Blackville, who was president of the NAACP's State Youth Conference; John Stroman of Savannah; and Benjamin Bryant of Mullins. In a statement issued February 24, President Turner called the demonstrators "noisy, discourteous and disorderly" and said, "The College administration will not deal with a rowdy and undisciplined mob."[45]

"The suspension of the three students galvanized the student body," wrote Hine.[46] After a series of meetings during the subsequent week failed to satisfy student leaders' demand for the immediate reinstatement of Hammonds, Stroman, and Bryant, a campus-wide boycott of classes was called on March 2 by Ike Williams, president of the senior class, and presidents of the other three classes, freshman Robert Cunningham, sophomore John Bishop, and junior Alexander Nichols. After some initial challenges to Williams's leadership, support of the boycott grew, and at its height, it was estimated that as many as 1,400 of the college's undergraduate student body of 1,695 were staying out of class.[47] Although Newman and student leader Williams were close friends and in regular communication, the NAACP chief was careful to remain at arm's length publicly from the student event, and he described his interest as that of being "a public-spirited observer first and as an official of the NAACP second."[48]

Both Newman and Williams were also protective of the NAACP's dominant role in the state's civil rights activity and declined the offer of intervention from Stokely Charmichael and the Student Non-Violent Coordinating Committee (SNCC). Newman called SNCC "outside interests," and he insisted that the NAACP's support of the South Carolina State students was limited to students who "maintain a promise to conduct the protest non-violently and [who] reject any participation in the boycott by outside agitators."[49] One news account quoted Newman as saying that the NAACP agreed to help the students if they would get rid of "outsiders who had come on the campus to cause trouble" and made it clear that he was referring to "some members of the Student Non-Violent Coordinating Committee, who had arrived on campus from other states."

Turner found himself isolated. After two meetings failed to break the impasse, his options narrowed and he turned to strong-arm tactics, threatening to close the school if necessary and directing faculty to continue keeping attendance records during the boycott. Newspapers reported that highway patrolmen and SLED and FBI agents had been dispatched to the campus.[50] In a March 6 memorandum to faculty and staff, Turner summarized the sequence of events leading to the stalemate and stated, "It is our feeling that we have made every effort to achieve a solution and that nothing further remains to be done, save to enforce the college regulations. You are therefore asked please to check class attendance regularly and report any unexcused absences. No date has been set by the Board of Trustees relative to closing of the college, but in the event that this undesirous result should occur, your salary will continue and you are asked to remain on duty."[51]

For their part, students incorporated into their demands additional requirements that called for the easing of restrictions on student activities and included the "end to mandatory attendance at Sunday vespers and lyceum programs, . . . the abolition of Sunday dress code for dinner, greater student control over student government," and other proposals designed to increase student involvement in campus decisions and activities. Turner showed some flexibility in dealing with student concerns over regulations and restrictions, but he drew the line with the reinstatement of Hammonds, Stroman, and Bryant. "'This,' Turner stated emphatically, 'is an ultimatum the college cannot accept.'"[52]

With that, doors slammed, rhetoric grew louder, and tensions were heightened. As the boycott neared its second week and as classrooms became increasingly vacant, McNair summoned Turner, Board Chairman Bruce White of Union, SLED Chief J. P. Strom, and Attorney General Daniel R. McLeod to his office for an assessment of the situation, and he later recalled that Turner seemed "personally hurt" by the attitude of the students. "He felt he had done a good job at State College, and he couldn't understand why the students had turned against him."[53]

In his seventeen years at the college, in fact, Turner had brought about some notable improvements. Additions to the campus included three new dormitories, housing for faculty, a new student union, a small football stadium, a new classroom building, and a new agricultural and home-economics facility. In addition, faculty salaries had improved, and the number of faculty with doctorates increased from two in 1950 to twenty-seven by 1967.[54]

Despite such evidence of progress, however, "The students had concluded that the issue involving the two instructors was merely the symptom of a deeper malady, and they turned their attention to the malady itself," according to I. A. Newby.[55] "The malady, they felt, was the administration's autocratic power over all facets of college life, including student conduct, its indifference to the quality of education, and its subservience to white authorities." It was, essentially, the same dilemma faced by Thomas E. Miller seventy-five years earlier, and after twelve years of protesting various aspects of civil rights and educational shortcomings, Orangeburg was still segregated and South Carolina State students were still unhappy with their president, Benner Turner.

McNair's meeting with Turner and others came on Wednesday, March 8, 1967, six days after the boycott had been called, and it did little to relieve the tension that existed in Orangeburg and on the State College campus. If anything, conditions only worsened in the aftermath of the meeting. McNair had chosen to back up Turner's hard-line position and to issue what was described in news accounts as a "stern ultimatum [to students] to end their classroom boycott by Friday [March 10], or face expulsion."[56] In response to a student request to meet with him, McNair issued an even stronger statement. "I have no intention to meet with any group of students who refuse to attend classes, who fail to abide by rules of responsible conduct, and who fail to recognize the necessity for settling grievances with the authorities who are legally responsible for the operation of the college they attend."

The governor's position in support of Turner only aggravated things. Ike Williams called the ultimatum "just the spark the students need to keep the movement going" and promptly announced plans to organize a massive student march to Columbia the following Saturday. It turned out that Newman had called an NAACP meeting later in the week in Columbia to "assess the situation at S.C. State College and to assess public reaction to the situation."

In the wake of McNair's meeting with the college's unpopular president, the NAACP meeting quickly became a forum for the state's black leaders to air their own thoughts and concerns about South Carolina State and to join in criticizing President Turner. "Turner doesn't know anything about the Negroes' problems," said Billy Fleming, longtime political activist and president of the Manning NAACP chapter. "Negroes have nothing to say about how the State College is run." Newspaper coverage the next day reported that "verbal support for the students came from Negro groups in Camden, Florence, Manning, Greenville, Darlington, Allendale, Barnwell, Union, Rock Hill, Aiken and Calhoun."[57]

The meeting also produced the clear message that McNair's support of Turner's hardline position could be a costly one. Even the usually diplomatic Newman told the politically powerful group that "the Negro bloc vote in the Second Congressional District alone turned out 97 percent for Mr. McNair in the last election [1966]. We have been kicked in the teeth." The rhetoric from the NAACP meeting was more than enough to convince McNair that the problems at South Carolina State were more serious than students staying out of classes. At the heart of it all was Turner, a man described at the NAACP meeting as an "Uncle Tom . . . who has done nothing for the Negroes in South Carolina since he has been president."[58]

McNair liked Turner personally and appreciated his predicament. But by then, he had also begun to understand that the president's days were probably numbered. "The faculty was upset, the students were upset . . . [and] . . . that's when . . . we all acknowledged that as much as we respected Dr. Turner, as much as we recognized the tremendous contributions he had made to State College and to South Carolina, he really needed to retire," McNair later recalled.[59]

McNair Takes on a Larger Role

McNair reluctantly began to realize not only that the autocratic Turner had to go, but that he—as governor—would have to engineer some of the changes himself. And while he later admitted that he did not relish direct involvement in the administration of the institution, "At the same time, when administrative decisions create massive problems . . . you get concerned about it."[60] "The direct communication with faculty committees and direct communication with student leaders demonstrated to me why they were frustrated," he said, acknowledging that he felt the protestors "had a legitimate complaint and a good cause that we felt we could do something about."[61] "The South Carolina State problem involving the faculty and administration was sort of the opener for me," he later said. "I think that . . . brought it to my attention better than anything else."[62] McNair's judgment was that "we needed a president at State College who was more progressive, who could communicate and would communicate with the faculty, with the students, and try to really build the institution and upgrade it." Turner, he felt, "had done his thing and resented any kind of interference."[63]

A day after the NAACP Wednesday meeting criticizing him and Turner, McNair dispatched an official car to Orangeburg to bring Ike Williams and his three fellow class presidents to Columbia for a secret summit meeting in his office. It was a remarkable moment. In a matter of hours, most of the issues that had triggered the boycott were conceded to the students amid what was described in press accounts the next day as "clandestine maneuvering between state officials and Negro leaders."[64]

McNair virtually assured Williams and his colleagues that the objectionable student restrictions would be lifted by Turner, and the reinstatement of the three students would be left to the judgment of a federal district court judge. McNair had called on his friend, Matthew Perry, whose firm of Jenkins, Perry and Pride had become the state's best-known black law firm, to handle the case, and he had also let Federal Judge Robert W. Hemphill of Columbia know that if the students were reinstated, the state would not appeal the decision.[65]

State newspaper reporter Paul Clancy wrote the next day,

> The deadlock was untangled earlier in the day [Friday] with the filing of a suit in U.S. District Court at Columbia. The suit asked the immediate return of three dismissed students. The court action, instituted by NAACP lawyers, was enough to convince boycotting State College students that their suspended colleagues would be back in school in a short time. Although the college board of trustees had stuck to its decision to keep the suspended trio out until August [1967], the court's decision could easily tie its hands.
>
> The court action was seen as a masterpiece of compromise.[66]

Less than a week later—on March 14—Judge Hemphill ordered immediate reinstatement of the students, saying that "this is not intended to condone" the student actions, but "no action on the part of this court could repair the damage which would have resulted should the suspension be allowed to continue."[67]

Boycott Ends, and Turner's Fate Is Sealed

For master compromiser McNair, however, there were other unresolved issues, one of them being the status of Turner. As the boycott ended and classes were scheduled to resume the following Monday, the South Carolina State president told reporters, "Now we can pick up the threads and get back to work."[68]

Such would not be the case, however. South Carolina State historian Hine wrote, "Though the trustees and governor continued to support him publicly and expressed appreciation for the manner in which he dealt with the crisis, he had demonstrated that he could no longer effectively manage the college. The black community, led by the NAACP, organized a petition calling for his removal. Many believed that campus protests would resume if Turner remained at the helm."[69] McNair had been even more direct. Hine reported that "when the students inquired about Turner's future, McNair's response was ambiguous, but hopeful. 'Now on that item, you gotta trust me to work it out.'"

McNair lived up to his word, but he later recalled it as being a painful experience. After arranging for a year's paid leave for the South Carolina State president to make him eligible for retirement, McNair called Turner to his office and described the settlement. When he was finished, McNair recalled Turner hesitating for a moment, then saying, "I guess I don't have a choice in this, do I?" McNair concurred. "No, sir, you don't."[70]

Two months later, on May 11, Turner's retirement was announced in newspaper accounts. According to one report,

> Turner announced his retirement Wednesday in the wake of mounting pressure for his removal. . . . His retirement statement said in part:
>
> "Influences of non-campus organizations and individuals and their effect on the work of the college have become so pervasive and continuing that the situation has become difficult with faculty, administration and the student body to carry on the normal routines." Trustees accepted the retirement and said Turner could have as much vacation time as he wanted until his retirement becomes effective Nov. 1.[71]

McNair praised Turner for rendering "a valuable and important service to South Carolina and particularly to State College" and said he had dedicated himself to "a constant upgrading and improvement of education for all the state."[72] Turner's departure was viewed as a victory for those wishing to bring more black control over the state's black college. McNair's role in championing students' position and easing out the unpopular Turner from the presidency was in sharp contrast to the legacy Tillman, Blease, and Thurmond had fostered in perpetuating white domination of the Orangeburg institution.

The moment was significant for other reasons. The reforms were recognition of the rising political influence of black South Carolinians and the importance attached both symbolically and substantively to the role of South Carolina State College. The issue was no longer one of simply dealing with rowdy students, as things may have been perceived in the 1950s and early 1960s. In the days subsequent to passage of the Voting Rights Act of 1965, the issue got new and higher priority attention, a reality facilitated by making registered voters out of hundreds of thousands of South Carolinians who had been disenfranchised by actions of a half-century earlier. South Carolina State now had a politically influential constituency, and that constituency was making it known that it was impatient with the overall treatment and perception of its institution. Black political power across the state was thrown behind the college through the intercession of the NAACP in the student boycotts. Black political power was also being felt in Columbia, where McNair was not only sympathetic to the need for changes at the Orangeburg campus, but would also soon introduce measures to address the college's long-standing financial and building needs.

For the moment, however, things became snarled over the choice of a president to succeed Benner Turner. Student interests rallied around popular professor Charles Thomas. In the meantime, the college's vice president for business and finance—a Columbia native, M. Maceo Nance Jr.—was serving as acting president, and his services were attracting favorable attention.

Nance was a graduate of Booker T. Washington High School, a veteran of service in the U.S. Navy in World War II with a bachelor's degree from South Carolina State and a master's degree in education administration from New York University. Compared to the Harvard-educated Turner and his autocratic style, Nance was a homegrown talent who claimed the unusual distinction of having had only one employer in his professional life, South Carolina State College. Where Turner had been stiff and distant, Nance knew the campus and its residents like family. While still in undergraduate school, he was a student janitor, and after graduation, he served successively as clerk in the business office, clerk in the bookstore, military property custodian, director of the student union, assistant business manager, and business manager before becoming vice president for business and finance.

He was also known and liked within state government circles through his budget presentations on behalf of the college each year to the Budget and Control Board and the House Ways and Means Committee.

A "Hands-On" Leader

Nance lacked a Ph.D. degree, a matter of concern to those sensitive to South Carolina State's academic status. He later said, "I've never thought of myself as an academician, and I have never had any desire to go into the classroom. I did graduate work at New York University in education. So that's the progression of my involvement here at this institution."[73]

That suited some of the college's decision-makers just fine. They felt the college needed a hands-on leader and a good manager, and Nance met those requirements. Support swung to Nance from the board and from McNair, and the governor recalled, "I remember the day I called Maceo to tell him he had been chosen permanent president, and his secretary said he was not in his office. He was downstairs shooting pool with the students. When he called me back, I told him that he was exactly the kind of man we needed for State College at the time."[74]

Nance remembered that as a high school senior in Columbia, he had ambitions to attend Lincoln University in Pennsylvania. "My father indicated to me that he thought I'd better come down here [S.C. State] for a year and he would see about sending me to Lincoln the next year. Well, I came, I fell in love with the place, and I had no desire to leave."[75]

Nance later acknowledged that he may not have "necessarily been Governor McNair's first choice" as South Carolina State's president to succeed Benner Turner in 1967. But he also said there were clearly recognizable differences in philosophies between him and his predecessor. "There was a difference between his style and my style," Nance said. "I don't mind saying that I think we should have been more aggressive than we were, aggressive simply meaning that it was a period of time that was right for progress in light of what had transpired, that is [in light of] laws having been changed and ability to demonstrate factually—and the records indicated it— that we had been short-changed. I thought that was the time to move aggressively and tell our story. I thought perhaps it could have been a little more aggressive."[76]

With the departure of Turner and the ending of the boycott, things grew calm on the Orangeburg campus for the moment, but not all South Carolina was pleased with the personal role McNair had taken in the settlement. One longtime board member, physician Howard G. Royal of Langley in Aiken County, resigned from the board on March 21, ten days after the boycott ended, saying, "I feel concessions were made to the students under duress." He was particularly critical of McNair's role and said, "As a physician, I am by nature conservative, but this was another matter, this usurpation of authority."[77]

More criticism came from Aiken's Republican senator, Marion H. Smoak, who asked the governor for a report on the compromise struck with the students. Smoak's criticism took the form of a proposed Senate resolution asking McNair for a policy statement on the South Carolina State incidents and saying that he found the governor's actions "incongruous." "The impression at this moment is clear that disorders, demonstration and riots bring results," Smoak said. "It is this impression that is of particular concern to me, and requires a policy statement before it invites other outbreaks of disobedience and lawlessness." McNair responded by saying that he "deplored his [Smoak's] trying to make an issue of the S.C. State situation for the purposes of political expediency" and contended that the issues of attendance regulations and chapel services [issues of concern to the students] had been settled before the boycott began.[78]

Conservative newspapers also weighed in against what one of them called "the student foolishness going on at State College at Orangeburg." The *State* newspaper, whose editor was prominent conservative and one-time Republican Senate candidate William D. Workman Jr., sided with President Turner during the boycott and contended editorially, "Immaturity is asserting itself as students seek to dictate what shall and shall not be done by the college's administration, not only with respect to retention of faculty but to reinstatement of student agitators. . . . We cannot predict to what extent the student body will go in trying to substitute its amorphous and immature judgment for that of college administration. We can predict that South Carolinians, regardless of race, will not permit public institutions of higher learning in this state to degenerate into academic anarchy."[79]

In a front-page editorial, the *Orangeburg Times and Democrat* took a similar tone, writing, "The time has come now for an end to compromise and concessions. The time has come for the administration to take a firm hand. If the students are foolish enough—and their leaders must be immature and adolescent—to go through with their march to Columbia, it might be a good idea to find the college closed to them on their return. . . . Enough is enough, kids."[80]

The *State* newspaper and Reverend Newman engaged in a lively exchange over President Turner and the role of the NAACP in the South Carolina State turmoil. The *State,* noting that Turner was black and that two of the college's trustees were black, asked, "What does the Negro community want?" And that inquiry, in turn, evoked another rhetorical inquiry, "Who speaks for the Negro community, assuming there is any such single group?"[81] Newman responded in a prominently displayed letter back to the *State,* observing, "There was ferment when he [Turner] was elected over other Negroes who had already proven their ability. They were turned down by the then all-white board in favor of Dr. Turner because they were identified with the Negro's aspiration for equality of opportunity. Dr. Turner was not so identified." He went on to attack "the pattern of race relations designed by white South Carolinians and by which the white power structure takes for granted that it can appoint leaders for the Negro community without first entering into dialogue with the Negro community concerning proposed appointments."[82]

In the aftermath of the 1967 boycott, at least two reporters speculated about the future of South Carolina State as an all-black institution. Writer Paul Clancy of the *State* wrote, "They [the students] had felt that bringing qualified white instructors to the campus would eventually bring white students to the campus. Having a desegregated student body at Orangeburg would make state leaders think more about the quality of education being served up [at] the school."[83]

Columnist Hugh Gibson of the *Charleston News and Courier* suggested that "S.C. State is an anachronism under today's civil rights laws. Almost certainly, the time is not far distant when Washington will compel what South Carolina could now do with good grace, voluntarily." Gibson's plan was to "end S.C. State's days as a Negro college and disperse students and faculty among other state-supported or private colleges and universities."[84]

That was not going to happen under a Nance administration. His view of the college's role—as compared to the utilitarian ideas of President Thomas E. Miller seventy-five years earlier—was broad and comprehensive. Both men saw a distinctly racial aspect to the institution's missions, but with Nance, it was the triumph of W. E. B. DuBois over Booker T. Washington.

> There were those in our society who immediately felt that after 1954, those institutions that we had—namely, education, our churches—that there was a desire to abandon them and merge ourselves into something else.

They were far from right. . . . There's very little that we as a people in our society have that we call our own. . . . There never has been any desire to be exclusively black. There was a desire to maintain something within our society that those of a certain ethnic background can associate ourselves with and feel comfortable in that kind of environment. That's what a historically black college does.[85]

Nance likened the historically black institutions with other colleges that had prominent religious and ethnic distinctions, particularly Notre Dame with its Catholic heritage.

To my knowledge, they've never turned down a Protestant [because he or she was not a Catholic], but they make it very clear—and a Protestant must understand—that they are associating themselves with an institution that's Catholic-oriented. Brigham Young has a certain kind of orientation, Mormon. Brandeis has a certain kind of orientation, Jewish.

There's nothing wrong with that, and one of the things that I think members of our society do not understand, or do not wish to accept, is that neither of these philosophies or orientations have anything to do with the quality of the education program. There isn't any Mormon mathematics; there isn't any Catholic mathematics; there isn't any black mathematics; there isn't any white mathematics. It's only mathematics.[86]

The 1967 boycott left a clearly visible impact on South Carolina State, on South Carolina politics, and on the administration of Bob McNair. With the departure of Dr. Benner Turner as president and the ascension of Maceo Nance to that position, even on an interim basis, the college took a significant psychological step toward liberation from the limited and white-oriented mission of its founding. Nance was a savvy leader who knew the value of the emerging black political power and how to use it. He accepted the new role of South Carolina State as a center of black cultural and political interests in the context of increasing black influence and authority. But Nance was a gradualist and set out to make the college's evolution consistent with the political tolerances of South Carolina's moderate political leadership.

For McNair, it was a full-blown battlefield experience in the state's growing civil rights conflict. For the first time, South Carolina saw its governor actively support a student-reform movement and use his influence to see that changes took place. They also saw a governor become deeply involved in the reshaping of the state's black college to reflect the interests of South Carolina's emerging black political constituency. It was a clear break with the influence and legacy still hanging over the college from the days of Ben Tillman and Cole Blease.

Events at Orangeburg also helped to reshape the state's increasingly volatile political agenda. South Carolina's left and right political elements were becoming more clearly defined after McNair's initiatives at State College, and the partisan issues that would dominate South Carolina for the rest of the century became more apparent. The boycott of 1967 brought racial politics into sharp focus and gave each side clear values to defend and pursue.

But for all the impact the boycott and its outcome had on South Carolina's racial, political, and educational world, unrest remained at South Carolina State, and for all the new interest and attention coming to the Orangeburg campus, unimagined tragedy lay less than a year away.

10

A Tragedy at Orangeburg

Settlement of the 1967 boycott at South Carolina State scarcely settled the simmering racial tensions that had been brewing in Orangeburg for years. Even though S.C. State's autocratic president had resigned and student rules had been relaxed, there remained significant unresolved issues within the college community and within the city of Orangeburg itself.

The quest for a replacement for Benner Turner as president had become a divisive issue on campus, and while Maceo Nance continued as acting president, many students and others were supporting the presidency of a popular professor, Charles H. Thomas Jr., a local NAACP official who had been a leader of the Orangeburg Movement five years earlier. Students who had protested vigorously the failure to renew the contracts of the two white professors a year earlier saw the presidency as another instance where State College's academic standing might be in jeopardy. Thomas had academic credentials, with an earned Ph.D.; Nance did not.

In a letter to McNair dated January 8, 1968, John Stroman, a boycott leader from the previous year, wrote, "We want a president who is qualified for this position to get along with others, interested in making this institution one of the nation's top colleges, able to let his job come first but thinks for himself, and [is] full of self-pride and respect. I know you and the board of trustees have a great problem in trying to find a president who possesses these qualities because a man with them would never come to a place like South Carolina State unless he happens to be here already. The last president was one the board of trustees maneuvered at will. The type of person we want is altogether different from Dr. Turner."[1]

McNair replied cordially to Stroman's letter, saying he was "terribly concerned about State College." In the letter to Stroman, he cited efforts to upgrade faculty salaries at State College and noted that the General Assembly had taken the unusual route of providing directly appropriated monies for new buildings at the college, as compared to other state institutions' use of tuition-supported revenue bonds for such purposes. McNair also called attention to four new members of the college's board of trustees, "three of them Negro leaders [I. P. Stanback of Columbia, James A. Boykin of Lancaster, and Samuel S. Bacote of Kingstree], and the other, James Rogers, the self-proclaimed liberal editor of the *Florence Morning News.* "The Board," McNair wrote, "is making a real effort to secure a President for the college."[2]

Also looming in those winter months of 1967–1968 were larger questions about the status of the overall civil rights implementation in South Carolina and some of the unfulfilled expectations growing out of landmark developments such as *Brown v. Board of Education,* the Civil Rights Act of 1964, and the Voting Rights Act of 1965. While black political muscle was beginning to be felt at the polls, the presence of black appointments to policy and legislative roles was lagging. Grassroots and student-based groups were becoming organized and active, and they were giving articulation to frustrations over slow civil rights progress in the state.

"We were looking for the opportunity to sit down at the table with the decision-makers," said Bill Saunders, a local organizer and civil rights leader in the Charleston area. "We let people know that if we can't sit down at the table with you, then we'll throw bricks at you."[3]

One of the leaders emerging in the grassroots/student movement was Cleveland Sellers, a South Carolina native who had served as program secretary for the Student Non-Violent Coordinating Committee (SNCC) and was a top lieutenant to the organization's leader, Stokely Carmichael. Sellers and Carmichael had stepped down from positions in SNCC earlier in 1967 during what was described publicly as a challenge to their leadership by James Forman and H. Rap Brown. Sellers has since denied the infighting, saying, "Stokely Carmichael and I ended our positions of our own volition when our terms came to a close. James Forman never challenged us and we were never in competition with H. Rap Brown. That notion about competition and dissension was a . . . disinformation ruse."[4]

Sellers was no newcomer to South Carolina. He was a native of Denmark, South Carolina, got his high school education at Voorhees Junior College, and met Carmichael when the two were students at Howard University. They were among SNCC's early activist leaders, and it was Carmichael who coined the term "Black Power" during a speech in Greenwood, Mississippi, on June 17, 1966. "The only way we gonna stop them white men from whuppin' us is to take over," Carmichael said on that occasion. "We been saying freedom for six years and we ain't got nothin'. What we gonna start saying now is black power."[5] The term became a rallying cry of defiance and impatience against a process that young blacks thought seemed stuck in inertia. It also came as a shock to white moderates who had championed the civil rights cause in the courts, the Congress, and in public demonstrations. It seemed antithetical to the message of racial harmony and Gandhian peace as articulated by Dr. Martin Luther King in his "I Have a Dream" speech in Washington in August 1963.

Forman, a leader in the aggressive SNCC, later acknowledged the impact of the change, writing that the shift in terminology from "civil rights movement" to "Black Power" provoked accusations of "extremism" and "racism in reverse." "Those accusations," Forman wrote, "reflected the fact that the slogan 'Black Power' was frightening to white Americans in general and the U.S. Government in particular because of its revolutionary implications."[6]

Orangeburg was a particularly polarized city at the time. Besides being a place where the emerging political influence of its two black colleges—Claflin and S.C. State—was being felt, it was also a hotbed of white conservative organizations such as the White Citizens Council, the Ku Klux Klan, and the John Birch Society. They were ideological opposites and, in later months, McNair and law-enforcement officials would worry about the possibility that the ideological opposites would actually clash with each other.[7]

"In Orangeburg," Sellers later recalled, "the 'peaceful and quiet' status quo was to segregate its citizens, deny credit to blacks, and for those who sought to change it, the answer was economic sanction and vigilante violence. Like Bull Connors's Birmingham, Orangeburg was known to use water hoses on student demonstrators. Perhaps some signs had been removed, but *de facto* segregation remained entrenched through the early 1970s. Let us be clear: maintaining the peace in Orangeburg was, in effect, supporting an apartheid regime."[8]

Sellers arrived in Orangeburg in October 1967, and by then—despite his South Carolina upbringing—he had been labeled an "outside agitator." "The 'outside agitator' moniker was brought to South Carolina by the FBI," Sellers later said, noting that it was also picked up by State Law Enforcement Division (SLED) chief J. P. "Pete" Strom and the mainstream press.[9] He also recalled an article in a local newspaper at the time that stated that a "'group of long-haired black militants' was traveling around the state trying to stir up trouble among the Negroes."[10] Sellers, who was joined in mid-October by SNCC organizers John Batiste and Bill Ballon, later wrote, "there was no question in my mind about the identity of those 'long-haired militants.'"

Sellers had actually been on the S.C. State campus during the student boycott earlier in the year. He recalled having had a hand in naming the S.C. State Coordinating Committee and linking the S.C. State students to other student organizations at historically black colleges and universities. He also established a student organization known as the Black Awareness Coordinating Committee (BACC), a group Sellers described as being politically moderate but with a high degree of interest in Black Power. Its membership fluctuated between twelve and thirty-five at a high, and its ideology was later described by the Southern Regional Council as being "not overly attractive to the largely rural-oriented student body."[11]

Sellers and Carmichael spent the Christmas holidays of 1967 on the islands below Charleston (James and Johns) and Beaufort (St. Helena), where they were guests of Bill Saunders, Esau Jenkins, James Jenkins, and the Penn Center, also a favorite retreat for King and his Southern Christian Leadership Conference (SCLC). The conversations, Saunders later recalled, ranged from discussions of local issues of education and jobs to broader topics of "the search for equal justice and the SNCC agenda of empowering people at the local level."[12]

Of particular concern to black Charlestonians at that time, Saunders recalled, was the tendency of white officials to appoint blacks to positions without consulting black leaders, and special attention was being called to the appointment of school-board members by the legislative delegation. A newsletter published by Saunders carried an article from a group called "Black Militant Group of Charleston County," saying that "if the Charleston Delegation does not appoint the three black men that we want, it would be the worst mistake that the white power structure has made since they fired on Fort Sumter."[13]

Much of the activity of Saunders, Sellers, and their colleagues was escaping the attention of state officials, who were relying on their traditional NAACP connections to remain informed and advised. McNair felt comfortable that he had built credibility at S.C. State when he took his stand with the students the previous spring, and he had confidence that Newman and his colleagues would bring anything important to his attention. What he knew of Sellers and his colleagues was coming largely from law-enforcement sources.

On the S.C. State campus, Sellers's influence and that of the BACC organization were considered mild at the time. "BACC members provoked discussions of contemporary social movements and personalities involved in them," the Southern Regional Council wrote. "Though popular with BACC, [Sellers] had little influence on the campuses [S.C. State and Claflin]. . . . Students interviewed, from the conservative to the radical, said he was respected for his ideas, but did not have a following."[14]

If Sellers's direct influence was limited, the influence of the Black Power message was growing. He later wrote, "The NAACP, which had a large chapter on campus, brought in several prominent speakers in order to combat BACC's influence, but this tactic backfired. Most of the speakers, instead of parroting the NAACP's moderate line, challenged the students to be more militant."[15] The NAACP fight with SNCC had burst into the open and taken on national proportions in the summer of 1967. Roy Wilkins, executive director of the NAACP, sent a "red alert" to local chapters, saying, "Don't just be against riots; be active in preventing them." SNCC chairman Rap Brown had told his followers, "We are at war, and we are behind enemy lines, so you better get yourselves some guns."[16]

The emergence of BACC in challenging the NAACP sent a signal that Black Power and its attendant aggressiveness were threatening the traditional civil rights movement and its more peaceful demonstration style as a force on the S.C. State campus. Black Power could destabilize the already shaky peace at S.C. State, and there were other destabilizing elements at work, as well.

A scant two blocks from the S.C. State campus lay Orangeburg's only bowling alley, the All-Star Bowling Lanes, owned by Harry L. Floyd. It was an establishment that had escaped legal challenge to the segregated, all-white status it had maintained in defiance of the 1964 Civil Rights Act requiring public accommodations to be desegregated.

It rankled black student and adult bowlers alike in Orangeburg that they had to drive thirty-five miles to Columbia when a bowling alley was only two blocks from the State College campus. Efforts to desegregate the bowling alley dated back "at least to 1963 and 1964 when massive demonstrations protested, and the Civil Rights Law ended for the most part, segregation of public accommodations in the city. Negotiations since then on the local level [and efforts to involve the national government] to desegregate the bowling alley had all failed."[17]

A big part of the problem, Maceo Nance later recalled, was its location. Not only was it within easy walking distance of State College and Claflin College, it lay along oft-traveled Russell Street, the main route between the campuses and downtown Orangeburg. It was located in a shopping center whose other stores had desegregated in compliance with the Civil Rights Act requirements, and it bore the telltale sign that stirred students' ire whether they were bowlers or not: "White Only."

"I suspect that very few of our students even knew how to bowl, even those students who may have come from metropolitan or urban areas," Nance recalled.

They just didn't have an interest in bowling. With no place to bowl, nobody bothered with it.

But then the sign. During that period, one's consciousness was raised. I don't know how long the sign had been there, but when one starts relating to these kinds of things, then every time you see [it], it strikes a chord, and that's what happened. The students' consciousness was raised because we were talking about public accommodations. This is what everybody was talking about.

Why would we accept this? This is against the law.[18]

Bowling had actually become an interest among Orangeburg's black adults before students took up the sport, according to Nance. "There was a bowling alley specifically for blacks in Columbia, out on Farrow Road. A new facility was built, and all of a sudden, bowling became of some interest [in] the black community, particularly in Columbia," he said. "There were several adults here, about a dozen, and they used to go up to Columbia to bowl."[19]

Nance also recalled early efforts to resolve the tensions over the Orangeburg bowling alley:

> Black people are reasonable, and perhaps [they] try to be too reasonable.
>
> The approach to that man [Floyd] was not to integrate his bowling alley, but to give one or two nights per week so that blacks could bowl. That was the first approach, and one of that group [was] Earl Middleton [a black businessman who later served in the S.C. House of Representatives]. That [negotiation] may have gone on for . . . a year or two, and there was nothing, no compromise. They just didn't get to first base.[20]

Both Nance and I. DeQuincey Newman believed that legal action could have headed off the February 1968 showdown, and both attributed at least part of the tragedy to the lack of enforcement of the Civil Rights Act of 1964 by federal and other authorities. "The federal government had been communicated with," Nance said, "Everybody was communicated with—the local authorities, the mayor, the city council, all of these people were involved."

Most of white Orangeburg had accepted the desegregation of public accommodations, if somewhat begrudgingly, he later recalled.

> You may not have been treated as courteously as you would have liked, but nobody called the police or tried to put you out or anything of that nature.
>
> This [the bowling alley] was the only vestige. The thing just provided a rallying point.[21]

Sellers later wrote, "The students wanted access to the segregated bowling alley; they were *not* interested in doing harm to the white patrons. . . . But the bowling alley was never the only issue. Police brutality and *de facto* segregation were what the students were also protesting."[22]

Like Nance, Newman believed legal action could have headed off confrontation over the bowling alley, and he included Orangeburg's black adults in his criticism. "It could have been avoided," he said.

> The bone of contention was a bowling alley. There were a number of adults in Orangeburg who got tired of having to come all the way to Columbia to bowl.
>
> Matthew Perry, Charles Thomas, who at the time was the President of the Orangeburg NAACP, and myself tried for three hours to persuade those adults to take action, legal action, against the owner of the bowling alley under the Civil Rights Act. We could have closed him up—and chances are—rather than close, he would have integrated. But the adults of Orangeburg, many of them leading citizens in Orangeburg, did not want to go on record as bringing legal action. We couldn't get them to do it.[23]

As the civil rights temperature in 1967–1968 Orangeburg thus rose, the bowling alley issue lay simmering, unaddressed by federal authorities, unresolved by local officials, and virtually overlooked by state officials. Even Sellers and the SNCC/BACC group initially declined to get involved in the matter. "BACC's members were approached on several occasions during the fall and winter by students concerned about a segregated bowling alley in downtown Orangeburg," Sellers later wrote.

> They had been protesting Floyd's exclusionary policy for more than two years, during which time the bowling alley had become a hated symbol of discrimination.
>
> BACC's members repeatedly refused to get involved in the bowling alley issue. They believed, and I supported them, that integration was an irrelevant issue. Despite BACC's position, a group of insistent students refused to let the issue die.[24]

Monday, February 5, 1968

The first major protest at the bowling alley came on Monday night, February 5, only nineteen days after McNair's letter to Stroman. A small group of students led by Stroman had been denied bowling privileges the previous week.[25] It was a larger group—some fifty students—that appeared early in the evening of February 5 and demanded that they be permitted to bowl. Things went peacefully, but not without some rancor. Floyd, who told authors Jack Bass and Jack Nelson that he had called Governor McNair that night and had been assured of "protection of the law," had changed his signage from "White Only" to "Private Club"[26] by that time. McNair later denied having any communication with Floyd, but said, "We were trying, through the people there, to get something worked out."[27] Floyd reportedly contended that lanes every night were contracted for by members of bowling leagues.[28] When the students refused to leave, according to a newspaper report, he left to seek warrants for their arrest, and in the meantime, Orangeburg police chief Roger E. Poston cleared the bowling alley and closed it for the night. "I am not going to ask my men to violate the law in interfering with those who are not breaking the law by being in your place," he reportedly told Floyd.[29]

While the Monday night incident went off without violence or arrests, it was sufficiently worrisome for Poston to alert SLED Chief Strom and Highway Patrol district commander Captain Carl Fairey that he might need "additional equipment or manpower to insure the safety of the citizens of Orangeburg . . . the coming night."[30] Poston's Orangeburg police force at the time numbered thirty officers. The following day, Tuesday, February 6, Strom; his deputy, Captain J. Leon Gasque; five other SLED agents; Attorney General Daniel R. McLeod; and one of McLeod's assistants, Carl Reasonover, arrived in Orangeburg.

They paid a call on Harry Floyd, and according to Strom, "We told him he couldn't violate the law." Floyd had lodged a protest with the city council earlier in the day over Poston's closing of his establishment Monday evening, and when he resisted Strom's appeal to desegregate the bowling lanes, Strom recalled, "We organized a very few law enforcement officers. We worked along with the city police, the sheriff, his deputies, SLED agents, and highway patrol."[31]

Strom was the trusted eyes and ears of the governor on law-enforcement matters and had built a reputation for being a peacemaker and a personal emissary of the governor's in potentially explosive instances. He had been particularly instrumental in the orchestration of the desegregation of Clemson and the University of South Carolina, and he was known on a personal basis to members of the civil rights community. The SLED chief reported directly to the governor, just as he had since 1956, and when McNair took office on April 22, 1965, to replace Donald Russell, the appointment of Strom was the first order of business. McNair said at the time, "One of the reasons I made the SLED appointment at the same press conference when we were going through the appointment of Mr. Russell to the U.S. Senate to fill that unexpired term was to emphasize my support and my confidence in Pete Strom. We were in a difficult period, and I wanted to make it clear that I supported the chief law enforcement officer of the state, and that I was going to put even more responsibility on him as we moved along."[32]

SLED's role was essentially an investigative one, likened by some to the FBI at the national level, but in instances of civil disorder, where more than one law-enforcement agency was involved, Strom became the unofficial "super boss." McNair recalled meetings with other state entities—particularly the Highway Patrol and the National Guard—in which "we discussed how we would react to given situations, who would be in charge, and how they would all function."

> I learned early on that you could not have three chiefs in an emergency. You could only have one, and my decision was that I had Chief Strom. He knew more by reason of his information system. He had more contacts with community people and community leaders than anyone else. And, since he was the so-called civilian chief, who was appointed by and responsible directly to the Governor, I felt he was the chief, and everybody understood that. When we had an emergency, they were all to work with and report to and generally take supervision from him.[33]

Under such an arrangement, Strom became the commanding officer for strategy and deployment in the Orangeburg operation, and it was under his direction that plans were made and orders were given for the full range of law-enforcement activities, including those of the Highway Patrol and National Guard. According to the FBI report, "By precedent, he could be considered the senior law enforcement officer at Orangeburg, South Carolina, even though he was never officially appointed as such. He was instrumental in formulating major policies and coordinating activities of the various law enforcement agencies."[34]

While Strom had become known for his political and diplomatic inclinations, he was first and foremost a traditional law-enforcement officer, and his instincts were those of a policeman. His views were influenced by the evolving reputation within law enforcement of SNCC as a dangerous threat to civil peace and public order. As the organization changed leadership through the 1960s, it came under closer scrutiny of the FBI, and on August 8, 1967, a sixty-nine-page internal FBI memorandum was filed, depicting "the evolution of the Student Nonviolent Coordinating Committee (SNCC) from a peaceful civil rights movement primarily devoted to direct-action voter registration in the Deep South to a hate group preaching violence and black supremacy." The memorandum went on to state, "Now, under the flagrantly incendiary leadership of H. Rap Brown, SNCC is motivated by a revolutionary, direct-action, anti-white ideology that places no faith in the normal democratic procedures. There can be no doubt that SNCC's present collision course with American society makes it a potent threat to racial peace."[35]

Over the years, Strom had become an insider with the FBI and could well have been privy to such communications from the Bureau about SNCC activities. In that context, Strom viewed the second night of protest at the bowling alley as a potentially dangerous event, and he acted accordingly. Unlike the orchestrated desegregation of Clemson and the University of South Carolina, and the much-organized desegregation of lunch counters in Columbia, there was nothing orchestrated about the Orangeburg bowling alley protest, and there was virtually no communication between demonstrators and law enforcement.

At that point, it was still considered a local issue by McNair, and he viewed his role largely as that of providing adequate law enforcement. It would also become clear that whatever contacts he may have developed within the NAACP the previous year were not going to be helpful as this event, driven by student activists, unfolded. As things developed on subsequent evenings, there was even some uncertainty as to which side the police were there to defend. Floyd considered the demonstrators as trespassers and contended his establishment did not fall under the Civil Rights Act of 1964. The demonstrators believed the bowling alley fell under the act and qualified them to enter the establishment lawfully.

Tuesday, February 6, 1968

Whatever may have been the various understandings and interpretations, students began gathering around seven o'clock Tuesday evening at the bowling alley parking lot to resume the protest. They found the doors locked and a small force of state and local police gathered in the corner of the shopping center where the bowling alley was located. It quickly became apparent that what McNair and Strom dreaded the most—a direct and spontaneous confrontation between the races—was in the making. White customers were inside the establishment bowling behind locked doors, and as the numbers of protesting black students grew, Strom positioned his twenty-five officers across the front of the bowling alley.

For a while, things were at a tense standoff. Then Strom and Poston offered students the opportunity to be arrested inside the bowling alley as a means of testing its segregation status. Stroman and fourteen others agreed to be arrested, but the ensuing action of escorting the students into patrol cars and driving them away only heightened tensions. Strom said he had hoped that the arrests would have the effect of "ending this matter as quickly as possible without injury to anyone."[36]

As word of the arrests got back to campus, however, angry students began streaming down Russell Street to the shopping center. "We moved toward the bowling alley along with a swelling stream of students," Sellers later wrote. He was among those in the move toward the bowling alley. "Many of the students were picking up rocks and bottles as they walked."[37]

Alarmed by the potential for violence, S.C. State officials went to Strom and Poston and asked that the arrested students be released to the custody of Dean of Students Oscar Butler, with the understanding that the students would return to the bowling alley and try to calm the tension. The agreement was reached, but no sooner did the arrested students return to the bowling alley than an Orangeburg City fire truck, summoned earlier by Chief Poston as a precautionary measure, arrived on the scene. It was taken as a hostile act by students, some of whom remembered being sprayed three years earlier during student-led demonstrations. Strom acknowledged, "We were planning on using water to disperse the crowd, but weren't able to do it because they took the truck over with so many students."[38]

Accounts vary as to the various causes of events that ensued. Student leaders and college officials contended the arrival of the fire trucks disrupted what would have been a peaceful conclusion to the protest. "Everyone was prepared to head back to campus when two large fire trucks pulled into the parking lot," Sellers wrote. "The students, who thought they had been tricked, were infuriated."

Law-enforcement officers later disagreed that the crowd was dispersing, but they also admitted the fire trucks were not a good idea. "As soon as the trucks arrived in the area, the crowd just went wild," Poston testified. "Rev. Nelson [Presbyterian minister Herbert Nelson] and possibly Dean Butler and some of the students who had been previously arrested and returned to the area came to me and said they're out of hand; we can't control them; you better send the truck out of here."[39]

Even as the trucks departed, however, things remained volatile. Next came a rush by students to force an entry into the bowling alley, and when they were met by a contingent of police, a melee ensued and one of the students kicked in a small window at the main entrance to the bowling alley. "The police, who had been relatively civil," wrote Sellers, "seemed to lose all composure. They raised their long nightsticks and began to flail away at the surprised young men and women. It didn't matter who they hit, male, female or innocent bystander. On the way back to campus, the fleeing students took out their frustration on white-owned stores along the route. Display windows were broken, trashcans turned over and mannequins upended. Rocks were scraped along the sides of parked cars and some radio aerials were broken. There was no looting."[40]

Law-enforcement accounts of the event were similar. Once the window was broken, said Strom, "things went completely out of hand, and by that time, the police were completely out of control. . . . When they [the students] threw the rock in the bowling alley, we at least believed they were fixing to go into the bowling alley . . . so we had to move in with what police we had." Like Sellers, Strom acknowledged that police "waded in with blackjacks and night sticks." Their purpose, he said, was to drive the students "off the parking lot and in the direction of the campus."[41] The Southern Regional Council wrote, "More than one witness told of a young woman held by one policeman, hit with a billy club by a second, also of a young woman begging not to be hit."[42]

Deputy SLED chief Leon Gasque later said, "It's important [to note that] no police officer pulled a pistol, nobody was shot, no guns were fired. . . . Chief [Strom] gave instructions to leave the students a place to retreat, so we did not follow them to campus, feeling that if we did, there would be real bloodshed."[43] Even so, in Gasque's words, it was "the biggest fist fight I've ever been in."[44]

Press reports subsequently called the parking lot fracas "perhaps the most serious racial incident in the state in years." One newspaper carried a picture of a fireman in position atop the truck, his hand on the coiled hose, surrounded by taunting students. Before it was over, eight South Carolina State students—seven men and one woman—had been injured, along with two law-enforcement officers, most with cuts and lacerations. One male student with a severe cut on his head was admitted to the hospital, as was a city policeman with a laceration. One highway patrolman was treated for tear gas in his eyes.[45]

Acting president Maceo Nance lodged a "sharp protest against police brutality" and—in contrast to the posture of his predecessor, Benner Turner, only a few years earlier—Nance assured student protestors that they had his and the faculty's support.[46] Nance also recommended an economic boycott of downtown Orangeburg, a ploy that had been used in earlier years to protest the city's resistance to desegregation initiatives. "We need to seal off downtown," Nance was quoted as saying, a suggestion that was also seen as a means of avoiding a black-white confrontation in the streets of Orangeburg.

For McNair, the Tuesday evening events provided a sobering realization that South Carolina—for all its New South aspirations of political and racial moderation—was not immune to violence. In their book, *The Orangeburg Massacre*, authors

Jack Bass and Jack Nelson quoted Lieutenant Governor John West as saying, "I've never seen him [McNair] more upset than he was." West had gotten word of an emergency underway and visited the governor's office late the evening of Tuesday, February 6.[47]

> He reported he had talked to the law enforcement people and that a real tense racial situation had developed and erupted to the point of violence. . . . I remember very vividly he told me Chief Strom said he had never been in a situation in which he feared more for the lives of his men.
>
> I remember him being quite concerned that we might be put in an almost untenable situation, that we are being asked to protect a business that might be found guilty of violating the civil rights law, and he said this in expressing his desire that there be some determination of whether Negroes had a right to go into this bowling alley or not.[48]

McNair recalled, "I got a report from Chief Strom that there had been an incident at the bowling alley . . . and that it had erupted into a confrontation. He reported that there had been a 'head-knocking' session in which everybody got roughed up . . . including some law enforcement officers and some students, and that that had really set off a problem."[49]

In his public comments carried in later press reports, McNair was quoted as saying he "would not tolerate 'brutality and violence'" and said he hoped negotiation could head off further confrontation. "We do not want to make it a major crisis," he said.[50] McNair also identified what he viewed as a limited role for the state at that point. "This is a community thing," he said. "We're not involved, except to keep order, and we will keep order."

To that end, the highway-patrol contingent was beefed up from 50 to 100 and a unit of the National Guard, the 250-man 1052nd Transportation Company with headquarters in Orangeburg, was mobilized and stationed in the Orangeburg Armory, about two miles from campus.[51] Strom recalled intermittent rock-throwing from the campus during the evening as his men began setting up roadblocks and preparing for the arrival of reinforcements from the National Guard.[52]

The instances of brutality to students were uppermost on the minds of students on campus later that Tuesday evening. "Later on that . . . night, I heard from a group of boys talking in the dormitory that a Negro girl and a Negro woman had been beaten up by police at the bowling alley," a student later said in an FBI interview the following week.[53] Student leaders and protest organizers returned to campus to discuss their own next steps, and Sellers's recollection was that things were still cautious and moderate, even though the "atmosphere was tense and filled with emotion." "Everyone wanted to do something about the bowling alley and other conditions in the town, but nobody seemed sure what was appropriate," he wrote. "At one point, I proposed that they use their bodies to block all traffic along

College Avenue, a main street adjacent to the campus. This relatively moderate suggestion was dismissed as being too radical."[54] The Southern Regional Council report identified other speakers, including Robert Scott, president of the S.C. State student body, and George Campbell, the student NAACP president, as supporting measures to continue the protest, and the evening ended with students agreeing to seek a city permit to march downtown the following day.

Wednesday, February 7, 1968

Given the tension of the previous evening, a downtown march was the last thing McNair, Strom, and the city officials wanted. "Recognizing that things had gotten real, real bad that evening as a result of the fight that took place at the bowling alley, we knew things were at a fever pitch," McNair later said.

> Then the reports began to come in about what was going to happen in Orangeburg. Demonstrations and marches downtown were planned, and the word we got was Orangeburg, the city [and] the business district—was sort of an armed arsenal and that everybody was bolting themselves in the stores and ready for almost anything that might happen.
>
> The word was . . . that it could end up in just a terrible situation. So we had to begin to talk about what we were going to do to keep the business community and the students from . . . getting into a real conflict. . . . The word I got was that there was not a single piece of ammunition left anywhere in that whole area. It had all been bought up, and the merchants were going to protect their property with shotguns. So we had to come up with a way of keeping the students from going down Main Street.[55]

By the next day, the city had a proposal to counter the students' request for a march permit. In a meeting attended by Orangeburg mayor E. O. Pendarvis, Chief Poston, and city manager Robert T. Stevenson, the city suggested a meeting in which the mayor, the city manager, and the heads of the Chamber of Commerce and the Merchants Association would appear before the students and attempt to respond to a list of twelve student grievances drawn up the night before. The grievances included the closing of the bowling alley and its subsequent reopening as a desegregated facility, investigation of police actions of February 6, immediate suspension and investigation of an officer who had fired a shot onto campus, establishment of a biracial human-relations committee in the city, full compliance with the Civil Rights Act of 1964, and various other matters that dealt specifically with conditions of segregation and discrimination in Orangeburg. Unlike the 1967 demands of the student boycott, these items covered a wide range of student, community, and even national issues.[56]

To the temporary relief of city and state officials, the students accepted the offer to meet, and the meeting for later that morning was scheduled. For all the hopes that the meeting would head off further confrontation and violence, however, the gathering of city officials and students turned out to be an almost unqualified disaster. The reasons for the breakdown, however, varied drastically, depending on the perspective. From the State College point of view, as articulated by Maceo Nance, "It would have been better had they not come, because they had nothing to say."[57] The effect of the meeting on the students was described as "devastating" in the Southern Regional Council report. "One who was there said it reflected glaringly both the inappropriateness of the white dignitaries' approach to the serious mood of the students, and the students' distrust of the dignitaries. When the mayor tried to say with Southern effusiveness that he was glad to be there, he was hooted. When he said the city believed in good race relations, he was hooted even louder. An assertion by the city manager that the city had not made a lot of progress in race relations, but had made some, met the same reaction."[58]

The city's version of the meeting made the event sound even more ominous. In his testimony at the trial of the highway patrolmen a year later, city administrator Robert T. Stevenson said, "We agreed that we would go to the State College campus to meet with a group of leaders on campus," but when he and his party arrived at White Hall for the meeting, they were ushered into a hall that was filled with six or seven hundred students.[59] To make things more difficult, Stevenson testified, the group of city officials had not received the student grievances they had been invited to discuss, and Stevenson said he did not receive the list until afterward. The meeting itself, he said, was conducted in "an atmosphere where no intelligent dialogue could be related to either side."

Attempts to speak were interrupted by taunts from the audience, Stevenson said. "He [Sellers] was whooping it up and as soon as he got through, he would pass the microphone to somebody else next to him as if things were planned this way."[60] Sellers, it turned out, was not the protagonist, as Stevenson believed. According to an eyewitness report, "Cleveland Sellers stood along one wall of the auditorium enjoying the predicament of the whites, but he asked no questions. However, the white officials apparently assumed he was playing a major role and thought he was the person with the microphone."[61] The actual questioner was BACC president Wayne Curtis, who "asked questions from the floor while holding a microphone, and other students laughed and jeered when the white officials tried unsuccessfully to answer."

In time, Stevenson said, "we were invited to leave. . . . I believe the President [Nance] suggested that we terminate the meeting and we were escorted off the campus."[62] Students expecting a response to their grievances were so upset with the outcome of the meeting, according to one of them in attendance, that "they considered ways in which they could express their displeasure. . . . We considered a march into Orangeburg and also a march to Columbia."[63]

In the aftermath of the fruitless meeting on Wednesday, the parties disengaged, and there was an uneasy suspension of organized contact or confrontation.

McNair was worried that "all it would take is one reckless rock throwing and one broken window . . . and then 'all hell would bust loose.' . . . So the more we got into it, the more serious we saw it, and the more aggravating the situation became. . . . Every report was worse than the one before."[64]

Searching for strategies to head off the confrontation, the governor had already turned to Washington, hoping that intervention by the Justice Department under the public accommodations provisions of the Civil Rights Act of 1964 would either close the bowling alley or order its desegregation. In either event, McNair hoped, federal action might provide at least a temporary respite from the hostilities.

A request had been hastily conveyed days earlier to U.S. Attorney General Ramsey Clark that he file suit in federal court against the bowling alley in hopes that there would be a speedy response.

> We felt the filing of the suit by the federal government would show some real action and that the students would have confidence in the Justice Department making a move . . . that maybe would calm [the students] down and let the matter be resolved in the court. We kept trying to get the thing served. We were telling everybody that they were going to do it. They committed to do it, and it dragged on from day to day and kept getting worse instead of better.
>
> . . . I can remember sitting in the mansion almost losing my patience and having Dan McLeod get them on the phone right then and there and saying, "Please get the thing served this afternoon."

McLeod also remembered, "I called a fellow from up in the Civil Rights Division . . .—I've forgotten who I talked to—and I asked him to pull that thing [the suit] off the desk and get it going. . . . If the United States government had come down and filed a suit on this thing, they probably would have succeeded. . . . Just bringing the . . . government after somebody down there then [who] wouldn't serve black people. It might have had a sort of cooling effect just from having that thing brought."[65]

Bass and Nelson identified McLeod's contact as Stephen Pollak, an assistant attorney general in charge of the civil rights division. A complaint had already been filed, they wrote, and McLeod and Pollak were trying to determine if the Civil Rights Act of 1964 applied to bowling alleys. "We wanted the federal government to institute the action, and bring it as quickly as possible," McLeod was quoted as saying.

McNair had a lot riding on the request for Justice Department intervention.

> We . . . had the people ready. We had alerted the Federal Marshal's office . . . to be prepared to have those papers served the moment they got them. We did not care whether it was five o'clock in the morning or ten o'clock at night. We wanted them served so the word would be out and everybody would know about it.

Why the delay I do not know to this day. We kept getting, "They are on their way; they are on their way. They are going to be done; they are going to be done."[66]

McNair speculated, "I think it was an internal foul-up. . . . I am not sure they recognized the fever pitch this thing had gotten to or the explosiveness of it. That's why . . . we were almost begging them to get the thing done and get it down here."[67] Bass and Nelson wrote that Pollak told McLeod that the matter was "on his desk," and McLeod reportedly replied, "For Lord's sake, put it on top of the pile and get the thing rolling."[68]

McLeod had a further thought: "Everybody was cussing the Civil Rights Division for coming down here and getting people in interstate commerce for being subject to the Civil Rights Act [1964], for interfering with business down here, luncheon room business and things like that. We'd just been through that. Now we turn around and ask them to come down here after saying, 'Stay out of here. We can run our business ourselves.' That may have been a factor in it [the delay], but . . . we were perfectly anxious for him to come on down here and act. Please come in and make this fellow straighten out his act."[69]

As the Justice Department intervention failed to materialize, McNair cast about for other avenues and options. He still hoped the matter could be contained as a community problem, and he decided to push indirectly for a negotiated settlement, working through the Orangeburg City Council at one level and keeping pressure on Washington for federal help at another level. He believed that closing the bowling alley would serve to buy some time, and he scheduled a meeting with members of the city council for nine o'clock, Friday morning, February 9.[70] By then, he hoped, federal action on the civil rights status of the bowling alley would be resolved, and such a ruling could be used as a basis for agreement. The meeting, as it turned out, would be a day late.

McLeod, in the meantime, worried about a breakdown in communication between the colleges and the city. "You have two camps sitting down here," he was quoted by Bass and Nelson as saying, "one out at the college, one uptown, both of them belonging to the same country, same state, same county, same city and it's a hell of a note when you have two groups of people parleying back and forth like a couple of warring nations."[71]

Wednesday proved to be an unsettling and disorganized day. Students unhappy with the outcome of the morning meeting with city officials and still angered by the violence of Tuesday seemed to drift into random and dangerous pursuits. "The events of Wednesday evening," the Southern Regional Council reported, "indicated the degree to which the situation had deteriorated during that day of meetings and indecision, frustration and anger. . . . Students from both campuses, mainly males, rampaged for several hours, shouting and moving in large crowds, and throwing rocks at automobiles passing the campuses. . . . Campus police and later state police moved to divert cars with white passengers from streets leading to the campuses. But cars were hit and the rampage went on for a matter of hours."[72]

As the evening progressed, students gathered on the west side, or front, entrance to the campus on College Avenue (Highway 601) and the one-block length of Watson Street, throwing rocks at passing cars. In an interview the following week with FBI agents, one student said, "The National Guard was at the corners of College and Russell and Watson and Russell Streets, to block traffic from entering the campus. There were some bricks and bottles being thrown by the students. Then the group I was with went to Claflin College. . . . We were throwing bricks and bottles [at] state police who were stationed across the railroad track."[73]

"They put so many rocks in the road . . . highway maintenance crews had to go out and pick up rocks, and trucks [were called] to clean up the road," Chief Strom later recalled. By the end of the uneasy Wednesday, law enforcement began taking up positions in key locations, with unarmed National Guardsmen patrolling the bowling alley parking lot and patrolmen and SLED agents stationed elsewhere. It was taking on the proportions of a military operation.

"We had to take our manpower and put them around the water supply [and] just behind the college was a large gasoline supply depot," Deputy Chief Leon Gasque recalled.

> We had to secure that, had to secure the several schools and the main electrical substation that fed the city. So that took [an] extremely large amount of manpower to secure all of those places, as well as . . . Main Street and the hospital.
>
> Then what was left was down at . . . East End Motors [on the corner of Watson Street and Highway 601 at the campus front], which was approximately a block away from the college.[74]

"I reported to the governor periodically by phone," Strom said, "telling him that we were doing everything we could to keep the peace and without anyone getting injured. . . . We never did have any idea to retreat, but we were hoping we would be able to contain the students without anyone getting hurt. We'd let them throw rocks at us personally [and at] automobiles. . . . We never fired a shot back and put up with all that and we didn't have any intention of going on campus because we felt like if we went on campus, we'd surely have trouble."

By then, Strom was operating with some measure of autonomy. Governor McNair "expected me to enforce the law," Strom said, "but he wasn't giving me orders. He was not on the scene, and . . . it's hard to give orders unless you're there because you don't know what's going to happen next. I think he had confidence in us, and he felt that we would protect the people in Orangeburg. Of course, we would protect the people on the campus if anybody bothered them. . . . We weren't protecting any particular people down there. We went down there to enforce the law in an emergency situation."[75]

Wednesday passed discordantly. Tempers and indignation were rising on the campuses, and forces were escalating on the law-enforcement side. Reports of gunfire from campus during the course of the turbulent day and evening had caused Strom and others to authorize the use of firearms for highway patrolmen if they were threatened, and by Thursday, the South Carolina State and Claflin campuses had been virtually sealed off by patrolmen and National Guard.

Thursday, February 8, 1968

Campus unrest spilled over into a Thursday meeting of S.C. State students. The Southern Regional Council reported that "there occurred a split between the Black Awareness Coordinating Committee (BACC) and other elements of the student leadership. BACC members learned that an agreement to refrain from marching had been reached without consulting them. They felt betrayed and voiced their disapproval of this change in plans. Moreover, BACC members felt that the students in the NAACP chapter and the other student leaders had compromised their original position.

> BACC members reportedly asked participants what was to be done in light of the "betrayal." A high-ranking member of the administration said, "Do what you want to do," and the meeting broke up with no one having decided on a course of action.
>
> Most students returned to their dormitories. Between 75 and 130 male students milled around the edge of the campus facing Watson Street and Highway 601. They were frustrated and without leadership. They wanted to do something.[76]

Earlier in the evening, state and local law enforcement pressed their plans to confine students to the campuses of S.C. State and Claflin in view of what officers considered "the vicious, violent and boisterous attitude, together with the utter disregard for law and order" the previous two nights.[77] By around 8:00 or 8:30 that evening, reports circulated that students were planning to break out of the confinement, and Strom stationed men along the busy intersection of Russell Street and Highway 601, across the street from the S.C. State campus. Police were also worried about reports that an effort might be made to burn the Russell Street home of an Orangeburg resident who had reportedly fired shots at three black students the night before.[78]

Students had been told earlier in the evening that they would be invited to a meeting and address by Reverend I. DeQuincey Newman on the Claflin campus, but when that invitation proved to be erroneous, many of them returned to their dormitory rooms or milled around the open areas where the two campuses join. Confined to campus and hemmed in by armed law-enforcement officers, most students seemed reconciled to another evening of random activity, and at that point, plans for major disruptions appeared to have been thwarted or perhaps exaggerated. Anxieties were still running high, however, and one patrolman later told FBI agents that the campus was cordoned off "to prevent them [students] from destroying the rest of the city and to protect the lives of the Orangeburg residents."[79]

But if there was little in the way of organized activity early on that Thursday, there was plenty of talk, and the excitement was palpable. Acting president Nance had circulated a memorandum Thursday morning telling students that

> your personal safety is in jeopardy, and we are requesting that all students remain on campus and refrain from throwing brickbats and bottles, as was the case last night. The shooting last night bears out the danger involved in this kind of violence and destruction.
>
> Until some semblance of order is restored, students are requested to remain in the interior of the campus.[80]

Reporters were wondering if BACC or SNCC had plans, and they had paid a noontime call on Cleveland Sellers at his off-campus home at 631 Boulevard, across the railroad tracks and Highway 601 from the Claflin and S.C. State campuses. "Like the governor, the mayor and seemingly every other white official in the state, the reporters were convinced that I was responsible for everything," Sellers later wrote.[81]

> "Everybody is looking for a scapegoat," I told them.
>
> They wanted to know what was going to happen next. I told them that I had no idea. They wanted to know if Stokely [Carmichael] was coming to town; it was obvious that they were hoping that he wouldn't.
>
> "Stokely probably won't come to town unless I'm incarcerated," I told them. I was hoping this information would get back to police. I was certain they intended to arrest me, and this comment was designed to make them change their minds.[82]

Sellers returned to the S.C. State campus, where he chose to remain in what he believed was the interest of his own personal security. He found that "the tension . . . was unbelievable. Everybody was talking about the beatings, the shootings, the bowling alley and the cops. . . . Everywhere I went I heard people say, 'Something's gonna happen. Something's gonna happen. Something's gonna happen.'"[83]

"Someone suggested building a bonfire on Watson Street," according to the Southern Regional Council. The students set about doing so around 9:30 or 10:00 that evening.[84]

The bonfire was built in the middle of the narrow street with an assortment of loose materials and set afire with a Molotov cocktail. As the fire began to catch and grow, demonstrators began vandalizing nearby property, uprooting two highway signs on College Avenue and ripping boards, screens, and pieces of the porch balustrade from the vacant Brunson house, which bordered the S.C. State campus and faced onto Watson Street.

Watson Street, a short, narrow street that connected Highway 601 and Russell Street at an angle, was bordered by a grassy bank that sloped up to the S.C. State campus. The street had little traffic, but it was within a few yards of busy Highway 601, which carried vehicles south from Interstate 26 into Orangeburg. Parallel to Highway 601 were railroad tracks, a freight depot, and a warehouse that lay between the adjacent S.C. State and Claflin campuses and downtown Orangeburg. To the south of the S.C. State campus, and only a few yards from Watson Street, was the Brunson house.

To Strom, private property needed to be protected, but the S.C. State campus should be kept off limits to law enforcement. That made the Watson Street bonfire strategically ambiguous. The fire itself seemed relatively unthreatening, but as the evening progressed, it was used to light other items that were carried or hurled in the direction of the warehouse, depot, the grass along the railroad track, and the Brunson house, raising fears that the spread of the fire could threaten other parts of town and triggering Strom's pledge to protect private property around the campus.

As the flames grew, some students gathered out of curiosity, and some chose to "throw rocks, sticks, glass, bricks and anything else they could find into the street and at various persons across the street." According to the FBI, "this fire became larger and larger and while the fire was being started and enlarged, the students took burning pieces of wood and 'fire bombs' and ran across the street [Highway 601] and threw these at an old warehouse."[85]

According to Strom, in a contention later disputed, "a private dwelling [the vacant Brunson house adjacent to campus] was set on fire. . . . We decided, as a matter of public policy, we couldn't let anyone burn, or stand by, and let people burn a private dwelling."[86] McNair had also been informed that the house was afire and recalled, "All I knew was Pete Strom calling me saying, 'We have got a problem, and I have had to send a highway patrol unit with the fire truck to put out a fire in a house that they had set on fire next to the campus.'"[87]

As it had been two days earlier, the decision to bring in a fire truck proved pivotal in shaping the events for the rest of the evening. Whether the fire did or did not pose a threat to surrounding property would become a matter of speculation for years to come. In the context of the events of Thursday evening, February 8, 1968, it seemed sufficiently dangerous to Strom and his law-enforcement colleagues to merit attention and to risk the escalation of hostilities.

In the aftermath, others would speculate that the decision to put out the fire was not necessary and was ill-advised. Nance was among those who felt patience might have been a better strategy. "They [the students] couldn't go anywhere. Nobody was going anywhere. They'd stopped automobiles from coming down [Highway] 601. So things were relatively quiet in terms of anything happening. I think what they were concerned about was they were determined they were not going to allow the students to go back downtown in mass. Now, whose decision it was to call to put out that little fire there in that street, I don't know. . . . But one can speculate. It's highly possible that if nobody bothered, that they [the students] would have gone on back. . . . Eventually, the students would have tired."[88]

McNair also speculated years later. "There is the old argument about the house which I had never seen. Why send a fire truck in there? Why not let it burn? Well, why not let all those old houses along the campus burn—and those were nice old homes along there. My understanding was that this house belonged to some . . . widow lady."[89]

Strom later recalled it was his decision to call the fire department, based on his belief that adjoining property was being endangered.[90] The decision to send the fire trucks also involved on-the-spot decisions and agreements by the city. Orangeburg administrator Robert Stevenson recalled in testimony at the highway patrolmen trial, "I went to the Fire Department and briefed the firemen on what was going on, [and said] chances are they would be called, and I made certain we had seasoned firemen on the truck, and that they were not armed and I assured them they would be protected if they were called to answer the fire."

When the decision was made to call the truck, Stevenson said, "I inquired as to the safety of the firemen. They [Strom, Poston, and National Guard Colonel Charles Leath] briefed me as to the plans to send the Highway Patrol ahead of the fire truck in order that the firemen would be protected, and I believe I told Chief Strom that the firemen were not armed, and they would be depending on them [highway patrolmen] for protection."[91]

Two trucks were dispatched from the Middleton Street station of the Orangeburg Fire Department to Watson Street around 10:30 P.M., and they made their way up Highway 601 to the campus entrance, turning off onto Watson Street, the pumper truck in front and the other about 125 feet behind.[92]

What they found was described by one of the firemen in an interview with the FBI eleven days later. According to the FBI account, in which specific names were blacked out, "As he got out of the truck and approached the fire, he said he saw a crowd . . . on the embankment at the edge of the S.C. State campus. He said he also observed bottles, rocks and pieces of wood being thrown into the street in the general area of where the police were standing and the area where his firemen were attempting to put out the blaze."[93]

In later testimony at the federal court trial of the highway patrolmen, fireman Edward W. Huffman described what he saw when he arrived on the scene:

> I saw Mr. Glover, another fireman, was with the fire truck [and] he was extinguishing the fire in the street. . . . I saw patrolmen, National Guardsmen, everybody, bunch of people, and someone yelled to cut the red light off, and I

stepped out of the truck and walked around to the front and then I could see dark shadows on the bank of the college.

I couldn't tell whether it was people or what. I do remember that.[94]

In the darkness of the evening, there was noisy confusion. Highway patrolmen from six districts around the state had been brought to Orangeburg during the three days of confrontation with the students, and on Thursday evening, they had taken up positions at various locations around the two adjoining campuses. Two units were located at the W. A. Livingston Warehouse across Highway 601 and the railroad tracks from the west end of Claflin and State College campuses to guard against efforts to set the warehouse afire. Another two units were stationed at the intersection of Highway 601 and Russell Street, sealing off the campus and directing traffic away from the area. A third unit was posted at Goff Street and Highway 601 west of the Claflin campus, and a fourth group was located downtown at the Orangeburg town square.[95] Each unit comprised twelve to twenty men, and officers carried service revolvers and batons. Some also carried carbines, and each unit was equipped with at least one shotgun. Some of the officers had been involved in the bowling alley fracas, and others had participated in the Wednesday night exchanges and cleanup. Others had arrived in Orangeburg only a few hours earlier as part of the further buildup of law enforcement in the area. When the fire trucks arrived, officers from three of the units were dispatched to accompany them and to shield them from students who had gathered on the west edge of the campus.

One of the students later recalled, "There were highway patrolmen with the truck to protect the firemen. A number of police and highway patrolmen also came down Watson Street and College Avenue [Highway 601] to the scene of the fire. Some of the police came through the bushes off Watson Street as if attempting to encircle the students. The students then began to pull back to the square at the center of campus."[96]

The officers initially cleared the students from around the bonfire and the grassy bank on the west edge of a large flat field. The area was about half the size of a football field across the front of the campus and stretched eastward toward dormitories. Students who had gathered to watch the fire and toss items onto it retreated toward the back of the flat field as the patrolmen arrived, and firemen set about dousing the bonfire.

"There were approximately 75 students with me on the bank and when the State Troopers . . . appeared, we moved off the bank away from Watson Street and toward Lowman Hall located on the State College campus. The . . . persons wearing helmets and carrying rifles [highway patrolmen] . . . appeared on the bank we had vacated," one student told FBI agents a week later.[97] "Shortly after . . . the fire engines came up . . . the patrolmen came up to the bank in front of the campus and other patrolmen came up on the campus," another of the students told agents.[98] "All of the students ran to the interior of the campus around Lowman

Hall." Another student recalled: "The officers started advancing up the incline and onto the campus. . . . The students retreated to both sides of State Street [the entrance to the campus], leaving the officers on State College campus."[99]

A highway patrolman gave the FBI this account several days later: "At about 10:15, Lt. [Jesse] Spell ordered the patrolmen of District 6 to proceed up Watson Street to the bonfire. As we proceeded up Watson Street, a fire truck arrived at the bonfire. . . . The group of about 30 students retreated back toward the State College campus where they joined in with a group of about 200 Negroes . . . on campus. When we got to the area on Watson Street which was in front of the old house [Brunson house] on the right side of the State College campus [we were ordered] to proceed up over the embankment in front of the old house."[100]

For a moment, there was distance between the students and the patrolmen. The demonstrators were moving toward the Lowman Hall dormitory, and the troopers held their positions at the western edge of the campus. Then there was reengagement. "[Some] of the students pointed out that the officers had no right to be [on] State College Campus," one student later said. "Whereupon the students began advancing toward the positions of the officers . . . the students were not running toward the officers, but walking."[101] "After we reached Lowman Hall," another student said, "we decided that there was no reason for our leaving and so we turned around and proceeded back toward our original position on the bank located on Watson Street."[102] Another student later said that "when the policemen arrived with their guns, the students moved back from Watson Street onto the campus . . . approximately 50 yards and stood . . . for approximately 10 minutes. At this point, someone among the students yelled something to the effect that the students should not be afraid and to move forward where the policemen were standing."[103]

The officers had their own accounts of the events. One reported that "when I got up on the bank, I saw a crowd who were now acting like a mob, moving toward us, yelling, cursing, throwing objects and waving their arms like they were charging us."[104] "I observed the students in retreat, but suddenly they turned, surged past the parked car or cars of campus police and came yelling and running toward us," another recalled.[105]

Another officer later gave this account:

I heard three shots and actually observed the muzzle blast from two shots coming out of the crowd coming toward us. The crowd of students then started running toward our position. My squad was lined up in the middle of Watson Street near State Street and was continuously ducking bottles, rocks, sticks and bricks being thrown from the campus.

When I heard the . . . three shots, I took cover at the bank along the Watson Street side of State Street. I was concentrating on my personal safety . . . I was armed only with my service revolver and a riot stick so I drew my revolver to protect myself and other members of my squad from the mob and the gunshots coming from the State College campus. I felt that we patrolmen, approximately 34 men, were so heavily outnumbered by the large number of students in the mob and since they were armed with guns as well as rocks and bricks, were in a very dangerous situation and had to defend ourselves. I felt that our lives were in jeopardy and the mob was uncontrollable. The mob was nearly on top of us.[106]

In testimony entered by stipulation into the federal civil trial record from the FBI report, Lieutenant Jesse Spell said,

I received instructions to move my squad forward to the campus to protect the firemen who had been called to put out the fire and protect the house from further damage.

My squad arrived at the edge of the campus near the vacant house and took up a position to protect the firemen. Just prior to arriving at our location, a group of individuals started throwing rocks, bricks, bottles and sticks at us.

I took my squad up the embankment as the group on campus, which was probably made up of 200 or more persons, retreated back into the campus area. I had to have my squad go to the top of the embankment to observe the mob and to protect the firemen from thrown objects.[107]

It was the moment that was not supposed to happen. Chief Strom had warned against having armed lawmen on campus. Acting President Maceo Nance had advised students to remain for their own safety on the interior of the campus. And yet, at variance with both admonitions, spirited students on the western border of the campus were moving toward edgy highway patrolmen who had taken up positions on the campus proper.

The first bloodshed came as patrolmen in Lieutenant Spell's squad moved through the trees and bushes around the vacant house toward the students. "One of my men [Officer David Shealy] was hit in the face and fell to the ground," Spell said. "I ran to where Patrolman Shealy was lying unconscious on the ground with blood all over his face. I told two of the men to take him to the rear and I ran back to a point in front of my squad. We stopped near the corner of the vacant house and the entrance to the campus. The mob of individuals numbering approximately two hundred at this time started moving toward us."[108]

In full view of many of the troopers, the downed patrolman was carried from the field by fellow troopers, taken down the embankment to Watson Street, and loaded into a squad car for transportation to the hospital. Sergeant Henry Morrell Addy, near Shealy when he was hit, later gave this account. "As I reached the [Brunson] house, Patrolman Shealy, who was directly in front of me, about four feet away, fell to the ground. . . . I didn't know whether Patrolman Shealy had been hit by . . . gunfire. I stopped to look at Shealy and saw that he was bleeding profusely about the face and observed him to be jerking rapidly. I assumed he had been shot by gunfire in the face. I looked toward the crowd on the campus in front of me, and saw there were 250 to 300 individuals in this group."[109] Shealy suffered multiple lacerations of the nose and septum area, and according to his attending physician, Roy C. Campbell of Orangeburg, "practically drowned in his own blood."[110] It was later determined that Shealy had been struck by a large wooden banister torn from the Brunson house and hurled toward the troopers in the area.

Also nearby was Officer Sidney C. Taylor, who later said,

> Patrolman David Shealy, who was slightly behind me to the left, hit the ground and I heard a patrolman yell, "Shealy's been shot." I went over to him and I rolled him over on his back. He was bleeding profusely around the mouth and nose. I yelled to get a car and then helped carry Shealy to a . . . police car which had pulled up nearby. . . . I then went back to the bank area facing the lawn of the campus. . . . I could see that the group of Negroes had reassembled and had started coming toward me and the other patrolmen on the bank. . . .
>
> I heard a small caliber weapon being fired from what seemed the rear of the group of Negroes. I yelled to get down behind the embankment and . . . at this time, the Negroes were about 25 yards from us and were throwing things at us. Some of the patrolmen were shouting "now?" "now?" and someone answered "now!"[111]

Spell recalled, "Someone, from the group [of students] threw a firebomb at the back of the house on our right [the Brunson house] and set it on fire. At this time, I realized the mob of people had to be stopped as they would not listen to the police and would injure and possibly kill some of the officers. . . . At this point, I ordered my squad to fire their weapons to stop the mob."[112]

Fifteen of the highway patrolmen later told the FBI they opened fire, some saying they heard orders to fire, others saying they fired spontaneously in self-defense, most of them saying the students were within a range of twenty-five to fifty yards. Nine of the patrolmen said they fired twelve-gauge pump shotguns loaded with double-ought buckshot. Three of the troopers reported firing .38-caliber Colt service police specials, and three other patrolmen said they fired .30-caliber carbines. Authors Bass and Nelson said the gunfire was set off by a single shot from a highway patrol carbine.[113]

Of the fifteen patrolmen who said they fired weapons, six said they fired into the air. The rest indicated they fired in the direction of the students, either directly into the crowd or low, at their feet.[114] During the course of the federal trial of the nine troopers a year later, it was stipulated the shooting lasted from eight to ten seconds, and that there were "around fifteen rounds of shotgun shells fired . . . in the direction of the crowd, and six 38-caliber bullets . . . there were 27 students who received buckshot wounds."[115] "I fired my gun in front of them," Spell said, "and had no intention of killing any of the group. . . . I am positive that if we had raised our weapons to a level position, we would have killed a large number of the group."[116]

Thirty-two students were wounded seriously enough to be seen in the emergency room at Orangeburg Regional Hospital. Eleven were admitted, and eighteen were discharged.[117] Three did not survive the barrage.

Sam Hammond, an eighteen-year-old student at S.C. State, died at 11:20 Thursday night, less than an hour after the shooting. Delano Middleton, a seventeen-year-old Wilkinson High School student from Orangeburg, died around two hours later, at 1:10 A.M. Friday morning. Henry Smith, an eighteen-year-old student at S.C. State, died at 1:45 A.M.[118]

Later lab studies revealed that Smith was shot at close range, that Hammond was hit from around thirty-five feet, and that Middleton was shot from around one hundred feet.[119] Smith and Middleton died of multiple wounds; Hammond was hit once.[120] Others near the front of the student surge also received multiple wounds but survived. Some students were hit by stray bullets as far away as the area around the Lowman Hall dormitory.

Among those shot was Sellers himself, who later wrote that he was close enough to the front to see Henry Smith hit. "I watched him spin and crumple to the ground," Sellers wrote. "Bullets seemed to be coming from all directions. The sound of the pistols and the shotgun blasts was deafening." Sellers was wounded in the shoulder. "It felt like a power-driven sledgehammer," he wrote. "I landed with a heavy thud. The air was knocked out of my lungs, but my mind was working fast. I was certain they had shot Henry [Smith] because they thought he was me. He looked just like me."[121]

In Columbia, McNair was awaiting word from Strom.

> "I had been getting reports about firebombs and things like that, and we were saying we had made a decision not to go on campus, not to go in the dormitories and try to pull out the bad guys, or something like that. We just said let us leave that alone.[122]

Things had seemed to calm down, McNair recalled, then, "Pete Strom was on the phone giving me a report, and he said, 'I have to go. All hell's busted loose. I will call you right back.'" The wait, McNair recalled, "seemed like hours. It was not long, but it seemed like hours before he called me back to tell me what had happened, that . . . several of the students . . . were wounded, and they were all at the hospital. . . . Some of them they thought were dead, and they were trying to get a count and he gave me a report as far as he could."[123]

Students who could do so crawled or ran back to the interior of the campus, and some of the wounded were helped by other students. Patrolmen moved onto the field to carry two of the students back down the bank and into emergency vehicles for transporting to the Orangeburg Regional Hospital.

In a matter of moments, it was over. The field fell empty and silent, and the patrolmen withdrew to positions across the railroad track and College Street. "We kept up our roadblocks, but we moved our people across the railroad track," Strom later said. "We didn't have any intention still of letting the students get off the campus and get in town because in our opinion Orangeburg would have been burned. . . . The people in Orangeburg were armed and had plenty of ammunition."[124]

The only arrest was that of Sellers, who was detained while awaiting treatment in Orangeburg Hospital for his gunshot wound. "They took me immediately to a doctor," Sellers wrote. "He examined my throbbing arm and told me that I was lucky. 'You're not hurt bad.' I was then taken back to the waiting room. Before I could regain my seat, a white man in shirt sleeves walked up to me and said, 'Come on.'"[125]

Sellers was arraigned at around 1:45 A.M. Friday morning, February 9, and was charged with "the crime of inciting to riot, arson, assault and battery with intent to kill and murder, destruction of personal property, damaging real property, and housebreaking and grand larceny." The sworn statement of arresting officer B. N. Collins, Orangeburg County deputy sheriff, stated that Sellers "did take, steal and carry away furniture from [the Brunson] residence and did burn same on the Street . . . and at the same time and place . . . did throw a bottle of flammable material against the said house thereby setting it on fire; and . . .did destroy personal property in said residence and did remove a post from the front porch of the said residence; and . . . did strike South Carolina Highway Patrolman David J. Shealy, with a heavy blunt object, thereby injuring him seriously and thereby attempting to commit the crime of assault and battery with intent to kill and murder."[126] Bail was set at $50,000 by magistrate Tom Friday, and Sellers was taken to the Department of Corrections in Columbia for incarceration.[127]

Friday, February 9, 1968

By Friday morning, Nance called on the South Carolina State Board of Trustees to suspend classes, saying, "It was bedlam. . . . We had to close the school."[128] The board responded by shutting down the college indefinitely.

McNair also moved quickly, declaring that a state of emergency existed in the city of Orangeburg and imposing a dusk-to-dawn curfew there. The language of the executive order cited "wide-spread acts of violence and threats of violence, common disregard for the law and disorders of a general nature which constitute a danger to the persons and property of the citizens of the community, and threaten the peace and tranquility of the State."[129]

At a press conference in his office in Columbia that Friday morning, McNair called it "one of the saddest days in the history of South Carolina." Flanked by Chief Strom, Attorney General McLeod, and Henry Lake, a McNair colleague and former legislator who had been on the scene the previous evening, the governor said in a prepared statement, "The years of work and understanding have been shattered by this unfortunate incident at Orangeburg. Our reputation for racial harmony has been blemished by the actions of those who would place selfish motives and interests above the welfare and security of the majority."

The statement, later criticized as not showing sympathy for the shooting victims, stated further, "It has become apparent that the incident last night was sparked by Black Power advocates who represent only a small minority of the total student bodies at South Carolina State College and Claflin College. . . . Everyone regrets the incident which caused the death of the three students and we hope that the responsible students of our State will pursue efforts toward eliminating any further outbreaks of violence."[130]

News accounts the next day carried pictures from the night before of patrolmen poised on the grassy embankment of the campus, some of them with weapons drawn, and pictures of the fatally wounded Middleton lying on the Watson Street sidewalk adjacent to the grassy bank. The front-page, eight-column headline in the hometown *Orangeburg Times and Democrat* the next day stated: "All Hell Breaks Loose—Three Killed, Many Wounded in College Nightmare."[131]

Initial reports, filed only minutes after the shootings, gave support to the law-enforcement account that students had initiated the shooting. Associated Press accounts filed periodically during the night and through most of the next day described "a heavy exchange of gunfire" and reported that "Negroes opened fire as city firemen and police moved to put out the fire."[132]

The *State* newspaper's story a day later by Dave Bledsoe provided this description:

> From a vantage point across Russell Street near the police lines, I could see the fire trucks coming with lights ablaze and sirens at full pitch. The line of troopers and Guardsmen moved down from the intersection toward the college entrance, screening the fire trucks. The patrolmen went up to a small cleared field not as large as a football field.
>
> The students were there. There was shouting and yelling from them as the fire fighters doused the flames with chemical extinguishers. On my way up the line—newsmen were finally admitted to follow the cordon as it swept down the street—I heard the persistent pap-pap-pap of a light caliber weapon. It had been heard all evening, but no officer was willing to pinpoint its exact location, and I could not see where it was.
>
> There was more shouting and yelling, and then the night exploded with the sudden booms and muzzle flashes of rapidly-fired shotguns. I heard no command to open fire, and Highway Patrolmen later said none was given.[133]

Elsewhere, Bledsoe's accounts reported that Officer Shealy had been "clubbed" and that "one patrolman fell after being struck by a bullet." The same story said that the patrolmen "returned the fire in a ragged volley."[134] An Associated Press account quoted a staff photographer as saying "a group of Negroes on campus started firing at about 50 officers."[135]

Bledsoe's story also supported the law-enforcement concern that white businessmen had become armed: "Apparently underlying the haste of the officers was the desire to avoid a confrontation between the Negroes and the businessmen."[136] Bledsoe later told of entering a furniture store near the campus and finding the proprietor and several others in the store armed with "two or three deer caliber rifles, 30/06 and above . . . two shotguns and a pistol." He described the mood of the people in the store as "very angry . . . very upset . . . extremely angry."[137] Bledsoe later testified at the trial of the highway patrolmen and described the scene as one of "vast . . . confusion. It's hard to convey exactly how confused the scene was."[138]

News Accounts Disputed

Sellers accused officials, including McNair, of trying to "white wash the entire affair" and said, "They claimed that the police fired in response to intense 'sniper fire from the campus.' The news media accepted and reported this lie as if it were the gospel."[139]

Later accounts gave less credence to the belief that students had initiated the gunfire, and within days, reaction was setting in across a wide range of issues. In New York, SNCC leader H. Rap Brown was referring to the event as "The Orangeburg massacre" and warned, "If we must die . . . let us die with the enemy's blood on our hands. . . . Let us die like men, fighting back."

Sellers later said the SNCC news release "had little effect."

> The organization just wasn't equal to the task. Unlike Selma, where SNCC was able to mobilize national support, within hours after the attack on the Edmund Pettus Bridge, there was almost no response to Orangeburg. SNCC's elaborate communications apparatus was gone.
>
> Moreover, there was no money for my bail.[140]

Within less than three weeks of the shootings, the Southern Regional Council in Atlanta issued a report challenging some of the initial contentions. It disputed the contention that the students had fired first and quoted Charleston newsman Warren Koon: "A line of patrolmen trotted, in orderly ranks, to the bank in front of the campus . . . to protect the firemen. They had rifles, pistols, and shotguns at port arms. Suddenly the line of patrolmen began shooting over the bank, toward the mob. It was a crackling gunfire, almost as if an order had been given for all patrolmen to shoot at once."[141]

The forty-three-page Southern Regional Council report, written by Pat Watters and Warren Rougeau, was based on interviews conducted with students, faculty, newsmen, and others who were involved in the events. It also contested, among other things, the belief that Black Power had been the chief instigator of the Orangeburg protests and demonstrators, and it agreed with Sellers that "the South Carolina press and its white public for the most part seemed to accept the official interpretation and justification of events at Orangeburg."[142]

The SRC also wondered, along with McNair, what had taken the Justice Department so long to take action in Orangeburg against violators of the Civil Rights Act of 1964. The suit McNair hoped might calm things early in the week came instead two days after the shootings, on Saturday, February 10, against Mr. and Mrs. Harry K. Floyd, owners and operators of the bowling alley, and Mr. and Mrs. E. C. Floyd, owners and operators of the snack bar on the premises, charging the four with "refusing to permit Negroes to use facilities on an equal basis in violation of the Civil Rights Act of 1964."[143] Two weeks later, U.S. District Judge Robert Martin issued a temporary restraining order enjoining the defendants from operating the establishment on a segregated basis.[144] The Justice Department also filed suit on February 13 against the Orangeburg Regional Hospital, alleging that "the Orangeburg Hospital practices racial discrimination in the assignment of rooms, floors, wards and wings, in its medical care treatment, service and training programs."[145] The SRC report said the Justice Department actions, coming within a week of the shootings, "at least raised the question of why they came so late—both in the life of the 1964 Civil Rights Act and in the day of Negro hope in Orangeburg."[146]

The SRC report had its critics, among them Highway Patrol Colonel P. Frank Thompson, who took issue with the contention that "some of the most responsible adult Negro leaders were in the aftermath of the shootings giving serious consideration to a theory that a deliberate effort was made to shoot Mr. Sellers. They cited as circumstantial evidence similarities in size, clothing or hair style to those characteristic of Mr. Sellers among the three fatalities."[147] Thompson called the claim "absolutely fantastic" and said, "As far as I know, none of the officers even knew Sellers. I know I didn't until I saw his picture published in the papers."[148]

Reliance on the FBI Report

As pressure mounted from various quarters for investigations of the Orangeburg events, McNair placed his confidence in the FBI, which had agents on the scene and launched an investigation days after the shootings. Some weeks later, he told interviewers on South Carolina ETV that the Justice Department probe and the FBI investigation were one and the same, and he called the federal agents "about the most impartial group I know."[149] A day later, in Washington for a Governors Conference meeting, he said the FBI work would be finished "in about two or three weeks" and would be sent on to the Justice Department before coming to the state.[150]

"Since the FBI was there and since we had seen what happened around the country," McNair later said, "we all knew what the aftermath would be."

We knew that there were going to be cries of police brutality and everything in the world. . . . We determined that, since we were in that posture, the best thing we could do would be to get the FBI to conduct a thorough and complete, comprehensive investigation.

We called on them, on the government, for that the very next morning [Friday, February 9]. [U.S. Attorney General] Ramsey Clark himself called to express his concern to me and his willingness to be helpful in any way he could. "What can we do to help you?"

I expressed my displeasure over their not bringing the action [against the bowling alley], and think I probably did it in rather strong language to the point that "if you had not dilly-dallied and delayed, we might have avoided this." But there needs to be a thorough, complete investigation, and we would like to ask the FBI to do it.[151]

McNair's request came at a time when the FBI and the Justice Department were hardly seeing eye-to-eye on much of anything. Attorney General Ramsey Clark and FBI Chief J. Edgar Hoover had serious differences over Hoover's surveillance techniques and had disagreed strongly over the use of wiretapping. In the months preceding and following the February 1968 Orangeburg shootings, the Clark-Hoover feud would reach brisk proportions. Their blowup would became so profound that, years later, Hoover, in an interview with the *Washington Post,* would say that Clark was "like a jellyfish . . . a softie. . . . If ever there was a worse Attorney General, it was Ramsey Clark. You never knew which way he was going to flop on an issue. He was worse than Bobby [Kennedy]. At least Kennedy stuck by his guns, even when he was wrong."

In his response, Clark told reporters, "For reasons that are unfortunate in my judgment, the FBI became ideological some time back. This has put a scale over its eyes." Clark reportedly lamented the "terribly wasteful use of resources" by the FBI and Hoover's "intolerance of different viewpoints." He was quoted as wondering aloud why the FBI was so bad at investigating "unlawful police conduct."[152]

All this was just beneath the surface as McNair put in his appeal for an FBI investigation of the Orangeburg shootings. What was known at the time was that President Lyndon Johnson had launched a major initiative after the July 1967 urban riots, and that "Johnson's pleas for help persuaded Hoover to expand its operations against the black power movement. In September 1967, Attorney General Ramsey Clark told Hoover to 'use the maximum resources, investigative and intelligence, to collect and report all facts bearing upon the question as to whether there has been or is a scheme or conspiracy by any group of whatever size, effectiveness or affiliation, to plan, promote or aggravate riot activity.'"[153]

The Orangeburg investigation came amid Hoover's stepped-up campaign against what he viewed as black militant organizations and only deepened the

Hoover-Clark rift. In an interview years later, Clark said he did not believe the FBI really had its heart in the Orangeburg investigation. "Like any other institution, if they didn't really believe in or empathize with an order . . . the investigation might be very poor, as in the Orangeburg massacre investigation."[154]

To some extent, public attention faded in the wake of the Orangeburg shootings, particularly among national observers. The Southern Regional Council wrote, "with the initial stance of white South Carolina, all the way up to the Governor's Office, adamantly supporting the state police, it was not surprising that national reaction was, if not indifferent, muted. There was no general public outcry for a fuller investigation of the specific incident, or the national implications."[155] To some, there must have been recollections of the labor disputes of 1930s, the shooting of six textile workers by special deputies in Honea Path in September 1934, and the subsequent silence within the state that remained unbroken for more than six decades.

Sellers spent three weeks in jail, had his bond reduced from $50,000 to $20,000, and was released only to face trial four weeks later for draft evasion, a charge for which he was found guilty. Facing charges in South Carolina and awaiting sentencing on the draft conviction, Sellers left for New York to rejoin Carmichael and to resume SNCC activity.[156]

In Orangeburg, things eased back into the appearance of at least surface normalcy over the next few weeks. Classes resumed February 26,[157] and two days later, McNair lifted the curfew, saying that "the situation looks extremely good."

Students March on Columbia

Just beneath the surface, however, things were anything but good among students returning to the campus. Within days, they were on the march—several hundred strong—to the State House in Columbia, where they descended on the governor's office and the Senate and House of Representatives with their protests and grievances. The BACC-sponsored event brought two hundred S.C. State students to Columbia in four buses, and they were joined by other students, increasing the group by several hundred.

Their visit to the Senate was a particularly boisterous one, as around ninety of the students interrupted proceedings with shouts from the gallery and the loud reading of grievances. Another seventy-five staged a sit-in in McNair's outer office, demanding to present him a list of grievances.

The governor refused to see the large group, saying he would meet with a representative group of five or six. The students refused. A day earlier, McNair had met with student-body officers and leaders of the student NAACP, both of which groups had presented him with lists of grievances.

The students spent much of their time milling around the State House lobby under the watchful eyes of law enforcement and edgy legislators, several of whom were reportedly carrying weapons. A few of the lawmakers made a point of joining the students and talking with them, including Senators J. Ralph Gasque of Marion and John Drummond of Greenwood. Drummond, a decorated World War II fighter pilot who thirty years later became president pro tempore of the Senate, said he was sympathetic to the students' needs and assured them he would work to improve conditions.[158]

A week later, the students returned to Columbia, their numbers swelling to seven hundred and the S.C. State contingent augmented by a busload from the institution where Cleveland Sellers had received his high school education, Voorhees College in Denmark, South Carolina. Only fifty students were permitted inside this time, however, and they presented grievances to Drummond and Lieutenant Governor John West, who had presided over the stormy confrontation in the Senate a week earlier.[159]

McNair was assailed from many elements of the civil rights corps, including moderate leaders such as NAACP president Reverend A. W. Holman of Columbia, Urban League president Colonel O. P. Taylor, Benedict College president Benjamin F. Payton, and NAACP attorney Matthew Perry. All of them laid the blame for the Orangeburg shootings on the governor.[160]

McNair chose to keep a low profile, declining suggestions that he go to Orangeburg and remaining essentially away from public view on the issue. News secretary Wayne Seal defended the governor's low-key strategy, assuring reporters that his lack of visibility was not a sign of low interest or involvement. "He is more involved than anyone," Seal said. "The fact that he has not gone out of his office should not be construed to mean he does not care. He feels that such appearances would gain publicity, but all he is concerned with is results."[161]

Among those results was an initiative that appeared two weeks later in the form of a financial package to address the needs of South Carolina State College. The package, proposed by McNair and approved by the Budget and Control Board, would provide for the construction of two new women's dormitories, additions to the student union, and other renovations. Unlike other college-bond issues, it was also provided, the debt would not be retired by revenue from S.C. State. It would come from the state's general fund. McNair also recommended that the college's operating budget request of $8.8 million for the upcoming 1968–1969 fiscal year be fully funded. The financial request was reported to be number one on the students' list of grievances.[162]

The proposal drew immediate fire from Republicans in the General Assembly, particularly from Newberry senator Eugene C. Griffith, who said McNair was attempting to "reward violence" with the proposals, an echoing of the charges Aiken Republican Marion H. Smoak had made a year earlier in opposing the 1967 compromises that liberalized student regulations and led to the ouster of President Benner Turner. This time, Griffith was challenged by Democratic senators Eugene

N. "Nick" Zeigler of Florence and Drummond, who "dared Griffith to say South Carolina has been . . . fair in apportioning funds to all its colleges."[163] The special bond issue, which included projects for other agencies and institutions, did not pass until the final day of the legislative session that year, withstanding Republican filibusters in the House by Representative Jerry M. Hughes Jr. of Orangeburg and in the Senate by Griffith and Smoak.

While McNair was successfully engineering his own kind of initiative for S.C. State in the wake of the February shootings, he was having less success in prying loose the FBI report on the events that February 8 evening. On March 12, McNair announced that he had asked the Justice Department to release the findings of its investigation of the February shootings. "A full disclosure of the facts is essential because of the concern and the confusion over the tragedy and because of the pressing urgency that the facts in the matter be made public," he said.[164]

Almost immediately, however, the Justice Department made it clear that it had no intentions "to make public or send to . . . Governor McNair the FBI report on the recent Orangeburg, S.C. riots that resulted in the deaths of three Negro students."[165] As the crucial months of 1968 passed, the FBI and the Justice Department were, in fact, deeply mired in internecine conflict fueled by philosophical, political, and personal differences. Caught squarely in the middle were the State of South Carolina, the Orangeburg investigation, and Bob McNair.[166] Following McNair's March 12 request, a Justice Department spokesman was quoted as saying the FBI routinely sent its findings to the appropriate division of the department, in this case the Civil Rights Division, for study. Information would be made public from the study only in the event of prosecution.[167]

Such, in fact, would prove to be the case. Excerpts from the dozens of interviews conducted by the FBI in the days and weeks following the February 8 shootings would be used more than a year later as the basis for much of the testimony when the Justice Department brought an unusual civil rights suit against the nine highway patrolmen who were identified as having fired into the group of students.

The suit was filed less than two months after a federal grand jury had refused to indict the patrolmen on similar charges. The grand jury, which included two blacks and five women among its twenty-three-member panel,[168] deliberated for more than two weeks behind closed doors, and some forty people were subpoenaed, including law-enforcement officers and students.[169] At the conclusion of the investigation, the jury returned no bill, and the record was sealed. The presiding judge, J. Robert Martin Jr., said at the time he "saw no reason why the families of the men should be subjected to this publicity since 'no bills' had been returned on the indictment."[170]

The Justice Department persisted, however, with or without an indictment. In what was known as a "criminal information," a direct criminal charge that bypasses a grand jury, charges were filed in December 1968, under the same statute that had been used in the grand-jury investigation of two months earlier. The subsequent trial would provide the most extensive public examination of the February shootings in or out of a courtroom, and it was hailed as such by at least one news account. AP writer Kent Krell suggested that the trial "may shed some light on the clouded circumstances involved in a bloody racial clash between young Negroes and South Carolina Highway Patrolmen in Orangeburg last year."[171]

The charges against the patrolmen, made under an 1870 act originally designed to protect the freedom of slaves, provided that the nine troopers "acting under the color of the laws of the State of South Carolina, did willfully discharge and shoot firearms into a group of persons on the campus of South Carolina State College . . . thereby killing, injuring and intimidating persons in the said group, with the intent of imposing summary punishment upon those persons and did thereby willfully deprive those persons of the right, secured and protected by the Constitution of the United States, not to be deprived of life or liberty without due process of law."[172]

Martin, the presiding judge, said the case was the "first he could find brought under the statute in which the defense of self-defense had been used under similar circumstances. He said in previous cases, law officers have generally been charged with violating the civil rights of persons in their custody."[173] "What makes it unusual," Martin later said, "is that it is a two-pronged situation. The two issues to be decided are that of self-defense and that of intent."[174]

The Trial of Nine Highway Patrolmen

The trial lasted ten days, between May 18 and May 28, during which many of the witnesses' statements made to the FBI, including all of the defendant patrolmen, were entered by stipulation as evidence in the trial record. None of the nine highway patrolmen actually testified. Representing the Justice Department were Tennessee-born Charles Quaintance, raised and educated in Oregon, and Robert Hocutt, a North Carolinian who had graduated from Wake Forest. The state's attorneys, defending the patrolmen, were veteran Assistant Attorney General J. C. Coleman, attorneys Frank Taylor and Geddes Martin of Columbia, and Orangeburg solicitor Julian Wolfe.

In Judge Martin's view, as he expressed to attorneys for both sides and the jury, the issue to be determined was whether the patrolmen acted in self-defense in firing on the students. He said there were four elements to be considered, the first of which he said had already been conceded by Justice Department, that the troopers "did not act wrongfully in moving to the State College campus with the intent to retain the students to the boundaries of the campus."[175]

The other three elements, he said, were being contended:

> . . . That the individual defendant . . . must have believed . . . that he was in imminent danger or peril of losing his own life, or of sustaining some serious bodily harm.

... that the circumstances must have been such as to have warranted such a belief in the mind of a person of ordinary prudence, firmness and courage. ...

... that the defendant had no other probable means of escape except to assault his adversary.[176]

The defendants, he reminded jurors, were not charged with murder, assault and battery, or a violation of any statute except the one under which they were being charged—depriving the students of their civil rights.

Justice Department attorney Quaintance argued,

we cannot say to these defendants [the patrolmen], or any other individuals, all right, three nights of this is too much. It's time we taught them a lesson by the fastest, most effective means available, gunfire. But isn't that what you say if you return a verdict of not guilty as to all these defendants?

... to return a verdict of not guilty ... would be to say when the going gets rough, the enforcers of the law are permitted to act beyond the law, and that those who are sworn to uphold the law may disregard it.[177]

For the state, J. C. Coleman attacked the Justice Department's extensive efforts to prosecute the patrolmen, likening it to the adage "The mountain has labored and brought forth a mouse."[178] "They [the Justice Department] have subjected to microscopic examination every piece of evidence that could be discovered ... they have come up with nothing." Coleman called attention to the dispute over whether there had been shots fired first from the students before the highway patrol opened fire. "Let's just say for the purpose of argument that there was no shooting in the [student] crowd. Where does that put us? That still puts us with an on-charging mob, throwing bricks, brickbats, balustrades, possibly iron pipes at the patrolmen. Frankly, I can't see it makes any difference." "It was necessary," he argued, "for them [the patrolmen] to get there, to hold the line, to stop this mob from going out and doing further violence."[179]

The jury of eight men and four women, a panel that included two blacks, reached a verdict in deliberations that took about an hour and half. They found, as had the grand jury six months earlier, that all nine patrolmen acted in self-defense and were therefore not guilty.[180]

There remained one more trial for the troopers, a civil action that came to trial a year and a half later, in November 1970, against the highway patrolmen by relatives of the three slain students contending, as in previous trials, that the students had been deprived of their civil rights and had been subjected to summary punishment from the troopers. NAACP attorney Perry represented the students' families, and Coleman once again represented the troopers.

It was an all-white jury this time that heard testimony similar to the earlier trial—students contending that the assault from the patrolmen was unprovoked, and the state claiming the patrolmen fired in self-defense. During the course of the four-day trial, all fourteen witnesses for the students said there was no shoot-ing before the patrolmen opened fire. All eight defense witnesses said there was. The jury believed the defense witnesses and cleared the patrolmen of liability after fifty-three minutes of deliberation.[181]

The Trial of Cleveland Sellers

It was in September 1970, more than thirty months after the shootings and four months before the second acquittal of the highway patrolmen, that Sellers came to trial. Even then, it was over some initial reservations of the cautious solicitor for the First Judicial Circuit [Dorchester, Orangeburg and Calhoun Counties], Julian S. Wolfe. Wolfe, a veteran Orangeburg attorney who had been in office since 1940, wrote McNair in December 1968, "I have conferred several times with Mr. J. C. Coleman . . . and Chief Strom, and they too feel that it is best that we not attempt the trial of the Sellers case or an alleged criminal assault case. As to do such, may cause a great deal of trouble which we are trying to avoid at this time."[182]

Some months later, in July 1969, Wolfe got a stinging reply from Lewie G. Merritt, the feisty retired Marine general who was providing legal assistance to the governor at the time. Merritt wrote, "the Governor feels definitely that Sellers should be brought to trial at the earliest practical time. He believes that the trial and conviction of this man, along with a stiff sentence, would serve as a warning to the others of like mind and disposition."[183]

Wolfe was still worried two months after Merritt's letter, writing to Coleman in September that "since Sellers is under bond and one of the provisions states that he remain at least five miles away from Orangeburg, and since he is under sentence in the Federal Court and an appeal has been taken . . . it might be wise that the case be continued."[184]

McNair answered this time himself, firing back two days later with a one-paragraph response that read: "In reply to your letter to J. C. Coleman on Sep-tember 8, I have told you on every occasion that I believe Cleveland Sellers should be tried. If we don't try people involved in riots, how can we ever settle them? In my judgment, this case should have been tried sometime ago."[185]

Wolfe continued to complain about workload and crowded dockets, and by October 28, an exasperated McNair wrote to Wolfe,

> As you know, I have always felt that Cleveland Sellers should be tried. It is difficult to send National Guardsmen, Highway Patrolmen and other police into dangerous situations that result in riot and death, and have the ringleader escape any punishment. . . .
>
> If you find that your court work has grown to such proportion that you need assistance, I would be most happy to have the Attorney General assign one of the other Solicitors to help you in a regular or special session, and also to

assign the Assistant Attorney General, J. C. Coleman, to help you in the preparation of the [Sellers] trial.[186]

By January 1970, Wolfe and the state's attorneys were in agreement to proceed, but the case was continued from the January session of court. Coleman's recommendation was for a September 14 start.[187] The trial eventually got underway September 21.

By then, Sellers's attorneys were seeking delays. One of his attorneys was quoted as saying that he was led to believe that the state would not pursue charges against his client[188] prior to initiating maneuvers to have the trial transferred from state to federal court. The request was denied by federal judge and former governor Donald Russell[189] in a decision upheld two days later by Judge Clement F. Haynsworth of the Fourth Circuit Court of Appeals.[190]

When the time came for jury selection, Sellers's attorneys submitted 192 race-based questions, and Judge John Grimball of Columbia had the number reduced to 25, saying, "I don't think the racial attitude of the juror has anything to do with the trial of the case."[191] A jury of nine whites and three blacks was eventually seated after daylong deliberations on September 24.[192]

Sellers was formally charged on three counts—inciting to riot, conspiracy to riot, and rioting—and testimony got underway the next day in a tense setting. Some two hundred students showed up for the trial, but only half could fit into the small Orangeburg courtroom. The rest remained outside, across the street. Twenty-one highway patrolmen were stationed upstairs in the balcony of the courtroom, and SLED agents were outside.[193]

As it turned out, the state's case quickly began to crumble. By the third day of testimony, Grimball had directed a verdict of acquittal in two of the three riot charges, saying that the state had "failed 'utterly' to prove that Sellers incited to riot or led a conspiracy to riot."[194]

In Grimball's judgment, the state had not even made much of a case for Sellers's presence at the Thursday-night disturbances. "You've had witness after witness," he told the state's attorneys, "[but] nobody has put this defendant in the area of the riot Wednesday or Thursday with the exception that he was wounded and that, to my mind, means very little."[195]

The trial also brought testimony for the first time from FBI agents that "several minutes elapsed between the small arms fire from the campus and the heavier Highway Patrol fire that killed three and wounded 27." Challenged about the relevance of the FBI testimony, Grimball said, "The materiality of the FBI investigation is that 30–40 agents investigated for four months and found nothing against your client [Sellers]."[196]

The remaining charge was that of rioting, and even on that one count, Grimball held that "the state had failed to prove—and the jury could not consider—the charges against Sellers for his actions on the nights of February 7 and 8."[197] That meant the state's only remaining chance to convict Sellers of anything was to prove he was guilty of rioting the evening of Tuesday, February 6, when students and police clashed in the parking lot of the bowling alley, and even on that charge Grimball had to allow some leeway for the prosecutors' sake. The indictment had specified that Sellers had rioted on February 8, the day of the shootings, but Grimball said that "since other parts of the indictment specified other days, [he] would consider the document as a whole, and allow the jury to consider the riot issue."[198]

"I expected the state's case against me to be much stronger than it was," Sellers later wrote. "Of the ten who testified against me—all of them were connected with law enforcement—only one could cite an incident where I was observed breaking a law. Chief J. P. Strom of the State Law Enforcement Division testified that I 'refused to disperse immediately when ordered.' Orangeburg Police Chief Roger E. Poston testified that he saw me 'move from group to group' during the disturbance but didn't hear me say anything."[199]

In his closing argument, Sellers's attorney, Howard Moore of Atlanta, said, "One's mere presence at the scene of a riot doesn't make him guilty of riot just because he was there."[200]

Under the circumstances, it came as something of a surprise two days later when the jury returned a verdict of guilty against Sellers on the remaining charge of rioting, and Judge Grimball sentenced him to one year in prison and imposed a fine of $250. Newsman Hugh Gibson described the atmosphere as one of "stunned silence," and wrote, "the apparent optimism of Sellers's Afro-styled admirers that he would escape conviction on the third and final riot charge lasted until the jury's 'guilty' verdict was announced."[201]

Sellers's attorneys blasted the verdict, calling the Orangeburg incident "the first one-man riot in history because their client was the only person singled out for prosecution." The *News and Courier* opined prophetically in an editorial the next day, "The argument over responsibility for the death of three young Negroes as the outcome of the 1968 disorders at Orangeburg will not be settled, we suppose, by the verdict of this jury in convicting Cleveland Sellers, any more than it was settled by the acquittal last year at Florence of nine State Highway Patrolmen accused of violating the civil rights of the demonstrators."[202]

Bail was set at $5,000 for Sellers, pending appeal, and he was granted by Grimball permission to travel out of the state after he agreed to waive extradition should the sentence be upheld. He told reporters at the time that during the appeals process, he "would probably go back to school."[203] During the interim period between conviction and final appeal, Sellers did return to college, earning a masters degree in education from Harvard.[204] His sentence began March 1, 1973, more than five years after the Orangeburg shootings, and upon his release seven months later he called on Governor John C. West to reopen the investigation into the shootings.

West, who had won praise as lieutenant governor for his diplomatic handling of the student petitions a month after the 1968 shootings, rejected Sellers's suggestion, saying, "I frankly don't see any useful purpose would be served by reopening matters which have been investigated and resolved in the courts." He added that "the events were most unfortunate. To reopen old wounds would serve no useful purpose."[205]

Sellers, who would later receive a doctorate in education from the University of North Carolina at Greensboro[206] and eventually return to South Carolina as a faculty member in African American Studies at the University of South Carolina, said at the time of his 1973 release, "We've been victorious in winning our freedom for a crime we did not commit. The forces of racism and capitalism have lost another battle."[207]

Twenty years later, at the intervention of journalist and author Jack Bass and Columbia businessman Rhett Jackson, Sellers was pardoned. Jackson, a member and past chairman of the state's Probation, Pardon and Parole Board, took up the cause and quietly lobbied the issue with colleagues on the seven-member panel, gaining all but one vote. Jackson, a fraternity brother of McNair's in their days at USC, was a lay leader of the Methodist Church and an active moderate in political and community issues.

The Subdued Aftermath

Public attention faded in the wake of the shootings and trials, at least partially because of the series of events that would make 1968 and the immediately subsequent years a period of remarkable and tragic violence across America. Two months after the Orangeburg shootings, Dr. Martin Luther King was assassinated in Memphis, and two months later, Senator Robert F. Kennedy was shot dead in Los Angeles during his campaign for the Democratic nomination for president. The aftershocks of those events, building on the assassinations of President John F. Kennedy in 1963, brought the country's nerves to the brink of hysteria.

The mounting sentiment against the nation's participation in the Vietnam War, and the attendant resistance to the draft of American young men to serve in that conflict, also tended to reshape the political agenda and priorities of the nation, and particularly those of the Democratic Party. With the death of King and the announcement by President Lyndon Johnson on March 31, 1968, that he would not seek another term of office, the nation lost two of its staunchest forces for the advancement of civil rights. Johnson's withdrawal was seen as a concession to the antiwar and antidraft elements of the party, and the subsequent eruption of violence and party disunity at the Democratic National Convention in Chicago that summer tended to replace civil rights with war resistance as the party's chief agenda item.

Orangeburg remained a matter of suspended anxiety and curiosity for many South Carolinians. McNair's reliance on the FBI investigation to clarify the issues of Orangeburg and to satisfy the interests of those seeking a South Carolina–based probe of the shootings proved to be something of a catch-22 since the report was not publicly released at the time. McNair later said that he was given a look at portions of the report at the behest of President Johnson and his FBI liaison "Deke" DeLoach. What he was shown was a report that shots had been fired toward the railroad warehouse across the street from the area of the Claflin and S.C. State campuses. The shots in question, however, it was later determined, were fired well before the patrol gunfire, and some one hundred feet from where the S.C. State shootings took place.

For McNair's part, he remained constant in his support of law enforcement, some say because of his enduring respect for Pete Strom and his colleagues, as well as an overall belief that anything less than full support for the police would have undermined the effectiveness of law enforcement in general.

The eight seconds of shootings in Orangeburg on February 8, 1968, left profound wounds on the state's conscience, many of which never fully healed. Oral-history interviews with survivors of the shootings and the families of those killed gives testimony to the long-term impact the incident had on the lives of the students. They told of physical and psychological ordeals, but they also told of a substantial number of men and women who had attained success in corporate, professional, and military careers. The events of February 8, 1968, Cleveland Sellers later said, "became the litmus test of civil rights in South Carolina."

Thirty years after the shootings, McNair, Ike Williams, and Cleveland Sellers sat down to lunch at the Capital City Club in Columbia and spent more than an hour in friendly discourse. Two years later, McNair attended a ceremony honoring Maceo Nance on the S.C. State campus, only months before Nance's death in 2000. McNair and Sellers greeted each other with civility, but through it all, there was little evidence that either had changed his mind over the issues and causes that lay at the heart of the 1968 crisis.

As years passed, McNair spoke more freely about the events and granted an interview with South Carolina State historian William Hine as part of an oral history of the shootings. Sellers and others observed the anniversary of the February 1968 shootings with various types of events. At the 2001 observance on the S.C. State campus—held in Martin Luther King Auditorium, not more than a few hundred feet from the site of the shootings—McNair was invited, but the serious illness of his son, Bobby, coincided with the scheduled event and caused him to decline the invitation. Governor Jim Hodges spoke, expressing the state's regret at the shootings, and two years later, newly elected Governor Mark Sanford issued an apology on behalf of the state.

Sellers also spoke at the 2001 observance on the S.C. State campus, tearfully recalling the events that had taken place thirty-three years earlier and the impact they had left on victims and their families. Present in the crowded hall were many who held distinct personal memories of the 1968 shootings, including activist John Stroman, as well as a number of survivors. There were families of the shooting victims, as well as other alumni, faculty, administrators, and members of the student body who had not even been born in 1968. Present were Ike Williams, leader of the 1967 boycotts, and Rhett Jackson.

In a 2004 presentation to the Kosmos Club of Columbia, Sellers renewed his contentions of previous years. "The State and its leaders deliberately distorted the facts surrounding the tragedy," he told the group of "town and gown" leaders. "Their response to this tragedy was to discourage real discussion or a search for the truth. A veil of secrecy and a cloak of silence were the methods employed to avoid responsibility or culpability. There has been no contrition and now only a state of denial."[208]

McNair's reluctance to join a public debate over the Orangeburg shootings left questions about his own personal sentiments concerning the 1968 tragedy. While he had spoken with friends and granted interviews on the topic, his relatively low public visibility left ambiguities for those seeking to bring some measure of closure to the event. He chose the publication of the present book to issue his strongest public statement to date on the Orangeburg shootings:

February 8, 1968 was one of the most tragic moments in our state's modern history. The fact that I was Governor at the time placed the mantle of responsibility squarely on my shoulders, and I have borne that responsibility with all the heaviness it entails for all those years.

My entire administration to that point in time—and after the tragedy—was predicated on the single principle that whatever policies we set, or actions we took, would be measured by what was best for all the citizens of the state. That something as devastating as the shooting deaths of three young men on a college campus could happen in South Carolina, particularly on my watch, was unthinkable. But it did happen. And it happened in spite of the fact that all our efforts had been directed toward avoiding just such a incident. All South Carolinians grieved with the families and friends of those young men, and I expressed my personal and deepest sympathy.

I knew we had to have a thorough and comprehensive investigation of the events surrounding this tragedy. I also knew that we as a state could not investigate ourselves, and I said so publicly at the time. As Governor, I requested an immediate, full and complete investigation by the United States Justice Department, knowing that such an investigation would be exhaustive and have full credibility. Following the investigation, the findings were adjudicated in the federal court system and all of those proceedings are matters of public record.

Those proceedings, however factual and conclusive, cannot diminish the gravity of the tragedy. It was a moment in time which should have never occurred, a moment we had fought so very hard to avoid, a moment which caused all of us to come together in prayer to ask guidance for the future of our state so that no such incident would ever happen again.

My hopes and concerns for our state are no less important to me now than they were when I first took the oath of office in 1965. The events at Orangeburg confirmed how essential it is to develop and maintain open and responsive lines of communication, dialog and strong diverse relationships. For the common good of our state, I believe it is critical that all citizens, no matter the circumstance of their birth or experience, commit to and remain diligent about continuing these efforts.

We must never allow another such tragic moment.[209]

11

The Rise of Soul Power

More than two months before highway patrol gunfire took the lives of three students at South Carolina State in Orangeburg, the seeds of a far longer and more complex dispute were being sown sixty miles away in Charleston. It was a large-scale, multitiered conflict with national implications, and it would stir deep passions that would again test the state's will to withstand violence. It would also bring to the fore a new cadre of black political leaders who would guide the state toward a decade and a half of significant African American influence in South Carolina's affairs.

At its outset, the 113-day strike of low-income hospital workers at the Medical College of South Carolina in the spring of 1969 exposed two of the state's rawest political nerves—civil rights and organized labor. It was, in the words of a later chronicler, the joining of "union power" and "soul power" into what organizers hoped would "[unlock] the secret to a whole tide of labor organizing among America's poor and unskilled."[1]

Even in ordinary times, the joining of those powerful forces of the 1960s would have had an enormous impact on a state that was at best politically lukewarm to either civil rights or organized labor. But coming during times that were far from ordinary, the strike caught South Carolina at its most vulnerable politically and socially. By the time the hospital's labor troubles came to the attention of the state as a whole in the spring of 1969, South Carolina was reeling from the tragedy at Orangeburg the previous February, and the newly forged politics of moderation were still highly suspect among many rank-and-file South Carolinians. For a place where racially divisive absolutes had ruled public policy for most of its three centuries as a political entity, five years of racial moderation scarcely constituted a secure and permanent mandate. If anything, backlash and skepticism in the wake of the

Orangeburg shootings were creating a new set of potentially incendiary conditions fueled by rightward drifts among whites and aggressive tactics by activist blacks.

"The killings of those youngsters [in Orangeburg] set us all on fire," said Bill Saunders, a friend of Cleveland Sellers and a grassroots civil rights leader in Charleston who would play a pivotal role in developing and ultimately resolving the issues of the hospital strike. "We were ready to work hard."[2]

The College's Troubled Past

As with many such conflicts, the causes of the hospital strike could be traced deeply into the state's racially troubled past. The Medical College had been born in Charleston in 1823, a conspicuously transitional time when the confidence and optimism of post-Revolution days in the state's powerful port city were beginning to give way to economic anxieties and political isolation in the years leading up to the Civil War. Charleston's longstanding affluence and prosperity had caused the number of physicians to increase rapidly in the state after the Revolution, and historian David Ramsey could boast in the early nineteenth century that "every operation possible in Paris or London could be equally well performed in Charleston."[3]

By the 1820s, however, Charleston was in the process of becoming what twentieth-century historian George Rogers termed "The Closed City." Its preeminence as a center of American shipping interests was challenged by the change from sail to steam as the source of power for oceangoing vessels, and the shift of cotton production westward into Alabama and Mississippi was damaging the fortunes of lowcountry planters. Coupled with the economic decline was the fear of slave insurrections, and, Rogers wrote, "the [economic] Panic of 1819, the Missouri Compromise debates of 1822, and the Denmark Vesey insurrection of 1822 jolted the city and changed ultimately her way of life—from a city that had looked outward to one that henceforth looked inward."[4]

It was during that time, in what Rogers called "the great shift" in the minds of Charlestonians, that the Medical College was born in 1823, a creation of the Charleston-dominated Medical Society of South Carolina. From its origins, the Medical College was beset with financial uncertainties and political bickering, and by 1831 rivalries between the college's faculty and the Medical Society led to the state chartering it as the Medical College of South Carolina. It eventually became a full-fledged state institution in 1913.[5]

By the mid-twentieth century, the college had shed neither the political eccentricity nor the racial inclinations of its nineteenth-century origins. An administrator newly arrived at the institution in 1967, John Wise, described himself as being "absolutely astounded by the archaic policies of the Medical College," observing, "they didn't even have a computer when I came here. . . . They were still doing bookkeeping by pen and ink."[6] Wise was also confronted with what a scholar later called "conditions at the Medical College [that] mirrored perfectly the paternalistic racism of the wider culture."

Its operating structure "was loose enough to allow this racism to manifest itself. The college had no black nursing students enrolled and the college's hospital had no black doctors on the staff.[7] Almost all of the lower-echelon non-professional positions—nurses' aides, practical nurses, orderlies, kitchen workers—were staffed by blacks. The organizational structure governing the operations of the hospital provided no job descriptions, no personnel procedures, and no vehicle for airing grievances."[8]

Even within South Carolina's notoriously fragmented governmental structure, the Medical College was an especially distressed case of organizational dysfunction. It was described as "a state-run institution [where] the absence of clear-cut operational procedure was consistent with the state government as a whole, where bureaucratic guidelines had failed to keep pace with a burgeoning public sector. Until the state legislature mandated the Board of Trustees to select a president in 1966, the Dean of the College of Medicine had run the hospital and the college—'out of his hip pocket,' in the words of one administrator."[9] McNair himself described conditions at the Medical College as "just terrible." He said, "There was . . . a total lack of personnel policy and personnel procedures."[10]

The Medical College's administrative deficiencies were not unknown to its president, Dr. William J. McCord, the burly son of American missionaries in South Africa who had served for twenty years as professor and chairman of the chemistry department before being chosen to head the institution in 1964. He had secured a $12 million grant from the U.S. Department of Health, Education and Welfare (HEW) for physical expansion and research, and he had also brought on board Wise, an Air Force veteran from Pennsylvania, to deal with the institution's operational deficiencies.[11]

To go with the visible signs of racial isolation came the less visible irritants. "The feeling of condescension with which most whites at the hospital traditionally viewed blacks increasingly came in conflict with the rising expectations of black workers," it was later observed. "Even though very few hospital workers had participated in the protests of the early 1960s, the civil rights struggles throughout the South had increased the workers' awareness of the prejudices that pervaded southern culture."[12]

The Makings of a Strike

In that setting, things came to a head on December 5, 1967, when five black nonprofessional workers were discharged at the beginning of their shift. Accounts varied as to the reason for their dismissal. One came from Mary Moultrie, the twenty-six-year-old hospital worker who was daughter of a Charleston Navy Yard worker and who would later become president of the fledgling Local 1199-B of the National Hospital and Nursing Home Employees Union. "The head nurse was in a bad mood. She refused to follow standard procedure, which was to review each patient's status with the workers before they made their rounds. She told them just to read the charts if they wanted to know anything. Of course, there are things on the charts which these workers wouldn't understand. That's why the review was required in the first place. These women came to me to see if I could help them. I talked to Bill Saunders about this and he agreed to help us try to get them back to work." The hospital's version was that "the 'uncooperative' workers 'increased their provocative attitudes to the point that the head nurse gave them a choice of carrying out instructions or leaving the job. They left.'"[13]

In the ensuing weeks, things simmered, and Moultrie and Saunders went to two members of Charleston's traditional black leadership, Reginald Barrett Sr. and J. Arthur Brown. They were members of an informal committee that had been organized in 1963 to investigate grievances of black workers and patients at the Medical College Hospital,[14] and within days, the workers were reinstated. Some said it took the intervention of the HEW—at the committee's behest—to restore the fired workers' jobs, and others said President McCord ordered the reinstatements at the HEW's "suggestion."[15]

Whatever may have been the fate of the five workers, however, the racial tempest had been stirred in Charleston and would not subside. Weekly meetings at Reginald Barrett's home involving Saunders, Moultrie, the reinstated five, and other workers not only kept the Medical College issues alive but also began to build forces that would eventually challenge the longstanding racial status quo not just at the Medical College, but in the city, as well.

Charleston, above all, treasured its gentility and refinement. The shabby condition of many of their once-elegant homes, some said, was because Charlestonians were "too poor to paint, and too proud to whitewash." University of North Carolina scholar Leon Fink observed, "Modern-day Charleston patriarchs had committed few of the rhetorical or physical excesses of a Bull Connor [Birmingham police chief known for using dogs and fire hoses on black demonstrators] in dealing with black expectations. Instead, they tended to smother dissent in an appeal to civic unity."[16] Charleston had withstood the wave of tensions accompanying lunch-counter sit-ins of the 1960s and had accommodated a successful NAACP suit challenging its segregated school system with the largely symbolic integration of its public and parochial schools. Even the significant civil rights work of Esau Jenkins and Septima Clark in the 1950s had been concentrated on nearby Johns Island and had left largely undisturbed the city itself.

Saunders, the foreman in the local Julius Weil mattress factory and a Korean War veteran, had been a product of the Progressive movement on Johns Island and was emerging as a recognized organizer of what whites would identify as Charleston's most militant wing of the civil rights movement. "Saunders, with his *Low Country Newsletter,* represented the voice of rising anger within the black community," wrote Fink. "Two important influences on him were Malcolm X and SNCC.

Saunders hosted SNCC leader Stokely Carmichael on a Christmas visit to the Charleston area in 1967."[17]

"He [Saunders] openly quarreled with older leaders. 'The situation got bad enough,' says Saunders, 'until in 1966 or 1967 I was elected to the OEO Commission and a group of black leaders got a petition against me that went to the governor [McNair] and he would not certify me as an elected commissioner.'"[18] McNair's refusal to certify Saunders threatened the Community Action Agency's federal funding until a rules change made it possible for the counties in the CAA coverage area to certify Saunders's election themselves.

Years later, Saunders would contend that the strike was not about civil rights per se, nor was the goal of the strikers the establishment of a labor union. The issue, he said, was simply economic. "Dr. King had gotten us the right to go to the Francis Marion Hotel," Saunders said, "but we didn't make enough money to afford it." Many workers at the Medical College were making below minimum wage, as were workers at other neighboring hospitals. "But Saunders said, 'we targeted the Medical College because we wanted to change the pay structure in the entire state system, and not just one institution.'"[19]

The weekly meetings of hospital workers at Barrett's home continued and attracted the attention of Isaiah Bennett, president of Local 15A, Retail, Wholesale and Department Store Workers' Union (RWDSU), which represented employees at a downtown cigar factory in Charleston. As the meetings swelled to between four and five hundred hospital workers, they outgrew Barrett's home, and Bennett's union hall became their headquarters. By October 1968, Bennett had linked the Charleston movement with another affiliate of his RWDSU organization, the New York Local 1199 of the Hospital and Nursing Home Employees Union, an ambitious union that had come to represent almost forty thousand hospital employees in the New York area in less than ten years of organizing activity.[20]

The affiliation with 1199, in turn, set off alarms within the arch-conservative Medical College administration, which countered by retaining in early October 1968 the prominent labor lawyer Knox Haynsworth Jr., a Greenville textile counsel and antiunion specialist. By October 14, President McCord had rejected a request for a meeting with Isaiah Bennett and had fired off to all nonprofessional staff of the hospital a testy, adversarial letter that said, in part:

> I have notified this union that I am sure that a majority of you would not want to get mixed up in an outfit such as theirs, and I, of course, have no intention of meeting with this tobacco workers union.
>
> In order that there be no misunderstanding as to exactly where the Medical College stands on this matter, I want to make our position crystal clear. WE DO NOT WANT A UNION HERE AT THE MEDICAL COLLEGE.

The letter closed with a not-so-veiled threat:

We, of course, consider this union matter to be extremely serious. It will affect both you and your family. It could affect you and your job here at the Medical College.

FOR THIS REASON IT IS OUR INTENTION TO RESIST THIS UNION IN ITS ATTEMPT TO GET IN HERE WITH EVERY LEGAL MEANS AT OUR DISPOSAL— MAKE NO MISTAKE ABOUT THAT.[21]

Saunders later contended that the letter and an antiunion cartoon had the opposite affect from that intended. "We got lots more members after [that]. I used to say Dr. McCord was our best organizer . . . and I almost felt guilty that we weren't paying Mr. Haynsworth ourselves."[22]

McNair's Early Concerns

As the battle lines were being drawn in Charleston and the sides were being entrenched, the alarms went off in Columbia, as well. It was clear to McNair that even as the state was still reeling from the impact of the Orangeburg tragedy, another major civil rights confrontation was underway. It was on a field that the embattled governor would not have chosen.

McNair's attention had been drawn to the Medical College's problems some time earlier, he recalled: "It [the hospital] never really had a good image. People were still going to Duke and elsewhere. The doctors in Columbia and above [the upper part of the state] really did not send their patients to Charleston. It never did become a real sophisticated teaching hospital where people from Greenville and Spartanburg would go, rather than Duke, if they had some real problem. . . . They would rather go somewhere else if they could afford it."[23]

The institution was also rife with what McNair considered the kind of political eccentricity that made it a troublesome place for progressive racial measures. "We apparently had a real festering sore down in Charleston, both in the administration, employee relations, employee practices, and all. We had been pouring money down there, and obviously, they had just been hiring people, just hiring bodies. After the fact, we determined that one of the main sources [of trouble] was attitudinal. . . . There was . . . a terrible attitudinal problem of the leadership from the top nurses to the blacks, who were nurses aides and support [personnel]." The problem, McNair said, was prevalent "even among the faculty."

"That was the hotbed of the so-called resistance movement," McNair said. "They were the John Birch conservatives. They were the leaders among that movement back then wanting to repeal the income tax, you recall. . . . The faculty were teaching very little and practicing a whole lot. Some of them . . . never walked into a classroom." It was, he said, a condition that should have surfaced earlier. "When you . . . look back on it, we have to take responsibility for not knowing about it and not delving into it."[24]

For all its complexity, however, the Charleston hospital strike was slow and deliberate in its evolution, giving McNair time to institute some of his own initiatives. Among them was the creation of a Community Relations Council in May 1968 to bring white and black leadership together in a structured setting to address Charleston's emerging racial troubles. A key member was banker Hugh Lane Sr., president of the Citizens and Southern National Bank of South Carolina (later purchased by Bank of America) and one of McNair's early supporters during his battle against the Broad Street Gang in the 1962 lieutenant governor's Democratic primary. Lane said, "After the problems in Orangeburg, the Governor was very concerned that we didn't have any communication mechanism set up to deal with these problems quickly and efficiently on the local level. He talked to me and other members of the Chamber of Commerce about forming a biracial committee to address racial problems and hopefully avoid any violence. We agreed that this type of committee was needed and the sooner we could set it up, the better."[25]

The committee comprised fifteen whites and fifteen blacks, chosen from lists compiled respectively by leaders in the white and black civic communities. Governor John C. West would use the same structure in 1971 in organizing a statewide Governor's Advisory Commission on Human Relations, the forerunner of the statutorily empowered State Human Affairs Commission. Included on the Charleston committee were Lane, liberal attorney Gedney Howe Sr., a Navy admiral, an Air Force general, an aggregation of older black businessmen, and Saunders.[26] "Its members varied from very militant to very conservative blacks, and from very liberal to absolute segregationist whites," according to one account.[27]

Anticipating a Long Hot Summer

The chairman of the group was Father Henry L. Grant, a black Episcopal priest who was director of St. John's Episcopal Mission and who saw his role as trying to "interpret the community one to the other."[28] Father Grant, a figure readily identified as an activist in civil rights matters, later recalled:

A few weeks before the committee was formed, I was asked to speak to the Charleston Rotary Club. They'd never had a black person attend one of their meetings, much less speak at one, but they were worried about the prospects of violence that summer of 1968, and I think they wanted me to reassure them that things in Charleston were quiet.

I didn't. A popular slogan at that time, which was voiced nationally by the Black Panthers and then picked up in the national media, was "it's going to be a long, hot summer." The white community was saying, "Law and Order. Law and Order." My message to the Rotary Club was that law and order is a two-way street and traffic is heavy on both sides. I'd had 40 summers and they had all been long and they had all been hot, and one more didn't bother me.[29]

McNair's effort to create a community forum to address the racial issues in Charleston was accompanied by a move he hoped would slow down debate on another element of the conflict in the port city, that of a labor union inside a government agency. "There were two sets of issues down there," McNair later said.

> One was jobs and better working relationships, and the other was recognition and bargaining [with a union]. We were caught in the middle of trying to improve the work relationships and improve the working conditions . . . without getting ourselves in trouble over on the legal side where it came to negotiating or recognizing [the union] or bargaining.
>
> So we tried quickly to define the issues . . . and make it clear by an enunciation of a state policy that the state was neither going to recognize a union nor engage in collective bargaining. Now, we did not say and did not intend to say that people could not join if they wanted to and belong if they wanted to. But we did say that in the public sector we were not going to recognize a union, and we were not going to engage in collective bargaining.[30]

"We recognized we had problems," he acknowledged, "and we had some justification on the part of the workers. At the same time, that [forming a union] was not the way to solve it."[31]

McNair, whose antiunion posture went back to his days in the House of Representatives as champion of the state's right-to-work law, staked out a position against public recognition of unions, a position that was based more on bluff and political clout than legal authority. There were various versions of the authority from which McNair drew his position. McNair himself said in early April 1969, "There is a law . . . under which the hospital, and other state institutions, cannot bargain with that union."[32]

Others contended that there was only legal precedent, among them Attorney General Daniel R. McLeod:

> Judge Singletary [Circuit Court Judge Clarence Singletary] issued what is the only decision that's ever been issued in the state on the question of whether a public employee has the right or whether or not the public body can bargain collectively with its employees. His holding was that it couldn't.
>
> It was not appealed, although we had hoped that it could be appealed so that we could have at least some definite adjudication of this issue by the Supreme Court of the state.[33]

The State's Case against Union Recognition

Others have cited McLeod as the source of the antiunion position. According to one account, "From the beginning, the hospital turned a deaf ear to all talk of negotiation, referring interested parties to the interpretation of the state statutes by Attorney General Daniel McLeod, who said that without specific legislation public employees had no right to collective bargaining and, further, that no state agency could authorize such discussions."[34] McLeod was also cited by Charleston attorney Kaye L. Koonce in her 1981 paper for the University of South Carolina Law School. "In 1965, South Carolina Attorney General Daniel R. McLeod issued an opinion that stated that neither the State nor any other political subdivision within the State has the right to recognize a union or to bargain with one. Mr. McLeod's opinion was not based on any State statute; there has never been a statute in South Carolina which by its plain meaning prohibits the State from recognizing and bargaining with a union. Even the State's right-to-work law does not apply to public employees."[35] Whatever may have been the source of authority, the all-white General Assembly stepped in on April 30, 1969, to pass a resolution "'affirming' Gov. Robert E. McNair's position that the state cannot lawfully bargain with striking hospital workers in Charleston."[36]

McNair followed up quickly with an address to the South Carolina Bar Association on May 10 in Myrtle Beach, stating, "In a sense this is not a simple test of will or a test of strength. This is a test of our whole governmental system as we have known it in South Carolina."[37] By the time the state got around to clarifying its legal position, however, much of the policy-setting and lawmaking was after the fact. The long, hot summer promised by Father Grant was well underway, and the political heat had preceded the summer heat by some months. In the fall of 1968 both sides—the union and the Medical College—became entrenched, and with little communication between the two sides, things were escalating significantly. In October 1968, the union was officially chartered 1199-B, the first out-of-state union for the Hospital and Nursing Home Employees Union. Mary Moultrie, a $1.33-an-hour nurse's aide at the Medical College, was elected president. Moultrie had been born and raised near the Medical College Hospital and had once served as a practical nurse in a New York City hospital. She was described as "possessing charisma, a strong physical bearing, and steely nerves."[38] Moultrie and Saunders had been introduced to activism by Charleston civil rights patriarch Esau Jenkins, and they had worked together on numerous occasions.

Neither Saunders nor Moultrie claimed they wanted a strike. "At the beginning, all the hospital administration had to do was meet with us and address the workers' legitimate complaints," Saunders later said. "We never wanted a strike and at first we didn't want a union. A strike was too expensive and it wouldn't get much support from the community."[39] Moultrie agreed. "Nobody wanted to go out on strike," she said. "We did everything we could to get things resolved."[40]

The stalemate persisted, however. Efforts by workers to meet with McCord were interpreted by the hospital to constitute negotiations with organized labor and were therefore considered to be prohibited under the McNair doctrine that the state could not recognize a union. One such rejection came when a group of workers tried to meet with President McCord in November, and attorney Haynsworth's position was that the Medical College Hospital and a sister institution, the Charleston County Hospital, were "political subdivisions" and therefore excluded from provisions of the National Labor Relations Act requiring good-faith negotiation.[41] It was not lost on the protesting workers that McCord's upbringing had been as a privileged white in the racially separated apartheid-era South Africa.

In December, things intensified, and some two hundred people set off the first of what became periodic demonstrations outside the Medical College administration building. In subsequent weeks, protesting workers met with members of the Charleston legislative delegation, and the HEW was requested to investigate wage and hour practices at the institution. Mounting political pressures from various workers' initiatives, it has been speculated, led eventually to the hospital administration agreeing to schedule a series of monthly meetings with workers to hear grievances.

The first meeting was set for March 19, and it proved to be a fateful turning point in the proceedings. Ground rules had been set for the meetings that provided that an equal number of employees from the pro-union element and from the workforce in general would be invited to discuss grievances. Accounts vary as to what actually took place at that critical meeting, but the meeting turned into a bitter confrontation out of which the actual strike quickly grew.

One account, carried in the pro-management trade publication *Southern Hospitals,* described events as follows:

> Each side accused the other of packing its representation to have a larger number present than the other side. Each side was to have seven representatives. Both sides showed up with a larger number than agreed upon. There is no question that approximately 100 employees of the Medical College Hospital left their jobs during the time this meeting was to be conducted. Some 30 to 50 of the employees left the designated meeting room and moved into the Board of Directors' room and began chanting and singing. They refused to leave the Board of Directors' room until Charleston City Police . . . gave them the option of leaving or being arrested. The employees leaving their work stations ranged from janitors and elevator operators to nurses' aides. Twelve of these employees were employed in the intensive care section of the hospital. . . . These twelve were the only employees working in this area at the time they left their jobs. The hospital discharged these 12 workers.[42]

Moultrie's account was at variance with that of the trade publication:

> President McCord issued an invitation to me and eleven other workers to meet with him to discuss grievances. Dr. McCord was not there; he had Mr. William Huff, one of the College's Vice Presidents, attend. We asked to see President McCord. He said that wasn't possible. Also, they invited more non-union members than us, so we were outnumbered, so we got others to come, too. We

went over to President McCord's office and we had a sit-in. There were more than 12 of us by then. People heard about it in the hospital and on their lunch break or rest break they came and joined us. Regardless of what was said, no one left a patient in any danger. First of all, we wouldn't do that—we were not irresponsible—and secondly, there were always other workers on the floors. We were angry that the newspapers reported that we left our posts and our patients. We were mad that they'd believe that sort of stuff. Anyway, we stayed in Dr. McCord's office until the police came and told us to go to work or go to jail. We went back to the hospital. But when we got back to our jobs, we got fired. That night we voted to strike.[43]

Charleston Strike Becomes a National Issue

What ensued was described as one hundred days that rocked Charleston "to its foundation." "In the one hundred days that it took to settle the strike, Charleston witnessed more than eight hundred arrests, hundreds of demonstrations and rallies, a dusk-to-dawn curfew, numerous fire bombings, and more than five hundred National Guardsmen with fixed bayonets in the city streets. This issue with such a deceptively inauspicious start soon mushroomed to include foremost civil rights and labor leaders in the nation, the state governor, the state legislature, both houses of Congress, the Secretary of Labor, the Secretary of Health, Education and Welfare, and the closest advisors to President Nixon."[44]

Suddenly, it was no longer a local issue. Within days, it became a national labor cause, and the *Wall Street Journal* was trumpeting the national organizing ambitions of the fledgling Brooklyn Local 1199. It was also rapidly becoming more than a labor issue. It was the opportunity viewed by many for the Southern Christian Leadership Conference (SCLC) to take up the cause of its assassinated leader, Dr. Martin Luther King, who had been killed a year earlier during the Memphis sanitation workers' strike. "1199 had . . . been preparing itself for some time for an escalating civil rights–based struggle," according to one later account. "Its ties to the campaigns of Martin Luther King Jr. and the SCLC, formalized symbolically in Coretta Scott King's honorary chairmanship in 1968 of the union's national organizing committee, now took on critical significance."[45]

In a statement supported by nine national civil rights organizations, including the NAACP, the Urban League, the Congress of Racial Equality (CORE), and the A. Philip Randolph Institute, Mrs. King noted that the right of public workers to unionize "is precisely the same issue that led to the tragedy in Memphis last year," referring to her late husband's assassination.[46]

The mushrooming proportions of the strike also began to cause some divisions. According to scholars Leon Fink and Brian Greenberg, "More moderate local figures, shy of the projected strategy, separated themselves, or were shoved aside, from the ensuing events." Among those were Isaiah Bennett, an original backer of the hospital workers, who was described as "openly opposed [to] the strategic arrangement with the SCLC" and who continued to "search for compromise through contacts with local authorities." The South Carolina Labor Council of the AFL-CIO, headed by longtime McNair ally Sinway Young, chose to remain on the sidelines, as did the Charleston branch of the National Maritime Union, which cited "racial overtones we cannot accept."[47]

"I have to give the AFL-CIO an awful lot of credit," McNair later said. "Sinway Young . . . took the position that this was not something they ought to be involved with. It should not be a labor dispute because we had pretty well made it clear that we were not going to recognize a union. . . . Sinway's bottom line was that it would hurt him and hurt the image of his union to get involved . . . so they stayed out."[48]

There were defections among the local black churches, as well, and the Inter-denominational Ministerial Alliance, a citywide association for the enhancement of black welfare, refused to commit itself.[49] The local defections created a perception of two-tiered leadership of the strike, with Saunders and Moultrie directing the local effort and SCLC increasingly viewed as the moving force at the national level. "The Charleston strike . . . offered the SCLC the chance to renew its purpose and strength," Fink and Greenberg wrote. "Ralph Abernathy's efforts in 1968 to pick up the mantle of King's Poor People's Campaign were seriously hampered by the mud, indiscipline, and generally unfocused strategy of the Resurrection City encampment in Washington, D.C. Organizationally, the SCLC was in disrepair, internally feuding over Abernathy's leadership. . . . The SCLC decided to make Charleston its priority battlefield."[50]

Legal machinery was quickly put in place. On March 20, 1969, the day pickets first appeared at the Medical College, Ninth Circuit Court Judge Clarence E. Singletary issued a restraining order barring all picketing on Medical College premises. A day later, Singletary amended the order to allow peaceful picketing so long as there were no more than ten picketers spread twenty yards apart.[51] Speaking later at a local football stadium, Moultrie said, "We could only put five people on this field from goal post to goal post. I think even the governor, as slow as he is, could get through a picket line like that."[52]

Singletary's ruling was actually seen as an early step toward moderate management of what was rapidly becoming an ongoing event of massively disruptive potential. "Judge Singletary . . . set the mark for successful containment of the civil disturbance by restraining overzealous prosecution of the strikers," one later analyst has written. "A graduate of the College of Charleston, the judge had taken his law degree at the University of Michigan and saw himself as an enlightened moderate on race and labor matters. To his dismay, however, hospital officials [who wanted a total ban on picketing] initially seemed to have 'no idea' of the possible violent repercussions of the strike. Singletary had them meet with the mayor's legal counsel, Morris Rosen, Chief of Police John F. Conroy, and State Law Enforcement

Division [SLED] representative Leon Gasque 'to make certain that the community understood the potential.'"[53]

SCLC Commits Its "People's Power"

SCLC leader Reverend Ralph David Abernathy made his first visit to Charleston on March 31 and committed the organization to a full-fledged display of "people's power" in the port city.[54] From that point forward, the SCLC became a powerful presence in Charleston, with lieutenants such as Andrew Young and Hosea Williams setting up shop on a full-time basis and Reverend Abernathy and Mrs. King making periodic visits. The first mass march came on April 21, and Abernathy promised to "sock it to Charleston."[55] By then, SCLC leadership had also discovered that they might have made a miscalculation about the state's antiunion resolve.

"Politically, the strike organizers discovered just how far removed they were from their traditional friends. Governor McNair, originally presumed to be open to compromise, simply would not budge on the issue of union recognition. Instead, he tried to avoid it by offering new material benefits to hospital workers," it was later reported.

McNair indeed was busy establishing the premise on which his strategy was based, namely that the strike was centered on two distinct issues: improvement of wages and working conditions for the hospital workers, and recognition of the union. The first issue could be broken down into political components and addressed with the kind of maneuvering that had characterized the settlement of the 1967 student boycott at S.C. State, and one that McNair had hoped in vain could be used to settle the Orangeburg eruption in 1968. The second issue, resistance to union recognition, challenged a political imperative that had helped propel McNair into public prominence years earlier and represented something that was—in the language of the times—nonnegotiable. The two issues, to McNair, were clearly separable. The separation also created another rift among the strike backers that McNair hoped to exploit, the presumption that there were divisions between local and national leaders of the strike effort. Such a division, in which local leaders like Moultrie and Saunders would presumably place the workers' well-being above the interest of national labor and civil rights organizations if given the choice, would provide a strategic avenue for a McNair-style centrist resolution. It was his plan to create the opportunity to make such a choice become a reality.

For the union to succeed, the two issues had to be seen as part of the same package. Improved wages and working conditions for the low-income hospital workers had to come through the auspices of organized labor; otherwise the mission of Local 1199 and its collaboration with SCLC were fruitless.

All the strategies and counterstrategies, however, were being played out against a backdrop of the largest civil disturbance and unrest the state had seen in decades.

"When you could not get the government to negotiate," Andrew Young said, "you had to mobilize the entire community, the churches and the high school students in a total program of non-cooperation or economic withdrawal."[56]

"It is only when you create the same kind of crisis in the life of the community as you have in the lives of workers," Young said, "that the community will give in." Employing tactics it had used in Birmingham in 1963, the SCLC "expected that disruptive but determinedly nonviolent crowd actions would provoke authorities into a massive counter-response that would end up paralyzing normal operations of the city. In the end, the 'economic power structure' [or self-interested business leaders] would bring the 'political power structure' [state and local officials] 'in line' [toward a compromise settlement]."[57] Young, who would later become mayor of Atlanta and ambassador to the United Nations under President Jimmy Carter, was impressing even his opponents in Charleston. McNair later called him "an articulate young leader" and said, "I think none of us were surprised to see him emerge in a leadership role later on."[58] Father Grant's long, hot summer would, as McNair later noted, be a test of wills.

Reverend Abernathy made good on his vow to "sock it to Charleston," and for weeks after his April 21 pronouncement, the city lay under siege from local and national forces. "The intensity of the movement grew in late April and May," according to one account. "April ended with ten marches in six days. Abernathy called for a boycott of classes by school children. A May 11 Mother's Day March, led by Abernathy, Coretta King and AFL-CIO President Walter Reuther brought an overwhelmingly black crowd of ten thousand. Finally, on May 24, the SCLC escalated an economic boycott of King Street businesses by conducting 'shop-ins' in which demonstrators would clog grocery aisles and cash register lines."[59]

The marches were accompanied by hundreds of arrests, including that of Abernathy, and by April 25 McNair had ordered out the National Guard. An evening march on April 28 was blocked by police, and vandalism along King Street business establishments occurred. Young's plan for community crisis was beginning to take place, and Charleston mayor Palmer Gaillard began nervously to seek solutions and call for resolution to the strike.

Tensions escalated on May 1 as the Guard complement was increased to 1,200 and McNair imposed the city's first curfew since 1945. The *New York Times* called the strike "the nation's tensest civil rights struggle," and as "rock throwing, fire-bombing and some looting portended worse," Mayor Gaillard later said, "I was going to have overwhelming lawful force to overcome unlawful force."[60]

Remarkably, the peace held, due—at least partially—to the efforts of Charleston Police Chief John Conroy, a former Marine officer from Niagara, New York, who earned the title "Mr. Cool."[61] He also gained the praise of Bill Saunders, who said, "Conroy did a magnificent job. [We] got along real bad. He locked me up over and over, but he was a fair person. I give him credit that there was no violence."[62]

There were other law-enforcement initiatives in the peacekeeping effort, one of them notably coming from Pete Strom, who had borne a large measure of criticism for the February 1968, shootings at S.C. State. He was credited with "subtle help in defusing the union coalition by undermining the mutual trust among its constituent parts," according to a later study. "Strom fortified community relations leader Rev. Henry Grant's mistrust of the union and SCLC 'outsiders' and encouraged him to play an independent role in settling the strike. Grant recalled Strom telling him, 'You know, you don't have to be with [the union]. They don't have the troops. We have the troops.'"[63]

Strom was also making contact with Saunders, who later remembered a meeting with the SLED chief at the Dorchester Motor Lodge during one of the periods of increased street activity. After a conversation in which Strom alleged some danger to Saunders from white union people, Saunders said he believed that Strom "was sincere in wanting to protect him." He recalled Strom once saying, "Here, I got a number I'll give you that anytime that you're having problems, the cops stop you, you call this number and then we'll handle it.'"[64] "In the end," Saunders said, "we got to be pretty good friends." And years later, he also recalled that he never used Strom's special inside number.

McNair Meets with Strike Leader

For McNair, there arose the opportunity to exercise the kind of personal politics that had been his stock in trade on many other occasions, and it led to something of a breakthrough in diplomacy with Saunders.

> I can recall my first sit-down conference with Bill Saunders. [It] was arranged through Hugh Lane and Chief Strom. I flew into Charleston and met him in the conference room at Hawthorne Aviation. Bill was . . . dressed in his white pants with his rope belt. . . . We had a rather tense first meeting, but we chatted a little bit.
>
> It normally was my pattern, before I got into discussions, to try to determine if I could develop a relationship . . . and maybe ease the tension. I can recall when I met him, [I said,] "What in the so-and-so are you doing creating all those problems for me down here when I am from just across the river over in Hell Hole Swamp, one of your Lowcountry fellows." We really started talking, and he turned to Pete Strom . . . and said, "He ain't a mean ole' bear after all," as he had been describing me.
>
> "We had a very good, very productive meeting in which we were able to talk. I was able to explain to him the position we were in as far as union recognition was concerned, while on the other hand we were concerned about the workers. We wanted to try to resolve the thing. We recognized there were problems, and we recognized that something had to be done about it, but we could not do so in an atmosphere of confrontation."[65]

The personal diplomacy initiatives came as other aspects of the strike and demonstrations were being tested, and a transformation was quietly taking place. During the first two weeks of May, according to a later account,

> 1199 leaders reluctantly [and privately] reached the conclusion that . . . "we just did not have the cards."
>
> Relying as they were on daily transfusions of outside aid to maintain their operation, the union forces faced not only the depletion of other resources in Charleston but growing strains on their services to 1199 members in New York. A grim reassessment of the situation brought up the difficult question of how, after focusing so much energy and attention in Charleston, could the union disentangle itself without suffering a humiliating national defeat.[66]

Softening of the union and the SCLC's strength coincided with developments elsewhere. An audit of the Medical College's compliance with civil rights requirements tied to some of its HEW grants, including the $12 million grant secured by McCord, had produced evidence of thirty-seven violations, enough to create some leverage for the federal regulators in dealing with the racially troubled institution. Contact between union officials and the Atlanta field office of HEW resulted in a noncompliance report and also produced the federal recommendation that the twelve union workers whose firing had set off the strike be rehired.[67]

In a June 5 letter, HEW contended that the Medical College, as a federal contractor, would be required to develop an affirmative action plan to comply with an earlier executive order from President Nixon. A newspaper account noted that "Failure to formulate an affirmative action plan will lead to a loss of funds eventually."[68]

McNair detected that there was some movement taking place among the parties, and he undertook a critical initiative of his own. "Sometime during May," it was later written, "Governor McNair determined that the strike had little hope for settlement as long as McCord directed the administration's efforts."[69] The vice president for development at the Medical College, William Huff, quietly took over negotiations at the governor's behest.[70]

A Turning Point in Negotiations

"Huff and Saunders set up a secret meeting of worker representatives and some moderate members of the hospital administration at the Santee-Cooper hydroelectric plant in Moncks Corner, some thirty-five miles north of Charleston. Neither McCord nor members of the union or SCLC was present. It was at this meeting that the basic terms of the settlement were hammered out face-to-face, on a personal level," according to historian Stephen O'Neill.[71]

Saunders called it "the real turning point" and said, "These black and white people got together."[72] The ice was broken at least partially by an injection of old-time Charleston civility, Saunders noted. The men "went and got chairs for the ladies to sit down . . . and the attitude began to change."[73] For McNair, it was a turning point in several respects. It represented a sharp departure from the arm's length hostility of McCord and the Medical College's labor attorneys. It also represented a returning of control of the strike to local leaders. "I give him [Saunders] an awful lot of credit for being perhaps the key figure in ultimately defusing the situation and getting it in a posture where we could resolve it," McNair said. "Bill had been a leader [when] all these national figures had come in. They had sort of taken over, and they had shoved people like him and some of the others aside . . . and made this a national thing."[74]

Saunders credited Huff with helping to open up communications and create an atmosphere of trust. "We looked on Dr. McCord as coming from that South African point of view," he later said. "Bill Huff was somebody we knew could talk our language."[75]

While the face-to-face work was underway under the prodding of Saunders and Huff, the other parties were retaining information loops into key centers of influence. Andrew Young recalled, "We began to just explore a kind of agreement. . . . We were calling this information to New York and they were calling this back down to the governor's office. And the governor then was calling McCord and the officials in Charleston. So we really never sat down in the same room with the governor and his people."[76]

All the pieces seemed to be falling into place for a settlement. "Governor McNair and the Board of Trustees announced that the rehiring of the twelve workers was no longer an obstacle for them. The state presented a pay hike . . . [the minimum wage was increased from $1.30 per hour to $1.60 per hour, effective July 1].[77] The workers softened their demands for union recognition, saying that a well-structured grievance procedure and a credit union would suffice."[78]

With the agreement apparently sealed, McNair went to Charleston on June 10 to meet with the still-disgruntled faculty for what turned out to be an unexpectedly hostile meeting. "I flew down to Charleston and made my persuasive argument to the boos of some and the cheers of others," McNair later recalled.

> That visit, I think, turned out to be a good thing because I got taken on strong and hard by many of the faculty who were so resistant to doing anything about this—you know, "surrender," and all of this sort of stuff. It gave me an opportunity to respond both in a very positive, pleasant sort of way and also to respond in a way I thought we needed to respond. "After all," I said, "we had to exercise some authority. We were the ones who had to resolve this thing, and we were going to resolve it. Not everybody was going to like it, and there was no way we could do it where everybody was going to be happy."[79]

The unhappy faculty and McCord, as it turned out, had one last card to play. The settlement depended on HEW holding the line on its insistence that the twelve workers be rehired as a condition of their retaining grant monies. "State and hospital officials, anxious to end the unrest in Charleston but politically constrained from appearing to appease the strikers, could now blame Washington for forcing concessions," it was later explained.[80]

McCord meanwhile was taking his case to the state's political community in Washington, and particularly to senior Senator Strom Thurmond, a White House insider who had been a major player in the southern strategy that had helped Richard Nixon win the presidency only months earlier.

White House Intervention

According to the account presented later by scholars Fink and Greenberg, "Only hours before the planned meetings (to announce the agreements on June 12), McCord reneged on his promise to rehire the 12 workers, claiming hospital staff opposition to the move."

McCord's action, in fact, reflected a shifting of larger political forces. On the morning of the projected settlement-signing date, Congressman L. Mendel Rivers [a member of the Hell Hole Swamp Gang and a conservative Democrat representing the First Congressional District, which included Charleston] and Senator Storm Thurmond reportedly prevailed upon then–HEW secretary Robert Finch to postpone his threatened fund cutoff to the Medical College Hospital "pending a personal investigation" after he returned from a planned vacation in the Bahamas.

This federal about-face was evidence of a larger conflict within the Nixon administration over civil rights enforcement. Liberal pressure for compromise and settlement of the dispute arose from a committed group of second-level administrative staff in HEW. Politically, however, Nixon's 1968 southern strategy had looked to a different constituency and was susceptible to different pressures. In this case, the demands of state party leaders and political advisors crucial to Nixon's narrow national electoral victory could not be ignored.[81]

State Republican Chairman Ray Harris had already placed Governor McNair and his fellow Democrats on notice for any waffling on the hospital issue. Now national Republicans were told to toe the line.[82]

It would not be the last time McNair would come into direct conflict with the Nixon White House and its staunch South Carolina GOP leadership over issues with direct racial implications. A year later, in the long-delayed court-ordered desegregation of South Carolina's public schools, Nixon and McNair would find themselves in day-to-day and week-to-week conflict in a bitter fight that proved to have dangerous and explosive outcomes for the state's schools.

The 1969 intervention of the White House in the Medical College strike also had an immediate and dangerous outcome. "Collapse of the projected settlement set off two more weeks of rising tensions, including night marches, fire-bombings, and threats to tie up telephone lines as well as transportation and major business arteries," according to one later account. Even the restraint of SCLC leaders broke, and Hosea Williams declared at a June 20 rally, "White folks are crazy. White America is insane. We have played around with Charleston long enough. We're going to march in Charleston or we're going to die."[83] The unleashing of violence in the wake of the White House intervention, as it turned out, gave the Nixon administration cause to reconsider its political loyalties to the entrenched and reactionary Medical College administration. Phone calls from a labor leader to presidential counselor Daniel Patrick Moynihan alerted White House strategists to the potential danger and brought a shift in responsibility for overseeing the issue from the vacationing Finch to the no-nonsense labor secretary, George Schulz.

"Look," labor organizer Moe Foner told Moynihan, "I'm not going to be responsible, but I think you have to know, the night marches are going to continue, and this town is going to burn."[84]

The weary town, the weary strikers, the weary union, and the weary civil rights community were ready for the event to be over; the Nixon partisans had misread the circumstances and had almost set off a racial catastrophe. Charleston banker Hugh Lane, McNair's key man in the effort to organize biracial harmony in the divided city, later said,

> I got a call from a very prominent Republican from the Midwest [Mr. Schulz is from Illinois] and he said that they were concerned that the hospital strike was going to move out of Charleston and become national in scope. He said they had the FBI involved and . . . the FBI [said] that I knew more about what was going on than anybody else and they wanted to read to me the FBI report. . . . It was extremely accurate. He said, ". . . what do you think we ought to do?" Well, the answer to that was very simple, really, because the public didn't have the vaguest idea what the truth was.
>
> It was being suppressed and the press didn't know and the administration at the hospital wasn't telling the truth. I said the answer very simply was to get Bob Finch . . . to pick up the phone and call down here and say, "If you won't play by the [HEW] rules, you don't get any more money."
>
> I got a call about an hour later and he said that's what we're going to do. I got to the Community Relations Committee meeting that night and it was the first time I personally was aware that we were to the boiling point. The blacks were ready to blow the lid off, but I pleaded for 24 hours more and they agreed. Sometime during the night, McCord was called and given the ultimatum. At 6:00 A.M. the next morning Ed [Medical College board chairman Edwin Schachte] called me and said, "It's been done." I headed for Florida and my boat.[85]

Minutes of the June 26 meeting of the Community Relations Committee tersely record the back-and-forth events of the preceding weeks, including the decision by the Medical College to withdraw its offer to rehire the fired workers because it had received thirty-six resignations from the nursing staff. The minutes also detail the exchange of correspondence between Dr. McCord and HEW concerning the rehiring of the twelve workers. In early June, McCord had agreed to do so, provided that HEW stated its position in writing. Such letter was received on June 5 from a Mr. Brimm, chief of the Contract Branch, HEW.

The minutes close: "Mr. Lane requested that a statement not be issued now, but that the committee be given a few days to try to expedite a settlement. Mention was made that as of Monday, June 30, 1969, there would be a sympathy strike by dockworkers and the port would be closed. It was agreed to give the committee an opportunity to negotiate."[86]

Strike Settlement and Its Conditions

Announcement of the settlement came on Friday, June 28, and news stories the following day described "bedlam . . . in Union Hall . . . when news reached striking hospital workers and their supporters that an agreement had been reached." McNair was said to express the hope that the settlement "will restore peace and calm" to the city, and Saunders said, "We are proud the situation has been brought to a close, not only for the community and ourselves, but for the state and country as well." He called the agreement "a victory for 25,000 workers, black and white, all across the state."[87]

There were five major conditions of the settlement:

1. The twelve discharged workers and any other strikers who wished to return to work would be rehired.
2. Employees hired as replacements during the strike were to be retained as employees of the Medical College Hospital.
3. The beginning wage would be $1.60 per hour for nonprofessional workers, up from $1.30.
4. A grievance procedure would be established that permitted employees to be accompanied by a worker of his or her choice when filing a grievance.
5. A job classification and a job description would be provided to each employee upon request.[88]

A front-page Sunday editorial in the conservative News and Courier carried a grudging concession that the settlement was "in a sense, a victory for the strikers, who have been offered their same jobs and other benefits; for the State of South Carolina, which has confirmed the policy of no union contracts for public employees; for the Medical College, which now can resume its mission of ministering to the sick and training people in the practice of medicine, and best of all, the people of

Charleston and the state as a whole." The paper saved its best praise for the city's treasured gentility, which it considered to be still intact: "The public endured patiently many inconveniences. . . . Charleston knows the value of harmony at home. Let us all get back to work and enjoy it while we can."[89]

There clearly were winners and losers in the tumultuous fray, and in the heralded merger of "soul power" and union power, both elements suffered serious setbacks. Perhaps the most conspicuous disappointment came for the union itself, which all but dried up its Charleston operation within a matter of months. "Whatever its indirect 'community' benefits," it was later written, "talk of 'victory' proved premature for hospital workers' Local 1199B. At the time of settlement, many of the second-level 1199 and SCLC staff left the city still convinced that the foundation for a successful union local had been laid."

> But during the months following the strike, the MCH [Medical College Hospital] administration not only refused to authorize checkoff [payroll deduction of union dues] through the credit union but undermined the union's authority in the grievance system by limiting the number of times that the same person could serve as a grievant's representative. In addition, local union leaders faced an erosion of both outside support and internal goodwill. When [Charleston] County Hospital followed the MCH settlement with nearly identical strike-ending terms . . . outside aid to Charleston workers all but dried up. The money was gone, the issue had lost its dramatic appeal, and perhaps most important, the New York union and SCLC had other priorities [90]

The SCLC itself also suffered. In the aftermath of the Charleston strike, "Friction within the organization and failure to score truly dramatic victories with its economic organizing strategy left SCLC increasingly demoralized," according to a later analysis. "Charleston itself proved to be one more drain on the sinking civil rights organization's resources. By the end of 1969, Andrew Young was already expressing doubts about the viability of an 'exhausted organization' and left shortly afterward to pursue a political career. Other resignations followed, until in 1973 a once robust staff of 125 had been depleted to 17."[91]

For McNair, the successful settlement of the Charleston strike provided, at least in some eyes, some recovery from the Orangeburg shooting and the tarnishing of his reputation as a racial progressive. In his own mind, the Charleston strike served to toughen his image as a no-nonsense leader in times of stress. "I think my perception then was that I had developed a reputation of being firm and stern," he later said. "But, people knew once we got to a certain point, and we said something, we meant it. . . . Otherwise, you really could not deal with the kinds of problems we faced."[92]

Perhaps the biggest winner in the hospital workers' strike was the black political community in Charleston. "The one hundred days of marches, meetings, and boycotts in support of four hundred black . . . strikers marked a significant departure from the weak black protest tradition in Charleston," one scholar later wrote.

> Poor people, especially, who had been all but silent during the civil rights years, mobilized for the cause of the workers. The local mass protest transformed the face of Charleston, shattering suppositions and self-perceptions that had governed the actions of black and white alike.
>
> The symbolic victory of 1969 paid tangible benefits in the 1970s. A new, more demanding black leadership emerged to supplement, or in some cases supplant, an older conservative elite that had, under the old system, forged close political ties with the city's white elite. Black voter registration skyrocketed, and for the first time in the twentieth century, black candidates were elected to public office in Charleston.[93]

Within a year, veterans of the hospital-strike leadership not only assumed political positions in the Charleston area, they were among the first black legislators elected in the twentieth century to the House of Representatives in Columbia. Funeral director Herbert Fielding was elected to the House of Representatives, along with minister Robert Woods in the 1970 elections. They were joined in the 1970 General Assembly by two more black legislators from Columbia—attorney and funeral director I. S. Leevy Johnson and attorney James Felder. Barely missing election from Charleston County was James E. Clyburn, the South Carolina State activist as a student who had become executive director of the South Carolina Farm Workers Association. Clyburn, who finished twelfth in a race for eleven seats from Charleston in 1970, went on to become the first black executive to be appointed to the governor's staff in South Carolina when he joined the administration of Governor John C. West in 1971. He later became the state's commissioner of human affairs from 1975 until 1992, and in 1992 Clyburn was elected the state's first black congressman of the twentieth century, representing the Sixth District. Saunders went on to serve for almost ten years as a member of the state's Public Service Commission, the agency that regulates electric utilities and transportation carriers.

One Confrontation Ends—Another Breaks Out

For McNair and his administration, however, there was hardly time to celebrate the peaceful conclusion of the Charleston strike. By June 1969, civil rights issues and incidents in South Carolina were multiplying and overlapping to such an extent that there was rarely a day in which at least one—and usually more than one—instance of racial tension was not erupting. Concurrent with the emerging tensions of the Charleston hospital strike was the aftermath of the Orangeburg shootings, and it was during the trial of the nine highway patrolmen in Florence, on May 18–28, 1969, that McNair, Pete Strom, and Bill Huff were initiating personal diplomacy with Bill Saunders and leaders of the strike to break the impasse at the Medical College Hospital.

Also during that period, violence broke out on another black college campus in South Carolina. This time it was at Voorhees College, a small Episcopalian institution in Cleveland Sellers's home town of Denmark. On Monday, April 28—the same day some six hundred marchers sympathetic to the hospital workers were blocked from proceeding down King Street in Charleston—twenty-four Voorhees College students armed with rifles, guns, and knives seized the administration building of the college. A day later they occupied the college's science building.

There ensued a delicate and disputed period of communication and negotiation in which the college's administration came to McNair for assistance to regain the buildings while faculty and the occupying students discussed a settlement to the dispute. The outcome was the arrival on campus that Tuesday afternoon, April 29, of National Guardsmen, highway patrolmen, and SLED agents to secure the buildings that had been in students' hands since the night before.

Their arrival coincided with the students' vacating their positions, reportedly having reached an agreement to their demands with two faculty members. Within moments of their leaving the buildings, however, the students were arrested by law-enforcement officers, taken to prison in Columbia, and charged with riot and unlawful assembly. Bond was posted two days later, and all but one of them—a student charged with possession of an unlawful weapon—were released.[94]

The incident set off a storm of protest from the civil rights community, and even as McNair was exploring diplomatic avenues for peaceful solutions to the Charleston strike, he was being assailed for the show of force at Voorhees by Allard Allston of the South Carolina Human Relations Council. Allston's position, endorsed by a cross-section of college and state leaders, including NAACP field secretary I. DeQuincey Newman, stated:

> The fact that the Board of Trustees of the college had laid the framework for state intervention does not exonerate Gov. McNair from his despicable attempt to obtain political aggrandizement from an unfortunate confrontation —a confrontation which had no violent overtures until the Governor, acting callously upon an apparently pre-determined plan, ordered troops onto campus.
>
> This action was taken despite what critics said was the request of the president of the college for additional time to finalize an amiable agreement between the administration and the dissident students.

McNair brushed aside Allston's attack at a news conference the same day: "The state is not in a position of negotiating with armed militants." He said it would be his policy that whenever "militant insurrectionists" take over property he would use whatever force is necessary to remove them "in the interest of public safety and society," and stressed: "Society cannot survive if we allow a band of armed insurrectionists to act like this."

McNair said that the intervention of law enforcement on the Voorhees campus came at the request of President John Potts and the chairman of the college's board of trustees. The request, he said, was made by telephone and came during a meeting he was holding with Dr. Martin Luther King Sr., father of the slain civil rights leader, and two of his associates to discuss the Charleston hospital strike. His visitors heard the request, McNair said, and the telephone conversation was taped to provide further verification. McNair also confirmed that President Potts had requested a delay in the arrival of law enforcement on the campus, but the request was denied, he said, because McNair felt it put the state "in the position of bargaining with insurrectionists."[95]

The ongoing press of crisis-level activity in the governor's office did not go unnoticed by at least one State House regular reporter. A day after the heated exchanges over the Voorhees College action, Charleston's Hugh Gibson noted: "A measure of peace returned to Gov. Robert E. McNair's office Friday as he prepared to end one of the most tension-filled weeks in his four-year administration."

"In rapid succession," Gibson wrote,

McNair had:

— Dispatched National Guard troops to the campus of Voorhees College where armed rebels had seized two college buildings. . . .
— Won General Assembly endorsement of his position that state policy prohibits bargaining with Charleston's striking hospital workers union.
— Beefed up National Guardsmen, highway patrolmen and SLED agents patrolling the strife-torn Port City, and followed that up Thursday by declaring a state of emergency and imposing a nightly curfew.
— Reaffirmed his "no bargaining" stand at a press conference the same day, and warned that any repetition of the Voorhees incident will bring similar state action.

Gibson surmised: "The hope—almost a prayer—was that the tranquility would continue through the night and weekend."[96]

It was Gibson who had hailed McNair's ascension to the governorship in 1965 as ushering in an era of good feeling. By 1967, the Charleston writer was calling him "a hard-nosed Scot from Berkeley County's Hell Hole Swamp country [who] today stands as undisputed master of South Carolina's government and claimant for the title of 'strongest' governor this state has known in decades."[97]

Whatever distinction and accolades McNair was gaining as the turbulent 1960s drew to a close were being tempered by the reality that the era Gibson had predicted would be one of good feeling had been anything but that, and had evolved into an era of danger and human risk for South Carolina. For all the political skills and persuasive powers that McNair had brought to the governor's office fifty months earlier, he was being tested even more severely as to the firmness and steadiness of his hand at the helm of the state's law-enforcement strategies and resources.

Where Gibson had wistfully mused about a tranquil weekend for the governor and his staff, there would—in fact—be few moments of peace as McNair headed into the final year of his administration. Lying ahead with certainty and with daunting complexity was the reality of South Carolina's long-deferred desegregation of its statewide public-school system. That moment of truth, coming a full sixteen years after *Brown v. Board of Education,* would be the ultimate test of McNair's abilities as a governor, as a political operative, and as a law-enforcement strategist. The year 1970 would also measure the state's tolerance for civil unrest, racial change, and political moderation. The newly energized two-party system, the growing anxiety over the Vietnam War, and an upcoming governor's election that might well be a referendum on the state's newly found middle ground on racial matters promised, above all, that there would, indeed, be few moments of tranquillity in the remaining months of the McNair administration.

12

South Carolina Runs
Out of Time, Courts

For all the state's professions of good intentions and goodwill, school desegregation in South Carolina entering the school year 1969–1970 was still largely a matter of legal resistance and token compliance. Fifteen years after the *Brown v. Board of Education* desegregation decree of the U.S. Supreme Court, and fourteen years after the court's admonition to desegregate "with all deliberate speed," the state had not made much headway toward either directive.

State Superintendent of Education Cyril B. Busbee had this description of conditions in South Carolina:

> Under pressure, the schools moved into a so-called freedom of choice system whereby black children and their parents were permitted to request assignment to previously all white schools. This was done with a required amount of publicity concerning the opportunity to transfer.
>
> While it was referred to as a freedom of choice system, freedom of choice was actually extended only to black pupils and the pattern of white attendance upon schools was generally maintained.[1]

Evidence of lingering inequality in the financing of public education, in fact, was clear across the South years after the *Brown* decision and its companion, *Brown II,* which in 1955 ordered that school desegregation be expedited. White schools, whose per capita annual funding was estimated to be 70 percent higher than that of black schools in South Carolina in 1954, still had 50 percent higher funding in 1960.[2] As late as 1966, in one sixteen-county area of Alabama, white schools and their contents were worth $981 per pupil, as compared to $238 per pupil in black schools.[3] While border states had desegregated thousands of all-black and all-white schools in the years shortly after the Supreme Court decisions, "it was in the Deep South that the collective heel dug in."[4]

In light of the lingering evidence of inequality among schools on a racial basis, civil rights activists fretted that there was a lack of teeth in the enforcement of the *Brown* decisions, a condition that they felt allowed defiant southern states to wriggle off the hook in meeting the requirements of the court's decisions. The teeth came with the Civil Rights Act of 1964, which created two enforcement mechanisms: Title IV, authorizing the Justice Department to file suit against school districts upon complaint that equal educational opportunity was being denied; and Title VI, which authorized the termination of federal assistance to school districts in defiance of the *Brown* desegregation orders. In the words of Leon A. Panetta, civil rights chief in the Nixon Department of Health, Education and Welfare, "the whole Title VI program became a North-South battleground as well as a liberal-conservative one."[5]

A year later, the Voting Rights Act of 1965 would facilitate black voting and provide political muscle to support the 1964 Civil Rights Act in abolishing the remnants of public-school segregation and its attendant inequalities. The two acts not only gave teeth and muscle to judicial and legislative initiatives out of Washington, they also affirmed the federal resolve to intervene in the South, where states had resisted full compliance with court decrees setting aside the tacit acceptance of segregation that had characterized federal-state strategies since the end of Reconstruction in the nineteenth century.

Those two acts, and their powerful historical implications, would change and influence South Carolina politics tangibly and almost immediately. Registered subsequent to the 1965 Voting Rights Act were 75,000–85,000 black voters, most of whom identified themselves as Democrats and whose addition to the voting rolls provided a significant part of McNair's victory margin in the governor's race of 1966. They would also form an increasingly important part of Democratic voter strength in subsequent elections for the rest of the twentieth century. And as Panetta had predicted, it was the 1964 Civil Rights Act, and its provision for enforcement of school desegregation, that would largely define political issues and political parties in the South and raise the level of political combat far above the years of "doing the right thing" and "orchestrating peace" in South Carolina. The era of good feeling that had ushered in McNair's term in 1965 would become a fond memory by the time he left office sixty-eight months later.

Richard Nixon and the GOP Emergence

South Carolina Republicans, who believed that they had lost only a battle in Barry Goldwater's crushing defeat by Lyndon Johnson in the 1964 election, were clamoring to win the war for the White House in 1968. Their candidate this time was Richard M. Nixon, defeated in 1960 by John F. Kennedy but looking to many

Dixie traditionalists like a man who could understand "the Southern mind and how to approach Southern problems."[6]

Nixon bought in on what was heralded as the southern strategy as early as 1966, seeing in Goldwater's strong showing in Dixie the makings of his own political comeback. Refashioned as a southern-style conservative, Nixon satisfied a significant element of the political South by saying he upheld the 1954 Supreme Court decision in *Brown,* rendered during his vice presidency under Eisenhower, but that he opposed busing "as a means of achieving racial balance in the schools."[7] The distinction was sufficiently acceptable to Thurmond to merit his calling "Nixon's position the most satisfactory of the candidates" (moderate Nelson Rockefeller and conservative Ronald Reagan were the others) and to declare for Nixon as having "the best qualifications in terms of experience and preparation. . . . He is the most acceptable and electable."[8]

Once aboard, Thurmond's job, and that of his key strategists, South Carolinians Harry S. Dent and J. Fred Buzhardt, was steering the 1968 convention away from the delayed candidacy of California governor Reagan. Using the southern strategy as their ideological centerpiece, they did just that, outflanking Reagan's forces in the South by gaining the support of 264 delegates to 65 for Reagan and delivering the Miami Republican convention to Nixon on the first ballot by a 25-vote margin.[9] The Thurmond-led Dixie GOP forces, still armed with their southern strategy, subsequently blunted the third-party candidacy of George Wallace in November, yielding to the Alabama governor five southern states (Alabama, Arkansas, Georgia, Louisiana, and Mississippi), losing one (Texas) to Democratic candidate Hubert Humphrey, and delivering to Nixon the rest (Florida, North Carolina, Oklahoma, South Carolina, Virginia, and Tennessee, as well as border states Missouri, Kentucky, and Delaware). The 89 southern electoral votes comprised 30 percent of the Republican's total and made the new president grateful and politically indebted to his newfound South Carolina allies.[10]

Nixon's South Carolina backers hoped that gratitude would be translated immediately into new strategies on school desegregation. However much Dent might have protested that the southern strategy was broadly designed to increase general southern political clout, it was interpreted by some as a loosely designed stratagem to delay or dilute the impact of school desegregation. As early as the Miami GOP convention in August 1968, newspaper headlines were greeting South Carolina readers with such reports as "Thurmond Tells Schools to Ignore New Demands, Wait for Better Deal." Columnists Rowland Evans and Robert Novak were writing that "Mr. Nixon will give the South just about what it wants, token integration under the 'freedom of choice' plans." Nixon spokesman and subsequent Reagan aide and presidential candidate Pat Buchanan told a Des Moines newspaper that "Nixon's position . . . coincides with that of Southern politicians and school officials who are seeking relief from this Supreme Court decision [the

Green decision of 1968, which weakened the use of 'freedom of choice' as a desegregation measure]."[11]

In South Carolina, where strategies of delay and a pattern of reluctant but peaceful acceptance of federally mandated desegregation had been in place for a decade, Nixon's election under the southern strategy produced what moderates believed would be a dangerously puzzling pattern of conflicts, contradictions, and uncertainty. For McNair, by 1970 well established as a moderate southern governor committed to peaceful desegregation, the ambiguities accompanying Nixon's arrival in the White House would aggravate an already complicated and potentially volatile set of conditions in South Carolina. During the fifteen years of tactical delays by which the state had avoided full implementation of *Brown,* a generation of white South Carolinians seemed to have accepted, perhaps begrudgingly, that desegregation of their state's public institutions was an inevitability. Many even took a degree of pride in the fact that their state had avoided the excesses and violence that had accompanied desegregation in states farther to the South.

Nixon's pronouncements, however, seemed to call into question the sense of inevitability by which the state had prepared for its desegregation experiences. McNair, whose administration had been beset for most of his elected term in office by a virtually unbroken chain of major incidents related to civil rights, was now facing a massive and complex desegregation event. It dwarfed in scale all the other protests, campaigns, and disturbances. Extensive desegregation of the state's public schools involved tens of thousands of students and teachers and reached into the homes of hundreds of thousands of South Carolinians. Such an undertaking not only called for major adjustments in the state's educational strategies and processes, it also presented hazards and threats to civil order all across the state. As the governor and his allies braced for the event, the last thing they needed was a newly inspired sense of resistance and the demoralizing emergence of confusion in the ranks.

When Nixon took office in January 1969, it was clearly with the expectation on the part of his new Dixie confederates that the pace of school desegregation, quickened by *Brown II* and the 1964 Voter Rights Act and accelerated even more by *Green,* would somehow be slowed by the president's embrace of the southern strategy.

Complications of the Southern Strategy

Those expectations, however, proved illusory, at least in the early days of the Nixon administration. As his southern hopefuls soon learned, the process of developing, ordering, and implementing school-desegregation plans was not a single, easily accessible, linear flow of activity. It was, in fact, a highly complicated, multilayered, and interlocking maze that had not one but many points of contact and deliberation. At any given time, the various desegregation plans could be within the jurisdiction of the courts, the Justice Department, or the Department of Health,

Education and Welfare, and sometimes more than one of those parties would be involved in a single case or set of cases. In addition, state and local entities representing school interests could form a second level of entanglements working with federal interests in either legal activity or some phase of plan development or implementation.

The clock that had begun ticking months, and even years, earlier in the processing of the South's many school-desegregation cases did not stop, or even slow down, when Richard Nixon took office on January 21, 1969. There were, in fact, awaiting the new administration what Dent called "desegregation booby traps,"[12] cases that required almost immediate attention. One of them involved five southern school districts, two of which were in South Carolina, whose Title VI funding was scheduled to be terminated nine days after Nixon's inauguration.

To complicate things further, there was no unity even within the Nixon inner circle itself. Political operatives who had made promises on the campaign trail as part of the southern strategy ran headlong into entrenched HEW functionaries little interested in interrupting the continuity of work that had been underway since the institution of enforcement procedures under Titles IV and VI. To overlay the built-in organizational conflicts, ideological differences emerged sharply with Nixon's appointment of Californian Robert Finch as his HEW secretary and his subsequent choice of Panetta as his civil rights chief. Panetta, who would subsequently become a Democratic congressman from California and eventually budget director and chief of staff in the Clinton administration, was a particular thorn in the side of the conservative wing of the White House, and his ongoing tilts with Dent and other Nixon strategists often left a blurred and indistinct message of actual federal policy and intentions.

Thus, for all the promise of relief from school desegregation that had been implied in the southern strategy of the Nixon campaign, the reality of things was somewhat less certain. The administration's best hopes for assistance to its southern allies often lay in the tactic of intervention in cases already underway, with the limited prospect of negotiating delays in the actual deadlines for implementing desegregation plans. Because such intervention was frequently in response to political inquiry or request, the process tended to be uneven and hurried, leaving the impression of erratic or inconsistent execution of civil rights policy. The sometimes vicious infighting within the administration on the school-desegregation issue also tended to cloud policy issues and send mixed, and sometimes contradictory, messages from Washington.

The early Title VI cases were examples of such improvised approaches. In the instance of the five districts scheduled for the termination of funds in January 1969, a sixty-day reprieve was granted, and the school districts were permitted to retain the funds in question pending the outcome of negotiation with HEW.[13] In the meantime, an additional seven districts were targeted for a cutoff of funds, and three of them lost their moneys with no grace period.[14] The southern strategy, it became increasingly clear, was just that, a strategy, and it could offer neither statutory change nor relief from court orders. Those who had been led to believe there would be instant change came away empty-handed and unhappy.

Disillusionment in South Carolina

In South Carolina, where expectations among Nixon's backers of relief from desegregation orders were particularly high, disappointment was registered early. One of the disgruntled school superintendents was Robert H. Gettys of Abbeville, whose district was one of the five scheduled for a cutoff of Title VI funds in the early days of the Nixon administration. "The situation has not changed," he was quoted as saying. "The desegregation guidelines have not changed. Only the people administering the guidelines have changed."[15]

State Superintendent of Education Cyril Busbee, whose election in 1966 had McNair's strong blessing, had a similar observation. Commenting on a letter he received from Panetta that informed him of a funds cutoff to Orangeburg County District Four (Edisto), Busbee said, "I have never gotten a nicer letter, but it still says that funds will be cut off."[16] Years later, in an interview shortly after he passed his ninetieth birthday, Busbee recalled: "we found that the Office of Education in Washington was telling one district one thing and tending to encourage them that—oh—you can get by or whatever, and others were telling them you're going to have to do it [desegregation]. My position was that you've got to do it, and you're going to have to do it."[17] It was an instance, Busbee acknowledged in the same interview, of his doing "some mighty unconservative things and [getting] by with it."[18]

Busbee's vigorous stand offered some state-level stability in an atmosphere that was becoming increasingly unstable at the federal level. McNair, a supporter of Hubert Humphrey in the 1968 presidential election, had good credentials in the traditional wing of the Democratic Party. He read and acknowledged the early disillusionment among Nixon supporters in South Carolina and took a jab at his GOP detractors. McNair told reporters that he believed many South Carolina voters "were confused about the issue of school desegregation during the presidential election."[19]

Dent was also picking up on the perceived disarray in the White House, later writing that southerners "could not understand how Nixon could say one thing in the campaign, back it up as President in news conferences, and then have HEW— and in some cases, the Justice Department—executing actions to the left of LBJ."[20] He singled out Panetta as one "who willfully disregarded orders, finagled Finch to get his way, leaked to the press and worked against administration policy on Capitol Hill and elsewhere."[21] Part of the problem, he contended, was "the President's tactic of using liberal friends [such as Finch and his eventual successor at HEW,

Elliott Richardson] to execute his conservative will without showing Nixon's hand."[22]

Awakening the Beast

For his part, Panetta was worrying that "any tangible retreat would mean the awakening of the beast again, the stirring of false hopes, the encouragement to be resistant—hell knows—maybe even the invitation to violent intimidation that we thought was dying out by the 1960s."[23] His counterpart in the Justice Department, Jerris Leonard, complaining about the injection of negotiation in the advanced stages of the desegregation orders, fumed, "We're fighting over the law to give something to a bunch of racists."[24]

Panetta, acknowledging that some saw him as a zealot, believed his job in the South was not one of pioneering or setting off on broad new campaigns, as may have been perceived by his critics. He felt that his task, instead, was one of wiping out the last pockets of resistance to school desegregation. He pointed out that during the fifteen years since *Brown,* three thousand school districts had "begun to end, or had ended discrimination under Title VI," noting that 89 percent of the districts in the South were in compliance with the law.[25] That left 11 percent he wanted to bring into compliance during the school year 1969–1970, and in that 11 percent (156 districts) there were twenty-one in South Carolina whose fate would be an issue of enormous importance within the Nixon administration and across the state, as well.

These twenty-one districts would provide the biggest confrontation to date for the feuding forces within the Nixon administration. According to Panetta, "[The] order requiring 21 school districts in South Carolina to develop desegregation plans could be crucial to the entire enforcement effort—politically and legally."[26] In South Carolina, Thurmond's clout with the president he helped elect would be severely tested, as would be the entire notion that a southern strategy made any difference at all. In Washington, in fact, the winners and losers would be defined even before the first of the twenty-one districts implemented desegregation plans.

The implementation order was issued by four federal judges on March 30, 1969, two months after Nixon took office. It gave the districts thirty days to "work out desegregation plans with officials of HEW." According to Panetta, the order "was a shock to the school officials involved . . . [and] a shock to Thurmond, too."[27] There ensued weeks of high-level attention from the White House, HEW, the Justice Department, and Thurmond himself. An initial thirty-day extension was granted by the federal court, pushing the deadline to May 30. Then some remarkable things began to happen.

One of those remarkable events was Nixon's offer to go to South Carolina himself. As Panetta and Gall quoted Finch as saying, "Thurmond is complaining that the plans prepared by HEW are too tough and that too few districts are agreeing to the plans. The President even suggested that he and I go to South Carolina . . . and see what we could do." Panetta's response was "The President of the United States and the Secretary of HEW negotiating plans with school boards in South Carolina. Wow!"[28]

Dent's recollection was that "the Nixon offer to negotiate the South Carolina cases sent shock waves through HEW. This had much to do with causing Finch to circumvent his staff on this and settle for less than Panetta was demanding. The deadline dates were moved to September 1970. The news media chalked up another loss for HEW and a victory for the South."[29]

Whoever may have been the winner or the loser in that exchange, the delay did have one momentous outcome: the new deadline placed the timing of the desegregation of twenty-one school districts squarely in the final weeks of the campaign to elect a new governor of South Carolina. It meant that school desegregation and its attendant racial emotions would unavoidably be a central issue of the campaign and that the state's strategies of restraint and orchestrated peace would be sorely tested. For all the composure and enlightenment it tried to show the outside world, and particularly industrial prospects, South Carolina was still a place of deep emotional vulnerability, a vulnerability especially strong among those who had only grudgingly accepted the changes being wrought in their school systems. Emotions had a way of going from vulnerable to volatile, as events in Alabama and Mississippi had proven. The prospect of a political donnybrook over public schools in the fall of 1970 revived those memories and resurrected fears that South Carolina had not yet escaped the demons of its past.

School Desegregation as a 1970 Campaign Issue

GOP gubernatorial candidate Albert W. Watson fired an early shot in the campaign with a January 24, 1970, statement. "It is high time," he said, "that the elected leadership of this state show . . . determination and courage in protecting the rights of our local school systems and our children."[30]

U.S. Congressman Watson hit several targets with that short comment. He stung McNair's Scottish pride with the reference to courage, a reference that the governor took personally and equated to being called a coward. Watson's attack also had a scattershot effect; by criticizing elected leadership, he hit both West, the Democratic candidate for governor, and McNair, giving things an anti-incumbency twist by which he could blast not only South Carolina leadership but also the Republican administration in Washington. It was an anti-incumbency tactic that would become a commonplace campaign ploy under GOP strategist, South Carolinian Lee Atwater years later.

The Watson comment also seemed to have the clear imprint of the White House. It bore an interesting similarity to the thrust of a lengthy policy statement Nixon issued two months later, a portion of which stated, "In achieving desegregation, we must proceed with the least disruption of the education of the nation's children."[31] Whether expressing plans to protect the rights of school districts or to proceed with the least disruption, the statements of Nixon and Watson were raising themes that touched parental fears and anxieties. Watson was clearly in tune with issues that were central to the southern strategy, and he would revisit them regularly in the months ahead.

There was one other message to come from that early statement. The Watson campaign would not eschew the use of emotion as a campaign technique. The congressman, almost evangelical in his tone, could excite an audience with his style, and he would not hesitate to make use of impassioned exhortations during the course of the campaign.

As the events of early 1970 unfolded, there was mounting evidence that the intramural struggle within the Nixon administration was tilting toward the side of the southern interests in the White House. As speculation began to rise about Panetta's possible resignation, Dent was credited with saying, "Panetta and those people are going to lose, because the die already has been cast. If they want to be martyrs and get run over by a Mack truck, then they'll be run over by a Mack truck."[32] The contest for control of White House policy on school desegregation was reaching a climactic moment and would resolve itself early in the second year of the Nixon term.

White House policy was one thing; the courts were another. As Panetta's influence ebbed in the spring and summer of 1969, the Nixon administration decided to test its clout in the U.S. Supreme Court to slow the desegregation process. Attorney General John Mitchell's Justice Department intervened on behalf of thirty-three Mississippi school districts seeking to delay compliance with Title VI deadlines. In the case, *Alexander v. Holmes County,* the Fifth Circuit Court of Appeals had granted the districts a deadline extension from August 25, 1969, until December 1 of that year.

As the case reached the Supreme Court on appeal and the Justice Department stepped in on the Mississippi side, Dent noted, "When the U.S. government appeared in court, for the first time the Department of Justice was seated at the same table with the South, rather than the NAACP."[33] Panetta, for his part, called the administration decision to represent the Mississippi school districts "the most significant civil rights retreat in the brief history of the Administration, and in the long and tragic history of school desegregation."[34]

Running Out of Courts

As it turned out, even with Nixon's recent appointee, Warren Burger, succeeding the retired Earl Warren as chief justice, the administration's presence, in the person of Deputy Attorney General Jerris Leonard, was of little influence. Ruling against the Mississippi districts and the Justice Department by a 9–0 vote, the Court found that "the obligation of every school district is to terminate dual school systems at once and to operate now and hereafter only as unitary schools."[35]

The court order was viewed by many as significantly weakening, if not outright removing, any lingering hope for freedom-of-choice plans or for prolonging the implementation of court-ordered desegregation plans. For Dent, there was an important strategic outcome, however. "The Southern reaction was one of placing blame on the court, and recognizing that Nixon had tried to be helpful," he wrote.[36]

For all the apparent clarity of the Court's position, there remained a clear reluctance on the part of the administration to associate itself with the firmness of the desegregation position. The notion of a president trying to be helpful to southern interests in the face of court orders prolonged hope that there was still some unspecified means by which the president could derail the fast-approaching desegregation deadlines. While hope may have been kept alive in such a scenario, there was also the danger of confusion and ambivalence being transmitted to a public unsophisticated in the complicated ways of government and its many inner conflicts and contradictions.

As early as February 1970, McNair addressed the ambivalence, telling White House representatives "that there were conflicting interpretations of the President's statements on school desegregation and that the varying interpretations were creating confusion in the public mind."[37] In that same series of interviews, North Carolina's Democratic governor, Robert W. Scott, expressed to the Nixon officials "concern over the public's lack of understanding of the relationship between the president and the courts."[38]

There was good reason for McNair's concern about the public's lack of understanding of school desegregation requirements. In mid-February—months before the delayed integration of the twenty-one districts—the state would be facing desegregation of two of its school districts under particularly difficult conditions. The districts—in Greenville and Darlington Counties—were under orders from the Fourth District Court of Appeals to carry out their desegregation plans at that time, an order that meant, in essence, that thousands of students and teachers would be assigned to new schools in the midst of the academic year. It was an unsettling prospect under any conditions, and it could be even more trying if parents were confused and uncertain about the legal necessity of the change.

Watson's opening shot on January 24 seemed to anticipate such confusion and uncertainty, raising doubts about whether state officials had displayed sufficient courage in representing the rights of schoolchildren. For McNair, the court order —having been issued after the case had been remanded from the Supreme Court in January—seemed to have less to do with courage and more to do with compliance and restraint. The Supreme Court's 9-0 ruling in the *Holmes* case in Mississippi seemed to slam the door even further on the exercise of options in the supposed interest of children's rights. The desegregation of the two districts would provide an early test of the impact the intensified political strategy would have on school desegregation in the state and might offer a preview of the integration of the other districts as the campaign reached the homestretch seven months later.

"Instant Integration" in South Carolina

The two districts targeted for "instant integration" could not have been more different. Greenville, in the industrialized northwest corner of South Carolina's upcountry, was large, populous, and economically aggressive. Its population of 240,546, second largest in the state, was 16.5 percent black, and the per capita income in its metropolitan area was third highest in the state.[39] As a high-growth area, Greenville was also a center of Republican strength, based not only on resident industrial interests but also on newcomers bringing GOP loyalties from other sections of the country.

Darlington, by contrast, was located across the state in the agricultural Pee Dee plain, and even though its history dated back to 1798, it had become widely known in recent years for tobacco farming and stock car racing. With a population of 53,442, Darlington's population was 38 percent black, and its per capita income was only slightly more than two-thirds that of Greenville. While traditionally Democratic, it also had strong George Wallace leanings.

As the implementation date approached for desegregation of the Greenville and Darlington districts, McNair was also concerned and complained publicly about the deadlines. "The illogical and unrealistic deadline imposed by the court is virtually impossible to meet," he said. "Even if the deadline could be met, the order would require the interruption of the school year at a time which would seriously impair the educational process for thousands of children."[40] Sensing more rebuff from the courts, McNair turned the tables on the Republicans, taking his complaint and his request for relief to the White House and to the Justice Department, strategically testing the "friendly" White House with a formal request for assistance on January 20, 1970.

For his part, Thurmond took two familiar paths: attacking the Supreme Court and keeping alive the ambiguous hope of a White House reprieve. "It seems sociologists have convinced the Supreme Court that integration is more important than education. . . ," he said. "I hope and pray that some way can be found to provide relief for the people of South Carolina from this judicial tyranny. I have urged the Nixon administration to explore every avenue that can possibly give relief from these decisions."[41]

Other Republicans, including state party chairman Ray Harris of Darlington, were still urging McNair to take the state's case back to the Supreme Court, even in the face of the January decision remanding the Darlington and Greenville cases back to the Fourth District, and in the face of the *Holmes* case in which the Justice Department, seeking delays in Mississippi, had suffered a 9–0 setback.

The Justice Department answered McNair's request for assistance tersely and directly. It came from Jerris Leonard, the deputy attorney general who had unsuccessfully argued the Nixon administration's case on behalf of the Mississippi school districts. As reported January 28, Leonard told McNair that, unlike its posture in Mississippi, the Justice Department felt it "had no standing to initiate any action in the South Carolina cases" and that "it is unlikely the Supreme Court will grant a review in light of recent decisions."

McNair took the Leonard statement as a case-closer as far as Darlington and Greenville were concerned. "It is apparent that Mr. Leonard closed the door on any possible recourse at the federal level and the citing of the recent U.S. Supreme Court ruling obviously closes the door to any appeal to the courts."[42] For whatever lingering abstraction of hope that may have been dangled toward South Carolinians, McNair at that point turned his attention toward preparing the counties affected for acceptance of instant integration.

His messages were beamed to television audiences in Greenville and Darlington, and they addressed directly the issue of confusion on the part of parents. "It is time," he said, "for everybody to be honest and sincere with the people of South Carolina and to quit holding out false hope. I think the situation we are in right now is too emotional and too important to let it get drawn into political chicanery."

Then he delivered the clincher in the context of the state's long-running strategy to use all the courts. "We have run out of courts and we have run out of time," he said. "We must admit to ourselves that we have pretty well run the legal course and the time has come for compliance or defiance. In South Carolina, we have always followed the law. We will continue to do so. We will comply with the court rulings."

In a press conference after the taping of the television program in Greenville, he said:

> We have seen what defiance led to in Arkansas and Mississippi and Alabama. I don't think the people of this state would want me to defy the order of the court after we have run the course legally.
>
> The state has built an image of obedience to the law. No society can continue to operate without obedience to the law.[43]

McNair Hailed as a Statesman

McNair's comments of late January were intended as something of a final statement designed to define with certainty a theme of moderate compliance that he had been articulating for some months. That theme had already caught the attention of ABC television newsman Howard K. Smith, who called McNair a "statesman." Smith said,

With emotion at a peak over school integration in the South, he [McNair] said things it took courage to say—stop defiance, accept law, comply.

There are no rewards for saying that. Segregationists, trying to make the water flow uphill, will scathe him. Blacks, getting some but not all, won't be happy. In any case, integration has become an ambiguous virtue. Whites get mad; Negroes derive little satisfaction from it; school quality often does decline, at least for now.

Those of us under less pressure should hasten to support Governor McNair by taking the view that makes sense—the historic one. The nation is in a confused, unsatisfactory interlude of dissolving 300 years of mistreatment of Negroes. Nothing that is done will be pleasing immediately. Integration has to be seen as the first step in a thousand-mile journey that will end in a united, color-blind nation.

A politician is a man who takes steps that will make him look good in the next election, one or two years hence. A statesman is a man who has the courage to sacrifice the short view to make history say that is what all our leaders should have done; that would have met the problem and saved the nation.[44]

Smith's contention that McNair's moderate stance would earn no rewards proved perceptive and prophetic. If television viewers were being told he was a statesman, many white parents in Greenville and Darlington, thought otherwise. Motorcades brought some three thousand people to Columbia to present the governor with petitions urging him to take action to halt the busing of students. Particularly disgruntled were parents from the small Darlington County town of Lamar, where a public-school boycott was being organized by a restaurant owner named Jeryl Best.

As the clock ticked down to the deadline, there was no intervention from the courts, from the White House, the Justice Department, or HEW. On Tuesday, February 17, the court order was carried out in Greenville County, with twelve thousand students and five hundred teachers being reassigned virtually overnight. The next day, Darlington followed suit, implementing plans that raised the number of black students in integrated schools from four hundred to seven thousand. Newspapers reported that both counties were peaceful, but that the boycott in the Darlington schools was "twenty per cent effective." Two days later, the boycott was reported to be up to 28 percent, resulting in some three thousand students being absent from classes in Darlington County.[45]

Panetta's Ouster at the White House

On February 20, three days after the "instant integration" of the two school districts in South Carolina, the White House furor over civil rights came to a head and Leon Panetta was forced to resign. A few weeks later, HEW Secretary Finch followed suit.[46] According to Panetta, Thurmond reportedly told fellow senator

Richard Russell of Georgia, "Dick, did you hear the good news? They just booted Panetta."[47] Dent wrote, "The Finch era ended as it began, with indecision, confusion and grief."[48]

Aside from the concerns in Greenville and Darlington, the waning weeks of February in South Carolina were marked by racial tension in several other locations. A second classroom boycott hit predominantly black Voorhees College at Denmark, fifty miles south of Columbia, and classes were suspended at Harleyville-Ridgeville High School, near Charleston, where fights had broken out involving more than one hundred black and white students.

South Carolinians were cheering the University of South Carolina basketball team, coached by Frank McGuire, after it finished a perfect 14–0 in the Atlantic Coast Conference, but they were also watching anxiously as antiwar student protests raged across California, bringing out six hundred National Guardsmen and leading to the burning of a Bank of America office in Santa Monica.

Closer to home, the *State* newspaper in an editorial was speculating that

in political stance, [John] West has identified himself with the moderate wing of the Democratic Party, much the same as Governor McNair. Watson, on the other hand, is a staunch conservative who is likely to benefit substantially from the discontent among white voters over current racial unrest in the schools and elsewhere.

. . . It seems significant that Watson has criticized McNair for the latter's recent refusal to meet with other Deep South governors, some of whom had individually expressed defiance of the latest federal court rulings on school desegregation. But it must also be remembered that Watson, along with Sen. Strom Thurmond, helped carry South Carolina for Richard Nixon over the Deep South's preferred third party candidate, George Wallace.[49]

Meanwhile, leaders of the school boycott in Darlington County stepped up their activity and scheduled a rally in support of "Freedom of Choice" at the Lamar High School football stadium for February 22. They invited McNair; West; Watson; a Democratic congressman, John L. McMillan, who represented Darlington as part of his Sixth District; and a Republican congressional candidate Arthur Ravenel of Charleston to attend and speak. Only Watson accepted.[50]

It turned out to be an interesting day. Watson was at his Sunday best, exhorting "God's blessing on anyone who will stand up for their children" and extolling boycott organizers as "leaders who will stand up and be counted."

"I choose to be with you and those concerned with quality education and freedom of choice," he told the crowd, which included boycott leader Jeryl Best. The congressman urged his audience to ignore "people who call you racist, bigot and redneck."

I've been called a racist, a bigot and a buzzard, but I intend to tell the people where I stand and tell it like it is. On controversial issues, it is often best not to take a stand, but you don't elect people to public office who refuse to take a stand on political issues.

There are some people who will criticize me, but even if it means my defeat, I will stand up and tell the people where I stand so far as regards freedom of choice. God bless anyone who is interested in their children. I'll stand with them and applaud them.[51]

News accounts reported that thousands cheered the Republican candidate, and three days later, boycott leader Best said that the leaders of the Freedom of Choice boycott at Lamar were putting plans in motion to abandon completely the public schools of the county.[52] Democratic gubernatorial candidate West said, "We don't need confrontation, just as we don't need defiance of the law."[53]

A week later, the state was visited by Georgia governor Lester Maddox, who preached in a Walterboro Baptist church to help raise money for a private school and urged that "prayer and Bible-reading need to be returned to schools."[54] A month earlier, a supporter of the Georgian's colorful style had suggested that Governor McNair "get yourself an ax handle and wave it around and call the Supreme Court names."[55] McNair reportedly replied, "I could have done that, and I'd be a lot more popular around the state, at least for now."[56]

Ax-Handle Politics and Violence in Lamar

McNair didn't get an ax handle, but eight days after Watson's impassioned speech in Lamar, the leaders of that town's boycott did. Apparently deciding that the process of petitions and boycotts was not swift enough, they took things into their own hands in trying to get Lamar High School closed down. According to newspaper reports, about two hundred persons gathered Monday morning, March 1, "in an apparent attempt to close the school."[57] Two demonstrators were injured, as was a highway patrolman.

Later that night, a crowd assembled again, described as "freedom of choice advocates . . . milling around in an area across from the high school." Columbia's *State* newspaper reported: "They brandished new ax handles, which were passed out from a pickup truck. Across the street, 50 highway patrolmen were lined up in front of the school . . . armed with riot control equipment."[58]

The next morning, as three school buses carrying mostly black children rolled up to the school, the mob turned violent. Wielding the ax handles, mace canisters, and homemade billy clubs, they charged the highway patrolmen, attacked the buses, and pelted them with debris. Only moments after the children had been rescued by state law-enforcement officers and escorted into the school, they turned two of the buses on their sides.

One witness said, "For 35 minutes it was hotter out there on that school ground than in Vietnam." A trooper called it "the meanest crowd I've ever seen."[59]

None of the children was hurt, but the next day fifteen people, including Jeryl Best, were arrested. McNair called the incident "unspeakable," and both Nixon and Vice President Spiro Agnew deplored the outbreak. "We will not tolerate violence or unlawful interference in efforts to desegregate," said Agnew.[60] Not overlooked in the aftermath was the rousing Sunday speech by Watson a week earlier and the possibility that his rhetorical fire may have been too close to the dry tinder of raw emotion this time.

Things were still simmering two months later when McNair visited Darlington County to deliver a Founders Day speech at Coker College in the town of Hartsville. Security officers were alerted that still-angry parents from nearby Lamar might try to "embarrass" the governor, and a contingent of around forty law-enforcement officers accompanied him.[61] The small Coker College campus was cordoned off as a precaution, but on this occasion, there were no instances of violence. The governor had words for the Lamar mob, as well as for the emerging presence of anti–Vietnam War protesters across the nation. In his prepared remarks, he said, "Problems are solved neither by those who raise their fists in defiance nor by those who shake their fists in outrage. It is time we open our fists and open our minds and undertake to find the reasonable alternatives to revolution on the one hand and suppression on the other."

It was good rhetoric for the moment, but four days later, another tragic event would threaten even further the already shaky civil order in South Carolina. The deaths of four students at Kent State University in Ohio by National Guard gunfire on May 4, 1970, intensified the already simmering antiwar insurgency, aggravated by the U.S. invasion of Cambodia, and brought the issue squarely and forcefully within the borders of South Carolina. Coming at a time when South Carolinians were still reeling from the impact of the S.C. State shootings two years earlier, the Medical College Hospital strike a year earlier, and the immediate and fractious desegregation of its public-school system, student uprisings on college campuses in May 1970 threatened to overload the state's already strained capacity for civil disorder.

Antiwar Protests in South Carolina

The emotional power of the antiwar movement in the state became evident within days of the Kent State shootings. South Carolinians who felt that student uprisings may have been something peculiar only to places like Berkeley, California, or New York City suddenly found themselves bracing for disruptions in the heart of their capital city of Columbia. "What's it like to be caught up in the violence at the University of South Carolina?" mused veteran newsman Charles Wickenberg, the onetime George Bell Timmerman aide and *Charlotte Observer* staffer who had become executive news editor of the *State*. "It's frightening, unnerving, exhausting, and a lot of things that are impossible to put into words, like, how do you describe 'mindless'?"[62]

For his part, Republican gubernatorial candidate Watson attributed it all to a left-wing conspiracy, commenting at a Spartanburg news conference, "The pity of it is that well-meaning, idealistic students were caught up in the emotion which the well-schooled, well-rehearsed ringleaders have been well taught to evoke." News accounts noted that Watson "said as the ranking member of the House Select Committee and as a member of the House Internal Security Committee, he knew of the anarchist aspirations to use campuses as battlegrounds."[63]

A contrasting view came from statewide political leader-to-be Dick Harpootlian, at that time editor of the Clemson student newspaper, the *Tiger,* and part of an activist group on the usually conservative upcountry campus. Harpootlian, who would later emerge as a circuit solicitor, a candidate for attorney general, and a chairman of the S.C. Democratic Party, fired off a letter to the editor published in the *Charlotte Observer,* in which he contended that

> Many Carolinians have delusions of Communist-paid agitators confusing and propagandizing the students into a violent frenzy. . . .
>
> This is completely wrong. . . . Students have become politically and socially aware, while those who make campus politics are still worrying about ACC championships or an addition to the football stadium. . . . Violence is abhorrent to every academic community, but so is petty politics. While university administrators keep appeasing state legislators, who view universities as training or trade schools, there will be only uneasy quiet at best, and violence at worst.[64]

Neither USC nor Clemson, in fact, would ever have been mistaken for hotbeds of student activism. When dissent began stirring in Columbia three days after the Kent State shootings, a voluntary classroom strike was called, but a spot check the first day indicated that attendance was still holding at 95 percent. A rally later that day attracted only five hundred of the estimated twelve thousand students enrolled at USC.[65]

By comparison, some six thousand students at the University of North Carolina in Chapel Hill rallied and marched through the college town, and a student strike was reported to "[involve] one-third of the campus' 16,000 students."[66] At USC, the student senate limited its action to that of adopting a resolution supporting a voluntary classroom strike, and the faculty was even less enthusiastic, rejecting a strike resolution and only affirming "the right of students peacefully to assemble for redress of grievances by proper democratic processes."[67]

Even with such lukewarm support from the institution's establishment, there were sufficient numbers on the USC campus to create high-visibility provocations, and for twelve days in May, there was a vigorous and often violent siege of the campus, much of it directed toward shutting down the institution. McNair, by then a veteran of disruptions at S.C. State, the Medical College, and various other schools and colleges around the state, vowed his full support to keep the university open, even if it meant posting military and law-enforcement officers on campus.

Rampage and Confrontation at USC

The governor's will, and that of USC president Thomas F. Jones, would be tested early. On the first evening of the student rally and voluntary classroom strike (May 7), demonstrators took control of the student center, the Russell House, and in so doing attracted more than three thousand jeering students to the site. It took local police, highway patrolmen, and National Guardsmen to quell the protest. Thirty-one students were arrested, and McNair was quoted as appealing to students to carry on with their classes and not become involved in the protests. Noting that law enforcement had restrained itself for three hours while the student dissidents held the building, he said officials "went the last mile and a half with the students today and I urge them not to expect it of us again."[68]

The governor's warning went largely unheeded, however, and while the classroom strike was still proving ineffective, two rallies on campus the next day (Friday, May 8) drew some one thousand students, and later that day, activists attracted some four hundred participants to a peaceful rally on the State House steps. After an edgy weekend, trouble broke out in earnest on Monday, May 11, while government offices were closed in observance of Confederate Memorial Day, a day that proved to be a bad time for the state to let down its guard. Meetings of Board of Trustees' committees dealing with discipline for students involved in earlier protests were scheduled for the Rutledge Administration Building that day, and they quickly proved to be magnets for dissident students, attracting several hundred to the building by midafternoon. By four o'clock, the crowd had swelled significantly, and the tenor of things turned nasty. Students rushed the front door, and finding security minimal, they stormed inside and occupied the building. The uprising caught state and university officials off guard. McNair, in fact, was in Washington attending a governors meeting, and only a skeleton staff was on duty in his office. As word of the urgency of the USC takeover reached the governor's staff and SLED Chief Strom asked for a complement of National Guardsmen to join the beleaguered officers on campus, the relaxed holiday schedule impeded communications and slowed response to the crisis.

Unable to mount a show of force, officers could not restrain students inside the building as they went on a rampage, destroying furniture, damaging equipment, destroying and scattering records, and scrawling obscene words and phrases on the walls. Students outside the building also turned destructive, damaging several automobiles parked in front of the Rutledge Building. It was nearly dark before sufficient National Guardsmen arrived to deal with the situation, and by then students evacuated the building and scattered across campus, shouting and vandalizing automobiles while drawing from pursuing guardsmen heavy doses of tear gas.

"We just weren't prepared," McNair's news secretary, Wayne Seal said afterward. "We couldn't have controlled the situation with the men we had there. The 'crazies' would have burned the place down." By the end of the evening, a concerned McNair, who had monitored events at USC by telephone during the day, returned from Washington and promptly declared a state of emergency, clamping a curfew of 9:00 P.M. to 6:00 A.M. on the campus and surrounding area. In the next day's newspaper coverage he was quoted as saying:

> I regret that this action is necessary because the majority of the students, who have maintained a respect for the University and its regulations and for the laws of South Carolina, are subject to the same restrictions and regulations which are imposed to control the few who are apparently determined to disrupt activities through destruction and violence.
>
> What happened today is a tragedy to the university and to the state and cannot be tolerated. We are prepared for any eventuality should any further threats be made against the peaceful operation. . . . I urge all students to attend classes tomorrow. All students and their parents can be assured that further disruptions will not be tolerated.[69]

Before the Monday night rampage had run its course, there were some six hundred guardsmen, one hundred highway patrolmen, and twenty to twenty-five SLED agents on campus, according to Seal, a key contact and point man for the governor's office with USC, described in one news account as "McNair's Johnny-on-the-Spot in civil disturbances."[70] Asked if the security contingent would be on hand to greet students attending class the next morning, Seal said, "We can only wait and survey the situation." Guardsmen, who had been armed only with tear gas the previous Thursday after the occupation of the Russell House, carried tear gas and bayonets on their rifles, and they were authorized to carry live ammunition clips on their belts.[71] For all the curfews, security precautions, and warnings, however, student dissidents made one last effort to provoke disruptions and close the institution the next day. McNair had agreed to meet late that Tuesday afternoon with five representatives of the dissident group to hear grievances and concerns, but the students turned abusive and presented the governor with only nonnegotiable demands. The meeting collapsed, and the disgruntled students headed back to rallies off campus at Maxcy Gregg Park and on the State House grounds.

It turned out to be the ugliest night of the campus siege, as students defied the curfew, taunted law-enforcement officers, and hurled bricks, rocks, and bottles in what was described as "guerilla-like skirmishes with authorities."[72] By the end of the evening, students variously estimated at between sixty-eight and eight-five persons were arrested, and pressure grew even stronger for the institution to be closed.

McNair, his Scottish stubbornness roused, was having none of that. The next day, at a televised midday news conference, he issued his most direct statement of the campus siege. "We have a group that has a strong determination to see the university closed. This is part of what is going on all over America today to close the major universities. We have a category of students who feel strongly about this." Keeping the university open, he said, would "take the cooperation of the whole university community and the people as a whole. Everybody has got to recognize that this problem exists and that as long as it does, there are difficult circumstances to which the students are going to be exposed."[73]

Cooperation, as it turned out, came in a surprising form from a surprising source—the USC faculty, which had held itself collectively at some distance from the fray. Among actions taken at a special faculty meeting on the fateful Tuesday was a resolution "to do everything possible to insure that the University remains open and completes its normal academic schedule." The faculty also "approved the idea to have faculty/student 'rap' sessions in residence halls."[74]

By the middle of the fractious week, a faculty cadre from remarkably divergent backgrounds had come together to spend the night in the nervous dormitories to quiet fears and deal with rampant rumors spreading among the students. Newcomers like Iowan John Mark Dean from marine science and Bill Caldwell from the mathematics department joined forces with faculty and administrative veterans like Don Weatherbee, Paul Fidler, Bob Alexander, and John Duffy to provide a calming influence within the jittery dormitories and to counter the influence of the radical student element.

Students by then were badly shaken by the turn of events on the usually placid campus in downtown Columbia. One of them, a sophomore named Bob Bigake from Columbia, was quoted as saying, "I'm afraid the governor is not going to close this school until somebody gets killed. That may be what it takes." A junior coed was quoted as saying, "The girls are all on tranquilizers, waiting for the governor to tell them they can go home."[75]

But as he had done a year earlier at the Medical College Hospital strike in Charleston, McNair willfully held firm in the face of public disruptions and violence. "McNair refused to let a group of about 200 hard-core radicals on a campus of 13,000 force him to close the university less than two weeks before the end of the year," one newspaper analysis observed.[76]

By midweek, with some 190 students in jail, the upheaval seemed to have run its course, and McNair shortened the curfew. Law enforcement was reduced on campus, and by Thursday, Chief Strom said, "Everything is nice and peaceful around here."[77] An appearance by antiwar icon Jane Fonda that night attracted a large crowd to off-campus Maxcy Gregg Park, and although some of the student rhetoric expressed at the rally was volatile, the evening passed peacefully and the campus rebellion passed with it.

By Monday, May 17, ten days after students had taken over the Russell House, security was removed from the student center and its governance was returned to student hands. A day later, the state of emergency was lifted, and faculty members met to express their "continuing confidence in the student body for their cooperation in returning protests to peaceful channels."[78]

Many reasons were offered for the peaceful resolution and the relatively low toll in personal injury over the twelve days of the USC incident. Experience gained from previous campus incidents in South Carolina and elsewhere around the country had left the painful lesson that academic chiefs often make poor law-enforcement officers. From the earliest days of the USC uprising, McNair established himself clearly as the emergency head of the university, with the full support of President Thomas F. Jones, a pleasant, bow-tie-wearing engineer who had come to USC only a few years earlier from Purdue to serve as president. Jones managed internal communications and maintained a busy schedule of meetings with faculty and students throughout the emergency.

McNair, whose office was only three blocks from campus, maintained a twenty-four-hour open-door schedule during the darkest days of the crisis, meeting regularly with protesting or other unhappy students and remaining in contact with concerned parents around the state. As dissident students attacked him as fascist in stereotypical rhetoric of the day, other students were reassured that the governor was, in fact, concerned about them and willing to listen.

Primarily, however, the protests lost their zeal—as had the strike at the Medical College Hospital a year earlier—because McNair would not budge from his stated position. As he had been with the refusal to recognize the Local 1199-B in Charleston, he was likewise adamant about not closing the university and bowing to the will of the student radicals. The get-tough stance endeared McNair to conservative South Carolinians who had been less than pleased with his position on school desegregation. His handling of the USC incident produced the greatest outpouring of favorable mail and public attention of the five-plus years of his administration.

Peaceful Summer, Hectic Autumn

The summer of 1970 found the state taking time to celebrate the three-hundredth anniversary of the first permanent European settlement on the coast, at Charles Towne (now Charleston). McNair spent a lot of time at ceremonial functions tracing the origins of the state's early settlers, traveling to London to meet with the Queen Mother in observing the state's British heritage, and doing his best to downplay the Confederate banner that hung atop the State House. McNair suggested that South Carolinians pay more attention to their role in the Revolutionary War than the more recent Civil War, "since that's the war we won." It was also possible that the South Carolina governor did not think the summer of 1970 was a particularly good time to recall a war whose principal issue was the state's right to permit the ownership of slaves.

Unlike the year before, when marchers occupied the streets of Charleston during the Medical College strike, the summer of 1970 passed in relative quiet. McNair stirred some sentiment by accepting an invitation from President Nixon to tour war operations in Cambodia, and his pro–Vietnam War statements rankled some of the antiwar elements that had worked vainly to close USC weeks earlier. By late June, the governor was resuming his jabs at Republican candidate Watson, telling a group of southern school-board officials "to reject those who hopelessly ensnarl the schools in the politics of this nation."[79]

Harking back to the state's economic development strategies, he said, "Change is the very nature of society, and we must develop the capability to respond to change and make it a resource of growth." As for the burgeoning movement to establish all-white private "academies," the governor said, "Those who abdicate the responsibility and turn against the concept of public education are turning their backs on reality."[80]

A week later, McNair would take a swipe at political foes and campus dissidents in general by saying, "Where free and open education is under attack, so, too, is the principle of a free society." Speaking to a College of Charleston commencement, he said, "Where institutions are made the targets of unrest and disruption, the process of logic and understanding is severely impaired. Intimidation is a poor substitute for reason and judgment."[81]

As the fall approached, the gubernatorial race appeared almost neck-and-neck. Large numbers of black voters, disenchanted at the perceived slowdown in civil rights progress and school desegregation, had formed their own party, the United Citizens Party and were running Columbia attorney Thomas Broadwater for governor. It was a potentially damaging development for Democratic interests, knowing their chance of electing Lieutenant Governor John West as governor rested heavily on the support of black South Carolinians. Polls taken by West backers in September showed an alarming indifference toward his campaign among potential black voters. September 1970 was also the deadline for the delayed enforcement of court-ordered desegregation of the twenty-one South Carolina school districts.

By that time, the governor had logged a full tour of rhetorical duty and was preparing for the final four months of his sixty-eight-month service. A dispute over the proposed location of a German-based industry near the state's lower coast was bringing to the state its first major environmental debates and was creating a public rift between McNair and West, neither the first nor the only disagreement between the two Democrats.

But there was no disagreement between them over the severity and potentially explosive nature of the major statewide desegregation that would be experienced that fall. West, himself a target of the Ku Klux Klan early in his political career, had established clear racial credentials on numerous occasions, including a visit to the S.C. State campus after the violence of February 1968. Fears spawned by public disruptions, both West and McNair realized, could polarize the population and turn the November election for governor into a referendum on race. As a Democrat, West would need not only a large turnout of black voters, but significant white support, as well. Voting along strictly racial lines could be West's worst nightmare.

Among the twenty-one S.C. school districts targeted for court-ordered school desegregation that fall, one stood out as having particular political status. It was Richland County District One, the district that served the capital city and many of its governmental and business leaders and the district, where two of McNair's daughters attended an already partially integrated middle school (Crayton).[82] It was also the district that caught attention in early conversations during the 1968 GOP convention between Nixon and Thurmond regarding places where a southern strategy might be applied. Efforts to negotiate a desegregation plan for Richland One had been rejected by HEW seven months earlier, prompting Thurmond to express disappointment and bringing from Watson an expression that he was optimistic that conversations he and Thurmond had with "officials at the White House and HEW will bring favorable results."[83]

Under the court-ordered, HEW-negotiated plans, schools opened peacefully that September in the twenty-one districts as well as in the rest of the state, and there seemed little evidence that another Lamar-type clash was brewing. Things were so calm, in fact, that McNair decided to schedule for early October long-deferred surgery on his right knee, first injured playing high school football and reinjured playing basketball at USC some thirty years earlier. The surgery was to take place at Columbia's Baptist Hospital on Friday, October 2, and the governor expected to be back at work early the following week in time for 1971–1972 budget hearings.

More School Violence, with a Political Twist

McNair had been back in the office little more than a week, still hobbling with the use of crutches and a cane, when news came that the school peace had been broken in—of all places—Richland One. An initial skirmish had taken place at midday on Wednesday, October 14, between black and white students at the district's suburban A. C. Flora High School. It initially went unreported in the local press, and it was not until the following day, when violence escalated alarmingly, that the Wednesday scuffle was brought to light, along with another curious detail, which would be discussed and debated much longer than the incident itself.

According to press and law-enforcement reports, things were calming down after the Wednesday clash when an automobile carrying two Watson campaign aides arrived at the front of Flora High and one of the aides began taking pictures. According to police accounts, students gathered around the car, rocking it, jumping on it, and clamoring to have their pictures taken. The overall effect, officers said, was one of creating new provocation and prolonging tensions on the shaky campus. One of the Watson aides later said that he was in the area with a fellow staff member working on a precinct campaign project when they observed the police cars at Flora. They stopped, he said, out of curiosity, identifying the other aide as "just a friend who likes to take pictures."[84]

Informed of the incident at Flora and noting that it had not been reported in the local press, Watson shifted his schedule and held a hastily organized press conference to call for immediate investigations into "spreading violence and disruptions in our schools." Watson said he called the press conference because "somebody had to bring it out" and, in words reminiscent of his remarks at Lamar eight months earlier, announced: "I have the courage to take a public stand on this issue and ask all parents, teachers, and principals to pick up their phones and call me or write me to advise me of the situation in their schools or communities."[85]

Scarcely had the Watson press conference ended than things blew out of control at A. C. Flora. The school, named for a former district superintendent, had been opened eleven years earlier as an all-white institution, and with its forty-four-acre campus, rambling architecture, and posh location in the middle of fashionable Forest Acres, just east of Columbia, it was the district's showpiece. On Thursday, October 15, however, it was a place where "all hell broke loose," according to Principal Clinton B. Harvey.[86]

News accounts quoted Harvey as saying that fighting broke out among some 50 students, and that another 300 of the school's 1,750 students watched in midday rain. The fights lasted several minutes, and then, according to Harvey, "pandemonium broke out for at least half an hour and sticks and rocks started flying."[87] "It was a pretty ugly thing," he said. Before it was over, police were required to restore order, and the high school was closed for the rest of the day. There were no serious injuries, but the attention given to the incident in South Carolina's capital accorded it a prominence matched only by that of Lamar six months earlier. For some, it seemed more than coincidental that there was a Watson presence, either in person or by staff, at the state's two worst school-desegregation incidents of the year. His exhortations for courage and for standing up were worrisome to those who may have opposed desegregation but who also feared the rhetorical unleashing of the state's pent-up racial emotions.

Watson subsequently denied that his staff caused any of the trouble at A. C. Flora, saying he would dismiss any aides who had done so. He went on to accuse state officials of a "conspiracy of silence" on school disorders and pledged to continue speaking out on the need for discipline in the schools.[88]

Later accounts would dispute the actual impact the presence of Watson's staff had on the incident. Richland County's sheriff, Frank Powell, reportedly in line for a high-ranking state law-enforcement position in a Watson administration, dismissed the role of the aides and blamed the incident on Principal Harvey.[89]

McNair's top law enforcement officer, SLED Chief Pete Strom, who was in line to continue his position under West, said he agreed with Forest Acres police that Watson aides "were at A. C. Flora High School looking for pictures of a racial incident when a disturbance occurred."[90] A month earlier, GOP moderate Cooper White, the mayor of Greenville, had withheld his support of Watson at least partly on the basis of Watson campaign ads featuring scenes of riots that had taken place in the Watts section of Los Angeles five years earlier.[91]

On the campaign trail, West vowed never to "inflame or polarize class against class, rich against poor, or color against color," and one of the state's larger newspapers, the *Spartanburg Herald,* urged the candidates to delete school desegregation as a campaign issue.[92] Except for perfunctory responses to press inquiries, however, McNair retained relatively low visibility in the incident. All that would change on Friday, October 16, two days after the first outbreak at Flora.

McNair Goes on the Attack

A scheduling coincidence provided McNair a public forum. Ground-breaking for a Law Enforcement Training Center, a national demonstration project funded jointly by state and federal sources and designed to provide, among other things, training for officers in coping with civil disorders, was scheduled for that day on the outskirts of Columbia. Nearby, in what was becoming a complex of criminal-justice facilities just north of the city, was the headquarters of SLED, the agency that had been the central coordinator and signal-caller of law enforcement activities in virtually all the instances of civil disorder that had occurred during the McNair administration. It was decided that following his ceremonial speech, McNair would proceed to SLED headquarters for a press conference to discuss the incident at A. C. Flora.

Flanked by Chief Strom and amid all the trappings of law enforcement, McNair was in a setting that called attention neither to school desegregation nor race relations; it provided him instead a pulpit from which to discuss the incidents of recent days and months in the context of the most fundamental of issues, public safety and the enforcement of the law. With uncharacteristic panache, the governor, still hobbling painfully on a cane, had created a moment of high political drama.

McNair began the news conference with a recitation of the state's previous disturbances, referring to the Medical College Hospital strike, the Voorhees student boycotts, the antiwar demonstrations at USC, and the overturned school buses in Lamar, among others.

> I think over a period of time that we have established a reputation as being a state that expected people to obey the law and that we would do whatever is necessary to see that there is obedience to it.
>
> We believe in law and justice. This applies to all of South Carolina.[93]

Then he warmed to the attack and got specific:

> I think the gentleman [Watson] should have learned from Lamar that inflammatory statements [and] over-reaction only add to the problem, rather than lessening it.
>
> We've had problems over the years in Newberry, in Chesterfield County, in Allendale County; we're having problems now in Edgefield and Barnwell, in addition to here in Columbia. . . . The public school officials of this state need our support . . . they don't need us adding to or creating problems for them.
>
> They [the problems] are severe enough, they're critical enough, they're great enough without us, who serve in government—or seek to serve in government—through personal statements, or through actions of staff people, actually involving themselves in these critical and frustrating problems at the local school level. I deplore this, and I can't deplore it too strongly.[94]

McNair's Scottish ire was rising as the session proceeded, something rarely seen by the reporters in attendance, most of them State House veterans who had known the governor for years. In the pre-Watergate days of less formally defined relations between press and public figures, McNair courted friendships of the press just as he did others he considered politically important. Reporters were regularly invited to social functions at the mansion as well as weekend hunting and fishing trips at the governor's farm and elsewhere. If there was a rap on McNair from the press, it was not his accessibility or personality. It was his publicly restrained style that rarely produced one-liners or quick sound bytes.

Such was not the case on that October 16, however. Jabbing the podium with his index finger for emphasis, McNair was raising the volume and intensity of his normally soft voice, calling his critic by name and harking back to Watson's contentions that South Carolina elected officials lacked sufficient courage.

> I think while the gentleman is calling and using terms of "cowardice" against those of us who serve in government that he should make a full explanation—and I speak of Congressman Watson—that he should make a full explanation of why his people were involved in the incident at A. C. Flora the day before we had the serious problem, in the first place; in the second place, I would like a full explanation of how they knew to be there when we didn't know it; Chief Strom didn't know that we were going to have a problem; and I'm sure the school officials didn't know there was going to be a problem.
>
> So while we [the politicians] are trying to exploit these things politically, I think the people of this state are entitled to explanations along this line, too. The public schools of this state are no place for partisan politics. They're too important to us. The lives and safety of these young children are too important to me to let any political candidate exploit it and use it for political purposes and reasons only.

Now, I would invite the gentleman to control himself and his staff until after the elections are over, because I want to make it clear and remind everybody who seeks public office and every citizen of this state that through January 19th, I am the Governor and I intend to be the Governor.[95]

It was as close as McNair would come to a public tirade, and while it would not have registered very high on a rhetorical Richter scale, it was sufficiently forceful to attract immediate attention. A local radio station was carrying the press conference in its entirety by the time the governor and his party had made the twenty-minute return trip to the State House in downtown Columbia.

From a strategic standpoint, McNair's popular handling of the USC demonstrations the previous spring had enhanced his image as a take-charge guy, giving him the pulpit to scold Watson for both Lamar and A. C. Flora and advancing the suspicion that the GOP candidate might be something of a loose cannon. John West's campaign slogan, "Elect a Good Man Governor," began to take on new definition, particularly as compared to the exclusionary tone of Watson's "Our Kind of Man." The perceived stridency by Watson, as the *State* had warned a year earlier, had "realistically, but perhaps unwisely, given public notice that they expect to get little or none of the Negro vote," and black support swung decisively behind West in the latter weeks of the campaign.

A Victory for Moderation

Many reasons were advanced for West's close victory sixteen days after the outbreak of violence at A. C. Flora. Thurmond blamed Nixon's vacillation over school guidelines and also accused reporters of painting a false impression of Watson as a racist. Republican Carroll A. Campbell Jr. of Greenville, whose victory in a South Carolina Senate race in 1970 launched him on a career that would lead him to Congress and eventually to the governor's office for two terms sixteen years later, also blamed the media. Watson credited the loss to what he called a low turnout. Black support swung strongly to West in the final weeks of the campaign and nullified Broadwater's third-party effort.

For his part, West stepped forward as an unabashed and avowed civil rights champion who was inspired by the strong black support of his candidacy. Even though he was a year older than McNair, his politics were not restrained by the accommodation to the senior elements of the traditional Democratic leadership. He launched openly a four-year term of state-level human rights initiatives with the promise to blacks of "no special status other than full-fledged responsibility in a government that is totally color-blind." He vowed in his inaugural address that the state would "break free of the vicious cycle of ignorance, illiteracy and poverty which has retarded us throughout our history."[96]

West acknowledged that his opportunity to address overtly the racial troubles of South Carolina had been made possible by the strategies by which McNair had held the state together during the tumultuous 1960s. It was McNair, West said, who had guided the state in withstanding the onslaught of violence and disruptions that threatened to split it into alienated camps of narrow interests and seriously impaired trust and confidence.

> If there has been a single factor which has influenced this phenomenal growth and progress more than any other, it has been the quality of leadership our state has had in the Office of Governor.
>
> I should like to say specifically to our retiring Governor, Robert E. McNair, that yours has been a period of unusual service and unprecedented accomplishment. You have served more consecutive years as Chief Executive than any other Governor in the history of our state, but your place in the history books will be for reasons other than length of term.
>
> Yours will be recorded as a period in which this state experienced its greatest human advancement. By reason of your distinguished service, you will unquestionably be accorded a well-deserved place as one of the greatest governors who has ever served the State of South Carolina.[97]

West's words bore out the remarkable transformation of the state. In the span of two decades, South Carolina had evolved from a state that had stubbornly resisted and only tacitly accepted racial equality to one that accepted the opportunities of racial liberation. The South Carolina that headed into the last three decades of the twentieth century was one that had gone to war with its past and had not only survived but faced its future with a new sense of purpose and direction.

It was a markedly different South Carolina from the desperately poor state that greeted Robert Evander McNair on his arrival as an infant newcomer to Berkeley County in 1923. It was a markedly different state from the one that had fought doggedly to sustain white supremacy in its political system in 1944, surrendering only when federal courts and federal legislation demanded black participation in what had essentially been a racially exclusive system for more than half a century. It was a markedly different South Carolina from the racially obsessed state in whose General Assembly he began service in 1951, a year in which the state charted its futile strategies for sustaining racially segregated public-school systems under the grimly deceptive "separate but equal" label.

South Carolina had shed its age-old reliance on agriculture and was stepping smartly into the kind of economic diversity that would eventually bring the sophistication of automobile assembly plants and millions of dollars of overseas investment to its shores. It had also discovered that long-term public investment in education was at the very core of its economic success, a lesson that would be recycled often during another generation of education-minded governors.

Such transformation did not come loudly in the form of revolutionary convulsions. It came at the painstakingly persistent prodding of leaders who practiced the politics of moderation. There was no overthrow of the state's political establishment; there was the step-by-step reconciliation of the state's traditional "friends and neighbors" politics with the reality of new court orders, new federal statutes, and new expectations of an increasingly enlightened population.

At the heart of that transformation was Bob McNair, the man who in many ways represented virtually all the elements of South Carolina's complicated past and its ambitious future. He understood the misery of rural poverty; he knew the ways of small-county politics; he learned firsthand the intricacies of the emerging black political force in the state. He worked his way into the confidence of often-conflicting elements within the state, and he respected above all the art of compromise.

It made him the ultimate negotiator for change and the powerful catalyst by which unity and consensus could be forged around seemingly disparate interests. The state's determination to pursue accelerated levels of support for public education in 1969 in the face of imminent desegregation of the state's schools a year later stood in stunning contrast to South Carolina's publicly articulated position only two decades earlier to abandon public education rather than desegregate.

McNair reluctantly delivered a final State of the State speech to the General Assembly in January 1971, days before he left office. He had questioned whether he needed to deliver a speech at all, since he had no legislative proposals, and presenting those had become the traditional use of the message. He was persuaded to deliver a short speech and use it as an opportunity actually to discuss the state of the state.

The speech was low key and impersonal, touching on economic growth, educational gains, and reciting the state's numerous instances of civil stress and disorder, including the Orangeburg shootings in 1968. It was not boosterism for the state, nor was it political or partisan in nature. It simply recapped events in what had been his unprecedented five-and-a-half years in office and included an understated and modest suggestion for the state's future. McNair spoke succinctly of the ambitions he had held and those that he passed along to his successor. He spoke of self-reliance and self-esteem for a state that at times had sold itself short and blamed others for its miseries. He also spoke of the human potential of a state that had a history of denying many of its people access to full opportunities.

"The time has come," he said in the same quiet voice with which he had spoken to the General Assembly five-and-a-half years earlier, "for the State of South Carolina to break free once and for all from the bondage of limited expectations."

Epilogue

Bob McNair chose not to seek public office again after his term as governor ended in January 1971. His name was mentioned occasionally as a prospect for the U.S. Senate, but those seats remained firmly in the hands of Strom Thurmond and Fritz Hollings, both of whom served into the twenty-first century.

Over the years, McNair devoted much of his energy to building the law firm that he and members of his executive staff—Wayne Corley and Jim Konduros—along with administrator Claire Fort, formed as he left office in 1971. Corley, who served as the firm's managing partner for ten years, recalled years later in a conversation with the author, "Most people thought he [McNair] was keeping us together because he was going to run for something else. He hadn't practiced law in ten years and Jim Konduros and I had never practiced law. As filing times passed, people said he must be serious about building a law firm and we set about to build it. From the beginning, he had told us he was not interested in returning to public service. He made it clear that twenty years was enough. Business began to come in, and since we didn't have any lawyers, we hired Bob Dibble and Mac Singletary. His [McNair's] goal was to build a law firm so that businesses wouldn't have to go to Atlanta or Washington."[1]

The firm developed five specialties: administrative/regulatory, business, intellectual property, legislative/governmental, and litigation/labor and employment. Over time, Corley recalled, McNair became known as much for his business acumen as his political skills, particularly among those business leaders who were "very young or not around at all" when he was governor.

Through it all, Corley said, McNair retained the same style as when he was governor. "He had the same manner, very benevolent," he said. "An article written about the firm called us a benevolent dictatorship, and that was accurate.

Even in his role as Governor, he very seldom said, 'Do this. This is what we are going to do,' without bouncing his ideas and his visions off other people. In the early years of the firm, he would call Konduros and me and say, 'Why don't you think about this?' He had his mind made up, but he wanted to give us buy-in."

The McNair, Konduros, Corley firm eventually became simply the McNair Firm, and its growth was steady. By the time Corley became managing shareholder in 1993, there were between 85 and 90 lawyers on board. By 2005, after the merger with the Bethea firm of Hilton Head, the McNair Firm had 133 lawyers, 218 support personnel, and offices in six South Carolina cities, as well as Raleigh and Charlotte.

"He wanted to develop the firm so that as we matured, it would not be dependent on one individual or any one group of individuals," Corley said. "We all knew it was his firm, and in the early going, 99.9 per cent of the business came in because of him. Today, we have a cadre of clients who are still here because he is here." Corley said McNair wanted to build a firm that would last "in perpetuity," and as the firm grew, "a lot of the rest of the lawyers have developed clients so that if he got hit by a truck, all the clients wouldn't leave. He designed it that way."

McNair remained active with the firm even after the leadership passed into younger hands. Except for his annual vacation in August at the Farm, he kept regular hours at the firm's headquarters across the street from the State House, where his corner office on the eighteenth floor of the Bank of America Tower continued to be a crossroads of the state's business, professional, and political communities. "It's always been nice to know he still sat in that corner office," Corley said.

As the firm prospered, McNair was invited to serve on numerous prestigious boards and commissions, including Southern Railway (later Norfolk Southern), NationsBank, Crum and Forster, Furman University, AIRCO, and Georgia Pacific, and he maintained an active interest and influence in the affairs of his alma mater, the University of South Carolina. Life after politics proved challenging, productive, and profitable for the attorney who had once launched a career with a typewriter on a wooden crate in Allendale, South Carolina.

In time, the McNair family itself grew. Three daughters, Robin Lee, Corinne Calhoun, and Claudia Crawford, joined eldest son, Robert Evander Jr., as South Carolina's first family during the late 1960s, and by the early years of the twenty-first century, Bob and Josephine McNair had six grandchildren and one great-grandchild.

For all his success in the professional and business world, however, McNair saw the political values that had undergirded his consensual power base in the 1960s give way to vastly different styles and strategies in the latter decades of the twentieth century and early years of the twenty-first. Centrism and moderation, seemingly unassailable virtues in a world trying to resist the violence and danger of civil disorder in the 1960s, became liabilities a few decades later. Flexibility and compromise were viewed as weaknesses in a world in which zealous partisanship had led to a winner-take-all mentality of power exploitation. In that setting, public policy became largely the product of political parties catering to their base of ideologically conforming followers.

The caution and patience that were the durable foundations of McNair's deliberative style gave way to the polarizing and aggressive politics of a generation in which "going negative" became a strategic norm for the time. Personal politics, the "friends and neighbors" practices of the state's rural political barons, were replaced by partisan machines that demanded conformity and discipline in their dutiful adherence to predetermined messages.

It was a long way from the coalitions that McNair had busied himself building to withstand the onset of legal, constitutional, and social change of the mid-1960s. But even in the 1960s, centrism had its clear opponents, and forces were building at either end of the philosophical spectrum. Barry Goldwater's GOP presidential campaign was defined by his comment of July 16, 1964: "Extremism in defense of liberty is no vice. Moderation in pursuit of justice is no virtue." He lit a torch that fueled a sequence of increasingly conservative—and increasingly successful—Republican campaigns, and in the process, he helped redefine political discourse in terms of ideological, spiritual, and personal themes. It was quite a contrast to the practical issues of economic growth, public education, health care, public safety, and others that McNair had viewed as the relevant themes for policy examination.

Republicans were not alone in their drift from the political center. McNair could see the leftward gravitation away from the center within his own Democratic Party. As early as the 1968 Chicago convention—best known for the explosive demonstrations at Grant Park that diverted attention away from the actual nominating process—McNair believed that the party's future lay with the state organizations, and to a great extent with the governors of those states.

A longtime friend of President Lyndon Johnson and a staunch believer in the big-tent theory of inclusive politics, McNair had been a vigorous member of governors' organizations at the national and regional levels. He also had broad experience serving in leadership roles in state-based organizations such as the Education Commission of the States and the Southern Regional Education Board, as well as federal-state partnerships such as the Appalachian and Coastal Plains Regional Commissions. He knew the potential for political and policy power that lay among the governors at that time, and he was part of a pact in 1968 that was urging the Democratic presidential nominee, Hubert Humphrey, to select a governor as his running mate. Longtime state Democratic leader Crosby Lewis believed McNair himself was in strong contention for that slot until the governors' bloc yielded under pressure to the selection of Senator Edmund Muskie of Maine to fill out the unsuccessful 1968 ticket.

The leftward drift within the party, identified at the time with the candidacies of Robert Kennedy and Eugene McCarthy and built around ideological adherence to an anti–Vietnam War theme, led to significant scuffling in the days following Humphrey's close loss to Nixon in 1968. McNair and many of the governors worried about incipient reform movements challenging the party's old guard and pitting governors against reformers who not only wanted a stronger ideological base for the party but were also working to reshape the party's governing and power structure.

In a speech given prominent coverage in *U.S. News and World Report,* McNair articulated the centrist position to the Democratic National Committee on September 18, 1969:

> There . . . is grave apprehension about the direction our party is taking and the alteration of basic philosophy which is under consideration. . . . If the zeal of reform has now brought us to the brink of extremism, then I suggest that we reassess our values.
>
> Extremism breeds extremism. . . . To yield our party now to either extreme would most certainly touch off a chain reaction which could reshape the entire political structure of our nation and permanently damage the traditional concept of our party's broad ideology. Unless I misread all the political signs in our nation today, I do not think our people are ready for a political party of extremism. I think the people of America today are looking for the politics of moderation.
>
> We are a party of liberals, we are a party of conservatives, we are a party of moderation encompassing that great collection of ethnic, racial, religious, economic, cultural, occupational and social minorities which have given our nation its perpetual regeneration of strength. Let us not now turn from this coalition of ideals into a single-minded party bent on purging certain elements from our midst.[2]

Among other things, McNair and the governors were worried about recommended party rule changes coming from a commission headed by South Dakota senator George McGovern that would significantly reduce governors' roles in party affairs and weaken the influence of states that did not support the Democratic candidate in national elections. McGovern defended himself against McNair's comments by saying, "In the past, political parties given a choice between reform and death have chosen death. It's so much more peaceful and easy. But we have chosen reform. We have chosen life. And that . . . is the way to future unity and future victory. Democrats have always prided themselves on their ability to fight and then make up in time to win elections. But seldom, if ever, have party differences been so bitter as now."[3]

Colorado senator Gary Hart, himself a presidential candidate at one time, put it more bluntly. "The moderate is suspect to all," he wrote in his 1993 book, *The*

Good Fight. "The passive centrist, the moderate, waits for activists in both polarized camps to seek the middle way, to discover their own moderates' leadership."[4]

As it turned out, it was McNair's words that proved painfully prophetic for Democrats. The party chose to follow McGovern, Hart, and their colleagues in a leftward march, and the result was the crushing political defeat at the hands of Richard Nixon in 1972. Democrats not only lost the election, they also lost the centrist power base that they had claimed since the days of Franklin Roosevelt.

Within South Carolina, there may have also been negative impact for the Democrats. Longtime party leader Don Fowler said years later, "The association with McGovern was damaging in South Carolina. When we got to the '74 [gubernatorial] election, we lost that. Now we didn't lose the '74 election because of McGovern, but it did create enough uncertainty in South Carolina so that when the Ravenel thing happened, there was enough looseness for the Republicans to win. So I think the McGovern experience was—I won't say it was conclusive—was an important experience that undermined the home base of the Democratic Party here."[5] McNair was right about some other things, as well. For the next eight presidential elections, the only Democrats to win were two former southern governors, Jimmy Carter of Georgia in 1976 and Bill Clinton of Arkansas in 1992 and 1996, both running as ideological centrists and strategic outsiders. Democrats who ran for president with backgrounds in the Senate—Walter Mondale, Al Gore, and John Kerry—were all losers. The Democratic Party of 2004 did not look or act much like the Democratic Party of 1968.

The McNair legacy, however, lay largely within the borders of South Carolina and took on many shapes and forms. Some were tangible and measurable. Others were indirect and less visible.

Most immediately evident were the outcomes of his aggressive and inventive approaches to economic development, outcomes whose influence remained for generations and which were already clear even as he left office. Per capita income grew by almost 80 percent during his years in office, a rate of more than 10 percent a year, and capital investments in new and expanded industry, estimated at $875 million for the first half of the 1960s, more than doubled during the latter half of the decade in which McNair governed the state.

In time, tourism became the state's economic pacesetter, fulfilling the expectations of a McNair initiative in 1967 with the creation of the Department of Parks, Recreation and Tourism. As manufacturing jobs left the state by the thousands in the migratory offshore movement of the 1980s and 1990s, the state's economy grew wobbly, and unemployment in a number of rural counties was chronically over 10 percent. Travel and tourism, taking on proportions scarcely imagined as the McNair vision of a PRT agency emerged in the mid-1960s, became the economic lifeblood in many of those counties and kept South Carolinians employed as manufacturing jobs went elsewhere.

Other parts of the legacy became similarly institutionalized with little public attention. It was under McNair's leadership that agencies were created to address the state's cultural heritage—a Commission for the Arts and a Department of Archives and History. As chairman of the Budget and Control Board, he oversaw the development of the current Capitol Complex, a four-block landscaped park at the center of which sits the South Carolina State House. Part of the initiative was the construction of underground parking, the erection of three new office buildings named for McNair legislative colleagues Solomon Blatt, Edgar Brown, and Marion Gressette, and the retrofitting of an older building named for Rembert Dennis. Senate Street was closed between Sumter and Assembly Streets to facilitate the gardens designed by Robert Marvin, a landscape architect from Walterboro. A small monument to McNair on the south grounds recognizes his role in the development.

It was under the leadership of First Lady Josephine R. McNair, whose ancestry could be traced back to the Calhoun family, that another cultural treasure, the governor's mansion, was rescued and developed. Organized informally first to help in acquiring suitable furnishings for the mansion, a commission was eventually given statutory authority to oversee the management of the mansion and grounds and to provide for expansion. Mrs. Herbert (Lilla) Hoefer of Columbia was its first chair. Acquisition of the Lace House and Boylston House made possible the current four-block complex that houses the governor, his family, and guests.

A great deal of the McNair legacy lay less tangibly, but perhaps more durably, in the Moody Report. Through that document, and the extraordinary exercise in political and governmental reform that accompanied it, public education was essentially rescued in South Carolina.

"I give Bob [McNair] the credit for really saving our public schools," former Governor John West said years later. "Looking back, and realizing that the private schools were growing up and taking away popular support for public schools, it took a lot of courage and leadership to say we're going to have a public school system and let's carry forward."[6] It was a vastly underrated moment in South Carolina history.

For scholars and serious public administrators, McNair was an innovator and a remarkably astute one, and his legacy had historical proportions. His administration, in the perspective of history's backward glance, was the last hurrah for the bygone days of South Carolina's personal, oligarchic government. Bob McNair took the old machine and got a few more good years out of it. He knew all its quirks and eccentricities, and he knew where to kick when it grew balky. He took on what was essentially the same form of government that had served South Carolina since the turn of the twentieth century, with many of its leaders in place for decades.

"He looked at it, he studied it and he reflected on it," said Fred Carter, a public administration scholar who became president of Francis Marion University and also served in an executive capacity on the staffs of Republican governors Carroll Campbell and Mark Sanford.

> I had just taken over as Governor Sanford's Chief of Staff, and I went over and had about a two-hour conversation with Governor McNair, talking about governance, talking about the cabinet, and the successive waves of reform that had come down the road.
>
> In those two hours—and remember now, this is a topic that I've studied not only as a practitioner, but also as an academic, for a number of years—I came away with a variety of perspectives that I had simply never entertained before. A lot of that had to do with being who he is at this point in South Carolina's history, and his being able to access a lot of different points of information and assimilate that information with his amazingly energetic intellect.[7]

Much of the McNair legacy lay unrecorded and best remembered for things that did not happen. His years as governor came during an era of unprecedented domestic conflict and confrontation in America. Racial violence was sweeping across the South and the rest of the nation. In big cities, entire neighborhoods and business districts were engulfed in flames of anger, and antiwar and antidraft student crusades were disrupting college and university campuses.

In South Carolina, all the makings of such destruction were in place. Pent-up racial feelings neared boiling points, and tensions were finding their release in demonstrations, protests, and disruptions of civic life. Antiwar sentiments were dividing the state politically and philosophically and were threatening to erupt into major public disturbances. South Carolina stood at the very brink of civil and societal mayhem.

The shootings at South Carolina State College in 1968 remained a deeply painful experience, and for many the tragedy was unresolved over the years. But it never happened again, and at least part of the reason was McNair's willingness to become directly involved and engaged in subsequent crises, particularly those at the Medical College Hospital in 1969 and the University of South Carolina in 1970. Painstakingly, McNair led the state through tensions connected with desegregation, antiwar sentiment, racial alienation, and labor disputes.

Other elements of the McNair legacy were even less tangible and more elusive to discover and describe. One was the manner in which he conducted business—a characteristic as much as anything else in his administration—which defined Bob McNair for those who knew and dealt with him. "He would break you down with that smile," his mentor, Speaker Solomon Blatt, said, and others had similar observations.

Longtime friend and colleague Don Fowler recalled, "He was a thoroughly nice person. The simple trait of being nice to people was a huge asset to him. People sensed that, and I think it was genuine. I don't think it was pretense and I don't think it was done just to try to please people. It was genuine. He genuinely respected people."[8]

Few political figures accomplished so much with the simple power of their personal will and good nature. McNair was not an orator, and his strength lay in the small rooms and not in the large auditoriums. His speeches were delivered in a conversational tone, and he never lost the distinctive sound and pronunciations of his rural lowcountry upbringing.

The quiet style and personal charm could be disarming, and they could also conceal the ultimate McNair weapon. He could simply out-think people. He possessed the extraordinary ability to apply his considerable intellect in a catalytic and analytical manner in practical situations. In instances where he might have been outnumbered politically, financially, or bureaucratically, he could prevail with whatever outcome he might have been seeking. "He knew where the leverage points were," Fred Carter said.[9]

"The man could walk into a room and he seemed to have a depth of knowledge in every crevice of government," Jim Konduros recalled. "People realized they were witnessing the enriched mind of an individual who understood the subject matter, and they knew he was asking them to look at things in a different way." McNair's style was one that often carried him into tangential conversations, inviting unguarded and relaxed chats and observations and winning confidence. "He took great mental notes," Konduros said, "and he had a pretty good view of the playing field." A lot of it was pacing and timing, and McNair had the capacity to size up his colleagues and judge their inclinations. At the moment he felt he had made some progress on a personal basis, Konduros said, "That's when he'd slide in his agenda."[10]

"He was smart," Fowler recalled. "He knew how to figure out people and how to work people."

> One thing that I've always marveled at. He could carry on a conversation and never let you know what he was thinking about a subject until he chose to. He could talk around anything in the world, and he could indirectly state things so that whatever he said that might have caused a negative reaction, he could back around it.
>
> One of the things McNair could do in a quiet way as well as anybody was inspire people. It was not like listening to Martin Luther King make a speech, but he could make people have confidence in themselves, and he could make people work together.[11]

Public life in the 1960s, for all its tensions and stresses, was conducted with civility. Before the days when personal attacks and partisan discipline turned political service into a contact sport, the business of government was carried out on a human scale. The smoke-filled rooms, and not the front pages of newspapers, were often the places where fights were fought and deals were cut. For whatever may have been its flaws and shortcomings, the 1960s were times when it was safe to disagree and acceptable to compromise.

In such an atmosphere, public attention was not always granted to the loudest or the angriest or the most ideologically pure. Unlike elsewhere in the South, dema-goguery was a low-value item in South Carolina in the 1960s. "It was a golden age," Fowler said. "It was the real blossoming of the New South in South Carolina. All the promise and the ambition and aspirations of the people of the state came to fruition."[12]

The victors in 1960s South Carolina were not the ideologues with the expensive media messages, spin doctors, and wedge issues. They were the masters of persua-sion and the purveyors of quiet influence. They were the negotiators and the com-promisers. They were the consensus-builders who could handle change and transition without uproar.

It was in that setting that civil rights change came to South Carolina. It was filled with the storms of protest and the tensions of confrontation. But it was accommodated by a political infrastructure that could absorb the forces and counterforces of change and not lose its equilibrium.

In their own way, they were good days for the American democracy. They were days in which the tree of liberty was being refreshed, as Thomas Jefferson envi-sioned two centuries earlier. And it was the precise moment in history in which Bob McNair could excel.

Notes

Chapter 1

1. Senator Johnston was particularly active in opposition to major civil rights acts of 1957, 1960, and 1964, proposals that significantly empowered the federal government to protect civil rights and enforce federal laws within the southern states. Southern resistance was formidable throughout and was fraught with parliamentary tactics. South Carolina gained some notoriety when Johnston's flamboyant colleague, Strom Thurmond, filibustered for twenty-four hours and eighteen minutes against the 1957 act. (See Nadine Cohodas, *Strom Thurmond and the Politics of Southern Change,* New York: Simon & Schuster, 1993.)

Johnston was also a vigorous opponent of efforts to abolish the poll tax as a requirement of voting, initiated as early as the Roosevelt administration in 1945. Johnston fought the creation of a Fair Employment Practices Act, a Truman proposal to prohibit discrimination in employment because of race, creed, color, or national origin. The Fair Employment Practices Commission initiative came from Truman's 1947 "To Secure These Rights" report, a document that led to the southern states' bolt from the Democratic camp in 1948 to run their own candidate, Thurmond, who at the time was governor of South Carolina, for president on the States' Rights, or "Dixiecrat," ticket. (See "Entire Senate Voting Record of Senator Olin D. Johnston by Subject from January 3, 1945, to October 13, 1962, Prepared and Compiled by the Senate Democratic Party Policy Committee," Papers of United States Senator Olin D. Johnston, box 98, South Carolina Political Collections, University of South Carolina.)

2. Johnston's scheme was dismissed in the South Carolina lawsuit challenging the all-white primary (*Rice v. Elmore,* 165 F.2d 387), a 1947 ruling in which federal judge J. Waties Waring offered the comment that "I cannot see where the skies will fall if South Carolina is put in the same class with other states. It is time for South Carolina to rejoin the union." (See Ernest McPherson Lander Jr., *A History of South Carolina, 1865–1960,* Chapel Hill: University of North Carolina Press, 1960, 172, and V. O. Key Jr., *Southern Politics in State and Nation,* New York: Knopf, 1949, 628.) Waring, whose subsequent rulings helped set the judicial stage for the landmark Supreme Court ruling overturning public-school segregation, *Brown v. Board of Education of Topeka, Kansas,* 347 U.S. 483 (1954), was scarcely overstating the impact a 1944 case outlawing the all-white primary (*Smith v. Allwright,* 321 U.S. 649) would have in South Carolina. In 1940, black-voter registration across the South "stood at a level not substantially higher than that to which it had been reduced by the disfranchising efforts of the late nineteenth and very early twentieth centuries" (David J. Garrow, *Protest at Selma,* New Haven: Yale University

Press, 1978, 6). In South Carolina, the total number of black registrants was estimated to be no more than three thousand, less than 1 percent of the voting-age black population and among the lowest in the South.

All that changed drastically after *Smith v. Allwright* and after Waring's South Carolina ruling in *Rice v. Elmore*. And, for some time, the political sky did fall. Strom Thurmond, the South's states' rights champion and Dixiecrat candidate for president in 1948, found his political stock significantly damaged in his home state only two years later by the "startling speed" with which blacks had registered (Garrow, 6).

3. Key, *Southern Politics,* 130.

4. *Greenville News,* February 4, 1998.

5. Donald Russell served on the Price Adjustment Board from January to October 1942; as assistant to the director of economic stabilization from October 1942 to May 1943; as assistant to director of war mobilization from May 1943 to September 1944; as deputy director, Office of War Mobilization and Reconversion, from December 1944 to July 1945; and as assistant secretary of state for administration from July 1945 to January 1947. He was also a member of the Wriston Commission, which reviewed the operation of the Foreign Service Act of 1946, and a member of the 1954 Hoover Commission on Government Reorganization.

6. Hugh Gibson, Charleston (S.C.) *News and Courier,* April 2, 1965.

7. Solomon Blatt, personal interview, Oral Histories of the Robert E. McNair Gubernatorial Administration (1965–1971), South Carolina Department of Archives and History, Columbia, 22 (hereafter cited as Oral Histories).

8. Daniel McLeod, personal interview, Oral Histories, tape 2, 8–9.

9. Al Lanier, Associated Press, April 23, 1965.

10. C. R. Canup and W. D. Workman, *Charles E. Daniel: His Philosophy and Legacy* (Columbia, S.C.: R. L. Bryan, 1981), 155–61.

11. Gibson, Charleston (S.C.) *News and Courier,* March 20, 1965.

12. Charles Wickenberg, Columbia (S.C.) *State,* April 21, 1965.

13. Fred Sheheen, personal interview with author, 1998.

14. McNair, personal interview, Oral Histories, tape 6, 13.

15. Ibid.

16. Blatt, personal interview, Oral Histories, 22–23.

17. *Charlotte Observer,* April 23, 1965.

18. Ibid.

19. Jack Claiborne, *Charlotte Observer,* April 25, 1965.

20. Charleston (S.C.) *News and Courier,* April 23, 1965.

21. State Senator Marion Gressette later contended that three members of the Senate, and not Governor Byrnes, originated the school-equalization plan:

> there were three of us in the Senate who just concluded that we had to do something if we were going to get education moving in the direction we wanted it to move. And those three of us were Dick [former Governor R. M.] Jeffries, who at one time was President Pro Tem of the Senate; Rembert Dennis, who [later became] Chairman of the Finance Committee, and myself. And we came up with the idea [in 1950] of the three percent sales tax and actually wrote that into the law.
>
> It went to the House. I imagine they considered it, but I got the impression that they wanted to make a big deal out of it, and they just didn't want to accept it because it orig-

inated in the Senate . . . so what they did then was they appointed a committee to study the three percent sales tax. We felt we didn't need a study; we needed the money.

And so what happened then was Fritz Hollings was elected chairman of that special committee [and] . . . the House studied the matter over the summer and then Byrnes was elected Governor in November of that year and he came in and approved the House committee's recommendation.

. . . Over the years I've had to stand by and hear them talk about how Governor Byrnes started the sales tax—and Governor Hollings—when I knew it was started with Governor Jeffries, Rembert Dennis, and Marion Gressette (Gressette Transcript, 18–19).

22. Robert McHugh, Columbia (S.C.) *State,* April 22, 1965.

23. Gibson, Charleston (S.C.) *News and Courier,* April 22, 1965.

24. Charleston (S.C.) *News and Courier,* April 22, 1965.

25. Lanier, Associated Press in Columbia (S.C.) *State,* April 22, 1965.

26. *Florence Morning News,* April 22, 1965.

27. Charleston (S.C.) *Evening Post,* April 22, 1965.

28. McNair, personal interview, Oral Histories, tape 6, 22.

29. Ibid.

30. Ibid.

31. Ibid., 6.

32. Ibid., 3–4.

33. Ibid.

34. By the start of the 1958–1959 school year, most of the black students in Missouri (94.2 percent) and the District of Columbia (82.3 percent) were enrolled in desegregated schools. To a lesser extent, Delaware (42.6 percent), Maryland (30.6 percent), Kentucky (28.9 percent), West Virginia (24.9 percent), and Oklahoma (23.9 percent) were proceeding with the desegregation process. Texas, Tennessee, Arkansas, North Carolina, and Virginia had taken barely measurable (less than 1.5 percent) desegregation steps. In Alabama, Florida, Georgia, Louisiana, Mississippi, and South Carolina, there was no reported desegregation (United States Commission on Civil Rights, "With Liberty and Justice for All," Washington, D.C., 1959, 123, 128).

By 1958–1959, in the years immediately after *Brown v. Board,* a total of some 216,000 black students were admitted to formerly all-white schools in eleven mostly border states and the District of Columbia. Of that number, more than 180,000 were in two states—Missouri (74,135) and Maryland (37,840)—and the District of Columbia (68,421) (*With Liberty and Justice for All,* 123, 128). Although much of the border states' willingness to comply voluntarily with desegregation orders has been attributed to the relatively low black population in those states, it has also been argued that desegregation in urban areas such as St. Louis, Louisville, Baltimore, and Wilmington, Delaware, involved "Negro numbers . . . as high as in some typically southern communities" (W. D. Workman, ed., "The Deep South: Segregation Holds Firm," in *With All Deliberate Speed: Segregation-Desegregation in Southern Schools,* edited by Don Shoemaker (New York: Harper, 1957, 60). The difference, it was speculated, came from "border state officials (who) from the first held the position that the law had been defined by the Court and it was up to the states to go along" (61).

35. Leon Panetta and Peter Gall, *Bring Us Together: The Nixon Team and the Civil Rights Retreat* (Philadelphia: Lippincott, 1971), 25.

36. Cyril B. Busbee, personal interview, Oral Histories, tape 1, 16. (The committee was known as the Gressette Committee after its chair, Calhoun County senator Marion Gressette.)

37. Harry S. Ashmore, *Hearts and Minds* (Washington, D.C.: Seven Locks, 1988), 186.

38. Lander, *History of South Carolina,* 202.

39. Ibid.

40. John G. Sproat, "Pragmatic Conservatism and Desegregation: The Case of South Carolina" (unpublished), 13.

41. Gressette, personal interview, Oral Histories, tape 1, 21.

42. John Egerton, *Speak Now against the Day: The Generation before the Civil Rights Movement in the South* (New York: Knopf, 1994), 609.

43. Ibid.

44. Columbia (S.C.) *State,* May 18, 1954.

45. Workman, "Deep South," 94.

46. Gressette, personal interview, Oral Histories, tape 1, 21.

47. Busbee, personal interview, Oral Histories, tape 1, 17.

48. Egerton, *Speak Now,* 589.

49. Barbara H. Woods, "Modjeska Simkins and the South Carolina Conference of the NAACP, 1939–1957," in *Women in the Civil Rights Movement,* edited by Vicki L. Crawford, Jacqueline Anne Rouse, and Barbara Woods (Brooklyn, N.Y.: Carlson, 1990), 109–10.

50. Ibid., 110.

51. I. A. Newby, *Black Carolinians: A History of Blacks in South Carolina from 1895 to 1968* (Columbia: University of South Carolina Press, 1973), 306.

52. Ibid., 278.

53. Ibid., 279.

54. John Lewis, *Walking with the Wind: A Memoir of the Movement* (New York: Simon & Schuster, 1998), 114.

55. Ibid., 347.

56. Ibid.

57. Ibid., 186.

58. R. Wright Spears, *One in the Spirit: Ministry for Change in South Carolina* (Columbia, S.C.: R. L. Bryan, 1997), 148.

59. Ibid., 147.

60. The Southern Regional Council, Atlanta, and the American Jewish Committee Institute of Human Relations, New York, N.Y., "The Continuing Crisis: An Assessment of New Racial Tensions in the South," May 1966, 6.

61. James Forman, *The Making of Black Revolutionaries* (Seattle: University of Washington Press, 1997), 224.

62. Ralph McGill, *The South and the Southerner* (Boston: Little Brown, 1963), 265.

63. Orville Vernon Burton, "The Black Squint of the Law," in *The Meaning of South Carolina History: Essays in Honor of George C. Rogers, Jr.,* edited by David R. Chesnutt and Clyde N. Wilson (Columbia: University of South Carolina Press, 1991), 163.

Chapter 2

1. See discussion in I. A. Newby, *Plain Folk in the New South: Social Change and Cultural Persistence, 1880–1915* (Baton Rouge: Louisiana State University Press, 1989), 26–30.

2. Robert E. McNair, personal interview, Oral Histories of the Robert E. McNair Gubernatorial Administration (1965–1971), South Carolina Department of Archives and History, Columbia, tape 1, 11 (hereafter Oral Histories).

3. Ibid., 2.

4. Ibid.

5. Ibid., 3–4.

6. Ibid., 10

7. McNair, personal interview, Oral Histories, Robert S. Davis tape, tape 1, 13.

8. By popular local story, Maxton took its name from "Mac's Town," after all the Scots who settled there.

9. Article in the Lumberton (N.C.) *Robesonian,* June 18, 1992, and a personal letter to Robert E. McNair from William C. Powell.

10. Letter from Roland Crawford to Claire Fort, February 7, 2000.

11. Ibid.

12. McNair, personal interview, Oral Histories, tape 1, 10.

13. Louis Towles, ed., *A World Turned Upside Down: The Palmers of South Santee, 1818–1881* (Columbia: University of South Carolina Press, 1996), 2.

14. Christian L. Larsen, *South Carolina's Natural Resources: A Study of Public Administration* (Columbia: University of South Carolina Press, 1947), 40.

15. Ibid., 9, 21.

16. McNair, personal interview, Oral Histories, tape 1, 15.

17. Ibid.

18. Ibid.

19. Ibid., 13–14.

20. Ibid., 15.

21. Ibld., 16.

22. Ibid., 16–17.

23. Ibid., 17.

24. Rivers, as longtime chairman of the House Military Affairs Committee, influenced the location of military operations in the South Carolina Lowcountry that improved significantly the area's economy. Bates was a two-time candidate for governor and was influential in settling peacefully the 1960s sit-ins at Columbia lunch counters. Dennis ended his legislative career as chairman of the Senate Finance Committee and president pro tempore of the Senate.

25. Exact figures are not available since Berkeley was part of Charleston County at the time, but estimates based on the 1860 population of parishes generally identified with the Berkeley territory would place the total slave population at more than 23,300.

26. Maxwell Clayton Orvin, *Moncks Corner, Berkeley County, South Carolina* (Charleston, 1950), 28–29, 35.

27. George Brown Tindall, *South Carolina Negroes, 1877–1900* (Columbia: University of South Carolina Press, 1952), 52.

28. David Duncan Wallace, *South Carolina: A Short History, 1520–1948* (Columbia: University of South Carolina Press, 1984), 620.

29. *South Carolina: A Handbook* (Columbia, S.C.: Department of Agriculture, Commerce and Industries and Clemson College, 1927), 102–3.

30. William J. Cooper and Thomas E. Terrill, *The American South: A History,* 2nd ed., vol. 2 (New York: McGraw-Hill, 1996), 653.

31. Ibid., 605.

32. Newby, *Black Carolinians: A History of Blacks in South Carolina, 1895–1968* (Columbia: University of South Carolina Press, 1973), 193.

33. *South Carolina: A Handbook,* 193.

34. Newby, *Black Carolinians,* 103.

35. Cooper and Terrill, *American South,* 605.

36. Harry S. Ashmore, in Walter Edgar, *A History of Santee Cooper, 1934–1984* (Columbia, S.C.: R. L. Bryan, 1984), 5.

37. V. O. Key Jr., *Southern Politics in State and Nation* (1949; repr., Knoxville: University of Tennessee Press, 1984), 131.

38. Ibid., 147.

39. Ibid., 135.

40. Ibid., 147.

41. Orville Vernon Burton, in Benjamin E. Mays, *Born to Rebel* (Athens: University of Georgia Press, 1987), xvi.

42. Democratic leader Martin Witherspoon Gary proclaimed what would become the state's policy for decades. "We regard the issues between the white and colored people . . . as an antagonism of race, not a difference of political party. . . . White supremacy is essential to our survival as a people" (quoted by Burton in Mays, *Born to Rebel,* xvii).

43. The last holdouts of black political influence were Beaufort County—at one time referred to by Tillman as the county of "niggerdom" (see Tindal, *South Carolina Negroes,* 61)—and Georgetown County, where the politics of "fusionism" made its last stand and where John Williams Bolts became the last black state legislator (elected in 1898 and 1900) until the election of Herbert Fielding of Charleston, James Felder of Columbia, and I. S. Leevy Johnson of Columbia in 1970.

44. George C. Rogers and C. James Taylor, *A South Carolina Chronology, 1497–1992* (Columbia: University of South Carolina Press, 1994), 132.

45. Burton in Mays, *Born to Rebel,* xviii.

46. Newby, *Black Carolinians,* 136.

47. Ibid., 148.

48. Ibid., 147.

49. Claudia Smith Brinson, *Columbia Record,* June 18, 1979.

50. Newby, *Black Carolinians,* 137.

51. bid., 157–58.

52. I. DeQuincey Newman, personal interview with author, 1981.

53. Barbara H. Woods, "Modjeska Simkins and the South Carolina Conference of the NAACP, 1939–1957," in *Women in the Civil Rights Movement,* edited by Vicki L. Crawford, Jacqueline Anne Rouse, and Barbara Woods (Brooklyn, N.Y.: Carlson, 1990), 101–6.

54. Mays, *Born to Rebel,* 2

55. *South Carolina: A Handbook,* 4.

56. James C. Cobb, *The Selling of the South: The Southern Crusade for Industrial Development 1936–1990,* 2nd ed. (Urbana: University of Illinois Press, 1993), 1–2.

57. *Houston Chronicle and Memphis Commercial Appeal,* in Roger Biles, *The South and the New Deal* (Lexington: University of Kentucky Press, 1994), 32.

58. Newby, *Plain Folk in the New South,* 352; for more discussion, see chapter 12, "Health," 352–86.

59. McNair, personal interview, Oral Histories, tape 1, 7.

60. Ibid.

61. Ibid., 5.

62. Biles, *South and the New Deal*, 54.

63. Larsen, *South Carolina's Natural Resources*, 191.

64. James F. Byrnes, *All in One Lifetime* (New York: Harper, 1958), 85.

65. Edgar, *Santee Cooper*, 4.

66. Ibid., 8.

67. McNair, personal interview, Oral Histories, tape 1, 5.

68. Byrnes, *All in One Lifetime*, 81.

69. Ernest McPherson Lander Jr., *A History of South Carolina, 1865–1960* (Chapel Hill: University of North Carolina Press, 1960), citing *Time*, 38 (August 26, 1936), 8.

70. W. D. Workman Jr., *The Bishop from Barnwell: The Political Life and Times of Senator Edgar A. Brown* (Columbia, S.C.: R. L. Bryan, 1963), 223.

71. Byrnes, *All in One Lifetime*, 104.

72. Ashmore, *Civil Rights and Wrongs: A Memoir of Race and Politics, 1944–1994* (New York: Pantheon, 1994), 22–23.

73. Biles, *South and the New Deal*, 123–24.

74. Robert A. Caro, *The Years of Lyndon Johnson: The Path to Power* (New York: Knopf, 1982), 220.

Chapter 3

1. Robert E. McNair, personal interview, Oral Histories of the Robert E. McNair Gubernatorial Administration (1965–1971), South Carolina Department of Archives and History, Columbia, tape 1, 23 (hereafter Oral Histories).

2. Secretary of the Navy, transmission to McNair, December 20, 2002.

3. McNair, personal interview, Oral Histories, tape 1, 23.

4. Robert Ross Smith, *Triumph in the Philippines* (Washington, D.C.: Center of Military History, U.S. Army, 1991), 30.

5. David Duncan Wallace, *South Carolina: A Short History, 1520–1948* (Columbia: University of South Carolina Press, 1984), 694.

6. McNair, personal interview, Oral Histories, tape 2, 4.

7. Ibid., 6.

8. Ibid., 5.

9. Ibid.

10. Compiled from individual biographical information contained in the *South Carolina Legislative Manuals* for 1946 and 1948.

11. *Charleston Post and Courier*, May 26, 1997, A1.

12. Armstrong Williams, Columbia (S.C.) *State*, February 5, 1995.

13. *South Carolina Legislative Manual*, 1975.

14. Marianna Davis, *South Carolina Blacks and Native Americans, 1776–1976* (Columbia, S.C.: State Human Affairs Commission, 1976).

15. John Egerton, *Speak Now against the Day: The Generation before the Civil Rights Movement in the South* (New York: Knopf, 1994), 218.

16. Ibid., 408.

17. See note 2, chap. 1.

18. "For the first time in any southern state," it was written by chronicler John Egerton, "a group of middle class black citizens organized a political challenge to the exclusively white institutions of privilege and control. They had taken the initial step at a meeting in

Columbia in November, 1939, when delegates from seven local branches came together to form the South Carolina Conference of the NAACP, and to declare that 'All the blessings of life, liberty and happiness are possible in integration, while in segregation lurk all the forces destructive of these values'" (227).

19. Egerton, *Speak Now,* 405–9.

20. Ibid., 428.

21. Ibid., 228.

22. David McCullough, *Truman* (New York: Simon & Schuster, 1992), 589.

23. Orville Vernon Burton, "The Black Squint of the Law," in *The Meaning of South Carolina History: Essays in Honor of George C. Rogers, Jr.,* edited by David R. Chesnutt and Clyde N. Wilson (Columbia: University of South Carolina Press, 1991), 163.

24. Department of Veterans Affairs, as reported in *Parade Magazine* (August 4, 1996), 4.

25. Egerton, *Speak Now,* 206–7.

26. Daniel W. Hollis, *University of South Carolina: College to University,* vol. 2 (Columbia: University of South Carolina Press, 1956), 339.

27. Ibid., 339.

28. Ibid., 340.

29. Ibid., 341.

30. McNair, personal interview, Oral Histories, tape 1, 18–19.

31. Ibid., 21–22.

32. Ibid., 22.

33. McNair, personal interview, Oral Histories, tape 2, 2.

34. McNair, personal interview, Oral Histories, tape 1, 20.

35. Jerold Savory, *Columbia College: The Ariail Era* (Columbia, S.C.: R. L. Bryan, 1979), 65.

36. Ibid., 11–12.

37. McNair, personal interview, Oral Histories, tape 1, 20.

38. Ibid., 20–21.

39. Hollis, *University of South Carolina,* 336.

40. McNair, personal interview, Oral Histories, tape 1, 21.

41. Frank H. Wardlaw, ed., *Men and Women of Carolina: Selected Addresses and Papers by J. Rion McKissick* (Columbia: University of South Carolina Press, 1948), 23.

42. Ibid., 161, 168.

43. W. D. Workman Jr., *The Bishop from Barnwell: The Political Life and Times of Senator Edgar A. Brown* (Columbia, S.C.: R. L. Bryan, 1963), 99.

44. Ibid., 99–100.

45. McNair, personal interview, Oral Histories, tape 2, 10.

46. Hollis, *University of South Carolina,* 208, 220.

47. McNair, personal interview, Oral Histories, tape 2, 12.

48. Mary L. Morgan, Carolyn R. Taylor, and N. Louise Bailey, *Biographical Directory of the South Carolina Senate, 1776–1985,* vol. 2 (Columbia: University of South Carolina Press, 1986), 1182–83.

49. McNair, personal interview, Oral Histories, tape 2, 17.

50. Walter Edgar and Inez Watson, eds., *Biographical Directory of the S.C. House of Representatives* (Columbia: University of South Carolina Press, 1974), 565; James E. Hunter Jr. and Watson, eds., *South Carolina Legislative Manual, 1946* (Columbia, S.C.: House of Representatives, 1946), 120.

51. Rembert Dennis, personal interview, Oral Histories.

52. Wallace, *South Carolina,* 624–25, 654.

53. Bailey et al., *Biographical Directory,* 1:377–78.

54. Dennis, personal interview, Oral Histories, tape 1, 2.

55. McNair, personal interview, Oral Histories, tape 2, 15.

56. McCullough, *Truman,* 710.

57. Nadine Cohodas, *Strom Thurmond and the Politics of Southern Change* (New York: Simon & Schuster, 1993), 84.

58. Ibid., 28–29.

59. Cole Blease Graham Jr., *Budgetary Change in South Carolina 1945–1971,* unpublished dissertation, University of South Carolina, 1971.

60. Cohodas, *Strom Thurmond,* 84.

61. Ibid., 96–97.

62. Ibid., 123.

63. Ibid., 101.

64. Ibid., 124.

65. McCullough, *Truman,* 586.

66. Ibid., 587.

67. Alberta Lachicotte, *Rebel Senator: Strom Thurmond of South Carolina* (New York: Devin-Adair, 1966), 47.

68. Ibid., 47, 49.

69. Cohodas, *Strom Thurmond,* 186.

70. Ibid., 189.

71. McCullough, *Truman,* 657.

72. Lachicotte, *Rebel Senator,* 61.

73. Harry S. Ashmore, *Civil Rights and Wrongs: A Memoir of Race and Politics, 1944–1994* (New York: Pantheon, 1994), 80.

74. McNair, personal interview, Oral Histories, tape 2, 17–18.

75. Ibid., 14–15.

76. Ibid., 20.

77. *South Carolina: A Handbook* (Columbia, S.C.: Department of Agriculture, Commerce and Industries and Clemson University, 1927), 228.

78. McNair, personal interview, Oral Histories, tape 2, 19.

79. Ibid.

80. Ibid.

81. Ibid., 23.

82. Ibid.

83. Ibid., 21.

84. Ibid., 22.

85. Ibid., 21.

86. Ibid.

87. Ibid., 22.

88. Thomas Lawton, personal interview, Oral Histories, 4.

89. McNair, personal interview, Oral Histories, tape 2, 24.

90. Ibid.

91. Ibid.

Chapter 4

1. James F. Byrnes, *All in One Lifetime* (New York: Harper, 1958), 406.

2. John Egerton, *Speak Now against the Day: The Generation before the Civil Rights Movement in the South* (New York: Knopf, 1994), 576–77.

3. Byrnes, *All in One Lifetime,* 408.

4. Annual Reports of the South Carolina Department of Education, as charted in *The Meaning of South Carolina History: Essays in Honor of George C. Rogers, Jr.,* edited by David R. Chesnutt and Clyde N. Wilson (Columbia: University of South Carolina Press, 1991), 176.

5. Egerton, *Speak Now,* 590–91.

6. Byrnes, *All in One Lifetime,* 412.

7. Egerton, *Speak Now,* 492.

8. Byrnes, *All in One Lifetime,* 407–8.

9. Ibid., 408.

10. Ibid., 409.

11. McNair, personal interview, Oral Histories of the Robert E. McNair Gubernatorial Administration (1965–1971), South Carolina Department of Archives and History, Columbia, tape 3, 12 (hereafter Oral Histories).

12. Ibid., 10.

13. Ibid.

14. Ibid., 11.

15. Ibid., 12.

16. Blatt, personal interview, Oral Histories, 25.

17. Ibid., 21.

18. Byrnes, *All in One Lifetime,* 408.

19. Egerton, *Speak Now,* 477.

20. Byrnes, *All in One Lifetime,* 412.

21. Sydnor Thompson, "John W. Davis and His Role in the Public School Segregation Cases—A Personal Memoir," *Washington and Lee Law Review* 52, no. 5 (1996):1685–86.

22. Harry S. Ashmore, *Hearts and Minds* (Washington, D.C.: Seven Locks, 1988), 187.

23. McNair, personal interview, Oral Histories, tape 3, 10–11.

24. Ibid., 4.

25. Ibid., 10.

26. Ibid.

27. Ibid., 23.

28. *South Carolina Legislative Manual,* 1985.

29. Blatt, personal interview, Oral Histories, 12.

30. Ibid., 13.

31. Ibid., 12.

32. Ibid., 1.

33. Ibid., 16.

34. McNair, personal interview, Oral Histories, tape 3, 5.

35. Blatt, personal interview, Oral Histories, 26–27.

36. John C. West, speech to State Executive Managers Conference, Hilton Head, S.C., January 23, 1971.

37. McNair, personal interview, Oral Histories, tape 3, 23.

38. Blatt, personal interview, Oral Histories, 27.

39. McNair, personal interview, Oral Histories, tape 3, 22.

40. Ibid., 15.

41. The film was a documentary produced for public television as part of a series titled *Point of View.* South Carolina Educational Television carried the series but did not air this broadcast.

42. William J. Cooper and Thomas E. Terrill, *The American South: A History,* 2nd ed., vol. 2 (New York: McGraw-Hill, 1996), 643.

43. Terrill, "No Union for Me," in *The Meaning of South Carolina History: Essays in Honor of George C. Rogers, Jr.,* edited by David R. Chesnutt and Clyde N. Wilson (Columbia: University of South Carolina Press, 1991), 206–7.

44. Ibid., 207–8.

45. Ibid., 208.

46. James C. Cobb, *The Selling of the South: The Southern Crusade for Industrial Development 1936–1990,* 2nd ed. (Urbana: University of Illinois Press, 1993), 100.

47. David McCullough, *Truman* (New York: Simon & Schuster, 1992), 466.

48. Cobb, *Selling of the South,* 101.

49. McNair, personal interview, Oral Histories, tape 3, 16.

50. Ibid., 17.

51. Cobb, *Selling of the South,* 101.

52. C. R. Canup and W. D. Workman Jr., *Charles E. Daniel: His Philosophy and Legacy* (Columbia, S.C.: R. L. Bryan, 1981), 163.

53. Ibid., 79.

54. Ibid., 76.

55. Columbia (S.C.) *State,* May 18, 1954.

56. *Brown v. Board of Education of Topeka, Kansas,* 347 U.S. 483 (1954).

Chapter 5

1. John K. Cauthen, *Speaker Blatt: His Challenges Were Greater* (Columbia, S.C.: R. L. Bryan, 1965).

2. Ibid. Nine years later, in 1962, as Blatt was turning down the opportunity to run for another seat on the Supreme Court, the *Anderson Independent,* whose publisher, Wilton Hall, was a sometime adversary of the speaker's, wrote, "Sol Blatt, Speaker of the House of Representatives for twenty-two years, undoubtedly could have been elected to the State Supreme Court vacancy if he had become a candidate. But Speaker Blatt, who has served Barnwell County in the House for thirty years, said he thought he could best serve his constituents and the State by remaining in the House. Speaker Blatt's powerful influence over the course of the State's affairs—earned over three decades . . . is not something to be lightly tossed aside, even for the robes of a Supreme Court justiceship" (quoted in Cauthen, *Speaker Blatt,* 124).

3. McNair, personal interview, Oral Histories of the Robert E. McNair Gubernatorial Administration (1965–1971), South Carolina Department of Archives and History, Columbia, tape 4, 1 (hereafter Oral Histories).

4. McNair, personal interview, Oral Histories, tape 4, 2.

5. Ibid.

6. Ibid., 2–3.

7. I. A. Newby, *Black Carolinians: A History of Blacks in South Carolina, 1895–1968* (Columbia: University of South Carolina Press, 1973), 346–47.

8. Ibid., 347.

9. Ibid., 349.

10. Ernest McPherson Lander Jr., *A History of South Carolina, 1865–1960* (Chapel Hill: University of North Carolina Press, 1960), 205–6.

11. Ibid., 203.

12. Ibid. The *State* newspaper, March 4, 1958, reported, "Dr. Saunders' home was damaged in a dynamite blast after his wife had written an article supporting gradual integration of the schools in a pamphlet entitled 'South Carolinians Speak.'"

13. Ibid., 202.

14. Ibid., 202–3.

15. James F. Byrnes, *All in One Lifetime* (New York: Harper, 1958), 411.

16. Lander, *History of South Carolina,* 211–21.

17. Ibid., 213.

18. Ibid., 214.

19. A South Carolina ad in the *Wall Street Journal* (April 8, 1958) declared, "South Carolina passes law reducing tax on industry; new flexible tax law offers optional methods of income tax computation to meet varying requirements of today's diverse industry."

20. Lander, *History of South Carolina,* 214–21.

21. Cobb, *The Selling of the South: The Southern Crusade for Industrial Development 1936–1990,* 2nd ed. (Urbana: University of Illinois Press, 1993), 1–2.

22. Lander, *History of South Carolina,* 225.

23. Ibid., 223–24.

24. McNair, personal interview, Oral Histories, tape 3, 24.

25. McNair, personal interview, Oral Histories, tape 5, 5.

26. Blatt, personal interview, Oral Histories, 16.

27. McNair, personal interview, Oral Histories, tape 5, 1.

28. Ibid., 3.

29. Ibid., 1.

30. Ibid., 3.

31. Ibid., 2–3.

32. Ibid., 3–4.

33. Ibid., 2.

34. Ibid., 5.

35. Ibid., 6.

36. Ibid., 7.

37. Ibid.

38. Herb Hartsook, personal interview with Crawford Cook, Columbia, S.C., March 26, 1997, 4. Cook was campaign manager in Marshall Parker's 1962 run for lieutenant governor, and he later worked in Fritz Hollings's winning 1966 race for the U.S. Senate. He went on to become Hollings's top aide in his Senate office in Washington, then formed an advertising and public relations firm in Columbia, which ran John West's successful campaign for governor in 1970.

39. McNair, personal interview, Oral Histories, tape 5, 8.

40. Ibid., 21.

41. Ibid., 17.

42. Ibid., 17–18.

43. Ibid., 15.

44. McNair identified several groups as members of his extended courthouse crowd during the 1962 primary election. "We had reformed the probate judge law . . . so the probate judges were almost unanimously strong supporters. Mayors were very important . . . mayors and city councilmen. Also, the municipal association was very, very important. The automobile dealers were people that had influence, saw a lot of people, and they could influence voters. Funeral directors were always a very, very strong influence. . . . My wife's father and mother happened to be in the funeral business, and they wrote letters around the state. . . . We worked at identifying and relating to groups . . . and getting two or three prominent, well-known, well-liked members of each group, not necessarily officers, but members who knew me personally. If I could get a banker to write all other small town bankers, it was a lot more effective than getting the bankers' association to write a formal letter. If I could get the president of my local Farm Bureau to write all the county farm bureau people, it would be more effective. . . . We even took on major family groups, like the Lawton family. My law partner, Tom Lawton, sat down and wrote every member of that clan in South Carolina, and—surprisingly—at Hartsville, which has a strong Lawton family, I had good support from them that I would not have had" (McNair, personal interview, Oral Histories, tape 5, 15–16).

45. Ibid., 13.

46. Hartsook, personal interview with Cook, 4.

47. Ibid.

48. McNair, personal interview, Oral Histories, tape 5, 8.

49. Ibid., 12.

50. Hartsook, personal interview with Cook, 3.

51. McNair, personal interview, Oral Histories, tape 5, 18.

52. Hartsook, personal interview with Cook, 4.

53. McNair, personal interview, Oral Histories, tape 5, 19. Cook said that Parker's "presence was very commanding and he spoke with great sincerity." See Hartsook, personal interview with Cook, 5

54. McNair, personal interview, Oral Histories, tape 5, 19.

55. Ibid.

56. Columbia (S.C.) *State,* June 2, 1962, B-1, 3.

57. McNair, personal interview, Oral Histories, tape 5, 19.

58. Hugh Gibson, Charleston (S.C.) *News and Courier,* May 2, 1965.

59. Columbia (S.C.) *State,* June 6, 1962, D-1, 5–8.

60. McNair, personal interview, Oral Histories, tape 5, 20.

61. Ibid.

62. Columbia (S.C.) *State,* June 9, 1962. In the statement announcing his candidacy for lieutenant governor on June 3, 1962, Parker had said, "As a small businessman in the dairy business, I have a first hand knowledge and an awareness of the problems and hardships suffered by our businessmen today. Being closely allied with our farmers, I have an intimate knowledge of the situation they are in, their need of help in financing, processing and marketing. Having lived among and worked with the employees of our industrial plants, I believe I know their basic values and understand their problems" (Columbia [S.C.] *State,* June 3, 1962).

63. Columbia (S.C.) *State,* June 20, 1962.

64. McNair, personal interview, Oral Histories, tape 5, 23.

65. Ibid.

66. Ibid., 21–22.

67. See Luther Brady Faggart, "Defending the Faith: The 1950 U. S. Senate Race in South Carolina," M.A. Thesis, University of South Carolina, 1992, 152–57.

68. Ibid., 156–57. Faggart writes,

> While Olin Johnston was not an advocate of "civil rights," he was a champion of economic programs which helped the poor, a category that included many blacks. In a post-election [1952] editorial, the *News and Courier* stated, "there seems little doubt that the colored vote for the most part went to Mr. Johnston. Probably the negro leaders acted on the theory that the candidate who was closer to the Fair Deal would be their better bet, regardless of his epithets . . . The negroes apparently supplied the margin of Mr. Johnston's victory.'

69. Olin Johnston was the crudest segregationist on the campaign trail that season [1950]; it was obvious that Strom Thurmond adhered to a rigid political ideology, modern states rights, which was developed to resist growing outside pressure to relax the racial separation of Jim Crow. Though he may not have given expression to it in the same blunt manner as the senator, Thurmond was no less of a racial hardliner than his opponent. Moreover, Thurmond was the spokesman for an emerging movement which offered less hope for social progress than the diverse coalition of the national Democrats. Black South Carolinians demonstrated their capacity for political pragmatism when they made the best of their isolated position and voted for Olin D. Johnston in 1950 (Faggart, 4).

71. Charleston (S.C.) *News and Courier,* May 23, 1965.

70. Columbia (S.C.) *State,* January 2, 1961, B-5:1–3.

71. Newby, *Black Carolinians,* 348.

72. Ibid., 349.

73. Ibid., 348.

74. Ibid., 348–49.

75. *Revolution in Civil Rights* (Washington, D.C.: Congressional Quarterly Service, 1965), 10–11.

76. McNair, personal interview, Oral Histories, tape 5, 25.

77. Ibid., 24.

78. Ibid., 25

79. Ibid., 25–26.

80. Ibid., 26.

81. Charleston (S.C.) *News and Courier,* May 2, 1965.

82. Wickenberg, Columbia (S.C.) *State,* April 7, 1963.

83. McNair, personal interview, Oral Histories, tape 6, 9.

84. Ibid., 10.

85. Johnston took 57.2 percent to Workman's 42.8 percent. See Numan V. Bartley and Hugh D. Graham, *Southern Elections: County and Precinct Data, 1950–1972* (Baton Rouge: Louisiana State University Press, 1978).

86. Columbia (S.C.) *State,* January 2, 1962, B-5:5–8.

87. Charleston (S.C.) *News and Courier,* April 16, 1965, 1–A.

88. McNair, personal interview, Oral Histories, tape 6, 12.

89. Columbia (S.C.) *State,* April 19, 1965

90. Ted Shelton, *Charlotte Observer,* April 27, 1965.

Chapter 6

1. Henry H. Hill to Governor McNair, McNair papers, May 17, 1965, South Carolina Political Collections, University of South Carolina.

2. Robert E. McNair, personal interview, Oral Histories of the Robert E. McNair Gubernatorial Administration (1965–1971), South Carolina Department of Archives and History, Columbia, tape 11, 1 (hereafter Oral Histories).

3. John G. Sproat, "Firm Flexibility: Perspectives on Desegregation in South Carolina," in *New Perspectives on Race and Slavery in America: Essays in Honor of Kenneth M. Stampp,* edited by Robert H. Abzug and Stephen E. Maizlish (Lexington: University of Kentucky Press, 1986), 11.

4. Ibid., 13.

5. Historian Ernest McPherson Lander Jr. offered the following insight into Timmerman's racial views: "As he learned that Eisenhower was preparing to use troops in Little Rock, he reacted as follows: 'I think the President has directed the people of Arkansas to mix the children of Arkansas against their will, he is attempting to set himself up as a dictator and this action may be taken as further evidence of an effort to communize America.' A few days later the Governor resigned his commission as a lieutenant in the United States Naval Reserve 'because of the recent change in official attitude on the federal level toward the personal and property rights of American citizens'" (Lander, *A History of South Carolina, 1865–1960,* Chapel Hill: University of North Carolina Press, 1960, 204–5).

6. Sproat, "Firm Flexibility," 13.

7. *Bourbon* is a reference to the name of the royal family of France, which was restored to the throne after the French Revolution. Critics observed that former plantation-based leaders returned to power in South Carolina "as if nothing had changed."

8. Sproat, "Firm Flexibility," 17.

9. In his essay "Firm Flexibility" Sproat wrote: "the elements of peaceful accommodation had been at work long before the *Brown* decision. . . . Of central importance were the peculiar dynamics of class in South Carolina. In comparison with other southern states, the Palmetto State's white population was a small, economically stable, relatively unified group, confronting a large, economically deprived, politically impotent population of blacks. The possibilities of control from the top were very different than, say, in North Carolina, where a large 'middling' class of whites was not necessarily amenable to the leadership of an establishment" (15).

10. J. Strom, personal interview, Oral Histories, tape 1, 10.

11. McNair, personal interview, Oral Histories, tape 12, 1.

12. Ibid.

13. Ibid., 2.

14. In his 1991 history of the *State* newspaper, veteran newsman Bob Pierce wrote:

Cooperating with the [28-member biracial] committee, eight downtown Columbia stores agreed to desegregate quietly their lunch counters on August 21. Despite the impact of this historic event, no story appeared in *The State* the next day. Or the next.

The State's leaders . . . were part of a well-meaning conspiracy to withhold the news of the integration in the interest of racial harmony.

Out-of-town newspapers, including *The Charlotte Observer,* trumpeted the full story. Soon everybody knew what happened in downtown Columbia, even though *The State* did not report the landmark event until August 24.

Pierce, managing editor of the *State* at the time, commented further:

> fair-minded observers who were less concerned about the segregation issue and more about the right of the public to know were disturbed for different reasons.

Finally, on September 11, 1962, the *State* reprinted an article from the *Pittsburgh Courier* [an African American newspaper] that provided details of the Columbia integration.

> Cauthen [the *State* newspaper editor Henry Cauthen, brother of textile executive John Cauthen] maintained to the end that *The State* followed the proper course, although many staff members groused about the ethical implications of the newspaper's decision to withhold the news.
>
> [The *State* newspaper executive editor Lloyd] Huntington, on the firing line, found it difficult to duck questions from the staff. But he did.

(See Robert A. Pierce, *Palmettos and Oaks: A Centennial History of "The State,"* Columbia, S.C.: State-Record Company, 1991, 197).

15. W. D. Workman Jr., *The Bishop from Barnwell: The Political Life and Times of Edgar Brown* (Columbia, S.C.: R. L. Bryan, 1963), 299.

16. Thirty-seven years later, under a headline "Do the Right Thing—Take the Flag Down," Robert C. Edwards wrote an opinion piece that appeared in the *State* newspaper urging the General Assembly to remove the Confederate battle flag from the dome of the state house in Columbia. At age eighty-five, Edwards observed:

> Throughout my eight-plus decades, one event stands out as an important learning experience I won't ever forget. Thirty-seven years ago, on a crisp, cold January 28 in 1963, during my fourth year as president, a high drama occurred at Clemson University (then Clemson College). A young man from Charleston, Harvey Gantt, became the first African-American student to enter an all-white S. C. institution of higher learning.
>
> While chaos reigned in states all around us, that enrollment was peaceful. Although the state Legislature had opposed integration with all the power it could muster, the Law of the Land was obeyed. There were no state troopers keeping order at Clemson. Instead, the plans that had been laid were followed to the letter, and students, faculty and staff—as well as other high-minded South Carolinians who did the right thing during a difficult time—accepted Harvey Gantt as the first of a long succession of worthy African-Americans who would enter the state's schools.

In addressing South Carolina's widely publicized conflict and debate over the Confederate flag during the year 2000, Edwards wrote:

> There are similarities between that day at Clemson during the quarrelsome '60s when South Carolinians fought integration and the current controversy about taking down the flag. Both issues are about change and doing the right thing for the state. Now, as in the '60s, we can take a step forward or a step backward.
>
> As it happened, the flag was raised [1962] just a year before Harvey Gantt entered Clemson. It went up rather quietly, but the time has passed when it can be run down the pole without notice.
>
> Now it will take political courage and personal commitment from our state's leaders to see that the right thing is done. Like many other South Carolinians, I hope the flag will come down with a show of respect for history that will be acceptable to those of both sides.

(See Robert C. Edwards, "Do the Right Thing—Take the Flag Down," Columbia [S.C.] *State,* February 21, 2000).

17. Workman, *Bishop from Barnwell,* 299. In its March 10, 1963, issue—less than six weeks after the admission of Harvey Gantt to Clemson—the popular weekly magazine the *Saturday Evening Post* gave the Clemson desegregation event national coverage in an article entitled "Integration with Dignity" (See George McMillan, "Integration with Dignity," *Saturday Evening Post,* March 10, 1963.) The lengthy article, which included pictorial coverage of the event and pictures of Gantt, Brown, Russell, Gressette, and Edwards, brought favorable attention to the state at a time when South Carolina's racial stance was scarcely differentiated from that of states in the deeper South.

Under the byline of George McMillan, the article noted that

> the peace with which Harvey Gantt entered Clemson was no mere lucky happenstance. Violence did seem clearly in the cards. South Carolinians are notoriously passionate when it comes to defending the South, or southern "customs." The logic of her traditions argued that Clemson would be another Oxford, Mississippi.
>
> South Carolina was the spiritual, cultural and financial center of the South when Mississippi was still Indian territory. The fact is that South Carolinians created the South as a politically self-conscious region, led it out of the Union, and then fired the first shot of the Civil War (17).

Tracing the lengthy process of preparing for Gantt's peaceful admission back to the summer of 1961, McMillan's article mused,

> Why hadn't something happened? What was the explanation for this astonishing turn of events? Had South Carolina learned a lesson from Oxford? Or was it something else? The question was important; if South Carolina could keep the peace, so could any other southern state.
>
> The answer is this: When South Carolina's turn came to face the inevitable fact of racial change, its responsible people, its leadership group, its 'power structure' took the initiative and handled the crisis with dignity, dignity for the Negro as well as for the white man. This is why the South Carolina story is one of the most significant—and reassuring—stories in the recent history of race relations in this country (17).

Years later, in 1999, South Carolina's highest ranking state senator, John Drummond of Greenwood—president pro tempore of the Senate and chair of the Senate Finance Committee—distributed reprints of the *Saturday Evening Post* article to his fellow legislators and other state leaders, urging them to support his efforts to have the Confederate battle flag removed from the state house dome in Columbia.

South Carolina benefitted from the Oxford, Mississippi, experience in at least one direct way. Through an acquaintance with Hugh Clay, at that time an administrator at the University of Mississippi, State Law Enforcement Division Chief J. (Pete) Strom visited the Ole Miss campus several weeks after the violence: "we stayed two or three days with him, and he told us the whole story," Strom recalled in a later interview.

> When we came back, [SLED Lieutenant Leon] Gasque and I got together, and others, and we tried to write out a plan and improve on every mistake they made. We had our plan set and we knew exactly what every man was going to do, where he was going to be

placed, and every responsibility of every agent. That included SLED, the highway patrol, the campus police, and the whole police community.

So after reviewing their problems and trying to improve on all their mistakes—when Harvey Gantt came to Clemson—you could hear a pin drop (Strom, personal interview, Oral Histories, tape 1, 27).

18. Workman, *Bishop from Barnwell,* 299.

19. McMillan, "Integration with Dignity," 21.

20. Leon Panetta and Peter Gall, *Bring Us Together: The Nixon Team and the Civil Rights Retreat* (Philadelphia: Lippincott, 1971), 30.

21. William Law Watkins, "Harvey Gantt Enters Clemson: One Lawyer's Memories," *Carologue* 13, no. 3 (1998): 8.

22. *Revolution in Civil Rights* (Washington, D.C.: Congressional Quarterly Service, 1965), 7.

23. Ibid., 68.

24. Ibid., 70.

25. Charleston (S.C.) *News and Courier,* September 14, 1965.

26. *Revolution in Civil Rights,* 8.

27. McNair, personal interview, Oral Histories, tape 10, 7–8.

28. McLeod, personal interview, Oral Histories, tape 3, 14.

29. McLeod enumerated various types of irregularities. "They were registering people from outside the county, forging names to registration certificates, issuing certificates to phony people, things of that nature." In recalling experiences with federal voting observers, he mentioned an incident where a state senator had to be restrained "from jumping across the table at one of them," and he remembered challenging a provision of the Voting Rights Act about assisting voters inside the booth. "Under the Voting Rights Act, they can have an observer, a federal observer. Under our act, [when there was] an illiterate person, you could have one of the managers and a bystander go in there. That's one, two, three, four people, at least. The voting booth is supposed to be, say, a yard square. . . . They had four people sticking in there watching some poor fellow that can't read or write cast his ballot. It couldn't physically be done" (McLeod, personal interview, Oral Histories, tape 3, 15–17).

30. Ibid., 3.

31. Ibid., 17.

32. McNair credited John Cauthen with having major influence on his position statement on the Voting Rights Act. "John Cauthen . . . who had been a forerunner and a leader in human relations councils to keep the peace and to help with the peaceful integration in Clemson and elsewhere, was a very close friend and advisor. John had real input into the drafting of that [speech on the Voting Rights Act]. In fact, it was his product, and I recall that the tone of his first draft was so strong that . . . we had to redo that one several times to get it into more of a moderate, but firm tone that I could be comfortable with. That was one of those difficult ones, because it was politically explosive at the time." (McNair, personal interview, Oral Histories, tape 10, 7–8).

Professor Sproat identified Cauthen, along with industrialist Charles E. Daniel, as the two who were "prime movers in bringing the state's industrial, commercial, and, ultimately political leaders to an acceptance of change." He described Cauthen, a journalist who became intimately involved in the state's political leadership during the wartime years and emerged as executive director of the state's powerful Textile Manufacturers Association, as a "deceptively mild-mannered" man who "worked quietly and carefully, but with dogged persistence, behind the scenes to persuade politicians and businessmen to accept a number of changes, including improved race relations, designed to bring South Carolina at last into the mainstream of economic and social development. No more an integrationist than Daniel, Cauthen nonetheless recognized injustices in the old order and understood that change, aside from making good political sense, had become a powerful moral imperative. Probably no member of the establishment better combined expediency and conscience in approaching the problem, and this posture made him an authoritative force in bringing about racial accommodation in the state" (Sproat, "Firm Flexibility," 30–31).

33. State of the state address, January 12, 1966, McNair papers.

34. McNair, conversation with the author, October 10, 2000, Columbia, South Carolina.

35. Thomas N. McLean, Columbia (S.C.) *State,* January 13, 1966.

36. McNair, personal interview, Oral Histories, tape 10, 8.

37. *Revolution in Civil Rights,* 18.

38. Panetta and Gall, *Bring Us Together,* 32.

39. *Revolution in Civil Rights,* 63.

40. Panetta and Gall, *Bring Us Together,* 32.

41. Letter from D. I. Ross Jr. to Governor Robert E. McNair, September 10, 1965, McNair papers, University of South Carolina, Modern Political Collections.

42. *Rankings of the States,* Research Division, National Education Association, January 1966.

43. McNair, conversation with author, Columbia, South Carolina, April 5, 2000.

44. *Rankings of the States,* 29–30.

45. Ibid., 30.

46. South Carolina State Budget, 1964–1967, State Budget and Control Board, Budget Office.

47. *Rankings of the States,* 20.

48. Ibid., 17.

49. Ibid., 39.

50. McNair papers, South Carolina Political Collections, University of South Carolina.

51. McNair, personal interview, Oral Histories, tape 16, 7–8.

52. South Carolina State Budget, 1967–1968, State Budget and Control Board, Budget Office.

53. McNair papers, Department of Educational Report, South Carolina Political Collections, University of South Carolina.

54. McNair, personal interview, Oral Histories, tape 16, 7.

55. Cyril B. Busbee, personal interview, Oral Histories, tape 1, 12, 15. Sproat believed that the language of *Brown* "played into the hands of the massive resistors." Citing a Louisiana study by Numan V. Bartley, Sproat has written that "the *Brown* decision was drafted in a manner to attract a consensus on the court; hence, it relied not upon the considerable body of legal precedent that had accumulated in recent years, but instead upon sociological and psychological arguments that ranged from the plausible to the theoretical. . . . In that the justices failed to include an implementation decree or to lay

down a precise timetable for compliance, their ruling in 1954 (and, more especially, the second *Brown* ruling the following year) invited delay at best, defiance at worst. The court's intent was to separate the constitutional issue of racial segregation from the delicate question of how southern whites would respond to a federal mandate on the issue. But the effect was to confuse the court's intent in the minds of moderates, as well as of racial extremists" (Sproat, "Firm Flexibility," 8–9).

56. McNair, personal interview, Oral Histories, tape 16, 8.

57. Ibid., 8–9.

58. Ibid., 9.

59. James E. Hunter Jr. and Inez Watson, eds., *South Carolina Legislative Manual, 1946* (Columbia, S.C.: House of Representatives, 1946), 1965.

60. Patrick C. Smith, personal interview, Oral Histories, tape 1, 5.

61. Ibid.

62. I. A. Newby, *Black Carolinians: A History of Blacks in South Carolina, 1895–1968* (Columbia: University of South Carolina Press, 1973), 303.

63. Smith, personal interview, Oral Histories, tape 1, 5.

64. Ibid., 6.

65. Ibid., 7.

66. Newby, *Black Carolinians*, 308.

67. The longtime legal counsel of the "Gressette Committee," David W. Robinson of Columbia, noting that the committee was created three years prior to *Brown*, defined its initial purpose in a 1983 memo as that of "studying what steps the State could take to protect its educational system and see that it was not injured in the event that its then racially segregated public school should be changed as a result of decisions of the United States Supreme Court." After *Brown*, Robinson wrote, "the Committee's principal problem . . . was how to implement those Supreme Court decisions without destroying the public education system of South Carolina" (Robinson Papers, South Carolina Department of Archives and History, memorandum to file dated 5–3–83).

68. Sproat attributed much of the state's racial peace to the Gressette Committee. "Unknown to the public until its work came to an end," he wrote, "were the committee's subtle adaptations to change and behind-the-scenes efforts to keep racial friction under control. It forestalled moves in virtually every county to abolish the public schools, its members and lawyers spending hours with, cajoling, sometimes threatening local school officials. On numerous occasions, it headed off violence before it could erupt. It had an appreciable influence on the White Citizens Councils, some of whose more restrained leaders, in keeping their hothead members in check, cited the committee's public avowal to maintain both segregation and law and order. Inundated annually with legislative proposals ranging from the mean to the crackpot, the committee as often as not proposed its own seemingly futile pieces of legislation simply to sidetrack more dangerous laws. Legislators from rural districts, in particular, regularly stoked up support among their constituents by introducing outrageous racist proposals, which then quietly disappeared into the committee's 'legislative trashcan'" (John G. Sproat, "Pragmatic Conservatism and Desegregation: The Case of South Carolina," unpublished, 14).

69. Newby, *Black Carolinians*, 308.

70. Jesse A. Coles Jr., interview by author, March 30, 2000.

71. Coles, interview by author, March 31, 2000.

72. McNair, personal interview, Oral Histories, tape 3, 12–13.

73. Sproat, "Firm Flexibility," 8.

74. McNair, personal interview, Oral Histories, tape 11, 15.

75. Ibid., 14–15.

76. Ibid., 15.

77. Ibid., 16.

78. Ibid., 17.

79. McLeod, personal interview, Oral Histories, tape 1, 12.

80. Ibid., 14–15.

81. McLeod, personal interview, Oral Histories, tape 3, 22.

82. McLeod, personal interview, Oral Histories, tape 1, 14–15.

83. Busbee later recalled that the "Dirty Dozen" was an element within the South Carolina Association of Superintendents and that "it wasn't even twelve. It was a baker's dozen, or some other (number) . . . it was an . . . informal organization of the superintendents of the twelve or fifteen largest school districts in the state. You had Guy Varn . . . in Columbia, and you had the superintendent in Spartanburg, Joe McCracken, . . . the superintendent in Greenville was M. T. Anderson. You had the superintendent in Charleston, who was Gordon Garrett, and he was a very key individual." Other districts and counties enumerated by Busbee were Florence, Anderson, Aiken, and his own Brookland-Cayce District. McNair, Busbee recalled, "could call them before there was trouble . . . this was not a public group in an sense of the word. In fact, they later had to be very careful because all the other superintendents took umbrage at the fact that they may have been calling more shots then they . . . should be calling" (Busbee, interview by author, January 17, 2001, 43)

84. Author and journalist Jack Bass described Busbee at the time as "a stocky man of no more than average height with a slight wave in his carefully parted gray hair. His dark suits suggest a banker's image. . . . He is a man who measures his words carefully. For reporters, getting a colorful quote from him is almost as rare as a bird watcher finding an ivory-billed woodpecker" (*Charlotte Observer,* September 5, 1971).

85. Busbee, interview by author, January 17, 2001.

86. Ibid.

87. Coles, interview by author, March 30, 2000.

88. Busbee, interview by author, January 17, 2001.

89. Ibid.

90. Coles, interview by author, March 30, 2000.

91. Al Lanier, Associated Press in *Greenville News,* October 17, 1966.

92. Paul Clancy, Columbia (S.C.) *State,* September 8, 1966.

93. Papers of Joseph O. Rogers.

94. Clancy, Columbia (S.C.) *State,* October 8, 1966.

95. Clancy, Columbia (S.C.) *State,* September 21, 1966.

96. Busbee, interview by author, January 17, 2001.

97. Clancy, Columbia (S.C.) *State,* September 1, 1966.

98. Charleston (S.C.) *News and Courier,* October 4, 1966.

99. *Sumter Daily Item,* October 5, 1966.

100. McLeod, personal interview, Oral Histories, tape 2, 15.

101. Rogers papers, quoted by Jack Bass in an undated article in the Columbia (S.C.) *State.*

102. Rogers papers, quoted by Hugh Gibson, Charleston (S.C.) *News and Courier,* February 22, 1966.

103. Rogers papers, "How Milton Justifies the Ways of God to Man."

104. Bass, Columbia (S.C.) *State,* September 25, 1966.

105. Rogers papers, quoted by Laverne Prosser, Charleston (S.C.) *News and Courier,* undated.

106. *Sumter Daily Item,* September 24, 1965.

107. William Rone, Columbia (S.C.) *State,* December 14, 1965.

108. Ibid.

109. Columbia (S.C.) *State,* September 12, 1966.

110. *Greenville News,* September 24, 1966.

111. *Anderson Independent,* April 15, 1966.

112. Charleston (S.C.) *News and Courier,* October 23, 1966.

113. A friendly editorial in the *Florence Morning News* summarized those positions, using reports from the South Carolina Education Association, which also supported McNair. The editorial listed "as quotations from the Governor":

— South Carolina will comply with the law.

— South Carolina is operating under a "freedom of choice policy."

— South Carolina is accepting all applications for entry and transfer to schools without regard to color, race, or creed.

— No South Carolina district is being asked to go beyond the requirements of the law to fulfill the requirements of the law.

— Every effort is being made to get specific information and clarification on the guidelines.

— It may be necessary for a South Carolina school district to test the legality of the guidelines.

— If a school district should choose to test the guidelines, the state stands ready to assist (*Florence Morning News,* October 6, 1966).

The *Florence Morning News* was edited by McNair friend and ally James A. Rogers (no relation to candidate Joseph O. Rogers). In an article published in 1997, two years after his death, James Rogers wrote:

It was lonely in the sixties for liberal newspaper editors in the South. During those years, the newspapers in South Carolina generally reflected the attitudes on the race question of their white readers, who by a vast majority stood by the "never" position on public school desegregation. Of the fourteen daily newspapers in the state, all but two sounded what might be called the "party line."

The two exceptions were the *Greenwood Index-Journal,* edited by the late Ed Chapin, and the *Florence Morning News,* which I edited. The story went around among some members of the South Carolina Press Association that when Ed Chapin and I went into a room and closed the door, the liberal press in South Carolina was in session.

Rogers, along with Methodist bishop Paul Hardin, Bob Davis, and an early McNair staffer, Bob Hickman, had traveled the state in the 1960s to attend "pre-arranged mass meetings in Methodist churches for encouraging whites and blacks to respond with Christian goodwill to the social revolutions swirling around us." Rogers continued active in state and local race-relations work, and as an editor, he later reflected, "Knowing all that I know now, I would not choose different years to be an editor than the years when I was in that role. During the early and middle years of the seventies, when so many of the civil rights battles had been won, the issues became somewhat blurred. But during the sixties, they stood out very sharply, requiring no special insight to see that history had overtaken and, indeed, was overrunning the segregated South" (Clinton [S.C.] *Evening Reader,* May 1, 1997, reprinted in *Furman Magazine,* Spring 1985).

114. Charleston (S.C.) *News and Courier,* October 23, 1966.

115. Ibid.

116. Charleston (S.C.) *News and Courier,* reprint from Jim Rogers, ed., *Florence Morning News,* "Had Enuff? News," Jospeh O. Rogers papers, Charleston (S.C.) *News and Courier,* June 17, 1966.

117. Charleston (S.C.) *News and Courier,* October 23, 1966.

Chapter 7

1. Columbia (S.C.) *State,* November 9, 1966.

2. *Legislative Manual* (1967), 373–74.

3. Columbia (S.C.) *State,* January 25, 1967.

4. *Legislative Manual* (1967), 372–73.

5. Ibid., 371.

6. Columbia (S.C.) *State,* undated, in the Papers of Joseph O. Rogers, South Carolina Political Collections, University of South Carolina.

7. Charleston (S.C.) *News and Courier,* August 12, 1969.

8. Rogers papers.

9. Hugh Gibson, Charleston (S.C.) *News and Courier,* November 27, 1967.

10. Laverne Prosser, Charleston (S.C.) *News and Courier,* January 19, 1967.

11. Text of McNair inaugural address, Columbia (S.C.) *State,* January 19, 1967.

12. Don Fowler, interview by author, tape recording, March 2004.

13. McNair inaugural address.

14. Blatt, personal interview, Oral Histories of the Robert E. McNair Gubernatorial Administration (1965–1971), South Carolina Department of Archives and History, Columbia, 23 (hereafter Oral Histories).

15. Fred Carter, interview by author, tape recording, August 16, 2004.

16. McNair, personal interview, Oral Histories, tape 12, 13.

17. Patrick C. Smith, personal interview, Oral Histories, tape 3, 7.

18. Philip G. Grose Jr., Columbia (S.C.) *State,* January 19, 1967.

19. McNair inaugural address.

20. Jo Anne Plyler, Charleston (S.C.) *News and Courier,* February 19, 1967.

21. Ibid.

22. Jim Konduros, interview by author, tape recording, September 22, 2004.

23. Carter, interview by author, tape recording, August 2004.

24. Robert Milton Burts, *Richard Irvine Manning and the Progressive Movement in South Carolina* (Columbia: University of South Carolina Press, 1974), 83–113.

25. Griffenhagen and Associates, *Extracts from Report of Griffenhagen and Associates . . . to the South Carolina Budget Commission of 1920* (Columbia: Printed . . . by the Joint Committee on Printing, General Assembly of S.C., 1924); James Karl Coleman, *State Administration in South Carolina* (1935; New York: AMS Press, 1968); South Carolina Preparedness for Peace Commission, *Report to the Governor and Members of the General Assembly* (Columbia, 1945).

26. South Carolina Executive Institute, State Budget and Control Board, "South Carolina's Perilous Journey: 1868–2003: The Evolution of Governmental Administration in the 19th and 20th Centuries," 3–6.

27. McNair, personal interview, Oral Histories, tape 12, 4.

28. Fowler, interview by author, March 20, 2004.

29. McNair, personal interview, Oral Histories, tape 12, 5.

30. Ibid., 7.

31. Ibid., 5.

32. State Budget and Control Board, Executive Institute, "Conversations with Three Governors," August 22, 1997, 3–4.

33. McNair, personal interview, Oral Histories, tape 12, 8.

34. McNair, personal interview, Oral Histories, tape 11, 21–22.

35. David Duncan Wallace, *South Carolina: A Short History, 1520–1948* (Columbia: University of South Carolina Press, 1984), 686.

36. McNair, personal interview, Oral Histories, tape 10, 12.

37. Ibid.

38. John West, Journal, South Carolina Political Collections, University of South Carolina, Thursday, June 8, 1967.

39. West journal, June 15, 1967.

40. The "brown bag" law proved to be a stopgap measure. During the administration of Governor John C. West, a constitutional amendment was approved authorizing the sale of "mini-bottles" of liquor in restaurants and bars. The "free pouring" from large, standard bottles became law January 1, 2006, after a public referendum.

41. *Greenville News,* February 1, 1969.

42. South Carolina Budget and Control Board, Economic Report for South Carolina, 1972, 88.

43. State Budget and Control Board, Division of Research and Statistics, Statistical Abstract, 1977, 161, and 1998, 361.

Chapter 8

1. James S. Konduros, interview by author, tape recording, September 22, 2004.

2. McNair, conversation with the author, 1967.

3. McNair, personal interview, Oral Histories of the Robert E. McNair Gubernatorial Administration (1965–1971), South Carolina Department of Archives and History, Columbia, tape 13, 8 (hereafter Oral Histories).

4. "Opportunity and Growth in South Carolina, 1968–85" (Moody Report), Moody's Investor Service and Campus Facilities Associates, 1968, 49.

5. McNair, personal interview, Oral Histories, tape 13, 9.

6. Moody Report, 83.

7. McNair, personal interview, Oral Histories, tape 13, 12.

8. Ibid.

9. Ibid., 15.

10. *Greenville News,* January 16, 1969.

11. Charleston (S.C.) *News and Courier,* January 24, 1969.

12. Jack Bass, *Charlotte Observer,* January 11, 1969.

13. *Greenville News,* January 16, 1969.

14. Ibid.

15. Ibid.

16. South Carolina Budget and Control Board, Economic Report for South Carolina, 1972, 60.

17. South Carolina Budget and Control Board, S.C. Statistical Abstract, 1974, 18.

18. South Carolina Budget and Control Board, S.C. Statistical Abstract, 1977, 79.

19. Louis Harris and Associates, "Priorities for Progress in South Carolina," 1971, 6.

20. Ibid., 19.

21. Moody Report, 2.

22. Fred Carter, interview by author, tape recording, March 31, 2004.

23. Konduros, interview by author, tape recording, September 22, 2004.

24. McNair, personal interview, Oral Histories, tape 13, 9.

25. Moody Report, 9.

26. Ibid., 7–9.

27. McNair, personal interview, Oral Histories, tape 16, 23.

28. Ibid.

29. Text of McNair inaugural address, Columbia (S.C.) *State,* January 19, 1967.

30. McNair, personal interview, Oral Histories, tape 16, 23–24.

31. *Charlotte Observer,* January 11, 1969.

32. Charleston (S.C.) *News and Courier,* January 24, 1969.

33. Columbia (S.C.) *State,* June 14, 1969.

34. Columbia (S.C.) *State,* January 14, 1969.

35. Associated Press report in Charleston (S.C.) *News and Courier,* June 23, 1969.

Chapter 9

1. William C. Hine, "S.C. State: A Legacy of Education and Public Service," *Agriculture History,* 65 (Spring 1991), 149.

2. Ibid., 151.

3. Ibid., 153.

4. Newby observed, "The most significant institutions of higher learning in black Carolina were Benedict College, Claflin and Allen universities. None of these was a bona fide college or university in this period (1915–17); two of them, in fact, had no college level programs at all. In 1915, Benedict's student body of 507 included 254 elementary, 205 secondary, 45 college, and 3 ministerial students. Claflin enrolled 597 in its elementary department, 177 in high school, and 26 in college courses. The 71 college students at Benedict and Claflin represented the entire college population in black Carolina in 1915. Allen University served 304 elementary and 140 secondary students and 6 special students. The state college, never more than a trade and normal school during these years, enrolled 529 elementary and 197 secondary pupils" (Newby, *Black Carolinians: A History of Blacks in South Carolina, 1895–1968,* Columbia: University of South Carolina Press, 1973, 107, citing U.S. Bureau of Education Bulletin, 1916).

5. Benjamin E. Mays, *Born to Rebel* (Athens: University of Georgia Press, 1987), 41.

6. Hine, "S.C. State," 157.

7. Ibid., 156–58.

8. Ibid., 158–61.

9. Hine, "Civil Rights and Campus Wrongs," *South Carolina Historical Magazine,* 97, no. 4 (October 1996), 310.

10. Ibid., 312.

11. Newby, *Black Carolinians,* 261.

12. Hine, "Civil Rights," 313.

13. Ibid., 318.

14. *The Reporter,* January 24, 1957.

15. Hine, "Civil Rights," 319–20.

16. Ibid., 322.

17. Columbia (S.C.) *State,* March 20, 1960.

18. Ibid.

19. Columbia (S.C.) *State,* October 22, 1963.

20. Hine, "Civil Rights," 324.

21. Ibid., 326.

22. McNair, personal interview, Oral Histories of the Robert E. McNair Gubernatorial Administration (1965–1971), South Carolina Department of Archives and History, Columbia, tape 21, 16 (hereafter Oral Histories).

23. Barbara W. Aba-Mecha, "South Carolina Conference of NAACP: Origins and Major Accomplishments, 1939–1954," *Proceedings of the South Carolina Historical Association,* 1981, 16.

24. Charles Wickenberg, Columbia (S.C.) *State,* April 6, 1992.

25. Barbara H. Woods, "Modjeska Simkins and the South Carolina Conference of the NAACP, 1939–1957," in *Women in the Civil Rights Movement,* edited by Vicki L. Crawford, Jacqueline Anne Rouse, and Barbara Woods (Brooklyn, N.Y.: Carlson, 1990), 115–16.

26. Ibid., 116.

27. Ibid., footnote 46, 120.

28. Wickenberg, Columbia (S.C.) *State,* April 8, 1992.

29. McNair, interview by author, April 27, 1981.

30. McNair, personal interview, Oral Histories, tape 27, 13–14.

31. The Reverend I. DeQuincey Newman, interview by author, April 21, 1981.

32. Ibid.

33. Ibid.

34. Newman recalled getting firsthand exposure to the delicacy of racial politics, 1950s-style, at the 1956 Republican National Convention at San Francisco. "I recall that in 1956," he said, "when Eisenhower was nominated for a second term, the South Carolina delegation visited Mr. Nixon [the vice presidential nominee] in his suite at the Mark Hopkins Hotel. As we posed for pictures, the black delegates were all lined up at one end of the group. Then, Mr. Nixon said, 'Now, let's get a picture for the northern papers,' and he moved the black delegates so that we were integrated in the line with the white delegates" (interview by author, April 21, 1981).

35. Claudia Brinson, *Columbia Record,* June 29, 2000.

36. Isaac "Ike" Williams, interview by author, June 21, 1981.

37. Newman, interview by author.

38. Williams, interview by author.

39. Brinson, June 19, 2000.

40. Williams, interview by author.

41. Newman, interview by author.

42. Newby, *Black Carolinians,* 355.

43. Wirth had a doctorate from the California Institute of Technology, and Fanning had a masters degree. In an interview with the *Orangeburg Times and Democrat,* Wirth said he had been told that "he had not followed 'proper channels in implementing his own ideas.'" The student handbook of the time provided that the college "reserves the right,

acting through its President, to terminate the appointment of any continuous (or tenured) faculty appointment or of any term appointment prior to its expiration, for . . . conduct detrimental to the best interest of the college" (Source: Manual for Faculty Members, South Carolina State College, 1964, 46, as cited in Hine, "Civil Rights," 326).

44. Hine, "Civil Rights," 326.

45. In the statement he issued on February 24, 1967, "concerning the present problem at South Carolina State College," President Turner stated, "There have been manifestations on the part of two groups of students at South Carolina State College. The smaller group, calling itself 'SAC' [Student Action Committee], never having applied for recognition at the College, having no list of officers nor members, having no statement of purpose and having no faculty advisor, is not recognized by the college. But, it has been noisy, discourteous and disorderly as evidenced by two demonstrations (at) the home of the President at night. As a result of the first, it was agreed that a small representative number of this group, namely 6, would be received to state the grievances and this offer as made for 10:45 a.m., Tuesday morning, February 21, 1967. Only one individual appeared, stating that he represented the entire student body, but was vague and inconclusive either as to grievances or desires. He stated that none of the administrative officers nor the elected student officers were trusted by him.

"The other group, which is the Student Council, also appeared on the same occasion at the same time with a mimeographed list of proposals, practically all of which were granted by the College Administration . . . The College Administration recognizes and deals with elected student representatives only. It does not recognize and will not deal with a rowdy and undisciplined mob group ("Statement concerning the present problem at South Carolina State College, February 24, 1976," in the personal collection of Isaac Williams).

46. Hine, "Civil Rights," 327.

47. Ibid.

48. Charleston (S.C.) *News and Courier,* March 8, 1967.

49. Ibid.

50. Hine, "Civil Rights," 327.

51. Benner C. Turner, Memorandum to All Faculty Members, March 6, 1967, in the papers of Isaac Williams.

52. Hine, "Civil Rights," 327–28.

53. McNair, interview by author, September 25, 2000.

54. Hine, "Civil Rights," 325.

55. Newby, *Black Carolinians,* 356.

56. *Orangeburg Times and Democrat,* March 9, 1967.

57. Columbia (S.C.) *State,* March 9, 1967.

58. Ibid.

59. McNair, personal interview, Oral Histories, tape 27, 12–13.

60. Ibid.

61. Ibid., 12.

62. Ibid., 10–11.

63. Ibid., 13.

64. Identified by President Turner as being involved in the maneuvering were McNair's friends Perry and Newman, the Reverend Herbert Nelson, and Isaac McGraw of the State Department of Education (Columbia [S.C.] *State,* March 11, 1967.)

65. McNair, conversation with author, September 25, 2000.

66. Columbia (S.C.) *State,* March 11, 1967.

67. Charleston (S.C.) *News and Courier,* March 16, 1967.

68. Columbia (S.C.) *State,* March 11, 1967.

69. Hine, "Civil Rights," 329.

70. McNair, conversation with author, September 25, 2000.

71. *Charleston Evening Post,* May 11, 1967.

72. Ibid.

73. M. Maceo Nance Jr., personal interview, Oral Histories, 5.

74. McNair, conversation with author, September 25, 2000.

75. Nance, personal interview, Oral Histories, 1.

76. Ibid., 15.

77. *Charleston Evening Post,* March 22, 1967.

78. Columbia (S.C.) *State,* March 23, 1967.

79. Columbia (S.C.) *State,* March 8, 1967.

80. "Enough Is Enough, Kids," *Orangeburg Times and Democrat,* March 9, 1967.

81. "Schizophrenia," Columbia (S.C.) *State,* undated.

82. "NAACP and State College," Columbia (S.C.) *State,* April 23, 1967.

83. Paul Clancy, "Unrest Still Grips State," Columbia (S.C.) *State,* April 23, 1967.

84. Hugh Gibson, "Bombs, Blossoms," Charleston (S.C.) *News and Courier,* April 9, 1967.

85. Nance, personal interview, Oral Histories, 8.

86. Ibid., 10.

Chapter 10

1. McNair papers, South Carolina Political Collections, University of South Carolina.

2. McNair, letter to John Stroman, January 17, 1968, McNair papers, South Carolina Political Collections, University of South Carolina.

3. William Saunders, conversation with author, March 4, 2005.

4. Cleveland Sellers, correspondence with author, February 2005.

5. Sellers, *The River of No Return: The Autobiography of a Black Militant and the Life and Death of SNCC* (Jackson: University of Mississippi Press, 1990), 166.

6. James Forman, *The Making of Black Revolutionaries* (Seattle: University of Washington Press, 1997), 458.

7. The Southern Regional Council, in its February 1968 report on the Orangeburg shootings, said, "A perhaps unusual degree of right wing influence has been at work in the city and county for some time. Besides the Klan, local residents said there exists a Wallace-for-President headquarters, a strong [White] Citizens' Council organization, strong John Birch Society organizations, a Carl McIntyre organization, and the home base of a state association of private schools" (Pat Watters and Weldon Rougeau, "Events at Orangeburg," Southern Regional Council, Atlanta, Georgia, 1968, 30).

8. Sellers, correspondence with author, February 2005.

9. Ibid., November 2004.

10. Sellers, *River of No Return,* 207.

11. Watters and Rougeau, "Events at Orangeburg," 28.

12. Saunders, conversation with author, March 4, 2005.

13. *Lowcountry Newsletter,* 1, no. 8 (November 4, 1967), the papers of William Saunders.

14. Watters and Rougeau, "Events at Orangeburg," 28.

15. Sellers, *River of No Return,* 207–8.

16. *Revolution in Civil Rights* (Washington, D.C.: Congressional Quarterly Service, 1965), 81.

17. Watters and Rougeau, "Events at Orangeburg," 1.

18. M. Maceo Nance Jr., personal interview, Oral Histories of the Robert E. McNair Gubernatorial Administration (1965–1971), South Carolina Department of Archives and History, Columbia, 29 (hereafter Oral Histories).

19. Ibid., 28.

20. Ibid.

21. Ibid., 30.

22. Sellers, correspondence with author, February 2005.

23. Newman, interview by author, May 11, 1981.

24. Sellers, *River of No Return,* 209.

25. Jack Bass and Jack Nelson, *The Orangeburg Massacre,* revised and enlarged edition (Macon, Ga.: Mercer, 1984), 22.

26. Ibid., 23.

27. McNair, personal interview, Oral Histories, tape 28, 17.

28. Watters and Rougeau, "Events at Orangeburg," 2.

29. Ibid.

30. Roger E. Poston, trial testimony, *U.S. v. Henry Morrell Addy, et al.* No- 68–313. U.S. District Court, District of S.C., Orangeburg Division, 654.

31. Strom, personal interview, Oral Histories, tape 2, 2.

32. McNair, personal interview, Oral Histories, tape 23, 1–2.

33. McNair, personal interview, Oral Histories, tape 28, 3.

34. Even though specific names were blacked out in the version of the FBI papers released under the Freedom of Information Act, the description could fit only Strom (FBI Report, Section 2). SLED deputy Leon Gasque later explained the arrangement by delineating between general and specific orders: "the governor gives him [Strom] general instructions, and he [Strom] gives them more specifically. Chief gave everybody general instructions, but the specific instructions as far as the National Guard was concerned was up to Colonel [Charles] Leath. The highway patrol, the riot team, was up to at that time, Lieutenant [Jesse] Spell" (Strom, personal interview, Oral Histories, tape 2, 14).

35. FBI files released under the Freedom of Information Act, Memorandum from R. W. Smith to W. C. Sullivan, August 8, 1967.

36. FBI Report, 10.

37. Sellers, *River of No Return,* 210.

38. Strom, personal interview, Oral Histories, tape 2, 4.

39. Poston, trial testimony, 675.

40. Sellers, *River of No Return,* 211–12.

41. Strom, personal interview, Oral Histories, tape 2, 5.

42. Watters and Rougeau, "Events at Orangeburg," 4–5.

43. Leon Gasque, personal interview, Oral Histories, tape 2, 6.

44. Columbia (S.C.) *State,* September 27, 1970.

45. Bass, *Charlotte Observer,* February 8, 1968.

46. Ibid.

47. Bass and Nelson, *The Orangeburg Massacre,* 33.

48. Ibid.

49. McNair, personal interview, Oral Histories, tape 28, 14.

50. *Charlotte Observer,* February 8, 1968.

51. Ibid.

52. Strom, personal interview, Oral Histories, tape 2, 8.

53. "Student 2 SW," FBI Report, 27.

54. Sellers, *River of No Return,* 212.

55. McNair, personal interview, Oral Histories, tape 28, 15.

56. The student grievances, as listed in the Southern Regional Council report, were "(1) closing of the All-Star Bowling Lanes and a change of its policy of segregation before reopening, (2) investigation of police brutality . . . the action of the SLED officers was uncalled for, especially the beating of the young ladies, (3) immediate suspension pending investigation of the officer who fired a shot unnecessarily in the State College campus, (4) establishment by the mayor of a biracial Orangeburg Human Relations Committee, with recommendation that each community select its own representatives, (5) that the Orangeburg Medical Association make a public statement of intent to serve all persons on an equal basis, regardless of race, religion or creed, (6) a fair employment commission, (7) a change (in) the dogmatic attitude of the Health Department and the segregated practices used there, (8) extension of the city limits of Orangeburg so as to benefit more than one segment of the community, (9) that officials give constructive leadership toward encouraging the Orangeburg Regional Hospital to accept the Medicare program, (10) the elimination of discrimination in public services, especially in doctors offices, (11) integration of drive-in theaters, (12) that officials fulfill all stipulations of the 1964 Civil Rights Act by leading the community so that it will serve all the people" (Watters and Rougeau, "Events at Orangeburg," 8–9).

57. Nance, personal interview, Oral Histories, 33.

58. Watters and Rougeau, "Events at Orangeburg," 7–8.

59. Robert T. Stevenson, trial transcript, 850.

60. Stevenson, trial transcript, 852.

61. Bass and Nelson, *The Orangeburg Massacre,* 29.

62. Stevenson, trial transcript, 852.

63. "Student 14–SW," FBI report, 93.

64. McNair, personal interview, Oral Histories, tape 28, 16.

65. Daniel McLeod, Oral Histories, tape 2, 33–34.

66. McNair, personal interview, Oral Histories, tape 28, 18.

67. Ibid., 19.

68. Bass and Nelson, *The Orangeburg Massacre,* 41.

69. McLeod, Oral Histories, tape 2, 34.

70. The bowling alley was closed, McNair said, "on my own initiative . . . under my emergency powers" (McNair, personal interview, Oral Histories, tape 28, 19). Orangeburg mayor Pendarvis was also reported to have contacted bowling alley owner Floyd, who agreed to the closure (Bass and Nelson, *The Orangeburg Massacre,* 41).

71. Bass and Nelson, *The Orangeburg Massacre,* 43.

72. Watters and Rougeau, "Events at Orangeburg," 10.

73. "Student 8 SW," FBI report, 55.

74. Gasque, interview with Gasque and Strom, January 4, 1992, 9.

75. Strom, personal interview, Oral Histories, tape 2, 10.

76. Watters and Rougeau, "Events at Orangeburg," 12.

77. FBI report, Section 2, 1.

78. FBI advisory to President Lyndon B. Johnson, February 8, 1968, Lyndon Baines Johnson Library, University of Texas, Austin.

79. FBI report, 537.

80. Sellers, *River of No Return,* 215–16.

81. Ibid., 216.

82. Ibid. Bill Saunders later recalled, "I was chairing an educational conference at Penn Center that weekend prior to the shooting. Cleveland [Sellers] was supposed to be there. We called him February 3rd asking him why he wasn't there with us. And he said, 'I can't come; because, if I leave here now, a lot of people are going to die.' We told him to stay put and take care of himself. Stokely Carmichael called us from New York and said he could not make it but he gave us a press release that ran in *The New York Times,* and parts of it ran in the [Charleston] *News and Courier*" (correspondence from Saunders to the author, February 8, 2005).

83. Sellers, *River of No Return,* 217.

84. Watters and Rougeau, "Events at Orangeburg," 12.

85. FBI report, 8.

86. Strom, personal interview, Oral Histories, tape 2, 10.

87. McNair, personal interview, Oral Histories, tape 28, 26.

88. Nance, personal interview, Oral Histories, 40.

89. McNair, personal interview, Oral Histories, tape 28, 26.

90. Strom, personal interview, Oral Histories, tape 2, 14.

91. Stevenson, trial transcript, 854.

92. By the time trucks arrived to put out the student bonfire, the Orangeburg Fire Department had already been called three times to respond to incendiary fires at the vacant Brunson house on Watson Street, once shortly before midnight (11:28 P.M.) on Wednesday, again three hours later (2:41 A.M.), and again at 8:41 P.M. on Thursday evening (Report of City of Orangeburg, South Carolina, February 12, 1968, in papers of Captain Carl Stokes).

93. FBI report, South Carolina State Archives, 876.

94. Edward W. Huffman, trial transcript, 69–70.

95. FBI report, 258.

96. Ibid., 70.

97. Ibid., 43.

98. Ibid., 21.

99. Ibid., 78.

100. Ibid., 405.

101. Ibid., 78.

102. Ibid., 43.

103. Ibid., 35.

104. Ibid., 331.

105. Ibid., 348.

106. Ibid., 362.

107. Spell, trial transcript, 493. The nine highway patrolmen actually did not testify at the trial a year later. By agreement of counsels and the court, their interviews with FBI agents were entered into the record as their sworn statements.

108. Ibid., 494.

109. Henry Morrell Addy, trial transcript, 486.

110. Roy C. Campbell, trial transcript, 99.

111. Sidney C. Taylor, trial transcript, 408.

112. Spell, trial transcript, 494.

113. Bass and Nelson, *The Orangeburg Massacre,* 65—an account supported in Walter Edgar's *South Carolina: A History* (Columbia: University of South Carolina Press, 1998), 442.

114. FBI interviews, 534–617.

115. Trial transcript, 1095.

116. Spell, trial transcript, 495.

117. Orangeburg Regional Hospital records, Lt. Carl B. Stokes, SLED agent on scene at S.C. State, Feb. 9, 1968. Papers in Stokes's possession.

118. FBI report, 640.

119. FBI memorandum, October 17, 1968, File Number 44-33410, Lab. No. PC-B2164 FAQ LU LX, pa., Stokes papers.

120. Trial transcript, 1096.

121. Sellers, *River of No Return,* 218.

122. McNair, personal interview, Oral Histories, tape 28, 26.

123. Ibid., 27.

124. Strom, personal interview, Oral Histories, tape 2, 19.

125. Sellers, *River of No Return,* 222.

126. Arrest warrant, Orangeburg County, February 9, 1968, McNair papers, South Carolina Political Collections, University of South Carolina.

127. Arrest Warrant and Department of Corrections records, Stokes papers.

128. Nance, personal interview, Oral Histories, 45.

129. McNair Executive Order, February 9, 1968, McNair papers.

130. McNair statement, February 9, 1968, McNair papers. The full text of the statement was also criticized by scholars, who noted McNair was in error in saying that the shootings occurred off-campus, that the situation had been worsened by the theft of ROTC rifles, an incident that took place after the shooting of the students, and that the patrolmen fired in response to the Officer Shealy's injury. With regard to the latter, the text correctly points out the lapse of time between Shealy's injury and the actual shootings.

131. *Orangeburg Times and Democrat,* February 9, 1968.

132. Associated Press news summaries, South Caroliniana Library.

133. Columbia (S.C.) *State,* February 10, 1968.

134. Columbia (S.C.) *State,* February 9, 1968.

135. Associated Press story in the *Charlotte Observer,* February 9, 1968.

136. Columbia (S.C.) *State,* February 9, 1968.

137. Dave Bledsoe, trial transcript, 874–875.

138. Ibid., 877.

139. Sellers, *River of No Return,* 224.

140. Ibid.

141. Watters and Rougeau, "Events at Orangeburg," 14.

142. Ibid., 19.

143. *New York Times,* February 11, 1968, 37.

144. *Orangeburg Times and Democrat,* February 24, 1968.

145. *New York Times,* February 14, 1968, 20.

146. Watters and Rougeau, "Events at Orangeburg," 24.

147. Ibid., 15–16.

148. Charleston (S.C.) *News and Courier,* February 25, 1968.

149. *Columbia Record,* February 28, 1968.

150. *Greenville News,* March 1, 1968.

151. McNair, personal interview, Oral Histories, tape 29, 14.

152. Ralph de Toledano, *J. Edgar Hoover: The Man and His Time* (New Rochelle, N.Y.: Arlington House, 1973), 365.

153. Richard Gid Powers, *Secrecy and Power: The Life of J. Edgar Hoover* (New York: Free Press, 1987), 424.

154. Ovid Demaris, *The Director: An Oral Biography of J. Edgar Hoover* (New York: Harper's Magazine Press, 1975), 229.

155. Watters and Rougeau, "Events at Orangeburg," 19.

156. Sellers, *River of No Return,* 226–27.

157. Columbia (S.C.) *State,* February 27, 1968.

158. Columbia (S.C.) *State,* March 8, 1968.

159. *Greenwood Index-Journal,* March 13, 1968.

160. Charleston (S.C.) *News and Courier,* March 10, 1968.

161. Ibid.

162. Charleston (S.C.) *News and Courier,* March 23, 1968.

163. Charleston (S.C.) *News and Courier,* March 27, 1968.

164. Charleston (S.C.) *News and Courier,* March 13, 1968.

165. Charleston (S.C.) *News and Courier,* March 18, 1968.

166. Mc Nair's request for an FBI investigation, in fact, had become lodged in the Hoover-Clark feud. Responding to a *Washington Post* article that the FBI report had been delayed because of attention being paid to the assassination of the Reverend Martin Luther King (on April 4, 1968) and the SCLC Poor People's March in Washington, FBI assistant director Alex Rosen wrote in an internal memo date My 28, 1968, "This allegation is entirely false. A 972-page report was submitted to the [Justice] Department on 3/8/68 and a closing report was submitted . . . 3/18/68. We received an additional request for investigation . . . on 4/22/68. . . . This was completed and a closing report submitted on 5/14/68" (Memo from A. Rosen to Mr. DeLoach, May 28, 1968, in the files of "Orangeburg Massacre," South Carolina State University Archives).

Six months later, McNair met with the FBI in a further attempt to dislodge the Orangeburg report. An internal memo documenting the meeting came this time from W. Mark Felt, the FBI official later identified as the "Deep Throat" source of information for *Washington Post* reporters Bob Woodward and Carl Bernstein during the Watergate investigation of President Nixon in 1972–73.

Felt's memo noted, "Governor McNair said he knew the FBI investigation was completed, but when he recently visited Attorney General Clark and requested the Attorney General to make some statement concerning the status of this matter, Mr. Clark informed him that as the investigation by the FBI was that of one law enforcement agency investigating another, it had been necessary to send Department attorneys into South Carolina to do another complete investigation."

The memo, dated 10/1/68, continued, "Governor McNair stated that the procrastination by the Attorney General was a serious slight to the State of South Carolina and created a very poor image of the state. . . . [He] realized that the delay was not the fault of the Bureau. He praised the effectiveness of the Bureau and expressed his appreciation for all the courtesies extended to him and his state by the FBI."

Felt concluded editorially, "Obviously, the Attorney General is attempting to blame the Bureau for delays attributable to his own shortcomings. He does not appear to have deceived Governor McNair" (Memo from W. M. Felt to Mr. Tolson, 10/1/68, "Orangeburg Massacre," South Carolina State University Archives).

A further memo from Rosen, following the grand jury refusal to indict the highway patrolmen and the filing of the criminal information by the Justice Department, stated, "Successful prosecution will require that the government prove the officers acted with the deliberate intent of denying the victims their Constitutional Rights. The situation is so controversial that it appears unlikely any jury can be convinced that the officers were guilty of the necessary criminal intent" (Memo from A. Rosen to Mr. DeLoach, December 24, 1968, "Orangeburg Massacre," South Carolina State University Archives).

167. Charleston (S.C.) *News and Courier,* March 18, 1968.
168. Eugene Sloan, Columbia (S.C.) *State,* November 8, 1968.
169. Al Lanier, Associated Press, in the Columbia (S.C.) *State,* October 22, 1968.
170. Sloan, Columbia (S.C.) *State,* November 9, 1968.
171. Kent Krell, Associated Press, in Columbia (S.C.) *State,* May 18, 1969.
172. Trial transcript, 1–2.
173. Lanier, Columbia (S.C.) *State,* May 27, 1969.
174. Lanier, Columbia (S.C.) *State,* May 23, 1969.
175. J. Robert Martin, trial transcript, 1195.
176. Ibid., 1195–96.
177. Charles Quaintance, trial transcript, 1124.
178. J. C. Coleman, trial transcript, 1131.
179. Ibid., 1135–36.
180. Columbia (S.C.) *State,* May 28, 1969.
181. Columbia (S.C.) *State,* October 27, 1970, and November10–14, 1970.
182. Wolfe, letter to Robert E. McNair, December 17, 1968, McNair papers.
183. Merritt, letter to Wolfe, July 10, 1969, McNair papers.
184. Wolfe, letter to Coleman, September 8, 1969, McNair papers.
185. McNair, letter to Wolfe, September 10, 1969, McNair papers.
186. Ibid., October 28, 1969.
187. Coleman, letter to Wolfe, July 30, 1970, McNair papers.
188. Columbia (S.C.) *State,* September 19, 1970.
189. Charleston (S.C.) *News and Courier,* September 22, 1970.
190. Charleston (S.C.) *News and Courier,* September 24, 1970.
191. Columbia (S.C.) *State,* August 20, 1970.
192. Columbia (S.C.) *State,* September 25, 1970.
193. Ibid.
194. Charleston (S.C.) *News and Courier,* September 27, 1970.
195. Columbia (S.C.) *State,* September 27, 1970.
196. Ibid.
197. Charleston (S.C.) *News and Courier,* September 27, 1970.
198. Columbia (S.C.) *State,* September 27, 1970.
199. Sellers, *River of No Return,* 265.
200. Columbia (S.C.) *State,* September 29, 1970.

201. Charleston (S.C.) *News and Courier,* September 29, 1970.

202. Charleston (S.C.) *News and Courier,* September 30, 1970.

203. Charleston (S.C.) *News and Courier,* September 19, 1970.

204. Frank Beacham, *Columbia Star,* February 8, 2001.

205. Charleston (S.C.) *News and Courier,* September 1, 1970.

206. Beacham, *Columbia Star,* February 8, 2001.

207. Charleston (S.C.) *News and Courier,* September 1, 1973.

208. Sellers, presentation to the Kosmos Club, Columbia, South Carolina, November 16, 2004.

209. McNair, correspondence with the author, March 11, 2005.

Chapter 11

1. Leon Fink, "Union Power, Soul Power: The Story of 1199B and Labor's Search for a Southern Strategy." *Southern Changes,* March/April 1983, 9–10.

2. Kaye Lingle Koonce, "The Political and Social Impact of the Charleston Hospital Strike," prepared for Prof. Dennis R. Nolan, Public Sector Labor Relations, University of South Carolina Law School, 2.

3. David Duncan Wallace, *South Carolina: A Short History, 1520–1948* (Columbia: University of South Carolina Press, 1984), 470.

4. George C. Rogers Jr., *Charleston in the Age of the Pinckneys* (Columbia: University of South Carolina Press, 1980), 138.

5. Wallace, *South Carolina,* 470.

6. Stephen O'Neill, "From the Shadow of Slavery: The Civil Rights Years in South Carolina," Ph.D. diss., University of Virginia, 255–56.

7. Ibid., 254.

8. Ibid., 254–55.

9. Ibid., 255.

10. McNair, personal interview, Oral Histories of the Robert E. McNair Gubernatorial Administration (1965–1971), South Carolina Department of Archives and History, Columbia, tape 21, 25 (hereafter Oral Histories).

11. Leon Fink and Brian Greenberg, *Upheaval in the Quiet Zone: A History of Hospital Workers Union, Local 1199* (Urbana and Chicago: University of Illinois Press, 1989), 131.

12. O'Neill, "From the Shadow," 257.

13. Koonce, "Political and Social Impact," 2.

14. Ibid., 6.

15. Ibid., 3.

16. Fink, "Union Power, Soul Power," 11.

17. Ibid.

18. Ibid.

19. Saunders, interview by author, tape recording, November 3, 2004.

20. O'Neill, 266.

21. Koonce, "Political and Social Impact," Appendix III.

22. Ibid., 12.

23. McNair, Oral Histories, tape 21, 23.

24. Ibid., 24.

25. Koonce, "Political and Social Impact," 4.

26. Ibid., Appendix I; Fink and Greenberg, *Upheaval in the Quiet Zone,* 132.

27. Koonce, "Political and Social Impact," 4.

28. Fink and Greenberg, *Upheaval in the Quiet Zone,* 133.

29. Koonce, "Political and Social Impact," 4.

30. McNair, Oral Histories, tape 22, 4.

31. Ibid., 6.

32. Jack Roach, Charleston (S.C.) *News and Courier,* April 2, 1969.

33. Ibid.

34. Fink and Greenberg, *Upheaval in the Quiet Zone,* 135.

35. Koonce, "Political and Social Impact," 13.

36. Levona Page, Columbia (S.C.) *State,* May 1, 1969, 1-A.

37. Columbia (S.C.) *State,* May 10, 1969, 1-A.

38. O'Neill, "From the Shadow," 258.

39. Koonce, "Political and Social Impact," 8.

40. O'Neill, "From the Shadow," 266.

41. Koonce, "Political and Social Impact," 13.

42. Ibid., 15.

43. Ibid., 15–16.

44. O'Neill, "From the Shadow," 268.

45. Fink and Greenberg, 140.

46. Bass, *Charlotte Observer,* April 21, 1969, 4B.

47. Fink and Greenberg, *Upheaval in the Quiet Zone,* 140.

48. McNair, Oral Histories, tape 22, 16.

49. Fink and Greenberg, *Upheaval in the Quiet Zone,* 141.

50. Ibid., 139.

51. Koonce, "Political and Social Impact," 16.

52. Fink, "Union Power, Soul Power," 13.

53. Fink and Greenberg, *Upheaval in the Quiet Zone,* 148.

54. Ibid., 140.

55. Ibid., 141.

56. Ibid., 139.

57. Ibid., 141.

58. McNair, personal interview, Oral Histories, tape 22, 7.

59. Fink, "Union Power, Soul Power," 15.

60. O'Neill, "From the Shadow," 279.

61. Ibid., 279–80.

62. Ibid., 280.

63. Fink and Greenberg, *Upheaval in the Quiet Zone,* 149.

64. Ibid.

65. McNair, Oral Histories, tape 22, 10.

66. Fink and Greenberg, *Upheaval in the Quiet Zone,* 151.

67. Ibid., 152.

68. Charleston (S.C.) *News and Courier,* June, 21, 1969.

69. Interview with Board Chairman Edwin Schachte, in O'Neill, 282.

77. O'Neill, "From the Shadow," 282–83.

71. Ibid., 284.

72. Ibid., 282.

73. Fink and Greenberg, *Upheaval in the Quiet Zone,* 152.

74. McNair, Oral Histories, tape 22, 11.

75. Saunders, interview with author, November 19, 2004.

76. Fink and Greenberg, *Upheaval in the Quiet Zone,* 152.

77. Koonce, "Political and Social Impact," 86.

78. O'Neill, "From the Shadow," 284.

79. McNair, Oral Histories, tape 22, 14.

80. Fink and Greenberg, *Upheaval in the Quiet Zone,* 153.

81. The *Washington Post* was editorially critical of HEW Secretary Robert Finch's role in the worsening of the strike. When it was proposed that HEW respond to the editorial by releasing a statement pledging to fulfill its legal responsibility in the area of equal employment in the Medical College strike, there was a holdup from the Nixon White House. In his book *Bring Us Together,* Leon Panetta—at the time civil rights chief in the Nixon HEW department—wrote that John Ehrlichman questioned the need for the release. When told that hundreds of blacks were demonstrating in Charleston, Panetta reported that Ehrlichman said, "Well, haven't we got some pressure on this from Thurmond? You know . . . the blacks aren't where our votes are."

Panetta, later a Democratic congressman from California and budget director in the Clinton administration, wrote, "I could hardly believe it. It was the first time I had heard the Southern strategy blown out in the open by . . . high-level Administration officials over a direct policy decision" (Panetta and Gall, *Bring Us Together*).

82. Fink and Greenberg, *Upheaval in the Quiet Zone,* 153.

83. Ibid.

84. Ibid., 154.

85. Koonce, "Political and Social Impact," 49.

86. Minutes of meeting of Charleston Area Community Relations Committee, June 26, 1969, papers of William Saunders.

87. Charleston (S.C.) *News and Courier,* June 28, 1969.

88. Koonce, "Political and Social Impact," 59.

89. Charleston (S.C.) *News and Courier,* June 29, 1969.

90. Fink and Greenberg, *Upheaval in the Quiet Zone,* 155–56.

91. Ibid., 157.

92. McNair, Oral Histories, tape 22, 20.

93. O'Neill, "From the Shadow," 4–5.

94. Charleston (S.C.) *News and Courier,* May 2, 1969.

95. Ibid.

96. Charleston (S.C.) *News and Courier,* May 3, 1969.

97. Charleston (S.C.) *News and Courier,* July 9, 1967.

Chapter 12

1. Cyril Busbee, address to public hearing on desegregation rules and regulations conducted by Minnesota State Board of Education, St. Paul, Minnesota, December 2, 1972, Busbee papers.

2. Orville Vernon Burton, "The Black Squint of the Law," in *The Meaning of South Carolina History: Essays in Honor of George C. Rogers, Jr.,* edited by David R. Chesnutt and Clyde N. Wilson (Columbia: University of South Carolina Press, 1991), 176.

3. Leon Panetta and Peter Gall, *Bring Us Together: The Nixon Team and the Civil Rights Retreat* (Philadelphia: Lippincott, 1971), 38.

4. Ibid., 25.

5. Ibid., 32.

6. Harry S. Dent, *The Prodigal South Returns to Power* (New York: John Wiley and Sons, 1978), 9.

7. Ibid., 82.

8. Ibid., 83.

9. Ibid., 101–2.

10. CQ, 1969, 133.

11. Panetta and Gall, *Bring Us Together,* 21–22.

12. Dent, *Prodigal South,* 121.

13. Panetta and Gall, *Bring Us Together,* 70–71; Dent, *Prodigal South,* 127.

14. Panetta and Gall, *Bring Us Together,* 86.

15. Ibid.

16. Levona Page, Columbia (S.C.) *State,* July 12, 1969.

17. Busbee, interview by author, Bob Hill in attendance, May 8, 2000, 20.

18. Ibid., 23.

19. *Greenville News,* February 13, 1969.

20. Dent, *Prodigal South,* 127.

21. Ibid., 126.

22. Ibid., 127.

23. Panetta and Gall, *Bring Us Together,* 178.

24. Ibid., 112.

25. Ibid., 168.

26. Ibid., 136.

27. Ibid.

28. Ibid., 176.

29. Dent, *Prodigal South,* 130.

30. Charleston (S.C.) *News and Courier,* January 24, 1970.

31. Dent, *Prodigal South,* 139.

32. Panetta and Gall, *Bring Us Together,* 208.

33. Dent, *Prodigal South,* 133–34.

34. Panetta and Gall, *Bring Us Together,* 216, 248.

35. Ibid., 300.

36. Dent, *Prodigal South,* 134.

37. Ibid., 142.

38. Ibid., 143.

39. South Carolina Budget and Control Board, S.C. Statistical Abstract, 1974.

40. Columbia (S.C.) *State,* January 22, 1969.

41. *Columbia Record,* January 22, 1970.

42. *Greenville Piedmont,* January 29, 1969.

43. *Greenville Piedmont,* January 28, 1969.

44. Columbia (S.C.) *State,* January 29, 1970.

45. Columbia (S.C.) *State,* February 18–19, 1969.

46. Dent, *Prodigal South,* 134; Panetta and Gall, *Bring Us Together,* 352.

47. Panetta and Gall, *Bring Us Together,* 365.

48. Dent, *Prodigal South,* 134.

49. Columbia (S.C.) *State,* February 26, 1970.

50. Columbia (S.C.) *State*, February 22, 1970.

51. Ibid.

52. Columbia (S.C.) *State*, February 25, 1970.

53. Columbia (S.C.) *State*, February 27, 1970.

54. Columbia (S.C.) *State*, March 2, 1970.

55. *Greenville News*, January 1, 1970.

56. Bob Gordon, United Press International, January 1, 1970.

57. Columbia (S.C.) *State*, March 2, 1970.

58. Ibid.

59. Columbia (S.C.) *State; Charlotte Observer*, March 4, 1970.

60. Columbia (S.C.) *State*, March 4, 1970.

61. Columbia (S.C.) *State*, May 1, 1970.

62. Columbia (S.C.) *State*, May 17, 1970.

63. Columbia (S.C.) *State*, May 12, 1970.

64. *Charlotte Observer*, May 19, 1970.

65. "Months of May," *University of South Carolina Magazine* 5, no. 2 (Summer 1970): 9.

66. *Charlotte Observer*, May 7, 1970, 1.

67. "Months of May," 9.

68. *Charlotte Observer*, May 8, 1970.

69. Columbia (S.C.) *State*, May 12, 1970.

70. Columbia (S.C.) *State*, May 13, 1970.

71. Columbia (S.C.) *State*, May 12, 1970.

72. Columbia (S.C.) *State*, May 13, 1970.

73. Columbia (S.C.) *State*, May 14, 1970.

74. "Months of May," 14.

75. *Charlotte Observer*, May 14, 1970.

76. Ibid.

77. *Charlotte Observer*, May 15, 1970.

78. "Months of May," 17.

79. *Columbia Record*, June 21, 1970.

80. *Florence Morning News*, June 21, 1970.

81. *Charlotte Observer*, June 27, 1970.

82. *Greenville News*, February 6, 1970.

83. Columbia (S.C.) *State*, February 25, 1970.

84. Columbia (S.C.) *State*, October 16, 1970.

85. Ibid.

86. Ibid.

87. Ibid.

88. Ibid.

89. Columbia (S.C.) *State*, October 31, 1970.

90. Columbia (S.C.) *State*, October 29, 1970.

91. Billy B. Hathorn, "The Changing Politics of Race: Congressman Albert William Watson and the Republican Party, 1965–1970," *South Carolina Historical Magazine* 89, no. 4 (1988): 233.

92. Ibid., 234.

93. Jay Latham, transcript of October 16 press conference, University of South Carolina.

94. Ibid.

95. Ibid.

96. Text of John C. West inaugural address, January 19, 1971, papers of John C. West, South Carolina Political Collections, University of South Carolina.

97. Ibid.

Epilogue

1. This and all subsequent quotes from O. Wayne Corley in the epilogue are from an interview by the author, March 21, 2005.

2. *US News and World Report,* October 6, 1969, 43–44.

3. Ibid., 44.

4. Gary Hart, *The Good Fight: The Education of an American Reformer* (New York: Random House, 1993), 94.

5. Don Fowler, interview by author, October 19, 2004. Fowler was referring to political newcomer Charles (Pug) Ravenel, who was the surprise victor in the 1974 Democratic primary, winning over party stalwarts Lieutenant Governor Earle Morris and Congressman Bryan Dorn. He was disqualified, however, when the South Carolina Supreme Court upheld a challenge that Ravenel, a Wall Street stockbroker, did not meet the constitutional residency requirement of having lived in South Carolina in the five consecutive years previous to his nomination. Dorn was subsequently nominated by convention as the Democratic nominee for governor and lost in the general election to Republican Dr. James B. Edwards, an oral surgeon from Charleston who became the state's first Republican governor in the twentieth century.

6. West, interview by author, October 24, 2003.

7. Fred Carter, interview by author, August 31, 2004.

8. Fowler, interview by author, October 19, 2004.

9. Carter, interview by the author, August 31, 2004.

10. Jim Konduros, interview by author, September 22, 2004.

11. Fowler, interview by author, October 19, 2004.

12. Ibid.

Bibliography

Major sources of material, and particularly many of the direct quotations from Governor McNair and those associated with his administration, are the transcribed interviews of the *Oral Histories of the Robert E. McNair Administration (1965–1971),* South Carolina Department of Archives and History, Archives and Publications Division

Ashmore, Harry S. *Civil Rights and Wrongs: A Memoir of Race and Politics, 1944–1994.* New York: Pantheon Books, 1994.
———. *Hearts and Minds.* Washington, D.C.: Seven Locks Press, 1992.
Bass, Jack, and Jack Nelson. *The Orangeburg Massacre.* New York: World Publishing, 1970.
Biles, Roger. *The South and the New Deal.* Lexington: University of Kentucky Press, 1994.
Black, Earl, and Merle Black. *Politics and Society in the South.* Cambridge, Mass.: Harvard University Press, 1987.
Burts, Robert Milton. *Richard Irvine Manning and the Progressive Movement in South Carolina.* Columbia: University of South Carolina Press, 1974.
Byrnes, James F. *All in One Lifetime.* New York: Harper, 1958.
Canup, C. R. (Red), and W. D. Workman. *Charles E. Daniel: His Philosophy and Legacy.* Columbia: R. L. Bryan, 1981.
Caro, Robert A. *The Years of Lyndon Johnson: The Path to Power.* New York: Knopf, 1982.
Cauthen, John K. *Speaker Blatt: His Challenges Were Greater.* Columbia: R. L. Bryan, 1965.
Chesnutt, David R., and Clyde N. Wilson, eds. *The Meaning of South Carolina History: Essays in Honor of George C. Rogers Jr.* Columbia: University of South Carolina Press, 1991.
Cobb, James C. *The Selling of the South: The Southern Crusade for Industrial Development 1936–1990.* 2nd ed. Urbana: University of Illinois Press, 1993.
Cohodas, Nadine. *Strom Thurmond and the Politics of Southern Change.* New York: Simon and Schuster, 1993.
Cross, J. Russell. *Historic Ramblin's through Berkeley.* Columbia: R. L. Bryan, 1985.
Dent, Harry S. *The Prodigal South Returns to Power.* New York: John Wiley and Sons, 1978.
Drago, Edmund L. *Initiative, Paternalism and Race Relations: Charleston's Avery Institute.* Athens: University of Georgia Press, 1990.

Edgar, Walter B. *History of Santee Cooper, 1934–1984*. Columbia: R. L. Bryan, 1984.

———. *South Carolina: A History*. Columbia: University of South Carolina Press, 1998.

Egerton, John. *Speak Now against the Day: The Generation before the Civil Rights Movement in the South*. New York: Knopf, 1994.

Federal Bureau of Investigation. Investigation of Orangeburg Demonstrations and Shootings, February 12–29, 1968. Report submitted, March 5, 1968. Made available by S.C. State University Archives.

Forman, James. *The Making of Black Revolutionaries*. Seattle: University of Washington Press, 1997.

Gordon, Asa H. *Sketches of Negro Life and History of South Carolina*. Columbia: University of South Carolina Press, 1971.

Halberstam, David. *The Children*. New York: Random House, 1998.

Hart, Gary. *The Good Fight: The Education of an American Reformer*. New York: Random House, 1993.

Key, V. O., Jr. *Southern Politics in State and Nation*. Knoxville: University of Tennessee Press, 1984.

Koonce, Kaye Lingle. "The Political and Social Impact of the Charleston Hospital Strike." Prepared for Professor Dennis R. Nolan, University of South Carolina Law School, May 9, 1981.

Lachicotte, Alberta. *Rebel Senator: Strom Thurmond of South Carolina*. New York: Devin-Adair, 1966.

Lander, Ernest McPherson, Jr. *A History of South Carolina, 1865–1960*. Chapel Hill: University of North Carolina Press, 1960.

Leuchtenburg, William E. *Franklin Roosevelt and the New Deal*. New York: Harper Torchbooks, 1963.

Lewis, John. *Walking with the Wind: A Memoir of the Movement*. New York: Simon and Schuster, 1998.

Mays, Benjamin E. *Born to Rebel*. Athens: University of Georgia Press, 1971.

McGill, Ralph. *The South and the Southerner*. Boston: Little, Brown and Company, 1969.

"The Months of May." *University of South Carolina Magazine* 5, no. 2 (Summer 1970).

Moody's Investor Service and Campus Facilities Associates. "Opportunity and Growth in South Carolina, 1968–1985," 1968.

Panetta, Leon, and Peter Gall. *Bring Us Together: The Nixon Team and the Civil Rights Retreat*. Philadelphia: J. B. Lippincott, 1971.

Rogers, George C. *Charleston in the Age of the Pinckneys*. Columbia: University of South Carolina Press, 1969.

Rogers, George C., and C. James Taylor. *A South Carolina Chronology: 1497–1992*. 2nd ed. Columbia: University of South Carolina Press, 1994.

Savage, Henry, Jr. *River of the Carolinas: The Santee*. New York: Rinehart, 1956.

Sellers, Cleveland. *The River of No Return: The Autobiography of a Black Militant and the Life and Death of SNCC*. Jackson: University of Mississippi Press, 1990.

Southern Regional Council. "Events at Orangeburg: A Report Based on Study and Interviews in Orangeburg, South Carolina, in the Aftermath of Tragedy," by Pat Watters and Weldon Rougeau. Atlanta, Ga.: February 25, 1968.

Southern Regional Council and the American Jewish Committee. Institute of Human Relations. "The Continuing Crisis: An Assessment of New Racial Tensions in the South." Atlanta and New York: May 1966.

Spears, R. Wright. *One in the Spirit*. Columbia, S.C.: R. L. Bryan, 1997.

Sproat, John G. "'Firm Flexibility': Perspectives on Desegregation in South Carolina," in Stephen Maiglish and Robert Abzug, *New Perspectives on Race and Slavery in America*. University of Kentucky Press, 1986.

———. "'Pragmatic Conservatism' and Desegregation: The Case of South Carolina." Paper presented to the Organization of American Historians.

Sproat, John G., and Larry Schweikert. *Making Change: South Carolina Banking in the Twentieth Century*. Columbia, S.C.: Bankers Association, 1990.

Tindall, George Brown. *South Carolina Negroes, 1877–1900*. Columbia: University of South Carolina Press, 1952.

Towles, Louis P., ed. *A World Turned Upside Down*. Columbia: University of South Carolina Press, 1996.

Wallace, David D. *South Carolina: A Short History, 1520–1948*. Columbia: University of South Carolina Press, 1951.

Workman, W. D. *The Bishop from Barnwell: The Political Life and Times of Edgar Brown*. Columbia, S.C.: R. L. Bryan, 1963.

Index

A. C. Flora High School, xviii, 288–90
A. Philip Randolph Institute, 251
Aba-Mecha, Barbara W. *See* Woods,
  Barbara A.
Abernathy, Ralph, 17, 252, 253, 254
Addy, Henry Morrell, 221
AFL-CIO, 254
African Americans: and Black Power /
  Black Nationalism, 18, 199, 200, 225,
  227, 228; and de facto segregation, 200,
  203; and demonstrations, xi, xvi, 48,
  85, 111, 176–77, 179, 185, 229–32;
  and disenfranchisement of, xv, 2, 9, 31–
  32, 34, 47, 115, 177; and grassroots
  political efforts, xi, 47; and out-
  migration, 33, 35; and political power,
  192; and school desegregation, 15, 16,
  21; and violent demonstrations, xi; and
  voting, 9, 34, 105, 119, 159–60, 267,
  287–88
African Methodist Episcopal Church, 35
Agnew, Hugh, 89
Agnew, Spiro, 281
agriculture, 22, 23, 36; and cotton, 6, 24,
  32, 77, 86–87, 242; and plantation
  economy, 22, 24; and tenant farming,
  5, 22, 32, 77; and timber, 24; and
  tobacco, 126
Aiken, Boone, 168
Aiken County, 132, 141
Alabama, 13, 14, 19, 26, 58, 109, 112,
  114, 266, 273, 277; Birmingham, 17,
  18, 101, 200, 254; Montgomery, 17,
  18, 101; Muscle Shoals, 39; Selma, 18,
  114, 226

Alexander, Robert E., 285
Alexander, Robert L., 145
Alexander v. Holmes County 274, 275, 276
Allendale County, xvi, 9, 11, 12, 44, 63,
  84, 89, 90, 93
All-Star Bowling Lanes, 202
Allston, Allard, 263
American Revolution, 23, 38, 242, 286
Anderson, Jesse T., 123, 125, 126, 132
Appalachian Regional Commission, 145
Ariail, J. Milton, 51
Arkansas, 19, 79, 86, 277
Ashmore, Harry, 33, 59, 70
Associated Press, 10, 134, 174, 225–26,
  232
Atlanta, Ga., 17, 19
Atlanta University, 41
Atomic Energy Commission, 86
Atwater, Lee, 273
Austin Peay University, 125
Aycock, Jim, 72, 130, 151

BAWI (Balancing Agriculture with Indus-
  try), 166
Babcock, Havilah, 51
Bacote, Samuel, 147, 199
Bailey, Lilly, 29
Bankers Trust, 169
Baptists, 35, 156, 157, 185
Barnett, Ross, 112
Barnwell County, 11, 40, 73, 102, 141
Barnwell Ring, 11, 53, 59, 71, 72, 112,
  160
Barrett, Reginald, Sr., 244, 245
Baruch, Bernard, 86

Bass, Jack, 165, 204, 209, 212, 213, 222, 237

Bates, Jeff, 130, 131, 135–36

Bates, Lester, 6, 30, 111

Beaufort County, 31, 63

Benedict College, 177, 178, 230

Bennett, Isaiah, 245, 251

Berkeley County, xvi, 11, 23–24, 26, 28, 30–32, 37–39, 90, 93, 100, 102

Best, Jeryl, 278, 279–81

Biles, Roger, 41

Black Panthers, 247

Blackwood, Ibra C., 39

Blatt, Solomon, 5, 7, 9, 11–12, 34, 53, 59, 62, 69, 87, 89, 137, 144, 149, 159, 300–301; and assessment of McNair, 82–84, 99–100, 160; and education policy, 71–76; and Moody Report, 164–66, 173–74; and role as Speaker of the House, 129, 130–31

Blatt, Solomon, Jr., 53, 72

Blease, Coleman, 110, 113, 178, 192, 196

Bledsoe, Dave, 225–26

Boineau, Charles E., 106

Boulware, Harold, 67

Boulware, Thomas, 63

Boykin, James A., 199

Boylston, Sam, 72

Briggs, Henry, 15, 67, 124

Briggs v. Elliott, xvi, 15, 16, 36, 67–68, 70, 85, 138

Broad Street Gang. *See* Charleston: and Broad Street Gang

Broadwater, Thomas, 287

Brooks, Woody, 146

Brown, Edgar, 5, 6, 8, 11, 12, 34, 112–13, 129–31,159, 300; and Budget & Control Board, 151; as legislator, 40, 53, 59, 62, 71, 75, 102–4, 149; and Moody Report, 166, 174; and reapportionment, 138

Brown, H. Rap, 199, 201, 206, 226

Brown, J. Arthur, 244

Brown, Walter, 57, 71

Brown II, 13, 179, 266

Brown v. Board of Education, xvi, 13–16, 32, 48, 68, 80, 110, 199, 265; and pres-sure to implement, 84–85, 117–22, 128–29, 161, 177; and resistance to, 266–68

Buchanan, Pat, 268

Burger, Warren, 274

Burroughs, Edward, 157

Burton, Orville Vernon, 34

Busbee, Cyril B., 14, 15, 122, 132–34, 135, 141, 149, 266, 271

Butler, Oscar, 207

Buzhardt, J. Fred, 268

Byrd, Levi, 182

Byrnes, James F., xvi, 4–6, 9, 13–14, 34, 41, 70, 166; and "Education Revolu-tion," 68, 69, 70, 80; as governor, 66, 75, 88; and industrial recruitment, 85–86; and sales tax increase, 68, 70, 118, 123, 165; and Santee Cooper, 39, 40; and school desegregation, 15, 16, 67, 68, 109, 124, 125; as senator, 41

Cain, Marshall, 136

Caldwell, Bill, 285

Calhoun, John C., 66

Campbell, Carroll A., 145, 292, 301

Campbell, Roy C., 222

Canup, Red, 79

Carmichael, Stokely, 18, 188, 199, 201, 216, 229, 245

Carter, Allen, 93, 94

Carter, James E., 54, 254, 299

Carter, Luther F., 145, 149, 170, 300, 302

Carter, Rex, 83, 84, 131

Cauthen, John K., 8, 82–83, 89, 112–13, 144, 156, 164, 168

Center for School Education Studies, 108

Chapman, Harry, 157

Chapman, Jim, 52, 168

Charleston, S.C., xvi, xix, 25, 30, 31, 35, 37–38, 70, 84, 86, 89–90, 93, 98, 102; and Broad Street Gang, 93–94, 247; and County Hospital, 249; and hospital strike of 1969, xii, xviii, 241–50; and Rotary Club, 247

Charleston County, 201

churches, 3; Betaw Christian Church, 26; First Baptist Church (Columbia), 156;

Jamestown Baptist Church, 27; Macedonia Christian Church, 27; Russellville Christian Church, 26; United Methodist Church, 19
Citadel, the, 54, 177
Civil Rights Act of 1964, 117, 119, 121, 128, 199, 202–3, 206, 210, 212, 227, 267
Civil Rights Commission, 117
Civil War, 22, 27, 28, 30, 31, 119, 242, 286
Civilian Conservation Corps, 37–38
Claflin University, 46, 101, 177–78, 180–81, 200–201, 214–6, 219, 225, 238
Claiborne, Jack, 8
Clancy, Paul, 191, 195
Clarendon County, xvi, 15, 16, 36, 67, 68, 85, 124, 138, 141
Clark, Ramsey, 212, 228, 229
Clark, Septima, 244
Clay, Cecil, 93
Clemson College. See Clemson University
Clemson University, xvii, 30, 49, 51, 112, 167, 172, 177, 282; and integration of, 3–4, 8–9, 12, 19–20, 60, 112–14, 116, 127, 205–6
Clinton, William J., 270, 299
Close, William H., 157
Clyburn, James E., 15, 180, 262
Cobb, James C., 79
Cohodas, Nadine, 56
Coker College, 19, 281
Coleman, J. C., 232, 233, 234, 235
Coles, Jesse A., Jr., 125, 133, 134
College of Charleston, 175, 252, 286
Collier, Becky, 144
Columbia, S.C., xix, 28, 35, 36, 96, 97; and desegregation, 126, 206
Columbia College, 51, 157
Communist Party, 182, 183
Community Action Agency, 245
Community Relations Committee, 259–60
Community Relations Council, 247
Confederate flag, 21, 110
Congress of Racial Equality, 251
Connor, Bull, 200, 244
Conroy, John F., 252, 254

Cook, Crawford, 92, 94, 95, 96
Corley, O. Wayne, xix, 146, 295
Covington, Jim, 96, 97
Crawford, Joseph Clark, 26
Crawford, Leona, 26
Crawford, Martha Susan Eatmon, 26
Crawford, Roland, Jr., 26
Crow, Ryan, 126

Dabbs, James McBride, 19, 57
Daniel, Charles E., 5, 79–80, 92, 112
Daniel, Jonathan, 14
Daniel International Construction, 79, 80
Darlington County, 102, 184, 274–79, 281
Davis, John W., 69–70
Davis, Robert S., 25, 132, 133
Davis, Thomas Hoyt, 47
Dean, John Mark, 285
DeLaine, Joseph A., 15, 67, 85
DeLoach, Deke, 238
Democratic Party, 4, 6, 8, 20, 282; and Lyndon B. Johnson, 41, 147, 237; and McNair, 65, 92, 99–101; and race relations, 2, 17, 34, 47, 58, 67, 112, 113, 267; and struggle against Republican Party, 31, 134, 138
Dennis, Adelaide "Tootsie," 144
Dennis, E. J., 55
Dennis, E. J., Jr., 55
Dennis, Rembert C., 30, 54–56, 60, 62, 75, 102–4, 149, 300
Dent, Harry, 135–36, 139, 268, 270, 274–75, 279
Depression, the, 1, 28, 38, 41, 44, 51, 78, 87, 135, 150, 168
Dewey, Thomas E., 56, 58, 62
Dibble, Bob, 295
Dixiecrats, 17, 56, 58–60, 66, 99
Douglass, Frederick, 36
Drummond, John, 159, 230, 231
DuBois, W. E. B., 35, 36, 195
Duffy, John, Sr., 285
Durham, Ralph, 126

Eaddy, Ed, 134
Eastland, James O., 14

Eddings, Inez, 141
Edgar, Walter B., xii, 39
education, 3, 42, 87, 91; and busing, 15, 67, 71, 124, 173; and desegregation, 12–13, 69, 108–13, 119, 123, 127, 137, 273–80; and drop-out rate, xviii; and Education Finance Committee, 123, 124, 125, 126, 127; and federal free-lunch program, 120; and funding process, 29, 95; and kindergartens, xviii, 69, 164, 165, 171, 173–74; and one-teacher schools, 28; and State Department of, 133, 134; and Title I, 120; and Title II, 120
Education Finance Act of 1977, 161
Education Improvement Act of 1984, 161
Edward, W. G., 168
Edward, Walter L., 89
Edwards, James B., 186
Edwards, Robert C., 8, 112, 113
Egerton, John, 15, 48, 49, 66, 69
Eisenhower, Dwight, 134, 139, 180, 184
Elliott, Tom E., 136
Ellis, Archie, 156, 186
Episcopal Church, 157
Evans, Rowland, 268

Fair Employment Practices Act, 57–58
Fair Labor Standards Act, 78
Fairey, Carl, 204
Fanning, Anthony, 187
Farm Bureau, 89
Federal Bureau of Investigation, xviii, 237, 259; and Orangeburg shootings, 200, 205–6, 214–15, 218, 220–22, 227–28, 231–32; and racial unrest at S.C. State, 188; and trial of Cleveland Sellers, 235
Felder, James, xix, 47, 262
Fidler, Paul, 285
Fielding, Herbert, xix, 47, 183, 262
Figg, Robert McC., 57
Finch, Robert, 258–59, 270–71, 278
Fink, Leon, 244, 251, 252, 258
Fisk University, 41
Fitzgerald, Martha Thomas, 71
Fleming, Billy, 190

Floyd, Harry L., Jr., 202–6, 227
Floyd, John, 89
Foard, John, 72
Fonda, Jane, 285
Foner, Moe, 259
Ford, Gerald, 135
Forman, James, 19, 199, 200
Fort, Claire, 295
Fort Sumter, 21, 201
Fowler, Donald, 143, 151, 299, 301, 302, 303
Francis Marion National Forest, 28
Francis Marion University, 145, 175, 300
Fraser, Charles, 157
Freedom of Information Act, 154
Freeman, Wayne, 112
Friday, Tom, 224
Frierson, J. Nelson, 53
Furman, Alester, 168
Furman University, 56, 296

GI Bill of Rights, 48, 179
Gaillard, Palmer, 254
Gaillard, Peter, 39
Gaines, Tracy, 83, 84
Gamarekian, Edward, 180
Gantt, Harvey, xvii, 9, 19, 20, 60, 114
Garrett, Gordon, 93
Garrett, William, 136
Gasque, J. Leon, 204, 208, 214, 253
Gasque, J. Ralph, 230
Gatch, Donald, 161
General Electric, 167
General Strike of 1934. See labor: and unions
George, Walter, 40
George Peabody College for Teachers, 108, 125
Georgia, 14, 19, 36, 48, 52, 56, 86, 114; Albany, 17; Augusta, 61; Elberton, 79; Savannah, 61
Georgia Pacific, 296
Gettys, Robert H., 271
Gibson, Hugh, 10, 97, 137, 142, 165, 195, 236, 263, 264–65
Goldwater, Barry, xvii, 17, 59, 127, 134–35, 139, 267–68, 297

Gore, Al, 299
Grace, John P., 39
Grady, Stella, 29
Graham, Cora, 143
Grant, Henry L., 247, 249, 254, 255
Grant, Wilbur, 102
Green v. School Board of New Kent County, 269
Greenberg, Brian, 251, 252, 258
Greenville County, 54, 93, 98, 102, 275–79
Gregory, George, 72
Gressette, L. Marion, xii, 34, 146, 300; and desegregation of public schools, 14–15, 125, 137; and legislature, 75, 102–4, 129–30, 149, 159; and Moody Report, 166
Gressette Committee, 14, 15, 108, 125, 137
Griffith, Eugene C., 230, 231
Grimball, John, 235, 236

Hamby, Dolly, 143
Hammond, Sam, 223
Hammonds, Joseph, 187, 188
Hampton, Wade, 31
Hampton, Wade, II, 34
Hampton County, 62, 63, 71, 79
Hardin, Paul, Jr., 19
Harley, J. Emile, 53
Harper, Walter, 166
Harpootlian, Dick, 282
Harris, Ray, 258, 276
Hart, Gary, 298, 299
Harvey, Clinton B., 289
Haskell, Alexander, 31
Hawkins, Maude, 51
Haynsworth, Clement F., 235
Haynsworth, Knox, Jr., 245–46, 249
Hell Hole Swamp Gang, 30, 93
Hemphill, Robert W., 191
Hester, Lawrence, 102
Heyward, DuBose, 158
Hickman, Bob, 144, 156
Higher Education Commission, 168, 172, 174
Hill, Henry, 108

Hine, William C., 177, 187, 191, 238
Hinton, James M., 48, 67, 68, 182, 183, 185
Hocutt, Robert, 232
Hodges, James H., 238
Hodges, Luther, 166, 167
Hoefer, Lilla, 300
Holder, Dwight, 157
Holland, Townes, 134
Hollings, Ernest F., 4, 8, 10–11, 13, 54, 60, 167; as governor, 108, 112–14, 150, 176; and race for lieutenant governor, 84, 88; and S.C. House of Representatives, 72, 76; and U.S. Senate, 98, 99, 100, 134, 136, 141, 295
Hollis, Daniel W., 49, 52
Holman, Alonzo W., 183, 187, 230
Hoover, Herbert, 36
Hoover, J. Edgar, 228, 229
Hope, James H., 123
Howard University, 18, 41, 199
Howe, Gedney, Sr., 247
Huff, William, 250, 256, 262
Hughes, Jerry M., Jr., 231
Human Affairs Commission, 147
Humphrey, Hubert H., 271, 297, 298

industrialization, 3, 24, 80, 85–86
Interdenominational Ministerial Alliance, 252
Internal Revenue Service, 182

Jackson, J. Rhett, 237, 239
Jackson, Jesse, 17
Jefferies, Richard M., 39
Jenkins, Esau, 244, 249
Jennings, Croft, 53
Jews, 12; American Jewish Committee on the Institute of Human Relations, 19; and anti-Semitism, 73
Jim Crow laws, 32, 67, 182
Jimmy's tax. *See* Byrnes, James F.: and sales tax increase
John Birch Society, 200, 245
Johnson, Charles, 41
Johnson, Daisy Dunn, 147
Johnson, I. S. Leevy, xix, 47, 169, 262

Johnson, Lyndon B., xvii, 2, 41, 114, 135, 139, 228, 237–38, 296; and 1964 election, 267; and the Great Society, 41, 146, 160; and War on Poverty, 169
Johnson, Mordecai, 41
Johnson, Sam Ealy, 41
Johnson, W. W. "Hootie," 169
Johnston, Gladys, 6, 8
Johnston, Olin D., xvii, 1–2, 4–8, 15, 17, 20–21, 34, 40–41, 47–48, 80, 106, 134; and friendship with McNair, 100; and race relations, 113; and U.S. Senate, 98, 99, 106, 145
Johnston, William, 6, 8, 106
Jones, Thomas F., 283, 286

Karesh, Coleman, 53
Kennedy, John F., xvii, 90, 101, 105, 184, 267
Kennedy, Robert F., 228, 237, 298
Kent State University riots, 281, 282
Kentucky, 57, 58, 79
Kerry, John, 299
Kershaw County, 54, 75, 92, 131
Key, V. O., Jr., 33
Kiawah Island, 91, 102, 155
King, Coretta Scott, 251, 253, 254
King, Martin Luther, Jr., 17, 18, 19, 36, 200, 201, 237, 245, 251, 252, 302
King, Martin Luther, Sr., 264
Kleberg, Richard M., 41
Konduros, James S., xix, 145, 149, 160–61, 170–71, 295, 296, 302
Koon, Warren, 226
Koonce, Kaye L., xii, 249
Krell, Kent, 232
Ku Klux Klan, 18, 19, 73, 85, 110, 131, 200, 287

labor, 69; and "right-to-work" legislation, xvi, 9, 78–79, 80, 82, 87, 249; and strikes, xv, xviii, 229, 241–50; and unions, xv, 40, 77, 78, 82, 135, 261
Lachicotte, Alberta, 58
Lake, Henry, 146, 224
Lake Marion, 39
Lake Moultrie, 39, 164

Lander, Ernest, 85, 86, 87
Lander University, 175
Lane, Hugh, Sr., 93, 168, 247, 255, 259
Lanier, Al, 10, 134
Lawton, Thomas O., 64
Leath, Charles, 218
Leevy, I. S., 184
Legare, T. Allen, 77, 92, 93
Legge, Lionel, 72, 76
Leonard, Jerris, 272, 274, 277
Lewis, Crosby, 297
Lewis, John, 17–18, 19
Lexington County, 133, 141
Limestone College, 104
Lincoln Emancipation Clubs, 48
Liuzzo, Viola Gregg, 18
Long, J. C., 93
Louisiana, 19, 56, 58, 114
Lumpkin, John H., Sr., 168
lynching, 58

MacArthur, Douglas, 43
Macedonia High School, 49, 91
Maddox, Lester, 280
Mahoney, Bill, 106
Malcolm X, 244
Mance, Robert W., 48
Mann, James R., 54, 72
Manning, Richard I., 150–51
Marshall, Thurgood, 48, 67
Martin, Geddes, 232
Martin, J. Robert, Jr., 227, 231, 232
Martin, John, 92, 103
Martin, Wade, 166
Marvin, Robert, 300
Maybank, Burnet R., Jr., 91
Maybank, Burnet R., Sr., 5, 34, 39, 88, 91, 100
Mays, Benjamin E., 36, 178
Mays, Marshall, 141
McCall, John, 140
McCarthy, Eugene, 298
McCord, William J., 243–46, 250, 251, 256–59
McCray, John Henry, 48, 182, 184
McCullough, Alex, 144
McCullough, David, 56

McCutcheon, Tom, 52
McDew, Charles, 180
McGill, Ralph, 19–20
McGovern, George, 298, 299
McGuire, Frank, 50, 279
McHugh, Robert, 9
McKaine, Osceola, 48, 182, 184
McKissick, Ellison S., Jr., 168
McKissick, J. Rion, 52
McLean, Thomas N., 116, 131
McLeod, Daniel R., 5, 115, 131, 132, 135, 136, 149, 152, 189; and Orangeburg shootings, 204, 212, 213, 224; and Medical College strike, 248–49
McMillan, John L., 279
McNair, Catherine McCallum, 26
McNair, Claudia Crawford, 23, 26, 27, 28
McNair, Claudia Crawford (daughter), 296
McNair, Corrine Calhoun, 296
McNair, Daniel Evander, 23, 25, 26, 28
McNair, Duncan, 26
McNair, James, 157
McNair, Josephine Robinson, 7, 44–45, 49, 53, 60, 63, 94, 103, 106, 300
McNair, Robert Evander, xi, 1; and A. C. Flora, 288–90; and Appalachian Regional Commission, 297; at Ballsdam, 23, 26, 27, 29, 30, 37, 38, 65; and Coastal Plains Regional Commission, 297; and commitment to education, 122–23, 162–66, 171–72; and desegregation, 108, 125, 129, 130, 146, 163–66, 274–80; and early life, 22–30, 40, 42, 43; and Education Commission of the States, 297; and elevation to governor, 7, 8, 9, 10, 11, 18, 21, 83–84, 128, 205, 264; and Lamar, 280–81, 288, 289, 292; and leadership style, 141–48, 161, 176, 253, 255, 296; as lieutenant governor, 102–6; and Medical College strike, 243–50; and Moody Report, 161–73; and race for lieutenant governor, 89–99; and move to Allendale County, 60–64; and opposition to unions, 248; and Orangeburg shootings, 198–240; and populism, xi; and race relations, 181, 200; and relationship with industry, 87–89; and S.C. House of Representatives, 54, 70–81, 83, 87, 102; and sales tax increases, 68, 69, 96, 97, 164–66, 174; and school desegregation, 15, 138; and South Carolina State, 189, 190, 198–240; and Southern Regional Education Board, 297; and tourism development, 154–58; and U.S. Navy, 43–44; and the University of South Carolina, 50, 51, 52, 53, 54, 72, 282–86, 292, 301
McNair, Robert Evander, Jr., 50, 53, 296
McNair, Robin Lee, 296
Medicaid, 160, 165
Medical College of South Carolina, 172, 174, 175, 241–50, 263, 281, 285, 286, 301
Medicare, 160
Meredith, James, 112
Merritt, Lewie G., 146, 234
Mickel, Buck, 168
Middleton, Delano, 223, 225
Middleton, Earl, 46–47, 184, 203
migration. See African Americans: and out-migration; South Carolina: and out-migration
Miller, Thomas E., 178, 179, 189, 195
Milliken, Roger, 92
Mills, Henry, 131, 141, 149, 151
Mississippi, 2, 13, 14, 19, 58, 79, 86, 101, 109, 112, 114, 166, 199, 273, 274, 277
Mitchell, John, 274
Mondale, Walter, 299
Monteith, Henri, xvii, 114
Monteith, Rachel E., 36
Moody Report, xviii, 161–73, 300
Morehouse College, 36
Morrah, Bradley, 136, 141
Morris, Earle, 72, 92, 98
Morris, James A., 116, 156
Morton, Beecher, 45
Morton, Robert, 41
Motes, Mason T., 136
Moultrie, Mary, 243, 244, 249, 252
Moultrie, William, 39
Moynihan, Daniel Patrick, 259

Mozingo, James P., 102
Murdaugh, Randolph, Jr., 63
Murray, Marvin N., 54–55, 60
Muskie, Edmund, 297
Myrick, Ed, 64

Nance, M. Maceo, Jr., 193–97, 198, 202–3, 208, 211, 215, 216, 221, 224, 238
National Association for the Advancement of Colored People (NAACP), 9, 14, 16–17, 35–36, 41, 47–48, 67, 68, 70, 85, 101, 109, 142, 176, 179; and McNair, 181, 201, 206; and Medical College strike, 244–51; and reaction against, 180, 182; and South Carolina State, 189–92, 198–240
National Guard, xviii, 112, 205, 209, 214, 215, 234, 264, 279; and Charleston hospital strike, 251, 254; and USC unrest, 283–86
National Labor Relations Act, 249
National Recovery Act, 78
NationsBank, 296
Nelson, Herbert, 207
Nelson, Jack, 204, 209, 212, 213, 222
New Deal, 37, 38 40, 42, 59, 99, 150, 155, 160, 168
New York, 38, 105, 115, 155
Newby, I. A., 16, 33, 35–36, 37, 85, 124, 125, 178, 189
Newell, Mike, 60
Newman, Isaiah DeQuincey, 35, 101, 160, 180, 181, 183; and NAACP leadership, 183–88, 195, 201, 202, 215, 263
newspapers, 37; *Charleston News & Courier,* 10, 140, 142, 195, 236, 260–61; *Charlotte News,* 58; *Charlotte Observer,* 6, 8, 281, 282; *Florence Morning News,* 85, 139, 199; *Greenville News,* 165; *Greenwood Index-Journal,* 139; *Lighthouse and Informer,* 99, 184; *Low Country Newsletter,* 244; *New York Times,* 254; *Orangeburg Times and Democrat,* 195, 225; *Raleigh News & Observer,* 14; *Spartanburg Herald Journal,* 290; Columbia *State,* 6, 7, 9, 80, 104, 106, 116, 138, 141, 180, 191, 194–95, 225,

280–81; *Tiger,* 282; *Wall Street Journal,* 251; *Washington Post,* 228; *Winnsboro News & Herald,* 40–41
Nichols, Alexander, 188
Nicklaus, Jack, 101
Nixon, Richard M., 13, 54, 59, 90, 117, 134, 142, 184, 251, 256, 258, 267–74, 288, 299
North Carolina, 23, 25, 48, 52, 86, 98, 114, 166; Gastonia, 77; Greensboro, 180; Wilmington, 26
Novak, Robert, 268

Oconee County, xvi, 9, 92, 93, 98
O'Dowd, Jack, 85
Ohio, 37, 155
Ole Miss. *See* University of Mississippi
O'Neill, Stephen, 256
O'Neill, Thomas P., 33
Opportunity and Growth in South Carolina, 1968–85. See Moody Report
Orangeburg County, 84, 100, 126, 180
Orangeburg Massacre, 208
Orangeburg Movement, 181, 198
Orangeburg shootings, xii, xviii, 198–240, 241, 253, 255, 281, 294, 301
Orvin, M. C., 31
O'Shields, Dexter & Hazel, 138

Palmer, John, 28
Panetta, Leon, 13, 114, 117, 118, 267, 270–74, 278
Parker, John J., 16
Parker, Marshall, xvi, xvii, 9, 92–95, 97–98, 100, 102, 104, 130–31, 134, 136, 140–42
Patterson, Dwight F., Jr., 6
Patterson, Elizabeth J., 6
Patterson, Grady L., 131, 132, 135, 136, 141, 149, 151
Payton, Benjamin F., 230
Pearson, Levi, 15, 67, 124
Pendarvis, E. O., 210
Penn Center, 201
Percell, Margaret, 147
Perry, Matthew, 9, 160, 181, 185, 187, 188, 191, 203, 230, 233

Philippines, 43, 44, 47, 52
Pickens County, 92, 98
Plessy v. Ferguson, xv, 32, 67, 70, 80, 124
Pollak, Stephen, 212–13
Porgy and Bess, 158
Poston, Roger E., 204, 205, 210, 218, 236
Powell, Frank, 289
Presbyterian College, 50
Progressive Democratic Party, xv, 47–48, 184

Quaintance, Charles, 232, 233

R. L. Bryan Company, 133
Ramsaur, Ned, 157
Ramsey, David, 242
Ravenel, Arthur, 279, 299
Reagan, Ronald, 59, 268
Reasonover, Carl, 204
Reconstruction, 22, 27, 31, 36, 110, 119, 126, 134, 267
Republican Party, 8, 17, 20, 31, 60, 76, 106, 133, 134, 136–41, 159, 258; and race relations, 113, 127, 128, 230; and rise in South Carolina, 275
Reuther, Walter, 254
Rhodes, E. C., 130, 132
Rhodes, William L., Jr., 7, 71, 72, 73, 74, 75, 79
Rice v. Elmore, xvi
Richardson, Elliott, 272
Richland County, 93, 102
Rigby, Robert, 157
Riley, Joe, Jr., 93
Riley, Joe, Sr., 93, 168
Riley, Richard, 157, 159, 186
Rivers, L. Mendel, 30, 93, 258
Roberts, Carlisle, 53
Robeson, Paul, 182
Robinson, William, 62–63, 65
Rockefeller, Nelson, 268
Rogers, George, 242
Rogers, Jim, 139, 199
Rogers, Joseph O., xvii, 135, 136–38, 139, 140, 141, 143, 181
Rone, Bill, 138

Roosevelt, Franklin D., 2, 33, 37, 39, 40, 48, 128, 131, 138, 299
Roper, Elmo, 58
Rosen, Morris, 252
Ross, Daniel I., Jr., 118, 121
Rougeau, Warren, 226
Rovetch, Warren, 171
Royal, Howard G., 194
Royster, William, 134
Rural Electrification Administration (REA), 38
Russell, Donald S., xvii, 4, 5, 10, 11, 101, 138, 143, 167; as federal judge, 235; as governor, 99, 100, 103, 106, 108, 109, 122, 147, 150, 172, 205; and race relations, 4, 112, 113, 114, 128, 176; and U.S. Senate, 6, 7, 8, 10, 134, 136; as USC president, 88, 114, 286
Russell, Richard, 279
Russell, Robert, 93, 168

S.C. Bar Association, 249
S.C. Coin Operators Association, 104
S.C. Farm Workers Association, 262
S.C. General Assembly, xvi, xvii, 4, 10, 11–12, 20, 31, 32, 34, 56, 65, 75, 114, 159–60; effect of one-man, one-vote ruling, 11; House of Representatives, xvi, xix, 7, 8, 11, 47, 98; and Public Education Committee (*see* Gressette Committee); and Santee Cooper, 39; and reapportionment, 138; and school desegregation, 14; and "Segregation Session of 1956," 85; Senate, 2, 11
S.C. High School League, 104
S.C. Human Relations Council, 263
S.C. Labor Council, 252
S.C. Municipal Association, 95, 96, 97, 146
S.C. State Chamber of Commerce, 79, 89, 90
S.C. State Highway Patrol, 204–5, 209, 218–20, 227, 232, 234, 236, 284
S.C. State Human Affairs Commission, 247
Sanders, Carl, 167
Sanford, Mark, 145, 238, 301

Sanford, Terry, 167
Santee Canal Park, 39
Santee River, 23, 27, 28, 38
Santee-Cooper Electric Cooperative, 38–40, 164, 168, 256
Saunders, Bill, 199, 201, 242, 244–47, 249, 252, 254–57, 259, 262
Savannah River, 61, 84
Scarborough, Y. W., 93
Schachte, Edwin, 259
Schulz, George, 259
Scott, Robert, 210, 275
Seal, Wayne, 144, 230, 284
Sellers, Cleveland, 18, 242; and All-Star Bowling Alley protest, 207–9; and involvement in Orangeburg shootings, 211, 216, 223–24, 226–27, 229, 230; as student leader, 199–201, 204; and Selma, Ala., 18; and trial, 234–38
Shaw-McLeod Company, 26
Shealy, David, 221, 222, 224, 225
Sheheen, Fred R., 6, 7, 144
Simkins, Modjeska, 36, 48, 182–84
Singletary, Clarence, 248, 252
Singletary, McLeod, 52, 295
Smith, Ellison D. "Cotton Ed," 2, 40–41, 59, 78, 99, 113
Smith, Henry, 223
Smith, Howard K., 277–78
Smith, James M., 135–36
Smith, Patrick C., 123–24, 126, 146
Smith, Winchester, 53
Smith v. Allwright, xvi, 47
Smoak, Marion H., 194, 230
Solomon, James, xvii, 114
South Carolina, 114; Aiken, 35, 86; Allendale, 50, 60, 66; Anderson, 6, 98; Barnwell, 7; Batesburg, 48; Beaufort, 35; and "Brown Bag Law," 156, 157; Cades, xv, 23; Camden, 86; Chester, 102; Coles, 126; and Constitution of 1868, 31–32, 119; and Constitution of 1896, 55, 61, 75, 80, 119, 124, 177; Darlington, 35; Denmark, 18; and Dept. of Parks, Recreation & Tourism, xviii, 144, 155, 157, 158, 299; and Dept. of Social Services, 186; and Dispensary State Board

of Control, 55, 155–58; Edgefield, 39; Edisto State Park, 85; and Educational Television Network, 77, 78, 227; Florence, 35; Greenwood, 36; Hell Hole Swamp, 23, 28, 29, 30, 37, 91; Hilton Head Island, 155, 158; Honea Path, xv, 78; Lamar, 280–81, 288, 289, 292; Lancaster, 97; Laurens, 6; Manning, xvii; McCormick, 102; Moncks Corner, 25, 39, 54, 55; Mullins, 125; Myrtle Beach, 28, 95, 97, 155, 157; Pinopolis, 164; Orangeburg, 35, 46; and outmigration, 33; and poverty, xix, 3; Rock Hill, 86; and sales tax, xvi, 9; St. Matthews, 14; and school desegregation, 14–15; Spartanburg, 4; State Budget & Control Board, 25, 57, 114, 126, 130, 146, 151, 193, 230, 300; State Development Board, 166; State Highway Commission, 54; Summerton, 15; and tourism, 154; Union, 4; Walterboro, 46
South Carolina National Bank, 168, 169
South Carolina School Committee. See Gressette Committee
South Carolina State University, xvii, xviii, 85, 101, 147, 172, 177–81; and Black Awareness Coordinating Committee, 200, 201, 202, 204, 211, 215, 216, 229; and boycott, 187–97; and history of, 177–79; and Orangeburg shootings, 198–240
South of the Border, 155, 158
Southern Christian Leadership Conference, 17, 18, 201, 251, 253–59, 261
Southern Regional Council, xii, 19, 201, 208, 210–11, 213, 215–16, 226–28
Sparkman, John J., 184
Spartanburg County, 83, 97, 98
Spears, Wright, 157
Spell, Jesse, 221, 222, 223
Springs Mills, 157
Sproat, John G., 109–10, 125, 126
Stanback, I. P., 147, 199
State Law Enforcement Division (SLED), 110, 188, 284, 290; and alcohol enforcement, 157; and investigations at S.C. State, 85; and Medical University

hospital strike, 252–53, 255; and Orangeburg shootings, 200, 208, 214, 235–36; and S.C. State boycott, 188; and USC unrest, 284; and Voorhees College unrest, 263–64

State Ports Authority, 169

States' Rights Party. See Dixiecrats

Stevenson, Adlai, 184

Stevenson, Robert T., 210, 211, 218

Strom, J. P., 110, 290, 291; and Medical University hospital strike, 255; and Orangeburg shootings, 200, 204–10, 214–16, 218, 221, 223, 224, 234, 236, 238; and S.C. State boycott, 186, 189; and USC unrest, 283, 285; and Voorhees unrest, 262

Stroman, John, 187, 188, 198, 204, 207, 238

Student Non-Violent Coordinating Committee (SNCC), 17–19, 180, 188, 199–201, 204, 206, 216, 226, 229, 245

Stukes, Taylor H., 82

Sumter National Forest, 28

Sumwalt, Robert, 63

Sumwalt, Vernon, 63, 64

Swinton, Sylvia Poole, 125

Taft, William Howard, 184

Taft-Hartley Act, 2, 78

Talmadge, Herman, 14, 56

Tarleton, Banastre, 23

Taylor, Claude A., 8

Taylor, Frank, 232

Taylor, O. P., 230

Taylor, Sidney C., 222

Tennessee, 19, 26, 125, 251

Tennessee Valley Authority, 39

Terrill, Thomas E., 77, 78

Texas, 19, 41, 47, 114

textile industry, xv, 5, 7, 22, 77, 83, 86, 160

Textile Manufacturers' Association, 79, 89, 164

Thomas, Charles, 193, 198, 203

Thompson, P. Frank, 227

Thompson, Sydnor, 70

Thornley, Sporty, 55

Thurmond, J. Strom, 2, 5, 8, 20, 34, 39, 139; and attacks on Supreme Court, 276; as governor, 75, 88, 130, 192; and politics, 56–57, 60; and race, 16–17, 58, 59, 66, 80, 99, 112, 113, 127–29; and switch to Republican Party, 134, 268, 279, 288; and U.S. Senate, 136, 142, 258, 272, 279, 295

Thurmond, J. William, 57

Tillman, Benjamin R., 31–32, 36, 52, 81, 110, 113, 120, 177, 192, 196

Timmerman, George Bell, Jr., 6, 75, 88, 109, 281

Tolbert, Joe, 184

Traxler, David, 146

Truman, Harry S., 4, 48, 56, 57, 58, 66, 78, 184

Tucker, Cecil, 126

Turner, Benner, xvii, 179, 180, 187–94, 196, 198, 208, 230

Tuskegee Airmen, 46

Tuskegee Institute, 41

U.S. Civil Rights Act, xvii

U.S. Congress, xi, 6, 38, 54, 57, 111, 251; House Committee on Un-American Activities, 182; House of Representatives, 46, 56; Senate, xvii, 1, 48

U.S. Constitution, 14, 22, 114

U.S. Court of Appeals, 16

U.S. Department of Education, 145

U.S. Department of Health, Education and Welfare, 243, 250, 256–58, 267, 269–73, 278, 288

U.S. Department of Justice, 117, 212, 227, 231, 233, 239, 267, 269, 271, 272, 274, 276–78

U.S. Supreme Court, xv, xvi, 13–14, 16, 32, 40, 47, 69, 70, 80, 108, 114, 122, 180, 266, 274

United Citizens Party, 287

United Fund, 101

United Methodist Church, 185

United Press International, 92, 95

University of Mississippi, 19, 112

University of South Carolina, xvii, xviii, 49, 63, 71, 77, 105, 126, 137, 149, 167,

University of South Carolina (*continued*)
172, 174; and integration of, 3, 4, 8, 12,
127, 205–6; and ROTC, 49; and
School of Law, 54, 56, 249; and unrest,
72, 282, 283–86, 292, 301
Urban League, 147, 230, 251

Vance, Robert, 168
Vesey, Denmark, 242
Vietnam War, 105, 139, 237, 265, 286, 298
Virginia, 16, 114
Volstead Act, 55, 156
Voorhees College, 230, 263–64, 279
Voting Rights Act of 1965, xvii, 18, 105,
109, 114–15, 117, 128, 143, 160, 192,
199, 267, 269

Wall, E. Craig, Sr., 168
Wallace, David Duncan, 77
Wallace, George C., 18, 112, 117, 142,
147, 268, 276, 279
Wallace, O. T., 77
Wannamaker, W. W., 136, 141
Waring, J. Waties, xvi, 16, 47, 67
Warren, Earl, 110, 276
Warren, George, 62
Washington, Booker T., 35, 36, 195
Washington, D.C., 2, 4, 5, 6, 13, 16, 101,
108, 129, 200
Washington and Lee University, 70
Watergate, 154, 291
Watson, Albert W., xviii, xix, 273–76,
279–82, 286, 288, 289, 291, 292
Watson, Inez, 145
Watters, Pat, 226
Weatherbee, Don, 285
West, John C., xix, 54, 75, 92, 102, 130,
131, 132, 136, 141, 149, 157; as gover-
nor, 172, 175, 186, 236–37, 247, 262,
287, 300; as lieutenant governor, 209,
230; and race against Albert Watson,
273–76, 279, 280, 288, 290

White, Bruce, 189
White, Cooper, 290
White, Walter, 41
White Citizens Council, 19, 85, 180, 200
Wickenberg, Charles H., Jr., 6, 9, 104,
144, 182–83, 281
Wilkins, Roy, 182, 201
Wilkinson, Marian Birnie & Robert Shaw,
178
Williams, A. P., 64
Williams, Arthur, 53
Williams, Hosea, 17, 18, 253, 259
Williams, Isaac, 185, 186, 187, 189, 191,
238, 239
Wilson, Reg, 146
Wilson, Woodrow, 70
Winter, Marion F., 55, 60
Winthrop University, 172, 177
Wirth, Thomas, 187
Wise, John, 242, 243
WIS-TV, 96
Wofford College, 50
Wolfe, Julian, 232, 234, 235
Wolfe, Katherine, 145
Woods, Barbara A., 16, 182
Woods, Robert, 262
Woodward, Isaac, 48
Workman, William D., Jr., 14, 17, 79,
106, 112, 194
Works Progress Administration (WPA),
37–38
World War I, 35, 150
World War II, 1, 3, 4, 16, 46, 54, 57, 70,
72, 77, 79, 81, 87, 88, 110, 131, 137,
150, 168
Worsham, G. Fred, 106
Wright, Fielding, 58

Young, Andrew, 17, 253, 254, 261
Young, Sinway, 252

Zeigler, Eugene N., 159, 230–31